Brief Edition

· · · ·

Principles
of
Speech
Communication

Bruce E. Gronbeck
The University of Iowa

Kathleen German
Miami University—Oxford, Ohio

Douglas Ehninger

Alan H. Monroe

🏭 HarperCollins*CollegePublishers*

Acquisitions Editor: Cynthia Biron
Developmental Editor: Ann Boynton-Trig
Director of Development: Betty Slack
Project Management, Art Coordination, Text and Cover Design: York Production Services
Cover Illustration: Jane Wooster Scott, *The Unveiling of Major Culpepper,* 1984. Collection of Ron
    Sunderland.
Art Studio: Dartmouth Publishing, Inc.
Photo Researcher: Carol Parden
Electronic Production Manager: Christine Pearson
Electronic Page Makeup: Alphabet Graphics, Inc.
Printer and Binder: R.R. Donnelley & Sons Company
Cover Printer: Coral Graphics Services, Inc.

Principles of Speech Communication, 12/e.

Library of Congress Cataloging-in-Publication Data

Principles of speech communication / Bruce E. Gronbeck . . . [et al.].—12th brief ed.
            p.   cm.
    Includes bibliographical references and index.
    ISBN 0-673-99176-8
    1. Public speaking.   I. Gronbeck, Bruce E.
PN4121.E36   1995
808.5'1—dc20   94-20248
                                                CIP

    95 96 97   9 8 7 6 5 4 3 2 1

. . . .

Principles
of
Speech
Communication

. . . .

CONTENTS

. . . . .

· · · ·

Origins of the Book 50 Years Ago

Principles of Speech Communication was written to go to war. It originated when the armed forces of the United States asked Professor Alan Monroe of Purdue University to write a brief textbook for officer candidates schools around the country during World War II. Monroe took his successful public speaking text-book, *Principles and Types of Speech,* shortened it, stirred in military examples, and brought out the "Military Edition" in 1943. It was such a hit that after the war he brought out the "Brief Edition" in 1945, modeled on the Military Edition. You have in hand the Twelfth Edition of "the Brief" on its fiftieth anniversary.

Principles of Speech Communication, Twelfth Brief Edition, is related to the larger book but has developed its own characteristics over that half-century:

1. *This text works hard at getting you into speaking situations and on your feet quickly and easily.* While every college-trained speaker needs a communication vocabulary to prepare and critique speeches, students in more practically oriented classes need less conceptual background. In this edition, the "Getting Started" chapter is the second one.

2. *The textbook focuses its examples on student life, but also draws them from the worlds of work, politics, and social activism.* We recognize that your college environment must be addressed, but we're also sensitive to the fact that you're being prepared for a lifelong endeavor—talking publicly.

3. *Within the safety of the college classroom, this textbook challenges you technically, intellectually, and morally.* Throughout your life, you will be expected to know how to accomplish goals (*technical skills*), how to analyze situations and propose courses of action (*intellectual skills*), and how to lead your social and professional life in trustworthy ways (*moral development*). Exercising your skills and thought processes now will make you a more effective communicator later. For these reasons, our textbook challenges you to try speeches on different topics and to use speaking techniques you've never tried before.

New Features

This textbook has always taught the basics, and it always will. Nevertheless, *Principles of Speech Communication,* Twelfth Brief Edition, like its predecessors, is still evolving. It strives to keep up with the latest thinking of scholars in rhetorical and communication theory and research and blazes new trails in speech communication pedagogy. In this way, you as a student are informed of the latest thinking in the field of communication studies. Some of the newest features of this textbook are:

1. *An increased awareness of ethics in speech communication,* which manifests itself in a discussion of speech ethics in the first chapter and, more importantly, in a series of special features entitled "Ethical Moments." These features pick up on today's concern with the ethics of communicating and help you to explore your own thinking about the do's and don't's of speaking. "Ethical Moments" were introduced in the last edition and now have been expanded, thanks to popular demand.

2. *A boxed feature that offers you a practical exercise or thoughtful commentary on speechmaking in society.* Called "Speaking of. . . ," these boxes offer a break from the primary subject matter, foreshadow situations in which you might find yourself, and occasionally ask you to look at the big picture—the role of public speaking in the operation and maintenance of a democracy.

3. *Reworked chapter-opening vignettes* which offer a real-world application of the topic to be discussed and set the tone for the subject to be explored.

4. *A separate chapter on finding supporting materials,* in recognition of the special information skills that you need in the age of the electronic superhighway. We first introduced this chapter in the last edition and have updated it to reflect additions to your collegiate electronic library.

5. *A full-page chapter-opener photo,* which sets the theme, and a *chapter summary,* which enumerates the main concepts of the chapter, to facilitate your review.

6. *Annotations on the major outlines and texts of speeches included in the chapters,* which point out how your speech preparation skills can be put to effective use.

Extended, Rewritten, Revised, and Restructured

In addition to adding new features to the Twelfth Brief Edition of *Principles of Speech Communication,* we've kept the text alive and vital by rewriting, revising, and restructuring the following elements and features:

1. *Full-color printing.* This book was the first college-level public speaking book to be printed entirely in full color. Students in the past have reacted positively to color, telling us how it improves the readability of the book, so we've increased the use of color.

2. *Critical-thinking emphasis.* With critical thinking increasing in importance as a part of speech instruction and overall education, we've expanded our coverage of it into many of our chapters, featuring it in two:

Chapter 3 on critical thinking and listening and Chapter 14 on critical thinking and argumentation.

3. *Streamlined chapters.* A group of previous users and manuscript reviewers told us to shorten and streamline most of the chapters so that more classtime could be spent on speechmaking skills and activities. We did that. We think you'll find the chapters in the Twelfth Brief edition easier to read than those in previous editions.

4. *Sample outlines and speeches.* As always, a key feature is the large number of sample outlines and speeches. In this edition, you'll find a number of new outlines and speeches that allow you to see how others wrestle and (usually) overcome the problems that all speakers face. In addition, we've added *annotations* to most of those outlines and speeches so that you can examine the rhetorical strategies being used in them.

5. *Rewriting of the central concepts developed by Monroe and Ehninger.* For years, Alan Monroe (1903–1975) and Douglas Ehninger (1913–1979) worked with students and teachers to develop a series of strategies for teaching public speaking to students of varied backgrounds and talents. As a student at the dawn of the twenty-first century, you are heir to the pedagogy they built:

   - Monroe's motivated sequence, the greatest formula for putting together a speech this century has seen.
   - A critical examination of the forms of supporting materials.
   - Exploration of types of imagery and of various kinds of introductions, organizational patterns, and conclusions.
   - A discussion of the factors of attention that help you capture and keep your listeners.
   - An emphasis on speeches to inform, persuade, and actuate (to move to action).
   - A chapter on argumentation that teaches you how to build an argumentative speech and analyze those of others.
   - Special materials on speaking in groups and on special occasions, to extend your skills beyond rudimentary speaking situations.

The Plan of the Book

Principles of Speech Communication, Twelfth Brief Edition, is organized into four parts, reflecting the four major emphases of most contemporary courses in public speaking.

1. Part one, "Public Speaking and Critical Listening," provides you with *an orientation to the communication process.* Most teachers help you to relate the particular skills involved in public speaking to a variety of real-world contexts. They want you (a) to see how those skills impact your success at work and in society, (b) to see the underlying conceptual or theoretical explanations of what's going on when you speak publicly, and (c) to adapt what you say and how you say it to the folks who make all the difference—the people in your audience. Part One of this book intro-

duces important ways to think about speechmaking even as, with the help of Chapter 2, you give your first classroom speeches.

2. If you try to think about all of the things you should be doing as you research and assemble your speeches, you'll drive yourself crazy. That's why Part Two, "Planning and Preparing Your Speech," offers a *step-by-step approach to speech preparation*. If you break down any complex task into its component parts, you can conquer it. Setting purposes and articulating central ideas or claims, finding and assessing supporting materials, organizing and outlining these materials, and building introductions and conclusions can be accomplished one task at a time with the aid of Part Two.

3. Building a speech is only half your battle. The other half is actually giving it—*putting your presentation into words, gestures, bodily actions, vocal patterns, and visual aids*. That's what Part Three, "Presenting Your Speech," is all about. You're communicating by way of four channels—language, sounds, movements, and visuals—every time you speak, so you've got to learn how to set and control the messages flowing through each channel. Even if your teacher doesn't assign each of these chapters, you would be well advised to read them, especially if you sense you're having trouble with some particular presentation skills.

4. So, you think, you finally know how to build a speech. In reality, of course, there are many different kinds of speeches, each with its own demands on you and with its own conventional rules. In Part Four, "Types of Public Speaking," we introduce you to *four broad types of speeches*—speeches to inform, speeches to persuade, argumentative speeches, and speeches for special occasions—as well as the particular formats you often will use when addressing various kinds of groups. In Part Four, as a result, you will really start to refine your speechmaking skills, learning how to adapt them to the demands of particular speaking occasions.

Resources for Instructors

If your teachers are going to work at their highest level and make your classroom even more challenging, they need to draw upon the latest in audiovisual support for instruction. The resources program for *Principles of Speech Communication,* Twelfth Brief Edition, includes the following eight instructional supplements:

1. *Instructor's Edition.*

2. *SpeechMaster Test Package.* Contains over 3,000 test items: true/false, multiple choice, short answer, and essay questions. The program contains editing features to create new questions or to modify existing items. Available for the IBM or Mac.

3. *SpeechMaster Test Package.* Print version of the computerized program.

4. *SpeechMaster Video Series.* Includes the classic speeches of our time and covers preparation tips and presentation techniques. An *Instructor's Video Guide* is available.

5. *Great Ideas for Teaching Speech (GIFTS).* A short guide to assignments successfully used by public speaking instructors.

6. *Instructor's Resource Guide.* An extensive bibliography and reference for media resources.

7. *The Speech Writers Work Shop Speech Outlining Software.* Designed to help students develop various types of speeches. This interactive software, available on IBM or Mac, will assist students with speech preparation, and enable them to write better speeches. This also contains a topic dictionary and a powerful bibliography documentation tool as well.

8. *Speaker Apprehension Video.* This professionally produced video addresses student speech apprehension and provides students with methods for overcoming anxiety in speaking.

9. *A Selection of Student Speeches.* Contains samples of introductions and conclusions as well as full speeches, presented by a diverse group of students.

ACKNOWLEDGEMENTS

• • • • •

This book is not simply the product of two professors and their predecessors. *Principles of Speech Communication* is the result of the efforts of many instructors and students who have evaluated and reevaluated its many features for over half a century. Feedback is as important for writers as it is for speakers. We thank a nationwide network of users who graciously completed questionnaires for us and many of whom who read portions of the manuscript to help us make even more improvement. That network includes: Gary Allen, Southeastern Illinois College; Douglas Brenner, University of South Dakota; Douglas R. Bruce, John Carroll University; Julie Adams Day, William Jewell College; Marvin E. DeBoer, University of Central Arkansas; Mickey Golden, Wayne State University; John Hart, Northeast Missouri State University; Joyce P. Harrington, Randolph Community College; Sidney Hill, Mississippi State University; Mark E. Huglen, Wayne State University; James Lee Hullinger, University of Nebraska; J. Daniel Joyce, Houston Community College; Jo Ann Lawlor, West Valley College; Melanie Mason, Wayne State University; Bradley A. Nies, Blinn College; Renee Reeves, Rose State College; Larry Reynolds, Johnson County Community College; Jonah Rice, Southeastern Illinois College; Helen R. Sands, University of Southern Indiana; Valerie Schneider, East Tennessee State University; Marsha Vanderford, University of South Florida; Chloe Warner, Polk Community College; and Sue Woodworth, Mesa State College.

A special thank-you is due to the Gronbeck children. Jakob and Ingrid are collegians who possess research skills useful to textbook writers. Their library research was especially important, as was their help in coming up with examples from a world younger than the one inhabited by the authors.

Finally, we owe our greatest debts to HarperCollins, which took on this revision as part of its commitment to offer the best pedagogical products in communication studies. In part, this revision was so successful because the full resources of contemporary electronic publishing were offered to the authors in the summer of 1993. Dan Pipp, acquisitions editor in communication, oversaw the project. An experienced and talented developmental editor, Anne Boynton-Trigg, had a clear vision of the tasks, recasting the vision when it became fuzzy for us, hammering on our language and our examples, and coordinating the writing with the rest of the book's materials. Picture editor Carol Parden captured the tenor of the book in its illustrations, while Allison Ellis of the permissions department kept us legal. We were most gratified, as well, with the marketing work done by Peter Glovin and the army of enthusiastic sales representatives who carried this book to you.

   You, the student of public speaking, are the bottom line. We thank you not only for using this book, but for your commitment to excellence in public speaking, in order both to improve your own fortunes and to make the world a better place for human beings. Your commitments make our work worthwhile, and we thank you for them.

Bruce E. Gronbeck
Kathleen M. German

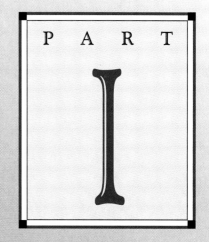

PART

I

. . . .

Public
Speaking
and
Critical
Listening

1

. . . . .

The "Public" Aspects of Public Speaking

Your best friend from high school was getting married, and you were to be the maid of honor. You knew that you would have to give a little speech at the rehearsal dinner. At first, fear gripped you: what could you say that was appropriate, sincere without being syrupy, serious yet light, and reflective of both your past relationship and your current friendship? You rolled this question over in your mind for weeks, but slowly, bits and pieces of ideas came to you. With the rehearsal dinner only two days away, you finally picked up a piece of paper and started a little outline. You recalled stories from the past, phrased expressions of happiness for the occasion, and gradually, a theme—"Weddings celebrate both the past and the future"—came to your mind, giving you a way to focus everything you wanted to say. You put the pencil down, breathing a sigh of relief. You were ready to face that room full of friends, relatives, and strangers with purpose, confidence, and something worth saying!

To be sure, you've been speaking all of your life. From the time you started gurgling in a crib, people have listened—sometimes intently, sometimes casually—to what you've had to say. Speaking to others, with others, has been a part of your normal life since shortly after birth. So, what are you doing in a public speaking class?

GOING PUBLIC

When you stand in front of a group—a group that's allowing or demanding that you present something we call "a speech," "a talk," or "some remarks," somehow the rules change. For most of us, "making a speech" is an activity that raises innumerable questions in our minds:

- How should I start? What should I say first?
- Why am I speaking? What do I want to achieve? What do others expect of me in this situation?
- How should I stand? What should I do with my hands? Where should I look?
- How loud am I supposed to talk, anyway?
- How can I remember what I want to say?
- What if someone asks a question that publicly embarrasses me?
- Is my fly unzipped or my blouse unbuttoned?
- What if I shake? throw up? pass out? just plain die?

Many people who speak publicly experience doubt, anxiety, and even fear. You've been talking all of your life, to be sure, more or less adequately most of the time and in most circumstances. Yet, somehow, public speaking—speechmaking, doing oral presentations, giving talks—seems unnatural, occasionally awkward, and sometimes terrifying. That's why you're here.

You're in this class because a lot of people in higher education believe that public speaking is something that well-educated and community-oriented people must be able to do well. Since the first schools of public speaking were set up in ancient Greece in the sixth century B.C., training in the arts of public discourse has held a special place in education for two reasons: the special demands of "publicness" and the needs of "community."

Publicness

To speak in public is to declare yourself to be a member, a worthy voice, in a community. By "going public" you demand that others consider you and your ideas worthwhile. Following the lead of Frederick Douglass, a former slave who urged the abolition of slavery, African Americans demanded the right to speak for themselves. They asserted their selfhood in public. In the language of his times, Douglass said, "Men may combine to prevent cruelty to animals, for they are dumb [mute] and cannot speak for themselves; but we are men and must speak for ourselves, or we shall not be spoken for at all."[1] Similarly, the women attending the Seneca Falls, New York, convention for women's rights in 1848 argued that they should be allowed to talk publicly. Originally, they had been assigned only to watch the proceedings from the gallery, but they were determined to define their own rights by exercising the freedom to speak afforded in the First Amendment to the Constitution.

Speaking in public, therefore, is a measure of your personhood, a recognition of your status in a group. Silence can make you invisible, a nonperson, a mere entity: the Jews of Hitler's Germany were talked about as "silent animals" in *Mein Kampf;* American slaves were thought of as chattel or personal property; Native Americans were viewed as children, to be seen and not heard; and whole segments of populations in Africa, Central America, and eastern Europe have been silently "cleansed" from their homelands. When whole peoples are forced or frightened into silence, they are in danger of being eliminated. There is an important connection between being heard publicly and being accepted as a human being.

Community

The other half of this proposition is that *communities*—the groups to which one belongs—are defined into existence by public talk. The words *community* and *communication,* of course, are intimately related; both come from a common Latin root—*cum,* meaning "with," and *munis,* denoting "public work." Communicating is doing public work—defining, exercising, maintaining, or saving *communities*—groups of individuals with shared characteristics and goals. Such groups are created and maintained symbolically, largely via public talk. Boy Scouts take their oaths together; churchgoers pray aloud and together offer creeds or public declarations of shared beliefs; the Pledge of Allegiance echoes through American schoolhouses every weekday; during lunch breaks, work groups indoctrinate new employees concerning the company's and the employees' expectations; Olympic athletes pledge to uphold the common ideals of international competition.

Public speech, whether ritualistic or creative, always has as a side benefit the maintenance of the communities to which one belongs. You'll even end up defining a community—an atmosphere, a set of rules for speaking and working together—in your speech classroom. You'll see first hand the power of public speech to create a community from a collection of strangers.

THE GOALS OF SPEECH TRAINING

Why, then, are you taking this course? You're taking it because the kind of communication that goes on publicly, especially in situations where you address many people at once, is important to you in achieving your goals in life and to others who make up your large and small communities. For now, in a collegiate community, you'll talk in classes, meetings of organizations or social groups, at rallies or demonstrations, in student government, or as a representative of your dorm floor. After you leave school, your life will present even more occasions for public talk: meetings of the PTA, church organizations, and your kids' scouting or 4-H groups; professional presentations; neighborhood get-togethers; city government hearings.

As a society, Americans traditionally have thought that self-development and social development are important enough to merit educating citizens and visitors in the art of public speaking. More specifically, you're taking a class in public speaking for four reasons:

> 1. *Bringing your communication skills to consciousness allows you to examine them and either keep or change them.* All of your life, most of your social learning has occurred "out of awareness," without your giving much thought to it. Most of your social education has consisted of formal learning or admonition (that is, when people have told you what to do) and informal learning or imitation when you've copied the behavior of others. Now, how-

ever, you're mature enough to move to the next stage of learning, which is technical learning. Technical learning is learning from the explanation of others.[2] You can handle a more technical analysis of your speech habits and understand the rationales for why you should try this or that speaking technique in a particular situation. A classroom makes you self-conscious in a positive way. In thinking about your speaking behavior and in listening to others discuss it, you can make some decisions about which techniques to keep and which ones to toss out.

2. *A speech classroom is a laboratory, an ideal place for experimentation.* Most of us have a comparatively limited repertoire of speech skills. You can try out new ones in the safety of the classroom rather than in the workplace, where experiments may affect your relationships with co-workers or customers. Use your classroom as a lab where you can experiment with different introductions, a more (or less) serious tone, special organizational patterns, or a variety of visual aids. You'll find numerous ways to improve your skills as you try different approaches and evaluate their usefulness to you and your lifestyle.

3. *Practicing public speaking in a classroom will make you much more audience-conscious than you now are.* Beginning speakers are very sensitive to themselves, their own hopes, fears, joys, and terrors; most beginning speakers are self-centered. A speech class forces you to focus as well on the other half of the communication process—the listeners. You talk not simply to hear yourself run at the mouth, but more important, to affect the thinking and lives of others. Becoming audience-centered is a key to becoming a more powerful speaker. You must learn to start where your *listeners* are, to work within *their* frames of reference, if your speeches are going to accomplish your purposes. A speech classroom is a great place to learn how to do that.

4. *Studying oral communication not only makes you a better speaker but also helps you to become a more shrewd consumer of oral messages.* You'll undoubtedly spend more of your life listening than talking. Whether face to face or via phone or mass media, you'll be exposed to innumerable oral messages. You'll meet hundreds, even thousands, of people who want a piece of your time, effort, money, and commitment. To protect yourself, you'll need to become a critical listener and thinker. You'll have to reason your way through complex arguments, often quickly, and decide how to proceed. As you listen to speech after speech in this class, you'll be making yourself into a critical listener and thinker. You're here to become better at both sending and receiving messages.

QUALITIES NECESSARY FOR SUCCESSFUL PUBLIC SPEAKING

Public speaking is an **interactive communication process.** One person (the **speaker**) offers a sustained, purposive message (a **speech**) to other people **(listeners),** who in turn offer **feedback.** That is, listeners react to the speaker directly (with questions or countercomments), indirectly (with frowns, puzzled looks, or laughter), and in a delayed fashion (when they do or don't do what the

Communication Studies and Your Career

What can you do in college to better prepare yourself for a job and career? Your school's career placement office will have some recent research on that question, but maybe not Al Weitzel's *Careers for Speech Communication Graduates*. Weitzel brings research findings to bear on the great variety of tracks in speech communication education; on the image that communication majors and the outside world have of speech students; on some career options (in particular, the skills needed for careers in training and development, public relations, law, teaching, and sales or marketing); on some techniques for maximizing employability (including working at internships, joining professional organizations, and improving your communicating skills); and on simple steps to find appropriate employment.

After you complete your communication training, you may choose to pursue either (1) "communication" careers such as education, politics, the ministry, advertising, sales, broadcasting, filmmaking, writing, editing; or (2) "noncommunication" careers that emphasize other special skills, such as accounting, scientific research, insurance, computer science, engineering, or nursing, which nonetheless still need people with good communication skills. No matter what you'll do after graduation, think of communication skills training as training for your life work.

FIGURE 1.1
The Process of
Public Speaking

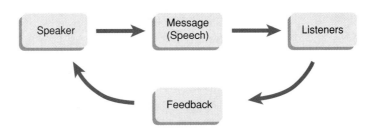

speaker recommends). Because there is interaction—back and forth communication initiatives—occurring during speaking (see Figure 1.1), you must develop the ability to identify, assess, plan, and execute responses to communication problems. Throughout this course, you should concentrate on six basic qualities: integrity, knowledge, rhetorical sensitivity, an understanding of human diversity, ethics, and oral skills.

Integrity

Your reputation for reliability, truthfulness, and concern for others is your single most powerful means of exerting influence over others. Integrity is important, especially in an age of electronic advertising and mass mailings—when every pres-

• A speaker can heighten the impact of a speech by increasing the audience's estimate of his or her trustworthiness, competency, sincerity, attractiveness, and dynamism. How are these elements of credibility probably influencing the listeners in this setting?

sure group, cause, and special interest can make its way into the public mind, often with conflicting analyses and recommendations for action. Listeners who have no personal experience with a particular subject seek information and advice from speakers they trust. You must earn their trust if you are to succeed. Your use of evidence, your willingness to recognize the weaknesses as well as the strengths of your proposals, your general temperateness—these are some of the ways you create a sense of integrity in speeches.

Knowledge

Expertise also is essential. No one wants to listen to an empty-headed prattler; speakers must know their subjects. So, even though you know a lot about a topic through personal experience, take time to do some extra reading, talk with other experts, and find out what aspects of the topic will engage your potential listeners. Audience analysis is the key to successful speechmaking. You must know both what you're talking about and to whom you're talking.

Rhetorical Sensitivity

The most successful speakers are "other-directed," concerned with meeting their listeners' needs and solving their problems through public talk. The best speakers recognize and respect their listeners and their listeners' needs. These speakers are rhetorically sensitive to others.

Rhetorical sensitivity refers to speakers' attitudes toward their listeners during the speech preparation process.[3] Rhetorical sensitivity is the degree to which speakers:

a. Recognize that all people are different and complex and, hence, must be considered individually. To treat listeners as a uniform mass instead of as people with individual needs is to dehumanize them. While a public speaker can't really talk to everyone individually, he or she can convey to the listeners a desire to do that.

b. Adapt their messages and themselves to particular audiences. Sensitive political candidates, for example, always make local references and shape their supporting materials (especially their examples) for the particular communities they address.

c. Consciously seek and react to audience feedback. In responding with clarifications to puzzled looks or audible listener reactions (laughter, murmuring), speakers turn public talk into interactive communication.

d. Understand the limitations of talk, sometimes even curtailing speeches rather than trying to express the inexpressible. In the face of utter personal tragedy, for example, perhaps the best we can do is to hug the victims, hold their hands, and say "I'm sorry"; more words may tend to make us appear insensitive.

e. Work at finding the right set of arguments and verbal expressions to make particular ideas clear and attractive to particular audiences. Senstive speakers draw supporting materials out of their audience's life experiences and employ language that is comprehensible and appropriate to the social groups being addressed.

Being rhetorically sensitive does not mean saying only what you think others want to hear. Rather, it is a matter of careful self-assessment, audience analysis, and decision making. What are your reasons for speaking? To what degree will they be understandable and acceptable to others? To what degree can you adapt your purposes to audience preferences while maintaining your own integrity and self-esteem? These questions demand that you be sensitive to listener needs, the situation, and your self-respect. Rhetorical sensitivity, then, is a way of thinking and acting.

Understanding Human Diversity

Related to rhetorical sensitivity is the speaker's need to understand **human diversity**—the fact that societies comprise people of two genders, multiple ages, varied ethnic backgrounds, innumerable religions, and diverse cultural backgrounds arising from geographical regions of origin (the South, the Midwest). America may think of itself as a melting pot, but we have never melted down to a uniform consistency. This fact has serious implications for the public speaker.

For most of the centuries since the rise of western oratory in ancient Greece, public speaking was a privilege reserved for white, economically secure, socially prominent males. Upper-class, white, propertied men ran the legislatures, the courts, the city governments, the churches; the voices of lower socioeconomic classes, nonwhites, and women were silenced.

The moves to emancipation followed John Locke's seventeenth-century treatises on government, and continued through the social and political revolutions of the eighteenth and nineteenth centuries. The various "rights" movements of our own times have empowered and given public voices to silenced segments of western societies in at least some arenas. While more progress toward public empowerment remains to be made, we've come far enough toward the goals of justice and equality to demand that public speakers keep human diversity in mind while preparing to speak. This is not a matter of liberal or conservative politics, just plain social fact. Nonwhites, the economically disadvantaged, women, the elderly as well as the young, all groups protected by the Americans with Disabilities Act, gays, lesbians, and heterosexuals—all of these segments of America will be represented in your audiences. Throughout this book, we'll occasionally stop and discuss how the fact of human diversity ought to affect how you talk publicly.

Ethics

Each time you speak publicly, you must remember that there are many ethical dimensions to the act of public speaking. Ethical principles are assumed values about thoughts and actions pivoting on understandings of justice and injustice, goodness and badness, rightness and wrongness. These go beyond the sense of integrity we discussed earlier. Whenever human beings gather to affirm each other's presence and personhood, to supplement each other's information, to offer advice, to attempt to change each other's beliefs, activities, or behaviors, ethical questions are intimately involved. Is it ethical to make explicitly racial references when describing an individual or a group? Should you tell both sides of the story when giving people information on a new wonder drug? Can you ethically suppress certain kinds of information when trying to change people's minds? These and hundreds of other ethical questions face you as you prepare and deliver speeches.

No one can presume to tell you precisely what ethical codes you ought to adhere to when giving a speech. Given a textbook's educational mission, however, we'll regularly raise ethical questions for your consideration. Throughout the book, you'll encounter "Ethical Moments," features that will confront you with a problem and ask you to think it through. Acknowledging and working through ethical dilemmas will make you a stronger and more thoughtful speaker.

Oral Skills

Fluency, poise, control of voice, and coordinated movements of your body mark you as a skilled speaker. These skills don't come naturally; they are developed through practice. Such practice is not a matter of acquiring and rehearsing a bag of tricks. Rather, your practice both inside and outside your classroom should aim at making you an animated, self-confident, and conversational speaker. You'll have many opportunities in this class to sharpen those skills.

• Some anxiety about performing publicly is normal. Symptoms of anxiety are experienced both physically and psychologically. How can you cope with the anxiety that accompanies performance?

Integrity, knowledge, rhetorical sensitivity to human diversity, ethics, and oral skills—these are the building blocks for lifelong satisfaction as a speaker in public.

A BASIC RECIPE FOR SPEECHES

In this book, you'll learn to work your way step by step through the process of preparing a good speech; we'll introduce the steps in Chapter 2 and tackle them in greater detail in Chapters 3–8.

But, now it's time to get you started—up on your feet and ready to develop your speaking skills. Like a cook, you need some ingredients and a recipe. Good cooks know that after they've used a recipe a few times they'll need to adapt it, altering the ingredients, proportions, and cooking techniques for their own tastes and skills. The same is true of speakers. First they learn some recipes; then they learn to vary them to produce better speeches.

The following is a recipe for a speech. It's not fancy, and it won't work all of the time, but it will get you up and talking. The precise order of some of the internal elements can be varied to suit you and your subject, but otherwise, you can mold a serviceable speech around this skeleton.

A RECIPE FOR A SPEECH

Introduction

1. Get your listeners' attention by introducing your subject and indicating its importance to them.

2. State your central idea—the idea you want them to believe or to accept.

3. Forecast the development of your speech—what you'll do first, second, third, and so on.

Body

1. First idea:
   a. Developmental or supporting material.
   b. More developmental or supporting material.

2. Second idea:
   a. Developmental or supporting material.
   b. More developmental or supporting material.

3. Third idea:
   a. Developmental or supporting material.
   b. More developmental or supporting material.

Conclusion

1. Summary of your main points.

2. Re-emphasis of what the audience should focus on, a restatement of your central idea.

3. Concluding idea, quotation, or anecdote.

From this recipe for a speech, three speaking strategies should be apparent. They are described in the paragraphs that follow.

A speech is divided into three main sections: the introduction, the body, and the conclusion. That's probably obvious; often, however, inexperienced speakers forget to *begin*—to draw their listeners into their speech, to orient them to what's going on. Sometimes speakers haven't composed a final sentence or two and so struggle to find a solid conclusion. And too often speakers don't divide up the main portion or body of their speeches into clearly logical sections, allowing listeners to follow along. Thus, it is important to build unmistakable introductions, bodies, and conclusions.

Ideas are the name of the game. The heart of a speech is the set of ideas you want someone to have when you're finished. State the ideas clearly, and then offer developmental material (explanations, illustrations, stories) to make them clear, or offer supporting material (testimony, statistics, specific instances) to make them acceptable. Clear, well-developed or well-supported ideas are what it's all about.

A speech, ultimately, is a well-formed or shaped piece of oral communication. You can see from the recipe that speakers don't just stand up, start talking, talk for a while, and then stop talking. A speech is not a casual recitation or musing, a monologue to be overheard by others. It's a way to achieve certain purposes by communicating to others. The ideas in a speech, therefore, are bent and shaped to fit in particular spots and to serve particular purposes. Some ideas help to engage listeners, others to orient them, still others to convince them that the speaker is right. For speakers, thinking rhetorically is a matter of knowing what materials they need in order to achieve their purposes, and them forming them into something called a speech.

So, you have a recipe. Now you can build a functional speech to get you started in this class. Chapter 2 will give you even more introductory help.

CHAPTER SUMMARY

1. While you have been communicating with others all of your life, public speaking offers you special challenges because of its publicness (you give yourself a significant voice in groups) and its ties to community (you help to create and sustain groups through shared talk).

2. To be successful, speakers need a range of skills and competencies: integrity, knowledge, rhetorical sensitivity, an understanding of human diversity, ethics, and oral skills.

3. All speeches are well-developed and formed public messages with introductions, bodies, and conclusions.

KEY TERMS

feedback (p. 5)   listeners (5)
human diversity (p. 7)   rhetorical sensitivity (p. 7)
interactive communication   speaker (p. 5)
    process (p. 5)   speech (p. 5)

SKILLBUILDING ACTIVITIES

1. Interview the leader of a local group that schedules public lectures, the director of the campus speakers' bureau, or another person in a position to discuss the speech skills that are characteristic of professional speakers. Bring a list of those skills to class and be prepared to share your notes with others.

2. Meet with a classmate to introduce him or her to the rest of the class. Concentrate on obtaining, selecting, and ordering your information for public presentation.

3. Prepare an inventory of your personal speech needs and speaking abilities. (Your instructor may make this the first assignment in a personal speech journal that you will maintain throughout the term.) In your inventory, complete the following statements:

a. I am _____

b. I am not _____

c. I want _____

d. I can _____

e. I cannot _____

Research

Richard Nelson Bolles, *What Color Is Your Parachute? A Practical Manual for Job-Hunters and Career Changes* (Berkeley, Calif.: Ten Speed Press, published annually).

Al R. Weitzel, *Careers for Speech Communication Graduates* (Salem, Wis.: Sheffield Publishing Co., 1987).

Al R. Weitzel and Paul Gaske, "An Appraisal of Communication Career-Related Research," *Communication Education* 33 (1984): 184–194.

REFERENCES

1. Frederick Douglass, "Speech at the National Convention of Colored Men [1883]," reprinted in *The American Reader: Words That Moved a Nation,* edited by Diane Ravitch (New York: HarperCollins, 1990), 172.

2. The first book in this country to seriously explore relationships between communication habits and culture was Edward Hall, *The Silent Language* (1959; reprint, New York: Fawcett, 1966). In it, Hall talks about culture as "out of awareness" and about three kinds of learning—formal, informal, and technical.

3. See Roderick P. Hart and Don M. Burks, "Rhetorical Sensitivity and Social Interaction," *Speech [Communication] Monographs* 47 (1980): 1–22.

Getting Started

"**W**ow! I didn't know you could talk like that in front of our whole class! That was great! You didn't look nervous or anything."

"Thanks," Jacinda replied. "I was nervous, but I spent so much time working on my speech and then practicing it that I probably could have given it in my sleep."

"I've been practicing mine, getting ready for class tomorrow, but I'm still worried," Taylor said.

"You'll do fine. Just don't panic. It really helped me to think about what I wanted to say. I practiced a lot too. I felt so sure of myself after giving that speech that I even answered a question in economics class!"

Chapter 1 introduced you to the role of public speaking in our society. While you can't learn everything at once about the intricacies of speech preparation and speechmaking processes, you can learn enough about the basics to begin speaking right away. As you prepare to speak, you'll have to make decisions about: (1) selecting and narrowing your subject, (2) determining your purposes, (3) analyzing your audience and the occasion, (4) gathering your speech material, (5) making an outline, (6) practicing aloud, and (7) delivering your speech. These may seem like a lot of decisions, but systematic planning is the key to platform success. You can save time and effort by planning carefully instead of wandering aimlessly through the library or waiting endlessly at your desk for inspiration.

There's no magical formula for getting ready to speak. However, if you follow the seven steps offered in this chapter—either in the order presented here or in another that works for you—you'll be ready for your audience. At the end of this chapter, you'll explore another subject you ought to think about before speaking: projecting self-confidence.

SELECTING AND NARROWING YOUR SUBJECT

The most difficult task for many speakers is to choose a subject. Sometimes the subject is chosen for you, but often you will chose your own topic for classroom speeches. You might begin the process of choosing a topic by asking yourself questions: What do you know something about? What are you interested in talking about? What topics do you think will interest your listeners? Does the occasion or situation suggest a topic for discussion? It's important to answer these questions carefully. Your answers will help you select and narrow your subject. A well-chosen speech topic is the first step to a successful speech. Let's examine in more detail the processes of choosing and narrowing a topic.

It's a good idea to begin selecting a topic by listing those subjects that you have knowledge of, circling the ones you're willing to talk about in front of others, and thinking about ways you can relate them to your listeners. If the purpose of your first classroom speech is to inform your classmates about a subject, you might come up with the following list of things you know something about:

> High school football (you played football)
> Sharks (you did a science project on this subject)
> Halloween (it's your favorite holiday)
> Nintendo (you like the game)
> Soap operas (you watch them)
> Caffeine (you drink a lot of coffee)
> Smoking (you quit two years ago)
> Careers in accounting (you're considering them now)
> Photography (you like taking amateur photos)
> Skin cancer (you're worried about the side effects of tanning)
> Weightlifting (you lift weights for exercise)

Next, you need to consider your audience. Which topics would interest them most? When you ask yourself this question, you realize that several of your topics such as Halloween, photography, and weightlifting are mainly of interest to you. You should probably cross them off your list.

You should also think about your listeners' expectations. What do they already know, and what do they expect to learn? They may already know more than you do about Nintendo, soap operas, and caffeine. You'll certainly need to eliminate these topics from your list. Now you have this narrower list of potential topics—those that will interest your audience and meet your listeners' expectations:

> Football
> Sharks
> Smoking
> Accounting
> Skin cancer

After some additional thought, you decide to inform your classmates about sharks because you've done a lot of research on this subject and you know you can interest your classmates in it. Within this general subject are more specific topics including:

- The types of sharks

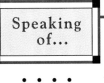

Speaking of....

Brainstorming to Generate Topics

Having trouble coming up with possible speech topics? Try this brainstorming exercise:

1. Get a large blank sheet of paper and a pencil.

2. On the left-hand side of the paper, write the letters of the alphabet in a column.

3. Then, as quickly as you can, write down single words beginning with each of the letters. Write down any word that comes to your mind. Repeat until you have the entire sheet filled. You might begin like this: A—apples, alphabet, alarm, alimony B—bazaar, balsa, baboon, bassoon, ballon C—comics, cologne, colors, confetti

4. Next, consider each of the words as a key to potential topics. For example, *apples* might suggest apple pie recipes, Johnny Appleseed and other early American legends, pesticide controversies, fruit in our diets, farm and orchard subsidies, or government price controls of farm produce. This is just the beginning. From one key word, you can derive many possible speech topics.

5. Obviously, not all of these topics would be great speech topics, but this exercise gives you a creative and quick way to generate lots of ideas.

- Sharks in scientific research
- The life cycle of the shark
- Endangered species of sharks
- Shark habitats and habits
- Famous shark stories
- Sharks as a source of human food
- Movies about sharks
- Shark attacks and how to prevent them
- The historical evolution of the shark

Given this list of subtopics, you should ask yourself additional questions to narrow the topic even further. How much time do I have to deliver this speech? What do my classmates already know about my topic? Which topics naturally fit together? After you answer these questions, you may end up with an informative speech focusing on three topics that cluster around the characteristics of sharks:

- The types of sharks
- The life cycle of the shark
- Shark habitats and habits

In selecting and narrowing your topic, you begin with a list of potential topics. Then, you select those that reflect your knowledge, the expectations of your listeners, and the requirements of the occasion. Finally, you consider the possible subtopics and choose several that fit the time limits and go together naturally. This kind of systematic topic selection is the first step in successful speaking.

DETERMINING YOUR PURPOSES AND CENTRAL IDEA

Once you know what you want to talk about, you need to ask yourself more questions. Why do you wish to discuss this subject? Why might an audience want to listen to you? And, why is what you're discussing appropriate to the occasion? The answers to these questions will require you to think about the reasons behind your topic choice. First, think about the *general purpose,* the primary reason you will speak in public. Next, consider your *specific purposes,* the concrete goals you wish to achieve in a particular speech. Finally, focus your thoughts on a *central idea,* the statement guiding the thoughts you wish to communicate. You may want to choose a working title for your speech. Selecting a provisional title early in the preparation process helps you to keep sight of your primary emphasis and lets you announce it to others ahead of time.

General Purposes

If you examine most speeches, you'll come up with three **general purposes** for speeches: to inform, to entertain, and to persuade. This chart summarizes the general purposes for speaking:

General Purpose	Audience Response Sought
To inform	Clear understanding
To entertain	Enjoyment and comprehension
To persuade	Acceptance of ideas or recommended behaviors

Throughout this book, we will emphasize speeches to inform and speeches to persuade. The reason is that these types of speeches dominate the speaking occasions you'll face in life. Chapter 15 explores speeches to entertain.

To Inform

The general purpose of your speech is *to inform* when your overall object is to help listeners understand an idea, concept, or process, or when you seek to widen their range of knowledge. This is the goal of scientists who report their research results to colleagues, of public figures who address community groups on subjects about which they are knowledgeable, and of college lecturers and work supervisors.

To create understanding, you must change the level or quality of information possessed by your listeners. They should leave your speech knowing more than they did before they heard it. For example, you might inform your classmates about herbal medicine, photographic composition, laser surgery, personal computers, tornadoes, Individual Retirement Accounts, anorexia nervosa, the battle of Bunker Hill, or any other number of topics. If you talk about laser surgery, for instance, assume that they already know what most of us know—that it is used in cataract removal and to break up kidney stones. To increase their understanding, you will need to focus on innovative surgical techniques using lasers, such as radial keratotomy, as well as the way lasers operate. You might even speculate about how lasers will change standard surgical operations in the future. By providing examples, statistics, illustrations, and other materials offering data and ideas, you expand your listeners' knowledge.

Not only must an informative speech provide raw data, but its message and supporting materials must be structured and integrated in such a way that listeners perceive the whole. For example, an informative speech on how to assemble a sound system must include the necessary instructions in an orderly sequence of steps. Some of your listeners may already be familiar with the information that you're presenting but may not have put the pieces together coherently. Your job as an informative speaker is to impart both knowledge and overall understanding. Understanding how to assemble a sound system depends not only on learning what to do but also on knowing when to do it and why.

To Persuade

If you seek to influence listeners' beliefs and actions, then your purpose is *to persuade*. While it may be argued that all speeches are persuasive to some degree, there are many situations in which the speaker's primary purpose is outright persuasion. Celebrities sell cars and shampoos; lawyers ask for the death penalty; activists exhort tenants to stand up to their landlords; politicians debate taxes.

As a persuasive speaker, you usually seek to influence the beliefs and attitudes of your listeners. You might want to convince them that John F. Kennedy was shot by several assassins, that education is the cornerstone of freedom, or that life exists after death. In these cases, you are altering beliefs or attitudes. Sometimes, however, you will want your listeners to act. You may want them to contribute money to the Humane Society, sigh a petition against a landfill project, vote for a new tax levy, or boycott a local video rental store. In this type of persuasive speech, called a speech *to actuate,* you ask your listeners to act in a specified way. You might ask your classmates to quit watching television, cut back on caffeine consumption, sign prenuptial agreements, start stock portfolios, or register to vote.

To inform, to entertain, and to persuade are the general purposes of speaking. By thinking about general purposes, you begin your orientation process and your assessment of the task you face. The next step is to focus on your specific purposes or goals.

Specific Purposes

Specific purposes are the actual goals you want to achieve in a speech. They can be extremely wide-ranging. For example, if your general purpose is to inform and your topic is aircraft, then your specific purposes might range from informing your audience about the history of aircraft and their role in military combat to outlining safety regulations governing air travel.

While some specific purposes are public, some are private—known only by you. For example, you probably hope you'll make a good impression on an audience, although you're not likely to say that aloud. Some purposes are short-term; others are long-term. If you're speaking to members of a local organization on the importance of recycling, your short-term purpose might be to convince them to save their aluminum cans while your long-term purpose could be to gather support for a citywide recycling program.

Theoretically, you have multiple private and public, short-term and long-term specific purposes whenever you speak. Practically, however, you need to reduce that mass of goals to a dominant one that can guide your speech preparation. A single specific purpose, one that you can articulate for an audience, focuses you on precisely what you want your audience to understand, enjoy, feel, believe, or do.

Suppose that you wanted to take on the challenge of getting more of your classmates to use your campus library. Consider various ways of wording your specific purpose:

- "The purpose of my speech is to tell students about the variety of library services" (understanding).
- "The purpose of my speech is to relate how the interlibrary loan program can put the resources of other libraries at your fingertips" (information).
- "The purpose of my speech is to reduce students' levels of anxiety about going to the library" (feelings).
- "The purpose of my speech is to destroy the old belief that librarians are mechanical automatons who care only about silence" (beliefs).
- "The purpose of my speech is to get half of the class to agree to come on a library tour" (action).

All of these purposes involve student use of the library, yet each has a different specific focus which makes it a different speech. Locking onto a specific purpose allows you to zeroes in on your primary target.

Central Ideas

Once you've settled on a specific purpose for your speech, you're ready to translate that goal into concrete subject matter. You first need to cast into words the controlling thought of your speech. This **central idea** (sometimes called a *thesis statement*) is a statement that captures the essence of the information or concept you wish to communicate to an audience. For example, your central idea for a speech on diamonds might be: "The value of a diamond is largely determined by four factors—color, cut, clarity, and carat." In a persuasive speech, the central idea phrases the belief, attitude, or action you want an audience to adopt. Your central idea for a persuasive speech on dieting might be: "Fad diets are dangerous because they create imbalances in essential vitamins and minerals and break down muscle tissue."

The precise phrasing of central ideas is very important because wording conveys the essence of your subject matter, setting up audience expectations. Examine Table 2.1 for examples of ways to word speech purposes. Then consider this example—assume that you've decided to give an informative speech on building a bird house. You might phrase your central idea in one of three ways:

TABLE 2.1   Speaking Purposes   This table provides a guide to the relationships between the general purpose, specific purpose, and central idea of your speech.

General Purpose	Specific Purpose	Central Idea
To help your listeners understand an idea, concept, or process (to inform)	To teach your listeners about the Federal Reserve Board	"The most important influence on interest rates in this country is the Federal Reserve Board."
To influence your listeners' actions (to actuate)	To get your listeners to walk to classes this week (short-term goal)	"You should start a fitness program today to improve the quality of your life."
	To get your listeners to develop a fitness program (long-term goal)	
To influence your listeners' thoughts (to persuade)	To increase your listeners' appreciation of the role of pure scientific research	"While science doesn't always yield a better mousetrap, it is still an important human activity."

  1. "With only minimal carpentry skills, anyone can build a bird house."

  2. "With some careful searching around the house and neighborhood, you can build a homemade bird house for less than $10."

  3. "Building an inexpensive bird house will give you a sense of accomplishment as well as hours of bird-watching pleasure right in your own backyard."

Note that the phrasing of the central idea controls the emphasis of the speech. The first version stresses the individual audience member's ability to complete the technical aspects of the task. Presumably, the speech would offer a step-by-step description of the construction process. The second version suggests a quite different speech, focused on obtaining free or inexpensive materials. In contrast, the third version concentrates on benefits to the listener.

Wording a central idea is essential to the planning of your speech because it determines the way you develop the whole talk—your main points, the data and information you'll need to find, the organization you'll present, and the ways you'll link the points.

Phrasing a central idea for a speech designed to persuade is especially critical, because the words you select can control your relationship with your audience. For example, each of the following claims varies the audience's perception of the speaker's intensity:

  1. "Getting an annual physical examination is a good idea."

  2. "Getting an annual physical examination is highly recommended."

  3. "Getting an annual physical examination can save your life."

As you move from claim 1 to claim 3, you are phrasing your feelings in progressively stronger language: each successive central idea expresses your attitude more forcefully. As a result, your audience should view each successive central idea as requiring more immediate action. Now look at the following central ideas to see how each would vary the impact on the audience:

1. "Make use of our campus gymnasium to reduce tension and stress."
2. "Make use of our campus gymnasium to improve your body tone and appearance."
3. "Make use of our campus gymnasium to meet people."

These three examples give listeners very different reasons to use the campus gymnasium. Which reason would motivate your listeners to use the gym? Your central idea should be phrased in a way that captures what you think will be the most compelling reasons for your audience.

The following central ideas would vary the approach of the speaker:

1. "The city's new parking garage is an eyesore" (aesthetic judgment).
2. "The city's new parking garage is in a dangerous location" (personal safety judgment).
3. "The city's new parking garage made several council members rich" (political judgment).

Each central idea condemns the city parking garage but in a different way. The first version judges the parking garage negatively on aesthetic grounds, the second on safety grounds, and the third on political grounds. To claim that the parking garage is an eyesore, you need to demonstrate that aesthetic qualities are important criteria for judging parking garages and that the parking garage is visible to a significant number of community members. For the second central idea, you need to argue that safety is a matter of public concern and that the location of this parking garage endangers citizens. In defending the third central idea, you need to document council members' financial gain from the construction of the parking garage. In each case, the phrasing of the central idea determines the main features of the speech.

The process of selecting your subject, determining your general and specific purposes, and phrasing your central idea is the process of narrowing. When you put it all together, here is the result for an informative speech:

Subject: The common cold

General Purpose: To inform

Specific Purposes: To explain how you catch colds, how your body fights back, and how you can cope with colds.

Central Idea: "The common cold is caused by over 200 different viruses and results in varied physical reactions that require time and patience for recovery."

Ethical
Moments

· · · ·

Ethics and Public Speaking

Occasionally, we'll include a boxed area devoted to "ethical moments"—ethical decisions public speakers must make in preparing and delivering their talks. Some of these moments will apply to you and your circumstances and some won't. In either case, we hope that you'll take an ethical moment to think about the problems presented and their solutions in your life. Some of these problems might be discussed in class.

Here are some typical ethical questions that you might face in the speeches you'll give this term:

1. You read a fascinating article about fund-raising ideas for organizations. Should you borrow these ideas and present them as your own at your next club meeting? Do you need to acknowledge everything you learned from others? Must you cite sources for everything?

2. You recognize that a major portion of a speaker's informative speech came from an article that you read last week. The speaker does not cite the source. During the critique session, should you blow the whistle on the speaker or should you talk with the person later? Should you tell your teacher or let it go?

3. An article says exactly what you intended to say about the use of tanning beds. Then you find a more recent article claiming that new research contradicts the first article. Should you ignore the new evidence?

4. An authority whom you wish to cite uses the words *perhaps, probably, likely,* and *often.* Should you simply strike those words from a quotation that you wish to use to make the statement sound more positive? After all, you're not tinkering with the ideas, only the strength of assertion.

5. There are four minutes left in your class period. If you keep talking, there'll be no time left for a critique of your position. Should you extend your speech by four minutes?

6. A student in your class disagrees strongly with your analysis of cheating on college campuses. You know that he was caught cheating in another class a year ago. You expect that if you bring this student's past up in response to his challenge, it will deflect focus from his point of view. Should you go for the deflection?

Ethical moments such as these will confront you regularly, both in your speech classroom and throughout the rest of your life. Taking a few moments to consider such situations and even to articulate your position in discussion can save you many, many embarrassments later. Know what your moral stands are and know why you take them before you face ethical dilemmas on the platform.

Work on your general and specific purposes before constructing your speech. Your speaking purposes clarify your relationship to your audience. They also guide your search for speech materials.

ANALYZING YOUR AUDIENCE AND THE OCCASION

Communication is a two-way street. That means you need to take your listeners into account when you are preparing to speak. It's tempting to focus only on yourself—your goals, your fears, and your own interests. However, if you want to speak so that others will know what you know, believe what you believe, feel what you feel, and do what you believe is in their best interests, then you've got to construct the speech from your listeners' viewpoint.

Regularly ask yourself questions such as: "How would I feel about this topic if I were in their place?" "How can I adapt this material to their interests and habits, especially if their experiences or understandings are different from mine?" Putting yourself in your listeners' shoes is what researchers call **audience orientation,** an ability to understand the listener's point of view. Being audience-oriented will push you to construct speeches from the receiving end of the communication process, investigating what aspects of the audience's psychological and sociological background are relevant to your speech.

Chapter 4 takes up the topic of audience orientation in detail. For now, you should find out how much your listeners already know about your subject so that you can adjust to their level. You should also discover their attitudes toward your subject. If they are apathetic, you must create interest; if they are hostile or favorable, you must adapt what you say. In a public speaking class, this type of investigation is easy enough to conduct—you can ask. Start asking those questions early—after all, your whole purpose in speaking is to connect with your listeners!

It is also important to consider the occasion on which you're speaking. The occasion is what brings people together, and, consequently, it usually determines listeners' expectations. Do they expect to hear a comic monologue on race relations or a lecture on the relationship between minority status and socioeconomic achievements in this country? In addition to answering these questions, you should consider the nature and purpose of the occasion. Is this a voluntary or captive audience? How many people will attend? Will the speech be delivered indoors or outdoors? Will the audience be sitting or standing? Will there be competing outside noise? Will you need to make special arrangements for equipment such as a public address system or audiovisual facilities?

Throughout the process of developing your speech, consider your listeners and the occasion. Your listeners' expectations and the reasons they have gathered to hear you will influence your choice of topic and the focus of your speech. As you examine the remaining steps in the process of speech development, remember that your ultimate goal is to communicate with your listeners.

GATHERING YOUR SPEECH MATERIAL

Once you've considered the subject and purpose of your speech and analyzed the audience and occasion, you'll be ready to gather the materials for your speech. Ordinarily, you'll start by assembling what you already know about the subject and deciding roughly what ideas you want to include. Nearly always, however, you'll find that what you already know is not enough. You'll want to supplement what you know with additional information—facts, illustrations, stories, and ex-

• The occasions that bring people together help to determine their expectations. How should speakers adapt to their listeners' expectations?

amples. You can gather some of this material from newspapers, magazines, books, government documents, or radio and television programs. You can acquire other information through interviews and conversations with people who know something about the subject that you do not know.

As you search for print materials, if you plan to deal with a current question of public interest, you should consult such sources as the "The Week in Review" section of the Sunday *New York Times, U.S. News and World Report, The Wall Street Journal, Harper's,* and *The Observer.* Many magazines of general interest are indexed in the *Readers' Guide to Periodical Literature* or can be accessed via electronic data base searches; numerous encyclopedias, yearbooks, government reports, almanacs, and other reference materials can be found in your college library. This important topic—locating supporting materials—will be covered in detail in Chapter 6.

MAKING AN OUTLINE

Early in your preparation, make a rough sketch of the points you wish to include in your speech. A complete outline can be drawn up once you've gathered all of the necessary material. When this material is at hand, set down in final order the principal points you expect to present, together with the subordinate ideas that will be necessary to explain or prove these points. Flesh out your ideas with supporting materials such as examples, statistics, and quotations.

FIGURE 2.1
The Essential Steps in Planning, Preparing, and Presenting a Speech
Systematic planning and preparation will save you time and frustration as you develop your speeches. These are the seven basic steps involved in effective speech preparation. Do you usually prepare your speeches in this order? Which steps are the easiest and which are most difficult for you?

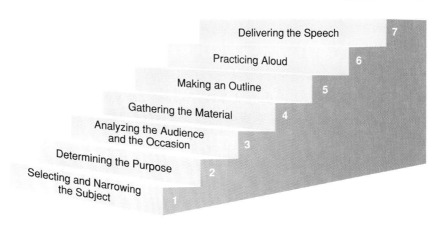

In Chapter 7, you'll find a number of specific patterns for arranging the ideas in a speech. There, too, you'll find the form that a complete outline should take. For the present, remember two simple but important rules: (1) arrange your ideas in a clear sequence and (2) make sure that each point is directly related to your specific purpose. If you follow these rules, your speech should be coherent.

PRACTICING ALOUD

Once you have completed your outline, you're ready to practice your speech (see Figure 2.1.). Even though you may feel silly talking to yourself, practice aloud to refine the ideas and phrasing of your speech and to work on your delivery skills.

Give practice a chance. It can mean the difference between an adequate effort and an outstanding speech. Repeatedly read through the outline until you've made all the changes that seem useful and until you can express each idea clearly and smoothly. Then write out a note card with brief cues for each of your main ideas. Next, try to talk through the speech by looking at your note card. On your first trials, you may inadvertently leave out some points; that's okay. Practice until all of the ideas come out in their proper order and the words flow easily. Talk in a full voice to get used to the sound—don't mumble. Finally, if possible, get a friend to listen to your speech, give you direct feedback, and help you practice making eye contact with a real person.

DEVELOPING CONFIDENT DELIVERY

Now you're ready to present your speech. Even if you've prepared fully, you still might be asking, "How can I deliver this speech? If I'm anxious, how can I convey a sense of self-confidence to my listeners?" If you understand communication anxiety, you will learn to cope with it. Let's look at the nature of anxiety, then offer some guidelines for coping with it.

Research distinguishes between two kinds of speech anxiety: state apprehension and trait apprehension.[1] **State apprehension** refers to the anxiety you feel in particular settings or situations. For example, perhaps you can talk easily with friends but are uncomfortable when being interviewed for a job. This sort of apprehension is also known as *stage fright,* because it's the fear of performing

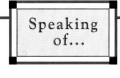

Speaking of...

• • • •

Practicing Your Speech

If you're ever learned to play the piano or drive a car with a standard transmission, you know that you can't do it all at once. You must practice to improve. The same principle can be applied to improving your public speaking skills. Practice repeated over time will result in more improvement than a single practice session. In addition, remember these guidelines:

1. Keep practice sessions brief. It's better to practice your speech for a few minutes at a time over the course of several days than to go through it repeatedly for two hours the day before it's due.

2. Practice in different settings. Deliver your speech as you walk to classes, in front of your friends, or in an empty classroom. This kind of varied practice encourages flexibility.

3. After you start your speech, finish it without stopping to correct errors or to restart it. You aren't going to deliver your speech exactly the same way every time you give it. Expect some changes in your speech delivery and phrasing.

---

that leads to your worries about failure or embarrassment. Extreme stage fright has physiological manifestations—clammy hands, weak knees, dry mouth, and a trembling or even cracking voice. Its psychological manifestations include mental blocks (forgetting what you're going to say), vocal hesitation and nonfluency, and an internal voice that keeps telling you that you're messing up. The knowledge that you're being evaluated by others brings on these anxious moments.

While some aspects of nervousness are characteristic of the situation, others are a part of your own personality. This kind of apprehension, called **trait apprehension,** refers to your level of anxiety as you face any communication situation. A high level of anxiety leads some people to withdraw from situations that require interpersonal or public communication with others. By attacking your trait fears of speaking before others, you'll be in a better position to reduce your overall level of anxiety.

Although there's no foolproof program for developing self-confidence, there are some practical ways to communicate confidently:

1. *Realize that tension and nervousness are normal.* They can even benefit you. Fear is a normal part of living; learn how to control it and make it work for you. Remember that tension can provide you with energy. As adrenaline pours into your bloodstream, you experience a physical charge that increases bodily movement and psychological alertness. A baseball pitcher who's not pumped up before a big game may find that his fastball has no zip. Similarly, a speaker who's not pumped up will undoubtedly come across as dull and lifeless.

2. *Be yourself.* Act as you would if you were having an animated conversation with a friend. Avoid a rigid or aggressive posture. At the same time,

don't become so comfortable in front of the group that you lean on the wall behind you or sprawl all over the lectern. When you speak, you want your listeners' minds to be focused on your ideas, not on the way you're presenting them.

3. *Look at your listeners.* Americans tend to mistrust anyone who doesn't look them in the eye. They also may get the impression that you don't care about them or that you aren't interested in their reactions to your message. Watch your listeners' faces for clues to their reactions. Without this essential information, you cannot gauge the ongoing effectiveness of your speech or make minor adjustments as you go along. If you notice looks of confusion or puzzlement on your listeners' faces, for example, you'll certainly want to adjust by further explaining your ideas.

4. *Communicate with your body as well as with your voice.* Realize that you are being seen as well as heard. Bodily movements and changes in facial expression can help clarify and reinforce your ideas. You might smile as you refer to humorous events or step toward your listeners as you take them into your confidence. Keep your hands free at your sides so that you can gesture easily. Let your body movements be natural and appropriate to your message. As you say, "On the other hand," you might raise your hand to reinforce your statement. Remember that your listeners won't detect the tremor in your voice or your hand. Your nervousness is much more noticeable to you than to your listeners. As you speak, your body uses up the excess adrenaline it generates. Shortly after you begin, you'll realize that your prior preparation is working in your favor and that you have the situation under control. The very act of talking aloud reduces fear.

5. *Talk about topics that interest you.* Speech anxiety arises in part because of self-centeredness; sometimes you're more concerned with your personal appearance and performance than with your topic. One means of reducing that anxiety is to select topics that are of deep interest to you, topics that will take your mind off yourself. By doing this, you make the situation topic-centered rather than self-centered. Have you ever wondered why you can talk at length with friends about your favorite hobby, sports, or political interests without feeling anxious but you find yourself in a nervous state when standing in front of your history class to report on something you've read? Talking about a subject that interests you may be part of the answer.

6. *Analyze both the situation and the audience.* The more you know about the audience and about what is expected of you in a particular situation, the less there is to fear. You will probably be less nervous during your second speech than during your first. You will be more comfortable with your audience and more aware of the demands of the situation. The same is true in other settings as well. The more you know about your audience and their expectations, the less natural fear of the unknown will occur.

7. *Speak in public as often as you can.* Having lots of public speaking experience will not eliminate your fears, but it will make them more controllable. Speaking frequently in front of your classmates will help reduce your anxiety. Repeated experiences with different audiences and situations also will increase your self-assurance and poise, which, in turn, will lessen your apprehension. Force yourself to speak up in class discussions, join in discus-

• Learning to speak in public requires thorough preparation. What essential steps should you follow before you address an audience?

sions with friends and others, and contribute as a member of organizations. Find time to talk with people of all ages. Attend public meetings on occasion and make a few comments. Maybe you'll decide to run for office!

There are no shortcuts to developing speaking confidence. For most of us, gaining self-confidence results from experience and from psyching ourselves up. The sick feeling in the pit of your stomach probably will always be there, at least momentarily, but it need not paralyze you. As you gain experience with each of the essential steps—from selecting a subject to practicing the speech—your self-confidence as a speaker will grow.

Sample Speech

• • • •
The following speech was given by David Mellor of Southern Connecticut State University at a speech contest. It's a comparatively simple, thought-provoking talk about diversity of educational goals. David opens with some reflections on the current job market and successful preparation for it. Then, he turns his attention to diversity. Using the unique life of Bill Veeck, David elaborates on his theme. Notice how the specific examples David uses make this speech interesting. The speech is easy to follow, thoughtful, and well adapted to student listeners.

Bill Veeck[2]
David Mellor

The speaker uses supporting material to show the problems in the current job market for college graduates. The answer he proposes is to take chances by choosing creative careers. Bill Veeck is an example.

By parents, peers and professors, we, as college students are pressured to succeed. This pressure is now at an all-time high. According to an April 19th article in the *New York Times,* "the job search for this year's graduates is the worst ever." Regardless of this hindrance, we see that in order to be successful, one must not only be intelligent but innovative and unique. In short, one must be creative. According to *The Journal of Higher Education,* we college students are anything but that. Over 33 percent of 1990 college graduates received business-oriented degrees. Of the remaining students, over half were divided between communications, political science, and computer studies. The problem is obvious: we need diversity. The solution is simple. We should not look to these overcrowded areas, but direct our attention towards individuals: people who chase chances rather than rest in routines. Baseball's business executive Bill Veeck was such a person. Of course, being a corporate baseball boss is not the only avenue to success. But the example shown to us by Veeck is an enlightening one. An amputee with . . . impaired vision and hearing, Bill Veeck far exceeded all expectations of him. It has been said ". . . when life gives you lemons, make lemonade." Bill Veeck did just this with his product: the game of America, the game of baseball; with his employees: our heroes, our idols, the players; and finally, with his patrons, all of us. We'll first see how Bill Veeck's creative product innovation made baseball the creative successful game that it is today. Next, we'll see how Bill Veeck's employee relations are not only the epitome of employee relations for baseball coaches, but for business executives everywhere. We'll finally see how Bill Veeck's patron appreciation has made him a man worthy of our admiration and praise. Unique, innovative individuals are hard to come by, as is success. Bill Veeck embodies a lesson we can all learn from./1

The speaker develops his first point. Bill Veeck introduced innovations to baseball, including the exploding scoreboard and the pitching cart.

From his autobiography *Veeck as in Wreck,* Bill Veeck stated ". . . baseball's greatest asset is the long sense of continuity that comes with a deep personal affiliation." Indeed Bill Veeck had long been affiliated with baseball. He merely followed in his father's footsteps when he purchased his first team. However, Bill Veeck was by no means a follower. His creative innovations upon baseball had never been seen before and may never be duplicated again. A typical day at the ballpark we'll hear, ". . . a deep drive to the center field fence, it's going, it's going, it's gone for a homerun. The scoreboard is exploding with light and a pitching cart will be out of the bull pen soon with a relief help." We hear that and it is commonplace, but we hear that courtesy of Bill Veeck. The exploding scoreboard was one of the many in-Veeck-ions that ignited both the crowd and the game of baseball. The pitching cart: a means by which the pitcher can make his grand tour of the stadium before taking to the mound—not quite. Bill Veeck created the pitching cart as a means by which to avoid lulls in the game and keep the action continuous by getting the pitcher from the bullpen to mound quicker. From the highly acclaimed business book, *Swimming with the Sharks without Being Eaten,* we see that Bill Veeck was correct in saying ". . . promotion is a state of mind long before it becomes a state of action." It was these creative innovations that brought us to Comiskey and ballparks all over the nation. This is because Bill Veeck owned several teams as a major league executive: the St. Louis Browns, the Chicago White Sox, and the Chicago Cubs just to name a few. Now some may see hints of inconsistency in wandering from team to team. Such is not present with Bill Veeck. What is present is his means by which to adopt an ailing franchise and help it achieve success. How was this done? By dealing all employees the same policy, honesty./2

The second point is expanded. Veeck earned respect from his employees by treating them honestly and equally. Examples of specific instances and testimony provide support for this point.

   In 1977, pitcher Steve Stone started out with Veeck's Chicago White Sox. After winning 18 games his rookie season, his demand throughout the league skyrocketted. Bill Veeck could not keep up with Stone's comparable offers. Though Stone wished to stay in Chicago, Bill Veeck referred him elsewhere. Now, Bill Veeck could have easily taken advantage of Stone's success and allegiance but did not. Steve Stone went on to win 25 games and the Cy Young Award in 1980, but went on to praise Bill Veeck as being the person who opened the door to his stellar career. Events such as this earned Veeck respect and admiration throughout the league. In his book, *A Hustler's Handbook,* co-author Ed Linn cites, ". . . if wealth could be measured by admiration Bill Veeck is indeed the richest man in the world." We see that Bill Veeck did have a rich reputation. But his treatment of Stone was not exceptional. Bill Veeck treated all players, major and minor leaguers, to that same honest policy and so strived to refine the echelons of his own business before intruding upon others. Such is seen with his treatment of the minor league teams. According to a 1989 *Sporting News* article, ". . . most today are mere drop-offs for hero has-beens." This was not the view of Bill Veeck. Bill Veeck looked to minor league teams as a means by which to recruit young talent, refine young ball players, and so set up a steady chain of progression from the minors to the majors. With Bill Veeck, few if any players were considered to be in the "minor league." The story of Eddie Gadell proves this fact. In 1951, Veeck sent the 3-foot 11-inch Gadell to the plate for the St. Louis Browns. Equal opportunity was provided at all levels of business under Bill Veeck. In turn, business was attracted to Bill Veeck./3

   Again from his autobiography *Veeck as in Wreck,* Bill Veeck stated

The final point extends the central idea of the speech. Veeck never forgot that the customer was the heart of the game of baseball. Examples of the pitchometer, team ponchos, checkerboard tarps, and other baseball fan involvement support this point.

". . . baseball consists of three dimensions, the customer brings a fourth." We all know that customers are the business to any business, but no one acknowledged this commonsense theory more than Bill Veeck. Most sports corporations today, be it Nike with the Air Jordan Shoe or Starter with the Pro-Line Jacket, offer a glitzy product but for a glitzy price. Bill Veeck took his product, the game of baseball, and not only made it affordable and accessible but enjoyable to all. An old archive rule in baseball states the pitcher must release the ball 20 seconds after it has been returned to him with the bases empty. Now some may protest this foolish rule, but Bill Veeck took full advantage of it. He went as far as to install a 20-second pitchometer that would bleep, scream, and siren every time the opposing pitcher exceeded 20 seconds. Baseball often falls victim to the weather. But rain did not foil the fun for the fan or Bill Veeck. Any day rain was expected fans would be given a team-emblemmed poncho upon entering the ballpark. Should the rain continue, the tarp that was rolled out onto the infield was also a chess/checkerboard on which the ground crew would be the pawns. Two lucky fans would then be recruited up into the press box and announce their moves over the public address system to the ground crew. Should chess or checkers not be the choice, the exploding scoreboard was also a movie screen that would show past highlights. We see that Bill Veeck confronted life's handicaps as he would hurdles, clearing them all. Be it with the exploding scoreboard, the checkerboard, or the complimentary ponchos, Bill Veeck has adopted all of life's abandoned apples and made a pie to please all. Eventually fans do have to leave the ballpark, but not without the continued gratuity and respect of Bill Veeck. Annually, he donated hundreds of thousands of dollars to clean up the communities beyond the stadiums. So be it in the ballpark or our own backyards, Bill Veeck is indeed worthy of our admiration and praise./4

The speaker summarizes the three main points of the speech, then returns to the idea of creativity that introduced this speech.

Veeck upheld many high traits. He was genuine, a true fan and follower of the game. He was grateful to have long been affiliated with baseball, and he was generous with his product, the game of baseball, to all of us, all of his patrons. Chances are many of us may have never made it to Comiskey. But Jerry Reinsdorf, owner of the Chicago White Sox, in the *New York Times* stated, ". . . memories won't leave, just the building is coming down." How true this is since the memory of the man who brought ivy greens to Wrigley Field and a midget to the plate in Eddie Gadell is everlasting. His employee relations, customer courtesy and creative innovations have made him a man of unequal imitation. Unfortunately college students today live in a world of imitation. It is time we seek alternatives. In this case, we need not address our congressman but rather the idea of our own originality and ingenuity. We need look no further than Bill Veeck./5

CHAPTER SUMMARY

Getting started is a matter of thinking about choices you have to make. Here are some considerations when plan and preparing your speech:

1. Select and narrow your subject, making it appropriate to you and your listeners.

2. Determine your general and specific purposes, then word the central idea to guide your development of the key ideas.

3. Analyze your audience and the occasion to discover aspects of both that may affect what you say and how you say it.

4. Gather your material, beginning with what you already know and supplementing it with library research.

5. Arrange and outline your points to package your ideas in clear and forceful ways.

6. Practice your speech aloud, working from outlines and then note cards, first alone and then with an audience.

7. Recognize that self-confidence can be developed by controlling speech anxiety.

KEY TERMS

audience orientation (p. 23)
central idea (p. 19)
general purposes (p. 17)

specific purposes (p. 18)
state apprehension (p. 25)
trait apprehension (p. 26)

SKILLBUILDING ACTIVITIES

1. For each group of statements, write a central idea for a persuasive speech that incorporates the three ideas. Compare your phrasing of the central ideas with those of your classmates.

    a. Many prison facilities are inadequate.

    b. Low rates of pay result in frequent job turnover in prisons.

    c. Prison employees need on-the-job training.

    a. Few doctors practice general medicine; most doctors specialize in one or two areas.

    b. The present system of delivering medical service is excellent.

    c. Rural areas have a shortage of doctors.

2. Rewrite each of the following statements, making it into a clear and concise central idea for a speech:

    a. "Today I would like to try to get you to see the way in which the body can communicate a whole lot of information."

    b. "The topic for my speech has to do with the high amount of taxes people have to pay."

    c. "A college education might be a really important thing for some people, so my talk is on college education."

    Now rewrite the last two statements (b and c) as central ideas for persuasive speeches. Be ready to present your versions in a class discussion.

3. Go to the library and read several popular magazines and newspapers from the week that you were born. Sort out the events of that week and write a clear central idea for a brief informative speech. Organize your ideas, and use some

illustrations or perhaps some expert testimony from the sources you examined. Follow the rest of the steps suggested in this chapter for developing a speech; then deliver it to your classmates.

4. To learn brainstorming, you must practice it. Form groups, appoint a recorder to jot down all ideas, then practice brainstorming with the questions listed below. Don't evaluate or editorialize until the brainstorming session has stopped. The goal is to list as many ideas as possible.

   a. How can an egg be packaged so that it will not break when dropped from the top of a 20-foot ladder?

   b. What can we do with all the disposable diapers clogging our landfills?

   c. What adjustments would our society have to make if there were three sexes instead of two?

   d. Pretend that aliens have been spotted hovering over our cities in spacecraft. How can we communicate with them?

   e. You are a scientist who has just discovered a potent narcotic. It has tremendous pain-relieving properties, but it is also highly addictive. What should you do with the drug?

REFERENCES

1. James McCroskey, "Oral Communication Apprehension: A Summary of Current Theory and Research," *Human Communication Research* 4 (1977): 78–96.

2. David Mellor, "Bill Veeck," *Winning Orations, 1991* (the Interstate Oratorical Association). Reprinted by permission of Larry Schnoor, Executive Secretary, Interstate Oratorical Association, Mankato State University, Mankato, Minn.

3

· · · ·

Public Speaking and Critical Listening

George called his neighbor Frank, who ran a trucking business. George said, "I want to ship three sows and seven sheep to market tomorrow." Frank said, "Fine, I'll be there at 6 A.M." At 5:50 A.M., George looked out his kitchen window to see a fleet of semis. Frank climbed out of the front cab, came to the door, and said, "We're ready." "Ready?" said George. "Why all those trucks?" "Well," replied Frank, "I figured that if you had 3,007 sheep to ship, I'd need every truck I have."

In your daily life, you spend more time listening than you do reading, writing, or speaking. While you may assume that you're a good listener from all that practice, you usually don't know about problems you might have until you miss something important. The fact is, you've probably never had any training in listening, especially for situations such as class lectures where you're expected to acquire technical or abstract materials aurally. Just ask Frank and George about the problems that can result from mishearing numbers!

Listening accounts for over 40 percent of your communicative time.[1] Through conversations, classroom lectures, group meetings, electronic media, and other forms of aural communication, you amass an amazing amount of information. You also learn to anticipate the actions of others and to gauge their feelings and moods through listening.

Listening is one of the two foundational activities in the communication process. As a speaker, you reach out to your audience; and in turn, as a listener, you respond. Both speaker and listener are active participants in communication events. As we noted in Chapter 1, listeners provide two kinds of feedback—immediate and delayed. **Immediate feedback** consists of verbal or nonverbal responses during a communicative exchange. Some immediate feedback is direct, as when questions are asked, while some is indirect, as when speakers look for

• The speaker re-
ceives verbal and
nonverbal feedback
both during and after
the communication
transition.

frowns, smiles, nodding heads, and other nonverbal cues to reactions. **Delayed feedback** consists of oral or visual signals received after the message has been transmitted—for example, voice votes on matters a speaker has recommended or written evaluations from your instructor.

After more fully introducing the idea of listening, this chapter will focus on practical listening techniques you can use in almost any situation in which someone else is doing most of the talking. We'll finish by suggesting how you can put new listening skills to work in your classes.

HEARING AND LISTENING

Hearing is the first step in the listening process. To listen to a message, you first must hear it. **Hearing** is the physiological process of receiving sound waves. Sound waves travel through the air and set up vibrations on the eardrum; these vibrations, in turn, are transmitted to the brain. Hearing is affected by the laws of physics and the neurophysiology of the body. Any number of factors can interfere with hearing—distracting noises in the environment, sounds too loud or too soft for the aural mechanisms, or impediments such as illness or hearing loss. Generally, the hearing process is beyond the speaker's control, except for the ability to change speaking volume, seating arrangements, or conditions in the room before talking.

• An example of delayed feedback—after the communication transition. What other examples of immediate and delayed feedback can you think of?

Listening, on the other hand, is the cognitive process whereby people attach meanings to aural signals. After sound waves are translated into nerve impulses by the middle ear and the auditory nerve, they're sent to the brain for interpretation. The process of interpretation—registering impulses, assigning them to meaningful contexts, and evaluating them—constitutes listening.

BARRIERS TO GOOD LISTENING

Listening is easy to define but hard to practice. You've probably developed some barriers to good listening. You'll have to remove those barriers from your mental habits if you're going to improve. Each of us has his or her own barriers, but many people share these four:

1. *Passive listening.* Many of us are just plain lazy listeners, hoping the speaker will be exceptionally clear. As a result, we forget more of the speech than we remember.

2. *Drifting thoughts.* You can comprehend many more words per minute than someone can utter; you probably can process about 400 words per minute, while most speakers produce only about 125–175 words per minute. A time lag is created in your mind that you probably fill with other thoughts. You may enter your **internal perceptual field:** the world of your own thoughts (about a friend, upcoming event, or tomorrow's term paper); or you

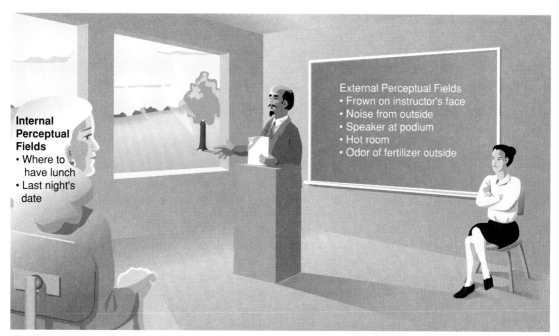

FIGURE 3.1   The Perceptual Fields of the Listener   Competing demands on our attention guarantee that we usually listen with only partial discrimination. That is, we hear and process only part of a spoken message. We rarely listen with full discrimination.

may be distracted by elements in your **external perceptual field:** things in your physical environment such as a loud truck, the sun's glare off your teacher's bald head, or a banging radiator. Listeners tend to drop in and out of speeches, taking time out to play in their internal and external perceptual fields (See Figure 3.1).

3. *Intrusion of the past.* We often bring our past—our feelings, values, and attitudes—into the speech setting. Memories of past events can be triggered by a mere word or a reference to a place. Many people spend time mentally debating with speakers, thereby remaining stuck on one idea in the past while the speaker moves ahead to others. Past feelings you remember from previous encounters with a speaker can color the way you understand the person today.

4. *Self-fulfilling prophecies.* Preset ideas can get in the way of good listening. You may have heard that Professor Rogers is a dull lecturer, so you enter the class expecting to be bored.

There's nothing wrong with having beliefs and attitudes about topics and people when you're in an audience. But, if you let your feelings, musings, and guesses get in the way of careful listening, you're likely to miss the important parts of speeches. You've got to become and remain an active listener.

PRACTICAL LISTENING TECHNIQUES

While hearing is a more or less natural physiological process for most people, listening is another matter. You've got to work hard to listen well. There's no alternative to serious brainwork if you're going to keep out of trouble when receiving oral messages. The good news, though, is that you can train yourself to listen better. Hard work can produce good listening habits. You can attack the problems of listening well in four ways: (1) know your purposes when trying to listen; (2) develop techniques that help you comprehend speeches; (3) design questions that help you evaluate or assess speeches on criteria that matter to you; and (4) sharpen your note-taking techniques.

Know Your Purposes

This may sound foolish, but the first thing good listeners do is figure out why they're listening. That's not really a silly thing to do, because, if you think about it, you know that you listen for different reasons on different occasions. On any given day, you may listen intently to your instructors in order to learn new concepts and facts, you may listen to your favorite music to relax, and you may listen attentively to be sure that a used car salesperson isn't skipping over some essential features of the machine's performance or the dealer's guarantee. Indeed, after reviewing a lot of research, Wolvin and Coakley[2] identified five kinds of listening that reflect purposes you may have when communicating with others: appreciative, discriminative, therapeutic, comprehension, and critical.

Appreciative listening focuses on something other than the primary message. Some listeners enjoy seeing a famous speaker. Others enjoy the art of good public speaking. On these occasions, you listen primarily to entertain yourself.

Discriminative listening requires listeners to draw conclusions from the way a message is presented rather than from what is said. In discriminative listening, people seek to understand what the speaker really thinks, believes, or feels. You're engaging in discriminative listening when you draw conclusions about how angry your parents are with you, based not on what they say but on how they say it. An important dimension of listening is based on relatively sophisticated inferences drawn from—rather than found in—messages.

Therapeutic listening is intended to provide emotional support for the speaker. Although it is more typical of interpersonal than public communication, therapeutic listening does occur in public speaking situations: for example, when a sports figure apologizes for unprofessional behavior, a religious convert describes a soul-saving experience, or a classmate reviews a personal problem and thanks friends for their help in solving it.

Listening for comprehension occurs when you want to gain additional information or insights from the speaker. This is probably the form of listening with which you're most familiar. When you listen to radio or TV news, to a classroom lecture on the four principal causes of the 1991 Gulf War, or to a school official explaining new registration procedures, you're listening to understand—to comprehend information, ideas, and processes.

Critical listening requires you to both interpret and evaluate the message. This is the most sophisticated and difficult kind of listening. It demands that you go beyond understanding the message to interpreting it, judging its strengths and weaknesses, and assigning it some value. You'll practice this sort of listening in class. A careful consumer also uses critical listening to evaluate commercials, political campaign speeches, advice from career counselors, or arguments offered by controversial talk show guests. When you are listening critically, you decide whether to accept or reject ideas and whether to act on the message.

Evaluating messages through critical listening requires you to identify mentally the key ideas and phrases. You might need to rephrase or reorganize the key ideas and note the signposts and other clues provided by the speaker. Summarize the message periodically. Ask yourself crucial questions about the information provided:

- Do I understand the ideas?
- What's the main thrust of the speech?
- Does the speaker's message coincide with other things I know to be true?
- Does the speaker provide supporting material and acceptable explanations?
- Do these explanations support the speaker's conclusions?

You may have many different purposes for listening, and that's why the first question you ought to ask yourself is: "What's my purpose in listening?" Do you expect to gain information and insight to make a decision? Or are you listening to enjoy yourself, to understand the feelings of another human being, to assess someone's state of mind, or to test some ideas? Knowing why you're listening will help you listen more efficiently and effectively.

Comprehend the Message

Listening for comprehension is the kind of listening you usually do and, in a sense, is the key to all the other types. Fully comprehending what's being said requires that you understand the three essential aspects of speech content: *ideas, structure,* and *supporting materials.* You've got to understand clearly what ideas you're being asked to accept, how they're related to each other, and what sorts of facts and opinions underlie them. Asking three questions will help you to comprehend a message:

1. *What are the main ideas of the speech?* Determine the central idea of the speech and look for the statements that help the speaker to develop it. These main ideas should serve as the foundation upon which the speaker builds the speech. The next time you listen to a soap commercial, listen for the main ideas: are you encouraged to buy it because of its cleaning ability, smell, sex appeal, or gentleness to your skin? Before you decide to buy a new brand of soap, you ought to know something about its characteristics. Transfer that same listening behavior to a speech: always know what ideas you're being sold.

2. *How are the main ideas arranged?* Once you've identified the main ideas, you should figure out and assess the relationships between them. If the speaker is recounting history, does the order of events seem reasonable, and are you getting a relatively complete rundown? (Always be on the lookout for speakers who leave out key events to make the story sound better.) Are causes and effects reasonably related to each other? (Let your experience in the world guide you here, but keep an open mind.) In other words, identify what the structure of ideas is, and then probe the speaker's use of that form.

Ethical Moments

Deliberately Misguiding Listeners

Some advertisers, politicians, sales representatives, and even friends have learned how to misguide their listeners without actually lying. They hope, of course, that you'll draw the conclusions they want you to on the basis of distracting or misdirective statements. Critical thinking and listening are musts in these situations.

When you recognize any of the following techniques, you should be alert to the possibility that you are being misguided:

1. *Percentages rather than absolute numbers.* Say you're told that women's salaries went up 50 percent more than men's last year. Should you cheer? Maybe not. Even if women got a 3 percent raise when men got 2 percent, there's such a differential in their salaries (with women still earning only about 60–65 percent as much as men in comparable jobs) that the gap remains wide. The actual dollar amount of women's and men's raises was probably about the same.

2. *Characteristics of the sample.* When the manufacturer tells you that "Four out of five of the dentists surveyed preferred the ingredients in Smiles-Aglow toothpaste," beware! How big was the sample? Were the dentists surveyed working in Smiles-Aglow labs, or were they in private dental practice? You need to know more about them to know whether this claim is solid.

3. *Generic substitution.* Also check out Smiles-Aglow's claim in a second way: notice that the dentists were not asked if they preferred Smiles-Aglow toothpaste but only "the ingredients" in it. Do most or all toothpastes have those same ingredients? The claim may be meaningless.

4. *Hasty generalization.* The neighbor who tells you that "Most folks on this block are against the widening of our street" may have talked to everyone, although that's not likely. He probably means "most folks I know on this block"—and then you'd better find out how many that it is. Press him for details before you accept or reject his judgment.

5. *Convenient bases.* Politicians talking about economic change carefully pick a base year for their analyses that makes their cases appear strong. For example, Republicans are fond of going back to 1981 to show how much inflation was reduced during the Reagan-Bush years, while Democrats prefer to go back to 1988 to show how much growth was slowed and the debt increased under Bush. Each party picks the base—and the economic yardsticks—that make its opponents look bad. You can't see much through only part of the lens.

These are just some of the distracting or misguiding techniques speakers use when they play with numbers. Be a critical thinker: Are the speakers lying? cheating? If they're not technically lying, are they nonetheless acting unethically? Where does ethical responsibility lie: with the speaker or with the audience?

Source: Andrew Wolvin and Carolyn Coakley, *Listening* (Dubuque, Ia.: Wm. C. Brown, 1982), pp. 3–11 and chaps. 4–8.

3. *What kinds of materials support the main ideas?* Consider the timeliness, quality, and content of the supporting materials. Are facts and opinions derived from sources too old to be relevant to today's problems? Is the speaker quoting the best experts? Ask yourself whether the materials clarify, amplify, and strengthen the main ideas of the speech. For example, if someone tells you to protest next year's 3.5 percent tuition increase, consider the following: If your school charges $15,000 or more per year, the protest may well be justified, but if it charges $25 per credit hour, protesting a $10–$15 increase would not be worth the effort. Examine the fact's ability to support the conclusion. Also, be sensitive to *types* of supporting materials; are you getting facts and figures or only some vague endorsements from nonexperts?

To comprehend the content, in other words, make sure you've got it straight so that you know what ideas, relationships, and evidence you're being asked to accept. Be an active listener. You should constantly *review, relate,* and *anticipate (RRA):*

- Take a few seconds to *review* what the speaker has said. Mentally summarize key ideas each time the speaker initiates a new topic for consideration.
- *Relate* the message to what you already know. Consider how you could use the information in the future.
- *Anticipate* what the speaker might say next. Use this anticipation to focus on the content of the message.

By reviewing, relating, and anticipating, you can keep your attention centered on the message. Using the **RRA Technique** keeps you on your toes. It keeps your head in the listening game by keeping *you* in charge of idea processing.

Assess the Speech

Once you've figured out why you're listening, how the ideas are arranged, and what supporting materials are being presented to you, you're in a position to form some opinions. You, after all, are the reason the speech is being given, so you're the one who must make the judgments: good/bad, beautiful/ugly, just/unjust, fair/unfair, true/false. Making such assessments is the only way to keep yourself protected from inflated claims, dated information, and no-good cheats. Completely assessing a speech could include asking yourself all of the following questions:

The Situation:

1. *How is the situation affecting this speech and my reception of it?* Is this the featured speaker or a warm-up act? Is the speaker expected to deal with particular themes or subjects? Am I in sympathy with this speech occasion? Speeches in churches, basketball arenas, and Rotary lunches are very different from each other, and you must adjust your judgment-making criteria accordingly.

2. *How is the physical environment affecting the speaker and my listening?* Is is too hot or too cold? Is the room too big or too small? Are other distractions affecting either of us? The physical environment can have an important

impact on your listening. You might have to compensate: lean forward, move up, or listen more closely.

The Speaker:

3. *What do I know about the speaker?* The reputation of this person *will* influence you whether you want it to or not, so think about it: are you being unduly deferential or hypercritical of the speaker just because of his or her reputation? Don't let it get in the way of critical listening.

4. *How believable do I find the speaker?* Are there things about the person's actions, demeanor, and words that make you accepting or suspicious? Try to figure out why you're reacting positively or negatively and then ask yourself whether it's reasonable for you to believe this person or not.

5. *Is the speaker adequately prepared?* Imprecise remarks, repetitions, backtracking, vague or missing numbers, and the lack of solid testimony are all signs of a poorly prepared speaker. For example, a speaker talking about how audiences influence TV programming decisions should discuss, among other things, the networks' use of focus groups. If the speaker doesn't discuss this, you'll know that he or she hasn't gotten very far into the topic. Similarly, if the speaker can't clearly explain the different rating systems, you should question the reliability of other information in the speech.

6. *What's the speaker's attitude toward the audience?* How is the audience being treated: cordially or condescendingly, as individuals or as a general group, as inferiors or as equals? Answering these questions will help you not only to assess your experience but also to form some questions for the speaker after the speech.

The Message:

7. *How solid are the ideas being presented?* We've been hammering on this point throughout the chapter because it's crucial for you to assess the ideas in terms of your own knowledge and experience. Just one warning: you could be mistaken yourself, so don't automatically dismiss new ideas. That's how you stagnate intellectually. But do listen all the more carefully when ideas seem strange, making sure that you understand them and that they're well supported.

8. *Are the ideas well structured?* Are important ones missing? For example, anyone who talks about the branches of the federal government but then ignores the Supreme Court has a defective set of ideas. Are logical links visible? The comparisons must be fair; the cause-effect links clear and logical; and the proposals for correcting social wrongs both feasible and practical. Structural relationships between ideas are what give them their solidity and coherence as a package.

9. *Is sufficient evidence offered?* You can skip ahead to Chapter 14, if you want, to see some of the tests of evidence and reasoning that you should make when faced with crucial decisions based on speeches you're hearing. The world is filled with slipshod reasoning and flawed evidence. Bad reasoning and a refusal to test the available evidence, after all, are what led the American high command to believe that Pearl Harbor was an absolutely safe port in 1941. Listen for evidence; write down the key parts so you can mull

it over, asking yourself if it's good enough to use as a basis for changing your mind or taking on some new job. Be demanding; adopt a "show me" attitude.

You certainly won't ask all nine of these questions every time you hear a speech. Remember that your listening purposes vary considerably from occasion to occasion. You will need all nine questions only when doing critical listening at times of important decision: which candidate to vote for, what lifestyle to follow, which side to support in a significant dispute. Tailor your listening practices to your purpose for attending the speech.

Take Good Notes

What we said earlier bears repeating: you're going to have to *practice* your listening skills to *improve* them. You've got to train yourself, and one of the easiest ways to do this while in college is to work on note taking. As you become a better note taker, you'll also become a better listener. Here are some tips for improving your note-taking skills.

First, get organized. Develop your own note-taking system and refine it. Some people like loose-leaf notebooks so they can add, rearrange, or remove notes; others like the tidiness of spiral or glue-bound notebooks. Whichever you choose, use separate notebooks for different courses and life experiences to avoid confusion.

Second, set aside a few minutes each day to review the syllabi for your classes, to scan your readings, and to review the previous class session's notes. This will prepare you to ask questions while the lecture or readings are still fresh in your mind and will help to keep you oriented to the class. Being oriented to what's going on helps you take notes on the most important materials.

A third suggestion is to leave a 2- to 3-inch blank margin when taking notes. When reviewing your notes later, that marginal area will allow space for making additional comments. A great way to review and study is to write critical comments about what you agree or disagree with, what you don't understand, what you think is significant or important, and what you have found to be confirmed or contradicted by another source. Such critical commentary is an important stage in merging the material in the notes with your own thoughts.

Finally, develop a note-taking scheme that works for you. Consider the possibilities:

1. *Outline form.* Making a conscious effort to outline a speech or lecture as you hear it will help you to isolate the important ideas, structure, and supporting evidence.

2. *Abbreviations.* Some abbreviations you'll want to use are obvious: the ampersand *(&)* for *and, btwn* and *w/o* for *between* and *without.* Some go with particular subject matters, as when business majors write *mgt* and *acctg* for *management* and *accounting* and when biology majors use the circle/arrow and circle/cross symbols for male and female. Others will be your own. Just make sure you can remember the ones you use!

3. *Textual space.* Leave enough space throughout your notes so that later you can add facts, clarification, and other alterations after comparing your notes with other students' or after doing related reading.

4. *Multicolors.* Many like to color-code their notes—say, black or blue for the main notes, red for questions or disagreements, green for additional content. Or, you may prefer to use highlighter pens to remind yourself of the most important parts of the material.

By taking these actions, you're no longer a couch (or desk) potato, a passive listener. You're an engaged, active listener who's demonstrating how public speaking works as a two-way communication channel. And the more you practice, the more effectively the channel will carry two-way traffic.

DEVELOPING CRITICAL LISTENING SKILLS IN THE CLASSROOM

As noted in Chapter 1, your speech classroom is set up to teach you multiple listening skills that will be of great use for the rest of your life. Listening is one of those skills you'll need to have to survive in the worlds of work, politics, and social life. You'll have to listen to understand work instructions, to make reasonable decisions between two political candidates who offer you a better life, and to follow a neighbor's instructions as she tells you how to rewire a light fixture. The ability to listen makes you money, helps you to be a good citizen, and keeps you from frying your fingers on a 110-volt circuit!

Your classrooms are excellent settings for practicing new listening skills and refining old ones. Use the Speech Evaluation Form in Table 3.1 on page 45 as a checklist when listening to speeches. It will challenge your skills, forcing you to consider a full range of speechmaking dimensions. During this term, we suggest that you improve your listening in the following ways:

1. *Practice critiquing the speeches of other students.* Practice outlining techniques; take part in postspeech discussions; ask questions of the speaker. You can learn as much from listening well as from speaking yourself.

2. *Listen critically to discussions, lectures, and student-teacher interactions in your other classes.* You're surrounded with public communication worth analyzing when you're in school. You can easily spot effective and ineffective speech techniques in those classes.

3. *Listen critically to speakers outside of class.* Attend public lectures, city council meetings, or political or religious rallies. Watch replays of presidential or congressional speeches on C-SPAN. You'll be amazed by the range of talent, techniques, and styles exhibited in your community every week.

4. *Examine the supporting materials, arguments, and language used in newspapers and magazines.* Refine your critical listening skills by practicing critical reading. Together, they represent the skills of critical thinking you need to survive in this world. **Critical thinking** is the process of consciously examining the content and logic of messages to determine their bases in the world of ideas and to assess their rationality. Critical thinking is the backbone of evaluation. It's what happens when you listen and read others' messages with your brain fully engaged.

Overall, then, listening indeed does make public speaking a reciprocal activity. Listeners seek to meet their diverse needs, ranging from personal enjoyment

TABLE 3.1   Speech Evaluation Form   Use this form to evaluate your own speeches.

The Speaker	The Audience
☐ Poised?	☐ All listeners addressed?
☐ Positive self-image?	☐ Their presence recognized and complimented?
☐ Apparently sincere?	☐ Their attitudes toward subject and speaker taken into account?
☐ Apparently concerned about the topic?	
☐ Apparently concerned about the audience?	**The Speech as a Whole**
☐ Apparently well prepared?	
The Message	Audience's expectations met?
☐ Suitable topic?	_____
☐ Clear general purpose?	_____
☐ Sharply focused specific purpose?	_____
☐ Well-phrased central idea or proposition?	_____
☐ Adequately supported (enough, varied, trustworthy sources)?	Short-range effects of the speech?
☐ Supporting materials tailored to the audience?	_____
☐ Introduced adequately?	_____
☐ Concluded effectively?	_____
☐ Major subdivisions clear, balanced?	_____
☐ Use of notes and lectern unobtrusive?	Long-range effects?
The Channel	_____
☐ Voice varied for emphasis?	_____
☐ Voice conversational?	_____
☐ Delivery speed controlled?	_____
☐ Body alert and nondistracting?	Possible improvements?
☐ Gestures used effectively?	_____
☐ Face expressive?	_____
☐ Language clear (unambiguous, concrete)?	_____
☐ Language forcible (vivid, intense)?	_____

to crucial decision making, through specialized listening skills designed for each listening purpose. When both speakers and listeners work at making the speech transaction succeed, public speaking reaches its full potential as a medium of communication.

CHAPTER SUMMARY

1. Listening is half of the communication process. Speakers reach out to audiences, who in turn respond via immediate feedback and delayed feedback.

2. Hearing and listening are two different processes. _Hearing_ is physiological. _Listening_ is a psychological process by which people seek to comprehend and evaluate aural-visual signals.

3. One way to improve your listening skills is to know why you're listening. There are five types of listening: appreciative listening, discriminative listening, therapeutic listening, listening for comprehension, and critical listening.

4. A second way to improve your listening skills is to sort out the essential aspects of speech content: ideas, structure, and supporting materials. The RRA Technique can help you listen more efficiently.

5. To improve your speech evaluation skills, practice assessing the situation, the speaker, and the message.

6. Work on note-taking techniques: getting yourself organized with a particular system; taking time to review course materials so as to learn what to listen for; leaving margins in which you can later write commentary; and developing a system of outlining techniques, abbreviations, internal spacing, and color-coding that works for you.

7. Practicing and refining your listening skills in your speech class and in other classes will help you to acquire important tools for success in the worlds of college, business, politics, and social life.

KEY TERMS

appreciative listening (p. 38)
critical listening (p. 38)
critical thinking (p. 44)
delayed feedback (p. 35)
discriminative listening
(p. 38)
external perceptual field
(p. 37)

hearing (p. 35)
immediate feedback (p. 34)
internal perceptual field (p. 36)
listening (pp. 36, 45)
listening for comprehension
(p. 38)
RRA Technique (p. 41)
therapeutic listening (p. 38)

SKILLBUILDING ACTIVITIES

1. Conduct a class discussion on a controversial topic: for example, doctor-assisted suicide, multiculturalism and political correctness, the rights of smokers, or the North American Free Trade Agreement (NAFTA). Establish the rule that before anyone can speak, he or she first must summarize to the satisfaction of the previous speaker what that person said. As a result of this exercise, what conclusions can you draw about people's ability to summarize accurately and fairly? How do good listening and feedback reduce the amount and intensity of disagreement?

2. Keep a listening log. For two or three days, record your oral communication interactions, noting (a) to whom you were speaking, (b) what your listening purposes were, and (c) how effectively you listened given your purposes. After completing the log, do a self-assessment: What are your strengths and weaknesses as a listener? What changes would make you a better listener?

3. Make a line drawing of an irregular geometric figure. Then describe it verbally to an audience and ask each listener to draw the figure when you're done. How good are you at helping listeners "see" what you've described?

REFERENCES

1. Andrew Wolvin and Carolyn Coakley, *Listening* (Dubuque, Ia.: William C. Brown Co., 1982), 3–11.

2. Wolvin and Coakley, Chaps. 4–8.

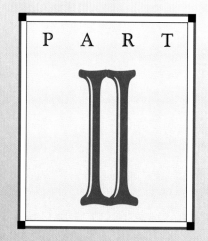

P A R T

II

· · · ·

Planning
and
Preparing
Your
Speech

Understanding Your Audience

"*L*adies and Gentlemen of the jury," the defense lawyer said, "my client has had to work hard for a living all of his life. He started out, like some of you did, at the bottom of the ladder. He's never asked for any special breaks, and he's always treated those of you who know him as a neighbor—fair and square. Why would he set fire to his own business—something he's worked so hard for? The night his building went up in smoke, so did half a lifetime's work and dreams—his and his family's. Arson is a serious crime, and it deserves our prosecution to the limits of the law. That's our duty as citizens of this country! But let's not get carried away and accuse someone who's never even gotten a parking ticket! Let's go after the real criminals, not honest law-abiding citizens like you and me."

This defense lawyer knows that effective public speaking is audience-centered. *She improves her chances of getting the desired response—a verdict of not guilty—by tailoring her communication to the individuals who make up the jury. People understand things in terms of their own experiences. This lawyer could have talked about definitions of arson, legal precedents, and reasonable doubt; but she didn't, because the jurors probably can't easily relate to technical legal arguments. Instead, she referred to starting out at the bottom, working hard, and being a good neighbor. These are the things her listeners probably have experienced in their lives. Imagine what this lawyer would say if the jury were made up entirely of senior citizens, professionals, fire fighters, or construction workers. To be most effective, she would analyze her listeners and select experiences common to the group.*

As previous chapters have stressed, you need to interact with the people you are addressing. Because of the richness and diversity of the American population, you can't assume everyone thinks and acts exactly as you do. As you select your speech topic, establish your purpose, and narrow your subject, think about your listeners. Each of the remaining steps in speech preparation—selecting supporting materials, arranging the sequence of ideas, and developing introductions and conclusions—also requires that you keep your audience in mind. Your effectiveness as a speaker depends upon adapting to your listeners.

Obviously you can't address your speech to each person individually. But you can identify common features among your listeners. Think of your audience as an onion. You peel away one layer and find others. The most effective way to understand your audience may be to peel away as many layers as possible. Identifying those layers or characteristics is the key to audience analysis. Once you have determined the primary features of your listeners, you can begin to adapt your ideas to them.

One theme will be stressed throughout this chapter: the goal of audience analysis is to discover what facets of listeners' demographic and psychological characteristics are relevant to your speech. When you understand who your listeners are, you can adapt your speech directly to them. This chapter will discuss the demographic and psychological features of listeners, how to find out about your audience, and how to use what you learn. Let's first turn to demographic analysis.

ANALYZING YOUR AUDIENCE DEMOGRAPHICALLY

Demographic analysis is the study of observable characteristics in groups of people. It encompasses features such as age, gender, education, group membership, and cultural and ethnic background. Since you can directly observe many of these things, it's a good idea to begin your audience analysis with these demographic factors. In any audience, you can identify traits that group members hold in common. You should determine your listeners' general age, gender, education, group membership, and cultural and ethnic background. Let's examine each of these factors individually.

Age

Are your listeners primarily young, middle-aged, or older? Does one age group seem to dominate a mixed audience? Is there a special relationship between age groups—parents and their children, for instance? Are your listeners your peers, or are you much younger or older?

Watch a nursery-school teacher talk to preschool children and you'll see how age gaps of 20 years or more can be overcome. Nursery school teachers know that they must adapt to their young listeners or risk chaos. They adapt partly by simplifying their vocabulary and shortening their sentences. If you've ever read a story to a child, you know another secret to engaging youngsters. You can command their attention through animation. If you talk like a wizard or a teapot or a mouse, you can see children's eyes widen. The point is this: even if your listeners are much younger than you are, you can still engage them by recognizing what captures their attention. In this way, you are using audience analysis to make your message more effective.

Gender

Is your audience predominantly male or female, or is the group made up of both genders? Do your listeners maintain traditional gender roles, or do they assume different roles? Ted chose date rape as the topic for a classroom speech. He was concerned about the lack of information about date rape on his campus and wanted to provide his classmates with the facts. But two things bothered Ted. First, one of his friends asked him why he was giving a speech on this topic. To the friend, it seemed like date rape was an inappropriate topic for a male speaker. Ted was surprised at his friend's reaction but also wondered if others in his class would have the same thought. In addition, Ted realized that both men and women were members of his class. He wondered how he could interest everyone in the subject.

After some thought, Ted decided to handle the problem of gender by convincing his listeners that date rape is not just an issue that affects women. Since they all date, they should all be concerned. In addition, Ted planned to present statistics showing the rising numbers of date rapes. In this way, he tackled the stereotype of the rapist as an unknown midnight assailant lurking in a dark alley. Finally, Ted would tell his listeners that he hadn't realized the extent of the problem until a good friend confided that she'd been raped by another student who offered to walk her back to her apartment after a party. With this three-point strategy, Ted was able to convince his classmates that date rape affected both men and women. They also wanted to listen to him because he was legitimately concerned about the problem. Ted's awareness of gender as a demographic variable allowed him to deal with his audience effectively.

Education

How much do your listeners already know about your subject? Does their experience allow them to learn about this subject easily and quickly? Obviously, people who have worked with a computer word-processing program, for example, will learn its new features more quickly than people who have not.

Knowing the educational background of your audience can guide you in your choice of language, kinds of supporting material, and organizational pattern. Assume that you are addressing the faculty senate as a student advocate of expanded student parking on campus. This audience will demand strong support for your arguments. You can express complex arguments in technical language. The general educational level of your listeners requires that you adapt your ideas and their development. However, when you are invited to speak to a local citizens' group about the proposal for expanded student parking, you will have to simplify your language, supporting material, and organization for a more diverse, probably less-educated audience.

Group Membership

Do your listeners belong to groups that represent special attitudes or identifiable values? Are they part of a formal organization such as a church, chamber of commerce, or scouting group, or have they spontaneously come together? Can you pick out common traditions or practices within the organization? What is the cultural climate of the organization?

In some ways, Americans are joiners. We form churches, fan clubs, hobby organizations, health groups—the lists seem endless. You can find a group to join for almost any purpose. We join together to share common experiences, to solidify common values, and to express feelings. Often group members share demographic characteristics. For example, doctors, lawyers, and dentists join professional societies based on occupational similarities. Consumer advocacy groups and support groups are united by purpose. Members of labor unions hold jobs and economic welfare in common. Homeowners' groups share geographic features. Political parties and religious groups attract people who share common values. Tee ball clubs, high school reunions, and associations of retired persons unite people who are similar in age. Groups share similar interests and goals that can be identified readily. Identifying these common interests is an important element of assessing your audience, as the following example illustrates.

The city council in Abby's hometown wanted to build an incinerator for disposal of solid waste. Abby was against the incinerator project and, after voicing her opinions at a backyard barbecue, she found herself representing a grass-roots group of local homeowners. This group shared a common concern for their property values and the environmental safety of their neighborhood. Abby attended the next city council meeting to express the views of the neighborhood. After thinking about the city council's actions, she realized that the primary argument for the incinerator had been to save money. She told the council that more money could be saved by recycling household plastics, selling aluminum cans, and mulching grass clippings. Those simple steps would reduce the waste significantly and make the building of an incinerator unnecessary. Abby's clinching argument was to remind council members that several of them were up for re-election. Her arguments hit a nerve; the incinerator project was canceled. As members of a group, the city council was dependent upon homeowners' approval for their jobs.

Cultural and Ethnic Background

Are members of your audience predominantly from particular cultural groups? Do your listeners share a special heritage? Can you identify common origins among listeners?

More and more, the United States is becoming a multiracial, multicultural society. Currently, over 25 percent of all Americans identify themselves as nonwhite. The number of nonwhites in this country is expected to grow rapidly in the next ten years. Many Americans celebrate their roots in other countries or cultures, and those strong cultural heritages may bear upon your speechmaking experience. It is important to recognize the cultural and ethnic diversity of your listeners, as the following example shows.

Ed, a student in mass communication, was invited to talk about American media to a group of visiting students sponsored by the Japanese Youth Exchange Program. He realized that some of his examples would be familiar to his listeners. Many Japanese are avid sports fans, follow the Simpsons, and have fan clubs for American celebrities. The Japanese also enjoy their own programs. Considering this, Ed decided to investigate Japanese television more fully. He found many examples of high-quality programs. After reading some particularly interesting research on Japanese soap operas, Ed discovered *"Oshin,"* the daily serial drama rated highest among television programs in Japan. He read about the series, which dramatizes the life of an early twentieth-century heroine. The struggle of new ideas with traditional values is featured in most episodes, and Ed realized how conflict characterizes both Japanese and American soap operas. This recognition of the similarity in television programming gave Ed an idea for his speech. He decided to focus on conflict in soap opera programming and to use both American and Japanese programs as examples. The speech was a hit. Like Ed, you should recognize when the background of your audience influences the speech topic and its development.

Using Demographic Information

The importance of demographic analysis does not lie in simply recognizing the variables present in an audience. This is just the first step. The key is to decide which of these demographic factors will affect your listeners' reception of your message. In other words, you must shape your message with your audience in mind.

Sometimes, several factors may affect your message. For example, if you've been asked to talk to a local kindergarten class about your baseball card collection, you must take age and education into consideration. You should adapt to your young listeners by using simplified concepts—talking about the number of hits rather than ERAs. You should also keep your talk brief to accommodate shorter attention spans. And, most importantly, you should involve children by using visual materials. Bring several cards for them to hold and examine.

If you were to talk about your baseball card collection to a group of local business owners, on the other hand, your message would be very different. The age and education of your listeners would still influence your message development, but since those demographic factors would be different, your message should be adapted to the changes. Since your listeners are older and better educated, they can understand more complex ideas. For example, you might focus on the investment potential of baseball card collections. As owners of businesses, their group membership suggests that they would be interested in the commercial aspects of your collection.

Demographic analysis helps you to adapt your message to your listeners more effectively. It can help you to select and develop your key ideas. It can also assist you in understanding your listeners by pinpointing the factors that are common among them.

ANALYZING YOUR AUDIENCE PSYCHOLOGICALLY

Careful psychological analysis of your audience may provide clues about how they think. This is especially important if you intend to influence your listeners. Before you can hope to alter their thoughts or actions, you need to know what ideas they already hold.

To analyze your audience psychologically, divide your listeners into groups much as you would group them by demographic characteristics. We call this analy-

Speaking of...

• • • •

The Changing Audience

Four major demographic changes are expected to occur in the United States during next 20 years. Some forecasters think that these shifts in the American population will have profound impacts on everything, including political decisions, consumer demands, and social values. Here's what they predict will happen:

1. Most of the economic growth in the United States will be fueled by people between 35 and 55 years old. People in the 35 to 50 age group will see the greatest increases in total income—almost 70 percent. People in the 45 to 55 age group will at least double their spending power.

2. The Hispanic population is both the youngest (with an average age of 22 compared to 26 for African Americans and 31 for white Americans) and fastest growing segment of the American population. By 2010, it is predicted that one-third of all Americans under 18 will be Hispanic.

3. Americans are aging at a rate faster than at any other time. There will be a boom in the number of senior citizens. By 2020, one-fifth of all Americans will be over 65.

4. Since World War II, women have entered the work force in increasing numbers. This trend, which is expected to continue, may be the single most significant trend of the twentieth century. As women continue to choose to work outside the home, birth rate patterns have changed, purchasing behavior has shifted, and income levels of families with two wage earners have risen.

What impacts do you think these four demographic changes will have on your future?

For more on this subject, see: Judith E. Nichols, *By the Numbers* (Chicago: Bonus Books, 1990).

sis **psychological profiling.** Beliefs, attitudes, and values are the key concepts in discussing the psychology of listeners. After we examine each group of concepts, we'll discuss ways you can use it to tailor your message to your listeners.

Beliefs

The first task of psychological profiling is understanding audiences' beliefs. **Beliefs** are convictions about what is true or false. They arise from first-hand experiences, from public opinion, from supporting evidence, from authorities, or even from blind faith. For example, you might believe "Calculus is a difficult course," based on your own experience. At the same time, you may also believe that calculus is important for your career because of what others have told you. And, you probably enrolled in college in the first place because your parents and high school teachers encouraged you to try college courses. Although each of these beliefs is held for different reasons, each is considered to be true.

Some beliefs can be demonstrated—these we call **facts.** Others are personal **opinions.** Facts are generally supported by strong external evidence. When you say, "Research has proven that infant blue whales gain an average of ten pounds per day," you're very sure of that belief. While you may not know much about baby blue whales, you have confidence in the researchers who do. You hold facts with certainty because you have hard evidence to support them.

Opinions, however, are another matter. An opinion is a personal belief that may not be supported by strong external evidence. You may think that all cats are nasty animals because you have been scratched by cats or because you are allergic to them. However, your experience is limited. Many people like cats. Normally, you signal to your listeners when your beliefs are opinions. You might say, "It's my opinion that cats are worthless creatures," or "In my opinion, cats are vicious." In this way, you are telling your listeners that your evidence to support your claims is limited. Thus, an opinion is a personal belief supported with less compelling external evidence than a fact.[1]

Since both facts and opinions are matters of belief, sometimes the difference between them is blurred. In colonial America, for instance, many people knew "for a fact" that regular bathing caused disease, just as their ancestors knew that the earth was flat and located at the center of the universe. If many people harbor similar opinions, those opinions may be taken for facts. It's important to recognize that opinions and facts are psychological constructs.

Once you have investigated your audience's beliefs, how can you use this information? You need to determine which beliefs will help you and which are obstacles to be overcome. Pretend that you oppose granting rights to gay personnel in the military. You want to convince your classmates to accept your point of view. Immediately you recognize the swirling controversy centering on this subject, about which people hold many different facts and opinions. First, consider what your listeners believe to be true. If they accept that gays already serve in the military and have served with distinction, then you may have to convince them that the presence of gays is disruptive. If, on the other hand, they think that the number of gays in the armed forces is negligible or that gay personnel do not make good soldiers, your job is much easier. Thus, determining your audience's beliefs will help you to focus your ideas.

Some beliefs are variable, or relatively open to change, while others are fixed. It is more difficult to change fixed beliefs than variable beliefs. **Fixed beliefs** are those that are highly resistant to change. They have been reinforced throughout a lifetime, making them central to one's thinking. Many early childhood beliefs, such as "Bad behavior will be punished" and "If you work hard, you'll succeed," are fixed. Some beliefs may harden in your mind and become resistant to change as you mature. For example, as you grow older, you may tend to vote for candidates from one political party and to purchase the same make of vehicles. The demographic variable of age may indicate to you that a more mature audience possesses fixed beliefs.

Some fixed beliefs can even be called *stereotypes*. A **stereotype** is the perception that all individuals in a group are the same. For example, we might believe, "All police officers are honest" or "Rich people cheat on their taxes" or "Never trust a politician." The problem with stereotypes is that not all police officers are honest, rich people may pay the taxes they owe, and many politicians are trustworthy. Stereotypes ignore individual differences and exceptions to rules.

In contrast, **variable beliefs** are less well-anchored in your mind and experiences. You might enter college thinking you want to be a chemist; however, after an instructor praises your abilities in a composition class, you may consider becoming a writer. Then, you take a marketing class and find out that you're good at planning advertising campaigns. This self-discovery goes on as you take additional classes. Your beliefs about your talents change with your personal experiences; since your beliefs are still not firmly fixed, they may change again as you encounter new experiences.

Before you speak, it's important to know which of your audience's beliefs are *fixed* (difficult to change) and which are *variable* (more easily altered). You can set more realistic expectations if you know that your listeners are unlikely to change their fixed beliefs, and you can concentrate on changing variable beliefs before you attack fixed beliefs. For example, consider trying to convince your classmates that education is a waste of time. Most likely, their belief that education is valuable is fixed and you'll have trouble changing it. On the other hand, you might have more luck getting them to change majors or take a class outside their majors. Their beliefs about which classes to take probably are variable.

TABLE 4.1   The Varieties of Belief   Beliefs of fact or opinion can be either fixed or variable. They are psychological constructs held by individuals or by groups.

	Beliefs of Fact	**Beliefs of Opinion**
Fixed beliefs	Vegetarians live longer, healthier lives.	Broccoli tastes good.
Variable beliefs	I might live longer if I didn't eat meat.	It might be fun to learn to cook vegetarian meals.

Attitudes

The second task of psychological profiling is to identify audience attitudes. **Attitudes** are tendencies to respond positively or negatively to people, objects, or ideas. Attitudes are emotionally weighted. They express individual preferences and feelings such as, "I like my public speaking class," "Classical music is better than rap music," and "Cleveland is a beautiful city."

Attitudes often influence our behavior. One dramatic example of the strength of attitudes occurred when the Coca-Cola Corporation introduced new Coke, a refigured formula, with disastrous results. Although extensive blind taste tests indicated that people preferred new Coke's flavor, consumers reacted negatively because of their loyalty to the classic formula. Their attitudes controlled their purchasing behavior, and the corporation wisely "reintroduced" Coca-Cola Classic.

As a speaker, you should consider the dominant attitudes of your listeners. Audiences may have attitudes toward you, your speech subject, and your speech purpose. Your listeners may think you know a lot about your topic, and they may be interested in learning more. This is an ideal situation. However, if they think you're not very credible and they resist learning more, you must deal with their attitudes. For example, if a speaker tells you that you can earn extra money in your spare time by selling magazine subscriptions, you may have several reactions. The thought of extra income from a part-time job is enticing. At the same time, you suspect that it might be a scam and you feel uncomfortable because you don't know the speaker well. These attitudes toward the speech topic, purpose, and speaker will undoubtedly influence your final decision about selling subscriptions.

Values

The third component of psychological profiling is understanding audience values. **Values** are the basic concepts organizing one's orientation to life. They provide standards for judging the worth of thoughts and actions. For many Americans, life, freedom, family, and honesty are basic values. These are deeply ingrained and enduring; as a result, they are very resistant to change. Imagine trying to convince a friend to cut all family ties and give up a steady income. No matter how noble your cause, you will probably meet powerful resistance because you are attacking fundamental values.

Values are more basic than beliefs or attitudes because they represent broad categories that may motivate attitudes and beliefs. Values serve as the foundations for the beliefs and attitudes that cluster around them (see Figure 4.1). For example, a person may hold a value such as, "Human life is sacred." That value can be expressed in multiple attitudes including "Abortion is wrong" or "Mercy killing is immoral." That value may also be expressed in beliefs such as, "A fetus should be treated as a human being," "Most Americans are opposed to abortion

• Listener's attitudes can vary dramatically. What attitudes could you expect to find in this situation? How might a speaker handle the expectations of these listeners?

rights legislation," or "Religious authority ought to be respected on questions of morality."

Values, then, underlie an individual's particular attitudes and beliefs. Former president Ronald Reagan, regarded by many as "The Great Communicator," frequently appealed to values in his public speeches. He often combined several val-

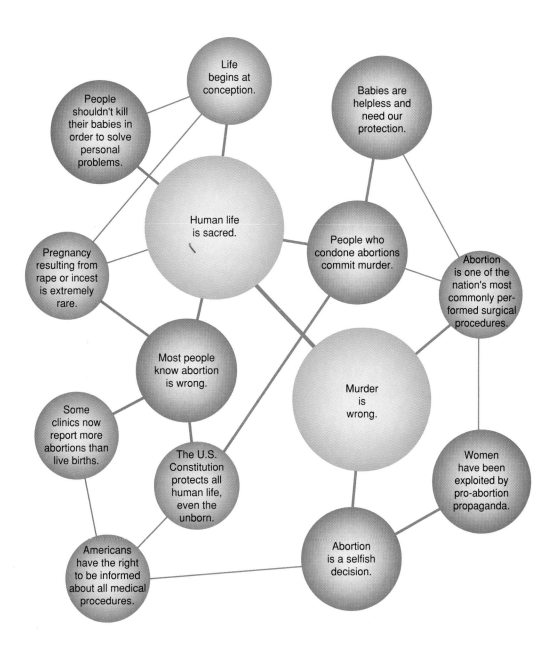

FIGURE 4.1   Belief, Attitude, and Value Clusters   Beliefs, attitudes, and values are interdependent. They often form clusters that reinforce each other.

ues in a single sentence. In his 1980 acceptance speech, Reagan declared that people from all walks of life, regardless of political party, were bound together "in the community of shared values of family, work, neighborhood, peace, and freedom."[2]

Discovering what values audience members habitually bring to bear on issues is a critical part of audience analysis. A search for *common ground*—shared values—represents a crucial step in audience analysis, because values organize and often influence the beliefs and attitudes of your listeners.

DISCOVERING DEMOGRAPHIC AND PSYCHOLOGICAL FACTORS

Now that you understand which demographic and psychological factors are important to consider when developing a speech, you should think about how you're going to discover this information. You probably already know the answer: you can ask your listeners for their opinions and you can observe them and draw inferences from your observations. Let's look at each option.

Surveying Your Listeners

Often, the best source of information about your audience is your listeners themselves. Ask them. You may not have the services of a professional pollster, but you can conduct informal interviews with members of the group or develop a more formal survey to assess their attitudes on a topic.

Suppose you are concerned about the rapidly rising number of sexually transmitted diseases among local teenagers. As the parent of a teenager, you are convinced that every effort should be made in the schools to halt this alarming trend, including making condoms available to all students. If you intend to convince the school board to take action on this issue, you need to know how the members of the board currently feel about the issue. Your plan is clear: you talk to the members of the board individually and find out.

However, you may also have to convince the local Parent-Teacher Association to support your plan. This presents an entirely different problem since there are thousands of parents in your school district. Even if you spent hours on the phone, you still probably couldn't interview every parent in the district. Your alternative is to talk to parents active in the organization or call them randomly to get an accurate profile of their views.

In each case, the questions you will ask are basic. You want action, so it's clear that you will ask how they would vote on the issue. It's also important to know whether they'll vote at all, so you will need to find out whether they regularly attend meetings. Finally, you need to understand why they feel the way they do about the issue. In this way, if you have an opportunity to talk about the issue, you'll have the basic points of conflict already outlined.

Observing Your Listeners

Sometimes you don't have direct access to members of your audience. If this is the case, then you must rely on indirect observation and inference for your audience analysis. Occasionally you'll have public statements, earlier conversations, voting behaviors, purchasing decisions, and other information on which to base your analysis. At other times, you will have direct access to your listeners. In your class, for example, you may interview or survey other students to find out how they feel about extending their college degree programs from four years to five years. You can also infer from informal comments about tuition and housing costs that students won't favor a five-year college degree.

If you aren't closely tied to the group you will address, you'll want to: (1) think through your personal experiences with identifiable groups in the audience; (2) talk with program chairpersons and others who can tell you who is in the audience and something about their interests; and (3) ask speakers who have addressed this or similar audiences what you can expect. Keep in mind that these strategies provide limited information. You can supplement this information by attending a few meetings of the group yourself or reading the constitution or other literature about the group. In combination, these indirect observations will help you to adjust your speech to your listeners.

Finally, you can consult published sources that provide demographic and survey information on broad segments of our society. Opinion polls, market surveys, political profiles, and demographic shifts are all available in your library in sources such as *Statistical Abstract of the United States, Survey of Current Business, Business Conditions Digest, Bureau of Labor Statistic News, Statistics of Income Bulletin,* and *Facts on File.*

Using Your Psychological Profile

After you have developed a profile of your audience's beliefs, attitudes, and values, how can you use this information?

1. *Understanding your audience's beliefs, attitudes, and values will help you to frame your ideas.* For example, if your audience believes childhood is a critical time of development, you can move from this belief to recruit volunteers for a day-care co-op. If they value family life, you can touch on this theme to solidify their commitment. On the other hand, if your audience is apathetic about childhood development, you must establish the critical nature of the early years of child development before you can hope to persuade them to support a co-op.

2. *Understanding your audience's beliefs, attitudes, and values will help you to choose your supporting materials.* If your audience analysis shows that your listeners consider statistics to be factual, you should use scientific studies or numerical data in your speech. On the other hand, if your audience believes in the divine inspiration of the Bible, you can cite biblical testimony to sway them.

3. *Understanding your audience's beliefs, attitudes, and values also allows you to set realistic expectations as you plan your talk.* Not all audience beliefs are equally amenable to change. You may encounter resistance if you try to destroy too many beliefs or beliefs that are firmly fixed. It is probably unlikely that you will convert a Muslim to Christianity or convince a millionaire to donate everything to you. If beliefs are rooted in strongly held values, you may never change them.

Psychographics

Marketers use a process called *psychographics* to understand consumers. They realize that groups of people with similar demographic characteristics don't always behave in the same way or purchase the same products. Even if the income, age, and educational levels of consumers are identical in suburbs of New York City, Seattle, Minneapolis, Atlanta, and Los Angeles, their purchasing behavior may vary dramatically. As a result, marketers have used demographic data to gain insight into consumers' minds. Psychographics is the result.

Psychographics evolved to synthesize the demographic characteristics of consumers with the underlying emotions and values that drive their choices among brands. Understanding how people think, combined with a demographic profile, gives marketers a tool to sell their products. But the process is hardly foolproof. One dramatic example of the failure of psychographic research occurred in the late 1950s. General Mills had developed a new cake mix to free cooks from the mixing and mess of conventional cake baking. The mix required the cook only to add water to a powder—the Betty Crocker Cake Mix. The results were disastrous. Even though it was easy to make and tasted fine, nobody liked it.

Imagine the confusion and concern among executives at General Mills. In order to solve the problem, General Mills hired Ernest Dichter, a psychologist who specialized in consumer motivations. Dichter interviewed housewives and discovered that they weren't satisfied with just adding water to a mix. They wanted to create something for their families, so they added eggs or milk to the mix as well as water and ruined the cake. The new mix left the cook out of the process. So, General Mills reformulated the mix, requiring the addition of an egg and water. The new mix made *Betty Crocker* a household word.

For more information on psychographics, see: Rebecca Piirto, *Beyond Mind Games: The Marketing Power of Psychographics* (Ithaca, N.Y.: American Demographics Books, 1991).

USING AUDIENCE ANALYSIS IN SPEECH PREPARATION

Audience analysis helps you search for clues to the way your listeners think and act. Identifying the demographic and psychological characteristics of your listeners is an important step toward good communication. Using these characteristics helps you to discover what might affect the audience's acceptance of you and your ideas. When you understand your listeners, you can plan your speech so that they can better understand it. Let's focus on how audience analysis helps you prepare to speak through audience targeting and audience segmentation.

As you consider your reasons for speaking, you need to determine what you can realistically expect to accomplish with your particular audience in the time you have available. As you think about your audience, four considerations should arise: your specific purpose, the areas of audience interest, the audience's capacity to act, and the degree of change you can expect.

Setting Purposes Realistically

Suppose you have a part-time job with your college's Career Planning and Placement Office; you know enough about its operations and have enough personal interest in it to want to speak about career planning and placement to a variety of listeners. What you've discovered about different audiences should help you to determine appropriate, specific purposes for each. If you were to talk to a group of incoming freshmen, for example, you would know that they probably:

- Know little about the functions of a career planning and placement office (have few beliefs in this area, none of which are fixed).
- Are predisposed to look favorably on career planning and placement (have a positive attitude toward the subject).
- Are more concerned with such short-term issues as getting an adviser, registering, and learning about basic degree requirements than they are with long-range matters such as finding jobs (are motivated by practical values).
- See you as an authoritative speaker and, consequently, are willing to listen to you (have a positive attitude toward the speaker).

Given these audience considerations, you would probably provide basic rather than detailed information about career planning and placement. You might phrase your specific purpose as follows: "To brief incoming freshmen on the range of services offered by the Career Planning and Placement Office." This orientation will include a brief description of each service and a general appeal to your audience to use these services to make some curricular decisions.

If you spoke to a group of graduating college seniors on the same subject, you would address the audience differently. You would discover that they:

- Are familiar with the Career Planning and Placement Office through roommates and friends who have used it (have beliefs that are fixed).
- Have strong positive feelings about career planning and placement because they are hoping to use such services to find jobs when they graduate (have a positive attitude toward the subject).
- Tend to think education has prepared them to "earn a decent living" (have a practical perspective on the topic).
- May view you as an unqualified speaker on this subject, especially if you aren't a senior or aren't employed full-time (have a negative attitude toward the speaker).

Given these factors, you should offer specific details in some areas. You might describe the special features of the office rather than simply outlining its general duties. Your listeners need to know the *how;* they already know the *what.* You could reassure them that the office successfully places many students and point out that the process is more successful when students allow ample time for résumé development, job searching, and interviewing. You could demonstrate your expertise by

Hostile Audiences

How do you gain a positive response from people who disagree with you? While it is unreasonable to expect to convert every member of a hostile audience, you can improve your chances of getting them to listen with the following strategies:

1. *Establish goodwill.* Let them know you are concerned about the issues or problems you're discussing.

2. *Start with areas of agreement.* Develop some common ground before you launch into controversial territory.

3. *Offer principles of judgment.* Determine the basis upon which you and your listeners can evaluate ideas.

4. *Develop positive credibility.* If your listeners respect you, they are less likely to reject your ideas.

5. *Use experts and supporting material to which your audience will respond.* Choose your supporting material with your audience in mind.

6. *Disarm your listeners with humor.* Mutual laughter establishes positive rapport.

7. *Use a multisided presentation.* Recognize more than one perspective on the issues.

Above all, be realistic when addressing a hostile audience. Remember that the more strongly an audience opposes your position, the less change you can reasonably expect to occur.

For more information, see: Herbert Simons, *Persuasion* (New York: Random House, 1986), pp. 150–160.

talking about career possibilities across a variety of fields—especially if you know what fields are represented in the group you are addressing. You might phrase your specific purpose as follows: "To inform graduating seniors about Midstate University's philosophy of career planning and placement, about ways that the office can help students find employment, and about specific types of information and assistance that the office provides to students." Audience analysis will help you to shape your specific purposes and determine which are most appropriate to your listeners.

Setting Audience Responses Realistically

As a speaker, ask your listeners to accomplish only what is within their capacity. You can often discover your listeners' potential for action through an audience analysis. Demographic factors will tell you about the channels of action available to your listeners. Voters can cast their ballots in elections, parents can teach their children, consumers can boycott products, and many people can contribute money. You can use the psychological factors that you discover through audience analysis to stimulate listeners' motivations to act.

You can also determine ranges of authority through an audience analysis, especially through analysis of demographic factors. For example, in speaking with a local school's Parent-Teacher Association about instituting an after-school program of foreign language and culture instruction, you're addressing an audience made up of school administrators, teachers, and parents. Each of these groups has certain powers to act. School administrators can seek funding from the school board; teachers can volunteer instructional time; and parents can petition the school board, enroll their children, and volunteer to help with the program. Your speech could include these specific goals for each group of listeners.

Be realistic about the degree of change you can expect from your listeners. How intensely can you motivate an audience to react to a topic? If your listeners are strongly opposed to downtown renovation, a single speech—no matter how eloquent—will probably not reverse their opinions. One attempt may only neutralize some of their objections. This is a more realistic goal for a single speech than completely reversing their opinions.

How much action can you expect after your speech? If your prespeech analysis indicates that your listeners vehemently oppose nuclear power plants in your area, you may be able to recruit many of them to work long hours picketing, lobbying, and participating in telephone marathons. However, if they moderately oppose nuclear facilities, you might ask for a small monetary donation rather than an actual time commitment. Audience analysis should help you to set more realistic communication goals.

Audience Segmentation

So far, we've focused on how audience analysis helps you to target your audience as a group. Keep in mind that no matter how close together people are seated in the room, they are still individuals. Sometimes you can approach each listener individually. However, such communication is time-consuming and inefficient when you're dealing with matters of broad public concern.

• Value orientations serve to motivate people to action. Speakers can appeal to these value orientations. What value appeals might work in this situation?

You can use an approach called **audience segmentation** to divide your audience into a series of subgroups or "target populations." A typical college audience, for example, might be segmented by academic standing (freshmen through seniors), by academic major (art through zoology), by classroom performance (A+ to F), or even by extracurricular activity (ROTC, SADD, Young Republicans, Pi Kappa Delta). You can direct main ideas to each of these subgroups.

Suppose you were to give a speech to members of a local community club, urging them to fund a scholarship. Your initial segmenting of the audience might tell you that the club is composed of medical professionals, social service personnel, educators, and business people. By thinking of the club as segmented into these subgroups, you should be in a position to offer each subgroup some reasons to support your proposal. You might outline the appeals this way:

> **Central Idea:**   The membership of the Community Club should fund a college scholarship for a local student.

Reasons

1. *For doctors and hospital workers:* Well-educated people take better care of themselves. They are more likely to seek early treatment for serious health problems.

2. *For social service workers:* The social-team concept means that working with everyone is necessary for the improvement of the community.

3. *For educators:* By denying education to capable students, we neglect to tap into one of the most important resources of our community—young people.

4. *For community business people:* Well-educated citizens contribute more to the financial resources of the community as investors, property owners, and heads of households.

You can see how each statement is directed to segments of your audience. These main ideas implicitly refer to the medical ethic of serving humankind, to the commitment of social services to helping people from all strata of life, to educators' beliefs and attitudes that youth are a national resource, and to business leaders' commitment to financial responsibility and success.

Understanding your audience is a key step in speech preparation. To become a competent speaker, you must make many decisions about your topic, specific purposes, and phrasing for central ideas and main ideas. Demographic and psychological analyses of audience members will help you to make these decisions. If you learn all you can about your listeners and use relevant information to plan your speech, you'll improve your chances for success.

Sample Audience Analysis

• • • •

In this chapter we have surveyed various factors that you will consider as you analyze your audience and occasion. If you work systematically, these choices will become clearer. Suppose you were invited by a community group to increase their understanding of the disease known as AIDS (Acquired Immune Deficiency Syndrome). You might prepare the following comprehensive analysis of your audience as you prepare your speech:

Understanding AIDS

I. General Description of Speech
   A. *General Purpose:* To persuade.
   B. *Specific Purpose:* To prove to members of a local political action caucus that AIDS poses a current national health threat.

II. *General Description of the Audience:* The political action caucus is a community group whose function is to promote political consciousness and action in the community. It consists of varied membership, including local homemakers, business owners, the mayor, the chair of the state Republican Committee, and approximately one dozen interested listeners. A synopsis of the monthly meeting is broadcast over local radio stations and included on the editorial page of the local newspaper (reaching a large secondary audience).

III. Audience Analysis
   A. Demographic Analysis
      1. *Age:* Most of the individuals attending the meeting are between 30 and 65. Except when I urge the audience to attend future events, age is probably not an important factor. I am significantly younger than members of my audience (21), and I will need to enhance my credibility as a speaker to compensate for my relative youth and inexperience.
      2. *Gender:* The caucus is a mixed group with slightly more women than men. Given the topic, the audience may initially have the attitude that AIDS only affects people who engage in high-risk behaviors.
      3. *Education:* Approximately one-third of the listeners have completed B.A. degrees in various fields including political science, pharmacy, nursing, home economics, and accounting. All but four of the remaining members have finished high school; several have taken college courses. While several health professionals in the audience are familiar with disease history and control, most listeners are acquainted with the topic only through media coverage.
      4. *Group Membership:* All listeners are politically active and registered voters. Although they do not necessarily share party affiliation, they all value participation in the democratic process.

5. *Cultural and Ethnic Background:* Ethnic background is primarily European. Most consider AIDS to be a problem associated with minorities, including homosexual males, hemophiliacs, and intravenous drug users. All members of the caucus were either born or raised in this small, midwestern community whose small-business economy is agriculturally-based.

B. Psychological Profile

1. *Factual Beliefs:* Anyone who contracts AIDS will die of it. There is no cure for AIDS. The disease is confined primarily to the East and West coasts. The only local resident to die from AIDS had visited New York—it is assumed that he contracted the disease during his visit.

2. *Opinions:* Homosexual behavior is morally wrong and should not be condoned.

3. *Attitudes:* Members of the caucus probably consider me naive and idealistic. While they were surprised by the recent news of the AIDS death of a community resident, they are probably not very concerned about the spread of the disease because they don't consider themselves likely targets of it.

4. *Values:* They are committed to the democratic process and take pride in community political involvement at the state and national levels. They see themselves as common people—"the heart of America"—fulfilling the American dream. Caucus members often point to community progress in civil rights issues, general educational reforms, and high voter turnout during elections.

With this prespeech audience analysis completed, the next steps in preparing the speech are clearer. The audience analysis points to the kinds of supporting materials needed. For instance, you need to supply accurate facts about the disease, especially its impact on those who are not considered to be at risk. You need to explain how AIDS can disrupt employees' lives, corporate health policies, and the community health care system. You can also heighten your listeners' understanding of the disease through examples of individuals who have contracted AIDS. To locate this information, you should:

1. Use the library's computerized data base to investigate the history of AIDS in the United States.

2. Find out projected levels of AIDS infection for the future.

3. Identify the populations that are currently infected by AIDS: men, women, and children.

4. Read local newspaper articles concerning the community resident who died of AIDS.

5. If possible, interview community residents who knew the local AIDS victim.

6. Search out examples of people who tested HIV-positive, including school children and heterosexual residents of midwestern towns.

7. Develop a "typical" disease profile, detailing what occurs in the body and how the body copes with the disease.

8. Interview local medical authorities to discover the kinds of treatment currently used and the chances of AIDS infection occurring in the community.

9. Prepare a list of other midwestern communities that have held community discussions or adopted measures regarding AIDS.

10. Anticipate and list potential questions and objections to the topic.

While this list seems extensive, it is more likely to yield useful information because it is *specific* than would a *general* search for facts on AIDS. With the demographic and psychological profile of the audience completed and research compiled, you can adapt your ideas and appeals to your audience. You might include the following main ideas in your speech:

1. Stress the listeners' commitment to the welfare of the community and nation, their belief in the democratic process, and their belief in the rights of citizens in minority groups. Encourage their feelings of pride in previous civic accomplishments and challenge them to face the AIDS crisis. In other words, show them that it is in their best interests to confront and discuss unpopular issues for the well-being of the entire community.

2. Make it clear that this is not simply a moral issue. While recognizing the importance of traditional national values, also stress the practical importance of treating disease, regardless of moral issues. Use projections of future infection rates to emphasize that everyone's health may be affected if the disease is allowed, through ignorance or neglect, to spread unchecked.

3. Point out that other midwestern communities have debated the issues involved as they were faced with enrolling infected children in local schools and treating AIDS patients in local hospitals. Emphasize predictions of future infection affecting broader populations. Overcome audience apathy and hostility by encouraging members to discuss the disease further.

4. Push for an open forum for continued discussion on the issue rather than demanding immediate commitments or political action.

5. Recognize the group's excellent efforts at political reform in local projects. Remember that listeners have taken the time to attend, and their commitment should be recognized. Stress the far-sightedness of the group on difficult issues such as this one. Point out that, in a democracy, fair play requires that each side be given equal time and consideration before anyone reaches a final decision. Aim the bulk of the speech at gaining approval for open-minded discussions.

CHAPTER SUMMARY

1. Public speaking is audience-centered.

2. The primary goal of audience analysis is to discover the facets of listeners' demographic and psychological backgrounds that are relevant to your speech's purposes and ideas.

3. Demographic analysis is the study of audience characteristics such as age, gender, education, group membership, and cultural and ethnic backgrounds.

4. Psychological profiling seeks to identify the beliefs, attitudes, and values of audience members.

5. Beliefs are convictions about what is true or false. Beliefs may be facts or opinions, fixed or variable.

6. Attitudes are tendencies to respond positively or negatively to people, objects, or ideas.

7. Values are basic concepts that provide standards for life.

8. Audience analysis allows you to identify audience subgroups for more effective selection of main ideas.

KEY TERMS

attitudes (p. 57)	opinions (p. 56)
audience segmentation (p. 66)	psychological profiling (p. 55)
beliefs (p. 55)	stereotype (p. 56)
demographic analysis (p. 51)	values (p. 58)
facts (p. 56)	variable beliefs (p. 57)
fixed beliefs (p. 56)	

SKILLBUILDING ACTIVITIES

1. Choose a speech text from this textbook, from *Vital Speeches of the Day* (or another anthology of speeches), or from a newspaper, such as *The New York Times*. Identify statements of fact and opinion in the speech. Determine the speaker's attitudes and values from statements in the speech.

2. Gather some magazine advertisements and bring them to class. As a class or in groups, share your advertisements. Speculate about the audiences for which they were intended. To what attitudes are the advertisers trying to appeal? Are they trying to create beliefs? What tactics do they use? How effective do you think these tactics are?

3. In a group or individually, pretend you are the chief speech writer for each of the individuals listed below. Decide which audience subgroups you will need to address. What values, attitudes, and beliefs are they likely to hold? What can you say in your speech to engage their attention and support?

   a. The president of the United States, addressing the nation on primetime television concerning the latest international diplomatic development.

   b. The president of your student government, welcoming first-year students to campus at the beginning of the academic year.

c. A defense lawyer, conducting closing arguments in a murder trial.

d. A ninth-grade teacher, cautioning a class about the use of illegal drugs.

REFERENCES

1. For more discussion, see Milton M. Rokeach, *Beliefs, Attitudes, and Values: A Theory of Organization and Change* (San Francisco: Jossey-Bass, 1968) and Rokeach, *The Nature of Human Values* (New York: Collier-Macmillan, Free Press, 1973.)

2. See Henry Z. Scheele, "Ronald Reagan's 1980 Acceptance Address: A Focus on American Values," *Western Journal of Speech Communication* 48 (1984): 51–61.

Using Supporting Materials

" I can't believe he marked me down on supporting material!" Angela was distraught. "I worked for hours in the library, running through government documents, Statistical Abstracts, *and even some of the bulletin boards on the Internet. My speech covered every base." "You missed the point," Jamie replied. "You had plenty of material—it was just too much of a good thing. Your audience was drowning in statistics by the time you were done. The numbers came so fast we couldn't absorb them. You didn't use any illustrations or stories that we could remember. If your supporting material can't be absorbed by anyone, it's not really support, is it?"*

As you put your speeches together, sooner or later you have to stop and look at the substantive aspects of your presentations: the material you've assembled and put into the speech. A speech that's on the move burns supporting materials for its fuel. If you're telling your classmates about local career opportunities, you need examples of entry-level jobs for students with various interests and talents. If you're arguing that "Coal-fired power plants are unsafe and should be shut down," you must authoritatively define *unsafe,* provide statistical and illustrative materials to support your contention that the plants are unsafe, and offer a plan to substitute safer forms of power. If you don't provide such materials, you're wasting your time as well as that of your listeners.

Chapters 5 and 6 focus on finding and using supporting materials, which are the media of exchange between your ideas and the audience. The functions of supporting materials are to clarify, amplify, or justify the beliefs, attitudes, and values that you're offering to your listeners. Just as a plant needs sun, water, and soil to bring it to life and sustain its growth, the ideas in a speech need supporting materials to empower them. First, we'll define and illustrate the various types of supporting materials. Then, we'll suggest some ways of finding, recording, and using these materials.

Devoting careful thought to finding and using supporting materials before you assemble your speech will pay off in efficient use of your preparation time, in confidence that you know what to look for when you search the library, and in self-assurance when you approach the audience. This chapter seeks to provide some of the critical thinking skills you need to use supporting materials to earn audience acceptance of your ideas. In Chapter 6, we'll deal with the search process.

FORMS OF SUPPORTING MATERIALS

The verbal supporting materials used to clarify, amplify, or justify your central ideas can be divided into six categories: (1) *explanations,* (2) *comparisons and contrasts,* (3) *illustrations and narratives* (hypothetical or factual), (4) *specific instances,* (5) *statistics,* and (6) *testimony* (see Figure 5.1).

FIGURE 5.1
The Forms of Supporting Materials
The supporting materials used to clarify, amplify, or justify your central ideas or claims are comparison and contrast, testimony, statistics, illustration, explanation, and specific instance. What should you consider when you choose each of the six kinds of supporting materials?

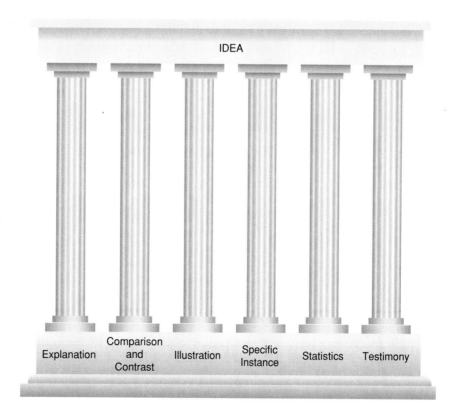

Explanations

An **explanation** is a description that makes a term, concept, process, or proposal clear or acceptable. Explanations tell *what, how,* or *why,* and they are useful in showing the relationship between a whole and its parts. They also may give meaning to a difficult-to-envision concept. Robert Lutz, president of Chrysler Corporation, wanted to explain inconsistencies in U.S. tariff rules and the unfair advantage they gave some Japanese auto exports to the United States. Here's the explanation he offered Cal-Berkeley students:

> *Let me tell you . . . the story of multipurpose vehicles, or "MPV's" for short. An MPV is a vehicle like, say, the Toyota 4-Runner sport utility. A funny thing happens to a 4-Runner when it's imported into this country. Four U.S. regulators all look it over. The fellow from the Environmental Protection Agency inspects and declares that it is "a truck," and will therefore only have to meet the emission standards for U.S. trucks, which are not as strict as those for cars. Behind him is the man from the National Highway Safety Administration, who certifies that it is indeed a truck so it won't have to have the same safety devices as a car. And then comes the inspector from the Department of Transportation, who also agrees that the vehicle is a truck so it won't have to meet the higher fuel economy requirements of a car. But then comes the fourth inspector. He's from the U.S. Customs Service. He looks at the 4-Runner and says, "Nope, this isn't a truck at all; it's a car!" And that means it pays a duty of only two-point-five percent instead of the 25 percent duty on trucks.*
>
> *Now what's going on here? Well, back in February of 1989, after intense lobbying by Japanese automakers, the U.S. Treasury Department, in a virtually unprecedented decision, overruled its own Customs Service and reclassified Japanese sport utilities and minivans from trucks to cars. It was, as President Clinton himself put it in a press conference last month, a "$300-million-dollar-a-year freebie to the Japanese for no apparent reason."[1]*

Notice the way this explanation works. Mr. Lutz sets up the four regulators, follows a Japanese MPV through them, offers the explanation, and then brings the audience up to date with a reference to President Clinton. He doesn't waste time with irrelevant details about the inspections, because he wants to keep our attention focused on the switch in definition.

Although explanations are good ways to clarify ideas, they shouldn't be too long or complicated and they shouldn't have to carry the weight of the argument. For example, Mr. Lutz's explanation was clear, but by itself it didn't point to a solution to the problem. Explanations clarify but seldom prove anything.

Comparisons and Contrasts

Comparisons and contrasts are useful verbal devices for clarifying ideas—to make them distinctive and focused. Pointing out similarities and differences helps listeners comprehend your ideas and opinions.

Comparisons

Comparisons are kinds of analogies that connect something already known or believed with ideas a speaker wishes to have understood or accepted. Comparisons, therefore, stress similarities. During the darkest days of the Civil War, when critics attacked the administration's policies, Lincoln answered them by comparing the plight of the government with that of the famous tightrope walker, Blondin, attempting to cross the Niagara Falls:

> *Gentlemen, I want you to suppose a case for a moment. Suppose that all the property you were worth was in gold, and you had put it in the hands of Blondin, the famous rope-walker, to carry across the Niagara Falls on a tightrope. Would you shake the rope while he was passing over it, or keep shouting to him, "Blondin, stoop a little more! Go a little faster!"? No, I am sure you would not. You would hold your breath as well as your tongue, and keep your hands off until he was safely over. Now the government is in the same situation. It is carrying an immense weight across a stormy ocean. Untold treasures are in its hands. It is doing the best it can. Don't badger it! Just keep still, and it will get you safely over.*

Contrasts

Contrasts help to clarify complex situations and processes by focusing on differences. A speaker explaining arena football would want to contrast it with the more familiar rules governing interscholastic football. To clarify the severity of the 1993 midwestern flood, the news networks contrasted the width and depth of rivers in more normal summers with their status that year. Contrasts can be used not only to clariy unfamiliar or complex problems, but also to strengthen the arguments that you wish to advance. H. Ross Perot testified against the North American Free Trade Agreement (NAFTA) before the Senate Joint Economic Committee in 1993. A series of contrasts helped him made his case:

• Explanations are enhanced usefully by visual materials that show the concepts about which you're telling the audience.

Let's contrast the burdens that businesses carry in our country. We're run-ning a business now. You're paying your manufacturers ten times what they make in Mexico. The minimum wage in the United States is, as you know, $4.25. The minimum wage in Mexico is 58 cents. The single most expensive item in making a car in the United States is health care. No problem in Mex-ico. Our companies also spend a great deal on retirement, worker's compen-sation, life insurance, and many other benefits not available in Mexico. The recently passed employee leave bill, while a very nice thing, adds to the cost of manufacturing. It's one more reason to head south. . . . Now, if all you want to do is make money, I'll give you some reasons to head south.[2]

Mr. Perot's contrasts were startling and, because there were several of them, cumulatively served as clear support for his central idea that the United States should junk NAFTA. Helping an audience reason along with you by visualizing differences is an excellent strategy for getting them to accept your ideas.

Comparisons and Contrasts Used in Combination

You can use comparisons and contrasts together to double your audience's abil-ity to see. For example, Professor Dudley Herschbach, Baird Professor of Science at Harvard and 1986 Nobel Prize winner in chemistry, gave the 1992 Phi Beta Kappa oration to the Harvard-Radcliffe chapter. To help his listeners understand relationships between human beings and dolphins, he used comparisons and con-trasts in tandem:

The evolutionary gulf between humans and dolphins is immense. We both evolved from land mammals, but the primordial ancestors of the dolphins re-turned to the sea fifty million years ago. Dolphins resembling those we know today appeared fifteen million years ago. Homo sapiens emerged much more recently—not more than about a quarter of a million years ago, following the earliest verions of humankind some three million years ago. . . .

In relation to body size, the brain of a bottlenose dolphin is comparable to ours. The cortex, seat of intelligence and language, is more convoluted and contains about 50 percent more cells. It has the same six differentiated layers but is thinner and much different in shape.[3]

Whenever using comparisons and contrasts, try to make sure that one of the items is familiar to listeners. Comparing arena football and interscholastic foot-ball will make no sense to an Irishman, who probably doesn't know anything about either one. You'd have to compare and contrast arena football and Euro-pean soccer to clarify the arena game for him.

Illustrations and Narratives

A detailed example of an idea you wish to support is either an illustration or a nar-rative. If the example describes a concept, condition, or circumstance, it's called an **illustration;** if it's in story form, it's called a **narrative.** An illustration or nar-rative is always, however, a big "for instance"—something concrete that makes abstract or general ideas easier to comprehend. Illustrations share many charac-teristics with explanations, the difference being that an illustration is always a "for instance" while explanations can take different forms.

Some illustrations and narratives are hypothetical (made up) while others are factual—recitations of events that actually happened or persons, places, and things that actually exist. If you were giving a speech on why students should move out of dormitories and into apartments, you might narrate a "typical" evening in a dorm: loud music, a constant flow of pizza delivery people through the hall, a traveling party, a false fire alarm, nonstop card games, illegal alcohol, and an engagement shower. Although not all of these occurred on the same night, asking listeners to imagine what life would be like if they *did* would help you to convey the intensity of your antidormitory feelings through a made-up narrative.

For many audiences, fact-based illustrations and narratives are more potent. President Ronald Reagan was famous for his reliance on homey little narratives. Hillary Rodham Clinton was equally successful using them in her travels around the country in search of a better health care system. Here's one of them:

> *Dr. Rob Barrinson, one of the practicing physicians who spent hours and hours working with us while also maintaining his practice, told us recently of an experience that he had as one of many. He admitted an emergency room patient named Jeff. Jeff suffered from cirrhosis of the liver. Dr. Barrinson put him in the hospital and within 24 hours received a call from Jeff's insurance company. The insurance company wanted to know exactly how many days Jeff would be in the hospital and why. Dr. Barrinson replied that he couldn't predict the precise length of stay. A few days later the insurance company called back and questioned whether Jeff would need surgery. Again, Dr. Barrinson said he wasn't yet sure.*
>
> *And what was Dr. Barrinson's reward for his honesty and his professionalism? He was placed on the insurance company's "special exemptions" list. You know, that's a list of troublesome doctors who make the insurance company wait a few days or a few weeks to determine the bottom line on a particular patient. From that point on, the insurance company called Dr. Barrinson six times in two weeks. Each time, he had to be summoned away from a patient to take the call. Each time, he spoke to a different insurance company representative. Each time, he repeated the same story. Each time, his role as the physician was subverted. And each time, the treatment of the patient was impeded.*
>
> *Dr. Barrinson and you know that medicine, the art of healing, doesn't work that way. There is no master checklist that can be administered by some faceless bureaucrat that can tell you what you need to do on an hourly basis to take care of your patients; and, frankly, I wouldn't want to be one of your patients if there were.*[4]

Guidelines for Choosing Illustrations and Narratives

Three considerations should be kept in mind when selecting illustrations and narratives, whether hypothetical or factual:

1. Is the illustration or narrative clearly related to the idea it's intended to support? If the connection is difficult to show, it won't accomplish its goal. If your hypothetical story about a typical night in a dorm is more attractive than repelling for some listeners, you're in trouble!

2. Is it a fair example? An audience can be quick to notice unusual circumstances in an illustration or story; exceptional cases are seldom convincing. Having parachutists landing on your dorm roof in your story, for example, would stretch the credulity of your listeners.

3. Is it vivid and impressive in detail? Be sure your extended examples are pointed, fair, and visual.

Mrs. Clinton's narrative met all three of these criteria, especially the third one. She also was very good at drawing lessons or conclusions from her story.

Specific Instances

Specific instances are undeveloped illustrations or examples; usually, they are grouped into a list, so that they pile one upon the other to drive the speaker's point home. They're undeveloped because their power comes from cumulative effort rather than vivid detail. You can get away with using a single specific instance if all you need is a quick example, for instance: "You're all familiar with the windows in this classroom, but you might not have noticed their actual construction. I want to talk about those windows—those double-glazed, low emissivity, gas-filled windows—and how the use of such windows contributes to reduced energy consumption on campus and in your life." More often, though, speakers pile them up to help establish a point. In his commencement address to Emory University, Donald Keough, retired president of the Coca-Cola Company, used specific instances when he urged students to keep on dreaming:

> *No matter how wise the prognosticators are, deep down they really don't know. They don't know. And usually I've found that they're far too pessimistic. Listen to some of these pearls of wisdom: (1) "Heavier than air flying machines are impossible." Lord Geldon, noted British physicist, 1895. (2) "Everything that can be invented has been invented." Director of the U.S. Patent Office suggesting that his operation close down, in 1899. (3) "The battle to feed all humanity is over. In the 1970s hundreds of millions of people all over the world are going to starve." Paul Erhlich, noted Stanford biologist and demographer, 1960.*
>
> *Occasionally, of course, these prognosticators have erred on the side of excessive optimism. Business Week in 1979 said, "With over 50 foreign cars on sale here the Japanese auto industry isn't going to carve out a big slice of the U.S. market." [Secretary of the Navy] Frank Knox, December 4, 1941: "No matter what happens, the U.S. Navy is not going to be caught napping."[5]*

With these accumulated instances, Mr. Keough demonstrated to his listeners that even new graduates ought to dream—to "seize the day," as he said.

Statistics

Statistics are numbers that show relationships between or among phenomena—relationships that can emphasize size or magnitude, describe subclasses or parts (segments), or establish trends. By reducing large masses of information into generalized categories, statistics clarify situations, substantiate potentially disputable central ideas, and make complex aspects of the world clear to your listeners.

Magnitudes

We often use statistics to describe a situation or to sketch its scope or seriousness; that is, its size or **magnitude.** Especially if one statistical description of the size of a problem is piled up on others, the effect upon listeners can be strong. Notice how the former U.S. Surgeon General Antonia Novello used multiple statistical descriptions of magnitude while urging citizens to think of violence as a community health problem:

> *Violence is a legitimate public health concern. It is your challenge—and mine. My friends, it is no small problem that: homicidal violence is now the leading cause of death among our youth; and that, in fact, every 14 hours a child younger than 5 is murdered. Firearms are now involved in one in every four deaths among 15- to 24 year-olds. And it is no small problem that domestic violence—along with child abuse and the abuse of the elderly—is found in every community and one-fourth of all American families; and up to six of ten married couples. Domestic violence today is the second most common cause of injury to women overall, and the leading cause of injuries to women ages 15 to 44. It is more common than automobile accidents, muggings, and rapes combined.[6]*

Not all uses of magnitudes, of course, need such piling up of instances. Simple, hard-hitting magnitudes sometimes work even better. For example, Brenda Theriault of the University of Maine, arguing that there is "very little nutritional value in a hamburger, chocolate shake, and fries," simply noted that "of the 1,123 calories in this meal, there are 15 calories of carbohydrates, 35 calories of protein, and 1,073 calories of fat."[7] These were all the numbers the listeners needed in order to understand the nutrition in a typical fast-food meal.

Segments

Statistics also are used to isolate the parts of a problem or to show aspects of a problem caused by separate factors; parts or aspects can be treated as statistical **segments.** In discussing the sources of income for a college or university, for example, you'd probably segment the income by percentages coming from tuition and fees, state and federal money, gifts and contributions, special fees such as tickets, and miscellaneous sources. Then you'd be in a position to talk reasonably about next year's proposed tuition hike. Student speaker Eddie Hunter used poll results in this fashion to show that incumbent politicians are not always unwanted by their electors:

> *Nobody forces people to vote for incumbents. Last October the* New York Times *reported a* New York Times-*CBS Survey, which found 44 percent of those surveyed believed their representative deserves re-election, while 40 percent say they want someone new. However, these percentages swing dramatically when people are asked about Congress as a whole. Only 20 percent then say most lawmakers deserve re-election, while 67 percent would give new people a chance. Apparently people perceive everyone else's legislator as the bad guy.[8]*

As Mr. Hunter's example illustrates, the most important value of statistics doesn't lie in the numbers themselves but in how they're interpreted and used—prepared for audience use. In using statistical data, always ask and answer the question, "What do these numbers mean or demonstrate?" In Mr. Hunter's case, when the separate polls are compared, there's support for the argument that, "If they're in, vote 'em out" doesn't apply across the board.

Trends

Statistics often are used to point out **trends,** or indicators that tell us where we were and are now, and where we may be heading. The comparison of statistical data across time allows you to say that a particular phenomenon is increasing or decreasing (see Table 5.1). An interesting use of a trend argument is found in testimony given to the U.S. House Subcommittee on Human Resources by Hortense Hunn, Executive Director of the California Preschool Services Department in San Bernadino County. She laid out what she considered to be a trend in spending on the Head Start program:

> There are numerous official fact sheets documenting Head Start's growth and development since its inception in 1965. I do not intend to reiterate the litany of glowing statistics which are readily available; suffice it to say that the National Head Start Program has grown from an "embryonic" program enrolling 561,000 children for about $96 million in the summer of 1965 to an "adolescent" program serving over 721,000 children and families for $1.7 billion in this year.[9]

Notice the cleverness with which Ms. Hunn framed her argument: she talked about "glowing statistics" in order to tell her audience to see them favorably; she used metaphors of maturation ("embryonic," "adolescent") to subtly project the need for further growth in Head Start (to "adulthood"); and she emphasized Head Start's direct service to children rather than its general family-services orientation, given that appeals to children usually are successful with listeners.

Using Statistics

When you use statistics to indicate magnitude, to divide phenomena into segments, or to describe trends, help your listeners by softening the numbers:

1. *Translate difficult-to-comprehend numbers into more immediately understandable terms.* In a speech on the mounting problem of solid waste, Carl Hall illustrated the immensity of 130 million tons of garbage by explaining that trucks loaded with that amount would extend from coast to coast three abreast.[10]

2. *Don't be afraid to round off complicated numbers.* "Nearly 400,000" is easier for listeners to comprehend than "396,456"; "just over 33 percent" or, better yet, "approximately one-third" is preferable to "33.4 percent."

3. *Use visual materials to clarify complicated statistical trends or summaries whenever possible.* Hand out a photocopied sheet of numbers; draw graphs on the chalkboard; prepare a chart in advance. Such aids will allow you to concentrate on explaining the significance of the numbers rather than on making sure the audience hears and remembers them.

TABLE 5.1 Types of Statistics In a speech to inform, a speaker might use three types of statistics to describe students at Central University. What other forms of supporting material could complement these numbers?

Magnitudes	Segments	Trends
"Three fourths of all Central University students come from the state."	"Sixty percent of all Central University students major in business; 25 percent are humanities majors; the remaining 15 percent are in fine arts."	"Since 1975, enrollment at Central University has increased by 20 percent every five years."

4. *Use statistics fairly.* Arguing that professional women's salaries increased 12.4 percent last year may sound impressive to listeners until they realize that women are still paid about a third less than men for equivalent work. In other words, provide fair contexts for your numerical data and comparisons.

Testimony

When you cite the opinions or conclusions of others, you're using **testimony.** Sometimes testimony merely adds weight or impressiveness to an idea, as when you quote Mahatma Gandhi or a clever turn of a phrase by Dorothy Parker. At other times, it lends credibility to an assertion, especially when it comes from expert witnesses. When Daniel Lashof of the Natural Resources Defense Council wanted to emphasize the point that serious steps toward control of toxic emissions must be taken now, he used testimony from one international conference and then indicated that other conferences had come to the same conclusion:

> *The Toronto Conference on the Changing Atmosphere, in June 1988, warned that "humanity is conducting an unintended, uncontrolled, globally pervasive experiment whose ultimate consequences could be second only to a global nuclear war," and called on the world to cut CO_2 emissions from fossil fuel combustion 20 percent by 2005. In the last two years the declaration of this ad hoc group of scientists, environmentalists, and policy makers has been strongly reinforced by the Intergovernmental Panel on Climate Change (IPCC), the Second World Climate Conference, and the Stockholm Environment Institute.[11]*

All testimony should meet the twin tests of pertinence and audience acceptability. When used to strengthen a statement rather than merely to amplify or illustrate an idea, testimony also should satisfy four more specific criteria:

1. The person quoted should be qualified, by training and experience, to speak on the topic being discussed. Athletes are more credible talking about sports equipment or exercise programs than they are endorsing breakfast food or local furniture stores.

2. Whenever possible, the authority's statement should be based on first-hand knowledge. An Iowa farmer is not an authority on a South Carolina drought unless or he or she has personally observed the conditions.

Ethical Moments

. . . .

The Numbers Game

The rise of science in this century has been accompanied by the rise of numerical data—and its public exhibition. By now you've been told by one poll that the public favors a liberalization of abortion laws two-to-one but by another poll that the public favors tightening abortion laws by an equal percentage. You know that four out of five dentists surveyed recommend a particular brand of toothpaste. You've heard that a brand of cigarettes has the lowest level of tar and nicotine—from more than one manufacturer. As both listener and speaker, you have to make some ethical calls when encountering such data:

1. Contradictory polls such as the ones on abortion usually result when questions are asked in slanted ways. "Do parents have to right to know when their underaged kids seek a dangerous abortion?" tends to encourage a positive answer, while "Ought women have the right to control their own bodies without external interference from others?" also encourages a positive answer—but one in favor of a very different public policy than the first. Questions can be loaded in favor of opposing public policies. You're wise to report the actual questions when quoting poll results.

2. Who were those "four out of five dentists surveyed?" Is it moral to cite statistics without reviewing how they were gathered and calculated?

3. If your favorite brand of cigarettes is one of five brands that all have the same low tar and nicotine content, technically, of course, yours has the lowest—and so do the other four brands. Is it moral, however, to claim your brand is "the lowest" or must you say that it is "one of the lowest"?

It's easy to fiddle with numbers: to round up or down, to compare only parts rather than wholes, to ignore key details that would properly contextualize information for listeners. It's easy, but if you play fast and loose with numbers, you might get caught. Learn to play the numbers game honestly so as to protect your reputation.

3. The judgment expressed shouldn't be unduly influenced by personal interest. Asking a political opponent to comment on the current president's performance will likely yield a self-interested answer.

4. The listeners should perceive the person quoted to be an actual authority. An archbishop may be accepted as an authority by a Roman Catholic audience but perhaps not by Protestant or Hindu listeners.

When citing testimony, don't use big names simply because they're well known. The best testimony comes from subject-matter experts whose qualifications your listeners recognize.

Finally, always acknowledge the source of an idea or particular phrasing. Avoid **plagiarism**—claiming someone else's ideas, information, or phraseology as your own. Plagiarism is stealing. Give your source credit for the material, and

TABLE 5.2 Checklist for Supporting Materials You should evaluate your supporting materials when you plan your speeches. Answer the questions on this checklist as you plan your supporting materials.

General Considerations

___1. Have I included sufficient supporting material?

___2. Are my supporting materials distributed throughout my speech?

___3. Do I provide extra support for confusing or controversial ideas?

___4. Are my supporting materials interesting and clear?

___5. Do I adequately credit the sources of my supporting materials?

Explanations

___1. Are my explanations short and direct?

___2. Do I provide other forms of support in addition to explanations?

Comparisons and Contrasts

___1. Is at least one of the items in a comparison or contrast familiar to my listeners?

___2. Is the basis of the comparison clear?

___3. Is the contrast distinct enough?

Illustrations and Narratives

___1. Is the illustration or narrative clearly related to the idea it's intended to support?

___2. Is the illustration or narrative typical?

___3. Is the illustration or narrative vivid and adequately detailed?

Specific Instances

___1. Have I provided enough specific instances?

___2. Can listeners easily recognize or understand the instances I mention?

Statistics

___1. Are my statistics easy to understand?

___2. Have I rounded off complicated numbers?

___3. Am I using statistics fairly?

___4. Should I use visual materials to clarify complicated numbers?

___5. Have I adequately interpreted the statistics I've cited for my listeners?

Testimony

___1. Is the authority qualified to speak on the topic being discussed?

___2. Is the authority's statement based on first-hand knowledge?

___3. Is the authority's opinion subject to personal influence or bias?

___4. Do my listeners know the authority's qualifications?

___5. Will my listeners accept this person as an authority?

give yourself credit for having taken the time to do the research. (See "Using Material Ethically" in Chapter 6.)

CRITICAL THINKING AND THE USE OF SUPPORTING MATERIALS

Most of us, with some effort, can gather and create supporting materials. The hard part is using those materials well. The effective use of supporting materials is an exercise in **critical thinking**—assessing the reasonableness of the connections between your assertions and your supporting materials. Furthermore, as we suggested in the opening paragraph of this chapter, you need to figure out how much support and what kind of support for your central ideas your listeners will demand. Think of both of these problems as matters of **rational requirements:** What would a reasonable (careful thinking) audience member want to know before he or she accepted your ideas as true, wise, and practical? More specifically, critical thinking about ways to use supporting materials involves four considerations:

1. The general standards of reasonableness the central idea of your speech suggests.

2. The range of supporting materials actually available.

3. The information a particular audience might demand to accept your central idea.

4. The generally perceived power-to-prove of particular forms of support.

Suppose you're asking your listeners to accept this central idea: "Universities should open technology and business innovation centers that can promote state economic growth." Think about what a critical audience might want to know:

1. *Standards of reasonableness*. To prove your point, you must demonstrate a relationship between university research centers and private-sector economic growth. What sorts of supporting materials might help you to make that demonstration? Comparing your state's situation to another's that has technology and business innovation centers would help. Describing the connection between research and economic development makes sense. Providing statistics on the number of jobs created by companies "incubated" in university innovation centers would work, as would testimony from experts.

2. *Range of available materials*. Can you find all of those materials? Do you have access to studies of other states? Are statistics on job growth available? Do the experts really believe university innovation centers spur local economies? In other words, it's one thing to guess at what constitutes good support and another thing to actually find the materials. You may have to settle for thin evidence in some areas simply because the needed data have not been gathered. Or, you might even have to modify your central idea to, say, "Universities should open computer design and technology centers to attract new investment to the state." That central idea is narrower and would be easier to defend. So stick with your central idea as long as you can, but alter it if necessary. Don't forge ahead without meeting the general standards of reasonableness.

3. *Audience demands*. What information does your particular audience need in order to make a positive decision on your central idea? An audience of university administrators would want to know what impact a technology and business innovation center would have on the campus: How many new faculty members would have to be hired? How many students would get access to it? What new facilities would be needed, and how much would they cost? Who would pay? In contrast, an audience of legislators might ask different questions: Is this another pipe dream by heads-in-the-clouds professors? Will our constituents accept the idea of spending state money to foster private business growth? Are the alumni from this school active voters? Is the governor behind this project? Different audiences expect you to answer different

questions with supporting materials. Remember the lessons of audience segmentation and targeting that we discussed in Chapter 4 and learn from them.

4. *Power-to-prove.* Any of the forms of support may be used to clarify, amplify, or strengthen assertions; however, some forms tend to accomplish those purposes better than others and are more effective with particular audiences:

    a. *Clarifying ideas.* Explanations, comparisons, specific instances, and segmented statistics are especially helpful in clarifying ideas. These materials allow the speaker to present information that simplifies an idea for an audience, and they're useful when listeners have little background or knowledge about the topic or when the subject matter is complex.

    b. *Amplifying ideas.* Explanations, comparisons, illustrations, and statistical magnitudes and trends can help a speaker amplify an idea, expanding on it so that the audience can better examine the concept. These forms of support may be especially useful when the audience has only minimal knowledge of the concept.

    c. *Strengthening ideas.* To strengthen or lend credibility to a point, a speaker can use factual illustrations, specific instances, statistics, and testimony. These forms strengthen the idea by making it vivid and believable. These techniques are beneficial when the audience is hostile or when acceptance of a particular idea is critical to the overall argument of the speech.

Of course, you're not always able to know exactly which ideas need clarifying, amplifying, or strengthening. However, by regularly asking yourself if the supporting materials you've provided make your ideas clear, develop them adequately, and give them the power to prove an assertion for some segment of your audience, you'll be evaluating your supporting materials carefully. If you find that some of the materials you want to include in your speech don't clarify, amplify, or strengthen your argument, drop them. Test the relevance of each supporting unit to be sure it contributes to your listeners' understanding and acceptance of your ideas. The two outlines that follow illustrate how supporting materials can be used.

Sample Outline for an Informative Speech

• • • •

The speaker establishes the comparison, an analogy, immediately upon starting the speech. Furthermore, short, simple sentences ("When we inhale, two things happen.") are used to aid clarity. The helpful speaker also would be pointing to parts of the body as they're mentioned—collarbone, shoulder bones, abdominal wall, diaphram. Demonstrative movements also would be appreciated by the audience: a lifting of the shoulders and chest cavity when talking about inhalation, a dropping of the rib cage and abdominal wall when describing exhalation. The visual and the verbal are brought together completely in the "How We Breathe" diagram.

Notice the summary: it works specifically from the comparison so that just as audience members understand how bellows work, they will now remember how their lungs work. The details of the full explanation now are left out since the formal aspects of the comparison (opening a bellows is to inhalation as closing a bellows is to exhalation [a:b::c:d]) are what can be easily remembered.

In the outline, note how the speaker has combined verbal and visual material to establish and develop the central idea. In this speech, the supporting material is used to amplify the idea.

How We Breathe

I. The human breathing mechanism may be likened to a bellows, which expands to admit air and contracts to expel it.
   A. When we inhale, two things happen.
      1. Muscles attached to the collarbone and shoulder bones pull upward and slightly outward.
      2. Muscles in the abdominal wall relax, allowing the diaphram—a sheet of muscle and tendon lying immediately below the lungs—to fall.
   B. This permits the spongy, porous lungs to expand.
      1. A vacuum is created.
      2. Air rushes in.
   C. When we exhale, two things happen.
      1. Gravity causes the rib cage to move downward.
      2. Muscles in the abdominal wall contract, squeezing the diaphram upward.
   D. The space available to the lungs is thus reduced.
      1. The lungs are squeezed.
      2. Air is emitted.
   E. The similarity between the breathing mechanism and a bellows is represented in this diagram:
      [Show "How We Breathe" diagram.]
II. In summary, then, to remember how the human breathing mechanism works, think of a bellows.
   A. Just as increasing the size of the bellows bag allows air to rush in, so increasing the space available to the lungs allows them to admit air.
   B. Just as squeezing the bellows bag forces air out, so contracting the space the lungs can occupy forces air to be emitted.

Sample Outline for a Persuasive Speech

• • • •

The body of this speech starts immediately with the central idea to be defended. The speaker immediately notes what the revolution is—interactive (two-way) television. A reference to the familiar telephone is offered to make sure listeners know what interactive means.

The heart of the speech explains three ways in which interactive television will revolutionize listeners' lives. The speaker cleverly talks about three different areas of effect— household life, political activity, and entertainment—in hopes of capturing different listeners interests with each. Here, therefore, the audience is not segmented by gender, age, ethnical background, etc., but by personal interests. That's a solid, safe strategy for a speech such as this one, in which a speaker might possibly offend listeners by talking demographically (say, about "men's" and "women's" television, the Black Entertainment Network, or Spanish-language channels). In this case, personal interests are the most useful grounds for segmenting and targeting listeners.

Study the following outline. Notice that the supporting materials are used to strengthen each of the points in the speech. The audience probably would not accept these ideas without further development. Although the proof of a single point may not require as many different supporting materials as are used in this outline, the variety of support shows how a number of different forms can be combined in a speech.

Cable Television—At Your Service!

I. Cable television soon will revolutionize your everyday life.
   A. Today, cable TV for most of us is a one-way "narrowcasting" system, bringing us various programs on channels numbering from a dozen to a hundred.
   B. The principal two-way electronic communications medium in most homes today is the phone, not the TV.
   C. But with the coming of interactive (two-way) cable communications, your TV will become part of the late twentieth-century communications revolution.
II. Interactive cable television will affect your household, political, and entertainment lives.
   A. On a rainy day a few years from now, you'll be able to run your household errands from your living room.
      1. On channel 37, your bank's computer will verify the amount of a recent withdrawal.
      2. On channel 26, you will ask the phone company to review the last month's long-distance charges.
      3. On channel 94, a supermarket will let you scan products, prices, and home-delivery hours.
      4. On channel 5, you will study a list of proposed changes in the city charter, getting answers to questions via an electronic checksheet.
   B. Your political life will be fully involved with your cable TV as well.
      1. Of course you'll be able to vote electronically.
      2. You'll also have access to candidate position papers and interactive contact with candidates' staff members and even with candidates themselves on electronic dial-in shows.
      3. Your city council representative and many of the city and county offices will be accessible via cable TV.
   C. Your entertainment will be expanded as well.
      1. You'll be able to interact directly with locally originated programs.

Because the second main point focused on possibilities, in the third point the speaker wants to emphasize actualities—what's already happening. Again, the speaker goes for a variety of current applications in local and franchised operations to convince listeners that a wide range of applications is already available.

The breadth of applications must be handled convincingly so that the fourth point—interactive TV is coming almost everywhere soon—seems reasonable. Here, the stress is on inexpensiveness (magnitudes) and ease of installation (specific instances), to make the penetration of two-way television into our daily lives seem almost a foregone conclusion.

The speaker now gets ready to conclude by reasserting the central idea, replete with an analogy and a piece of expert testimony. The analogy helps to reinforce the central idea conceptually, while the testimony gives it supporting authority.

2. You'll have instant access to hundreds of first- and second-run movies from a pay-per-view channel.

3. You'll also be able to program an evening of music videos from your favorite chair.

4. And of course you'll have access to the entire professional baseball, football, and basketball seasons for a price.

III. Once only dreams, these possibilities are becoming actualities across the United States.

   A. All cities with cable TV already have public-access channels filled with local talent and political programming ready to become two-way when the coaxial cable is installed.

   B. Ann Arbor, Michigan, and Columbus, Ohio, have been leasing channels to private firms and public utility companies.

   C. Many hotels already have satellite-fed movie channels giving you multiple pay-per-view films when you want them.

   D. Telephone and cable companies are working out their economic and political relationships even today.

IV. Cable television soon will be available to virtually every household in the United States at a reasonable cost.

   A. Because the cost is shared by licensee and householder alike, no one bears excessive burdens.

      1. Commercial users find that leasing a channel costs little more than their computer-accounting systems and print/electronic advertising services.

      2. Studio facilities for the public-access channels are made available at cost in most cable TV contracts—normally about $35 per hour.

      3. Current cable installation charges range from only $15 to $50.

   B. The technical characteristics of cable television render it inexpensive.

      1. Some existing phone lines and equipment can be used.

      2. The conversion box mounts easily on a regular television set.

      3. Studio costs are minimal.

V. Given the actual and potential uses plus the positive cost-benefit ratio, interactive cable TV will indeed revolutionize your everyday life.

   A. Just as the wheel extended our legs and the computer extended our central nervous system, so will cable TV extend our communication capabilities.

   B. In the words of Wendy Lee, communication consultant to new interactive cable-television franchises, "We soon will be a nation fully wired for sight, sound, and backtalk. We will rid ourselves of the need for short shopping trips and long doctors' lines. We will put the consumer and the constituent into the front offices of corporate suppliers and political servants. Interactive cable television will make us into a fully operative, electronic community of neighbors and shopkeepers."

CHAPTER SUMMARY

1. Supporting materials clarify, amplify, or justify the beliefs, attitudes, and values that speakers ask listeners to accept.

2. Explanations are descriptions that make a term, concept, process, or proposal clear or acceptable.

3. Comparisons and contrasts point out similarities and differences between things that are familiar and things that are not.

4. Illustrations and narratives are detailed examples of ideas or statements you want listeners to accept. Illustrations are in explanatory form; narratives, in story form. Some are hypothetical (fictional), and some are factual ("real").

5. Specific instances are undeveloped illustrations, often used in groups or clusters to add power to ideas.

6. Statistics are numbers that show relationships between or among phenomena. Some emphasize size or magnitude; some describe subclasses or segments; and some establish trends, or the directions in which matters are heading over time.

7. Testimony is made up of the opinions or conclusions of credible persons.

8. To effectively use forms of support, you must learn critical thinking skills to: (a) assess the general reasonableness of your central ideas and what others would demand to know before accepting them; (b) understand how the range of materials actually available may force you to alter your central ideas; (c) respond to demands for particular kinds of supporting materials from particular kinds of audiences; and (d) estimate what kinds of supporting materials clarify, amplify, and strengthen ideas.

KEY TERMS

comparisons (p. 74)	plagiarism (p. 82)
contrasts (p. 75)	rational requirements (p. 84)
critical thinking (p. 83)	segments (p. 79)
explanations (p. 73)	specific instances (p. 78)
illustrations (p. 76)	statistics (p. 78)
magnitudes (p. 79)	testimony (p. 81)
narratives (p. 76)	trends (p. 80)

SKILLBUILDING ACTIVITIES

1. Read one of the speeches in this textbook. Identify its forms of supporting material. How effective are those materials in supporting the central idea of the speech? How well do supporting materials seem to be adapted to the immediate audience? What else might the speaker have done to improve his or her use of supporting material?

2. Prepare an outline for a short speech that explains one point or idea clearly. State the central idea; amplify it with an explanation, a comparison/contrast, and an illustration; then restate the idea in other words. Submit the outline to your instructor for evaluation. You may be asked to deliver the speech later.

3. Prepare an outline for a short speech proving a point. State the central idea; support it with statistical materials, a comparison/contrast, and an illustration; then restate the claim in other words. Submit the outline to your instructor for evaluation. You may be asked to deliver the speech later.

REFERENCES

1. Robert Lutz, "Managed Trade: Spring of Hope or Nuclear Winter?" *Vital Speeches of the Day* 59 (1 July 1993):554.

2. H. Ross Perot, "Testimony Before Senate Banking, Housing, and Urban Affairs Committee," 22 April 1993. *The Impact of the North American Free Trade Agreement on US Jobs and Wages,* Senate Hearing, 103rd Congress (Washington, DC: U.S. Government Printing Office, 1993), 10.

3. Dudley Herschbach, "1992 Harvard-Radcliffe Phi Beta Kappa Oration," *Harvard Magazine* 93, no. 3 (Jan.–Feb. 1993):57–58.

4. Hillary Rodham Clinton, "Health Care—We Can Make a Difference," *Vital Speeches of the Day* 59 (15 July 1993): 583.

5. Donald Keough, "The Courage to Dream—Seize the Day," *Vital Speeches of the Day* 59 (15 July 1993): 600.

6. Antonia Novello, "Your Parents, Your Community—Without Caring There Is No Hope," *Vital Speeches of the Day* 59 (15 July 1993):591, italics in original.

7. Brenda Theriault, "Fast Foods," speech given at the University of Maine, spring 1992.

8. Eddie Paul Hunter, "Term Limits: A Solution Worse than the Problem," *Winning Orations, 1991:* 90.

9. Hortense Hunn, "Testimony Before House Subcommittee on Human Resources," 8 April 1993. *Oversight Hearing Regarding the Head Start Program,* House of Representatives Hearing, 103rd Congress (Washington, D.C.: U.S. Government Printing Office, 1993), 88.

10. Carl Hall, "A Heap of Trouble," *Winning Orations, 1977.*

11. Daniel Lashof, "Testimony Before House Subcommittee on Energy and Power," 3 March 1992. *Global Warming,* House of Representatives Hearing, 102nd Congress (Washington, D.C.: U.S. Government Printing Office, 1992), 1.

Finding Supporting Materials

*D*avid had avoided the library since his freshman year in high school. He still performed adequately in his classes. His parents had a set of old encyclopedias and he often used them to write reports and do research papers. Then, disaster happened. His communication teacher assigned a "birthday speech." David had to find out what happened the day he was born and report on it. He finally managed to walk into the library and ask a librarian for help. Within an hour, David located periodicals he hadn't known existed, he found reference books, and he learned that he could use a computer to search data bases for additional information. The speech earned him a B+, but even better than that, David felt like he'd accomplished something. He even planned to visit the library again the following week to work on a chemistry assignment.

You are living in a communications revolution. You have at your disposal the miracles that result from the harnessing of electricity: the computer chip, television, satellites, fax machines and electronic mail, and digital sound reproduction. Electronically, you can access and experience wildly diverse people, places, and events all over the world. You can now retrieve more data than at any other time in history.

The thought of limitless knowledge is exhilarating but also dumbfounding. You have access to staggering amounts of information. Of course, you can't learn it all. You don't have the time or the resources for total knowledge. Rather, you need to know where to look for the information that you're interested in and that will improve your life. This chapter explores the challenge of finding and assembling the materials relevant to your speeches, your audiences, and the occasions on which you're speaking.

Finding supporting materials should be a purposeful, targeted search, not an aimless bibliographical spree in the library. You must develop some sense of the supporting materials you will need, of the location of those materials, and of efficient ways to record the information you find. You will also need to know how to use other individuals' materials ethically. In this chapter we won't deal with these matters exhaustively, because your own libraries will have their own particular ways of organizing and handling materials. However, we do hope to get you off to a good start.

DETERMINING THE KINDS OF SUPPORTING MATERIALS YOU NEED

At the end of Chapter 5, we discussed how you need to think in order to guide your choice of supporting materials. You need to consider your main ideas, the range of available materials, and the kinds of supporting materials required by your audience.

These critical guidelines for selection should govern your search process. Suppose, for example, that you have become interested in emotional depression because a friend has been diagnosed with it. You want to give an informative speech on this topic to an audience of college students. What kinds of supporting materials do you need?

1. *Rational requirements.* However you phrase your central idea, speeches on this topic reasonably require certain sorts of supporting materials:
   a. Statistics on the number of people who have been diagnosed with depression.
   b. Statistics on the incidence of depression among various age groups.
   c. Testimony from people who are afflicted with the condition and from medical experts who study or treat it.
   d. Symptoms associated with depression and consequences of the condition.
   e. A summary of current medical treatment and avenues of research.
   f. Theories about who gets the disease and why.

The statistics provide a general picture and develop the scope of the problem; testimony, examples and illustrations, and comparisons and contrasts depict details and develop audience interest.

1. *Available materials.* Do you have access to these kinds of materials? Your library might have the following sources:
   a. Medical journals with up-to-date research (see *Psychological Abstracts*).
   b. Computer access to special bibliographies on the topic (check computerized databases like MEDLINE and PSYCHINFO).
   c. Government statistics (see the *Statistical Abstract of the United States, American Statistics Index,* and *Statistical Reference Index*).
   d. Pamphlets put out by the federal government's National Health Information Center (begin with the *Monthly Catalog of U.S. Gov-*

ernment Publications, CIS/Index, and *Index to U.S. Government Periodicals*).

e. General magazines with articles on depression (check the *General Science Index* and the *Social Sciences Citation Index*).

f. Newsletters and periodicals put out by groups specializing in treatment of and support for people with depression (look up your subject heading in *Ulrich's International Periodicals Directory, Gale's Directory of Publications, Standard Periodical Directory,* and *Newsletters in Print*).

g. Books on the history of mental and emotional disorders (listed in the card catalog).

2. *Audience demand.* Your specific audience is probably most interested in the occurrence of depression on campus. They may have inaccurate ideas about who is likely to become depressed and the symptoms and the causes of the disease. They may also be unaware of the variety of treatments currently available for depression.

3. *Power to prove.* As you conduct your research, you should realize that you will discover many forms of support. However, some will be more effective with your audience than others. Your classmates may want to know how depression affects their lives. They may also have little background or knowledge about the topic. Explanations, statistics, and illustration will help you develop the topic so your listeners can better understand it. Specific instances and testimony will lend interest to the topic.

No matter what forms of support you choose, merely citing the findings of research is clearly not enough; you also have to test the authorities and their special interests in making and defending claims. You also have to ask, "Who are my listeners likely to believe? What is most relevant to their lives?" And, "Do these conclusions represent prevalent thought on the topic?"

Your review of initial considerations suggests the following search strategies for supporting materials:

I. Topic: Mental depression among college students
II. Sources
    A. Background examples and illustrations from popular magazines
    B. Demographic studies of magnitude of problem and medical studies of symptoms and treatments (from MEDLINE computerized search)
    C. The opinions of experts from MEDLINE search, from government pamphlets, and from on-campus interviews with medical professionals if available
    D. Illustrations of effects of depression from interviews with officials at local treatment centers
    E. Comparisons and contrasts from interviews with patients and clinical supervisors

This initial thinking about your topic: (a) helps you clarify your central idea, (b) guides your search for the specific materials you'll want to examine, (c) determines whom you should contact to interview, and (d) indicates what supporting material you should include in your speech.

How Much Is Enough?

Have you ever found yourself wondering, "How much supporting material should I use in my speech?" You probably realize that there's no absolute rule governing the number or kind of supporting materials. However, you need enough support to establish your points, and this varies according to the quality and kind of supporting materials. Here are some guidelines for choosing your supporting materials:

1. *Complex or abstract ideas are enhanced by concrete supporting materials.* Visual aids, specific examples, or factual illustrations will make complex or abstract ideas clearer. A speech on chaos theory would be clarified by a graph or an example from daily life.

2. *Controversial points require a lot of authoritative evidence.* This means that a speech for raising property taxes would benefit from statistics, budget trend information, and well-respected testimony.

3. *Speakers with low credibility need more supporting material than speakers with high credibility.* If you plan to speak on educational reform for the next century but your only experience has been as a student, you should use a lot of supporting material.

4. *If your topic is abstract or distant from your listeners' experiences, use concrete supporting material.* Illustrations, examples, testimony, and explanations will establish some identification with listeners. A speech on life in a medieval castle doesn't come alive until you insert specific details and concrete examples.

5. *If your audience's attention or comprehension is low, use more examples.* Stories command attention, and most of us can understand them.

SOURCES OF SUPPORTING MATERIALS

Where and how do you find the kinds of supporting materials we've been discussing? Several sources are available to you: publications of many kinds, computerized searches, printed materials, interviews with experts, broadcasts, and letters and questionnaires.

Computerized Searches

Your library undoubtedly subscribes to one or more computerized databases. These work much like printed indexes—only much more quickly and thoroughly. Electronic databases are usually updated regularly, making them much more timely than printed indexes. The average university library probably has access to nearly 200 data files such as ERIC, BIOSIS, PsychInfo, AGRICOLA, Datrex, and MEDLINE. Computerized searches, run intelligently, can be invaluable tools for research on speech topics.

1. Pick the database likely to have the information that you want. With the help of a reference librarian and the descriptive material on the databases, you'll know to go to ERIC if you want scholarly and educational papers written by humanities professors and to MEDLINE if you can make use of psychological and scientific studies of diseases and other medical problems.

2. Try some of the public databases as well as library bases. If you have access to a personal computer and modem, you can reach BRS/After Dark, CompuServe, Prodigy, Dow Jones News/Retrieval, and other general bases giving you a wealth of general information, news events, economic indicators, and the like.

3. Be smart when picking key words for searches. Computerized searches can give you too much information if you select only broad categories such as *television.* The more you're able to narrow and coordinate key words, the more likely you are to get usable material. So, if you're interested in television anchor people, coordinating the key words *television* and *news reporters* will get you what you want.

Searching library shelves for books can be rewarding; often you'll find an even more useful book next to the one you wanted. But, for sheer volume of information, nothing beats a computerized search.

Printed Materials

The most common source of supporting materials is the printed word: newspapers, magazines, pamphlets, and books. Through the careful use of a library, and with the help of reference librarians, you can discover an almost overwhelming amount of materials relevant to your speech subject and purpose.

• Libraries provide many forms of information, including print and nonprint media. What materials can you expect to find in your library? How can you locate these materials in a systematic and efficient way?

Newspapers

Newspapers are obviously a useful source of information about events of current interest. Moreover, their feature stories and accounts of unusual happenings provide a storehouse of interesting illustrations and examples. You must be careful, of course, not to accept as true everything printed in a newspaper, since the haste with which news must be gathered sometimes makes complete accuracy difficult. Your school or city library undoubtedly keeps on file copies of one or two highly reliable papers, such as *The New York Times, The Observer, The Wall Street Journal,* or the *Christian Science Monitor,* as well as the leading newspapers of your state or region. If your library has *The New York Times Index,* you can locate the paper's accounts of people and events from 1913 to the present. Another useful and well-indexed source of information on current happenings is *Facts on File,* issued weekly since 1940.

Magazines

The average university library subscribes to hundreds of magazines and journals. Some, such as *Time, Newsweek,* and *U.S. News & World Report,* summarize weekly events. *Omni* and *Harper's* are representative of monthly publications that cover a wide range of subjects of both passing and lasting importance. *The Nation, Vital Speeches of the Day, Fortune, Washington Monthly,* and *The New Republic,* among other magazines, contain comment on current political, social, and economic questions. More specialized magazines include *Popular Science, Scientific American, Sports Illustrated, Field and Stream, Ms., Better Homes and Gardens, Byte, Today's Health, National Geographic,* and *The Smithsonian.*

This list is, of course, just the beginning—there are hundreds of periodicals available covering thousands of subjects. To find a specific kind of information, use the *Readers' Guide to Periodical Literature,* which indexes most of the magazines you'll want to consult in preparing a speech. Or, if you'd like more sophisticated material, consult the *Social Sciences Index* and the *Humanities Index,* now computerized in most libraries. Similar indexes are available for publications from technical fields and professional societies; a reference librarian can show you how to use them.

Yearbooks and Encyclopedias

The most reliable source of comprehensive data is the *Statistical Abstracts of the United States,* which covers a wide variety of subjects ranging from weather records and birth rates to steel production and election results. Information on Academy Award Winners, world records in various areas, and the "bests" and "worsts" of almost anything can be found in the *World Almanac, The People's Almanac, The Guinness Book of World Records, The Book of Lists,* and *Information Please.* Encyclopedias, such as the *Encyclopaedia Britannica* and *Encyclopedia Americana,* attempt to cover the entire field of human knowledge and are valuable chiefly as initial reference sources or for background reading. Refer to them for important scientific, geographical, literary, or historical facts; for bibliographies of authoritative books on a subject; and for ideas you do not need to develop completely in your speech.

Speaking of...

• • • •

What Well-Read People Read

You may have noticed that people who command respect frequently have ideas to contribute on a wide range of subjects. These men and women not only provide social commentary on many matters but also make observations that reflect the understanding of complex social, economic, religious, and political forces. The basis for thoughtful living is often cultivated by extensive reading. For many, the habit of reading, thinking, and speaking begins early— in high school or college.

Recently investigators drew up a list of respected American intellectuals: Noam Chomsky, William F. Buckley, Norman Mailer, Barbara Jordan, Daniel Patrick Moynihan, and others. They surveyed this elite group to discover what periodicals they regularly read to stay informed. Among the 42 journals cited, those most frequently read were:

The New York Review of Books
The New York Times Book Review Section
Commentary
Harper's
Partisan Review
The New Republic

The most highly regarded individuals in the group were also the ones who read most widely.

Other researchers surveyed college and university faculty members to determine which popular periodicals they read regularly. At the top of the list were:

Newsweek
Time
U.S. News & World Report
The New York Times
Saturday Review
The New Yorker
The Wall Street Journal
The New York Review of Books
Science

If you want to become better informed or more fully comprehend the events around you, consider what the experts do to become well informed— expand your reading. In other words, learn to read and think before you speak.

For further reference, see: Julie Hover and Charles Kaduchin, "The Influential Journals: A Very Private Club," *Change* 4 (1972): 38–47; Everett Carl Ladd, Jr., and Seymour Martin Lipset, "The General Periodicals Professors Read," *The Chronicle of Higher Education* 9 (1976): 14.

Documents and Reports

Various government agencies—state, national, and international—as well as many independent organizations publish reports on special subjects. The most frequently consulted governmental publications are the hearings and recommendations of congressional committees on the publications of the United States Department of Health and Human Services or Department of Commerce. Reports on issues related to agriculture, business, government, engineering, and scientific experimentation are published by many state universities. Such endowed groups as the Carnegie, Rockefeller, and Ford Foundations and such special interest groups as the Foreign Policy Association, the Brookings Institution, the League of Women Voters, Common Cause, and the United States Chamber of Commerce also publish reports and pamphlets. Though by no means a complete list, *The Vertical File Index* serves as a guide to some of these materials.

Books

Most subjects suitable for a speech have been written about in books. As a guide to these books, use the subject-matter headings in the card catalog of local libraries. Generally, you will find authoritative books in your school library and more popularized treatments in your city's public library. You can now access the card catalog via computer in many libraries. This often makes your search more efficient and productive.

Biographies

The Dictionary of National Biography, the *Dictionary of American Biography, Who's Who, Who's Who in America, Current Biography,* and more specialized works organized by field contain biographical sketches especially useful in locating facts about famous people and in documenting the qualifications of authorities whose testimony you may quote.

Radio and Television Broadcasts

Lectures, discussions, and the formal public addresses of leaders in government, business, education, and religion are frequently broadcast over radio or television. Many of these talks are later mimeographed or printed by the stations or by the organizations that sponsor them. Usually, as in the case of CBS's *Meet the Press* or National Public Radio's *All Things Considered,* copies of broadcasts may be obtained for a small fee. Other broadcast content, such as national news broadcasts, is indexed by Vanderbilt University; your library may subscribe to that index, which is helpful in reconstructing a series of events. There are also computer databases that track media programs.

If manuscripts or transcripts are not available, you may take careful notes from videotaped or audiotaped programs. Be exact! Just as you must quote printed sources accurately and honestly, so, too, are you morally obligated to respect someone's radio and television remarks and to give that person full credit.

Obviously, you won't have to investigate all of the foregoing sources of materials for every speech you make. The key concept is relevance: go to the sources that will yield relevant materials. You are more likely to find historical statistics

Speaking of...

• • • •

Recognizing Primary and Secondary Sources

To read and think critically, one must be able to distinguish among sources of information. One way to differentiate is to distinguish between what historians call *primary sources* or eyewitness/first-hand accounts and *secondary sources,* accounts based on other sources of information. The diary of a pioneer woman crossing the Great Plains in 1822 would be considered a primary source, since she herself recorded her experiences. The history of the westward movement based on many accounts of pioneers is a secondary source. Both are subject to biases. Obviously, the pioneer woman may not have had a "typical" experience, or her own personal prejudices may have influenced what she recorded. The same may be true of the historian. Furthermore, sometimes the sources a historian works from color the resulting history.

Consider the following sources for a speech on breast cancer. Which are primary and which are secondary sources? When would you use each?

1. A summary of breast cancer research from 1983 to 1993 in an American medical journal.

2. Your aunt's account of her mastectomy.

3. A local newspaper article on the seven warning signs of cancer.

4. A book titled *Surviving Cancer Surgery.*

5. The meeting notes of a local cancer support group.

6. A radio commentary on the importance of annual mammograms.

7. A journal written by a cancer specialist who underwent breast cancer treatment.

8. A U.S. government study evaluating the success of various treatments for breast cancer.

in print materials than in a television program or to find a viewpoint on a local problem in an interview than in a computer search. Use your head in selecting sources of materials to investigate and then carry out the search carefully. If you do, you'll find the materials to make your speech authoritative and interesting.

Interviews

When looking for material, many of us forget the easiest and most logical way to start—by asking questions. The goal of an **informational interview** is to obtain answers to specific questions. In interviewing someone, you seek answers that can be woven into the text of your speech. Interviews increase your understanding of a topic so that you will avoid misinforming your audience, drawing incorrect inferences from information, and convoluting technical ideas. Your interviewee may be a content expert or someone who has had personal experience with the issues you wish to discuss. If you're addressing the topic of black holes, who is better qualified to help you than a physicist? If you're explaining the construction of a concrete boat, you might contact a local civil engineer for assistance. If you wish to discuss anorexia nervosa, you might interview a person who has suffered through the disorder. Interviews can provide compelling illustrations of human experiences.

You need to observe three general guidelines in planning an informational interview:

1. *Decide on your specific purpose.* What precise information do you hope to obtain during the interview? One caution: if you are interviewing a controversial figure, you should avoid engaging in an argument or assuming a belligerent or self-righteous tone. Even if you disagree with the answers being given, your role is not that of Perry Mason, seeking to win a jury's vote by grilling the witness. Nevertheless, your interview can encompass tough questions or questions that seek further clarification for answers that seem "not right." Simply raise such questions without provoking an argument.

2. *Structure the interview in advance.* The beginning of an interview clarifies the purpose and sets limits on what will be covered during the session. You also can use this time to establish rapport with the person being interviewed. The middle of the interview constitutes the substantive portion, during which the information being sought is provided. Structure your questions in advance so that you have a clear idea of *what* to ask *when.* The interview may not follow your list exactly, but you'll have a convenient means of checking whether all the information you need has been covered. You'll also find the list useful as you summarize your understanding of the major points, a process that can prevent misinterpretation of the meaning that the interviewee has given to specific points.

3. *Remember that interviews are interactive processes.* There is a definite pattern of "turn-taking" in interviews that allows both parties to concentrate on one issue at a time and assists in making the interview work for the benefit of both parties. This interactive pattern requires that both parties be careful listeners since one person's comments will affect the next comment of the other. You'll need to remain flexible and free to deviate from your interview plan as you listen to the answers to your questions. You'll also have to listen to what's said and almost simultaneously think ahead to the next item on your list of questions to decide if you should forge ahead or ask intervening questions to clarify or elaborate on a previous response.

From this discussion of interviewing, it should be clear that adept interviewers must have certain communicative skills:

1. *A good interviewer is a good listener.* You should listen carefully to what is said and accurately interpret the significance of those comments. Because questioning and answering are alternated in an interview, there's plenty of opportunity to clarify remarks and opinions.

2. *A good interviewer is open.* Many of us are extremely wary of interviewers. We're cynical enough to believe that they have hidden agendas—unstated motives or purposes—that they're trying to pursue. Too often interviewers have claimed only to want a little information when actually they were selling magazine subscriptions or insurance. Frankness and openness should govern all aspects of your interview communication.

Speaking
of...

• • • •

Conducting an Interview

What follows is an example of a format you might follow in an informational interview:

I. Opening
   A. Mutual greeting
   B. Discussion of purposes
      1. Reason information is needed
      2. Kind of information wanted

II. Informational Portion
   A. Question 1, with clarifying questions as needed
   B. Question 2, with clarifying questions as needed
   C. [and so on]

III. Closing
   A. Summary of main points
   B. Final courtesies

If you were preparing to interview your high school counselor for information to develop a speech on violence at school, you might come up with the following questions:

I. Have you encountered the problem of violence on school grounds?
   A. How many times in the past school year?
   B. Is the problem increasing?

II. Are some students more likely than others to become violent?
   A. Is gender a factor?
      1. Are males more prone to violence than females?
      2. Why?
   B. Does the incidence of violence peak in a certain age group?
      1. Are some adolescents more likely to become violent because of their family background?
      2. Does violence occur more frequently among students who perform poorly in the classroom?
   C. Can you provide other characteristics of students who tend to resort to violence in school?

III. What are the effects of violence?

IV. What measures does your school take to deal with violence on school property?

V. If you had an unlimited budget and staff, what would you do to solve the problem of violence among students?

3. *A good interviewer builds a sense of mutual respect and trust.* Feelings of trust and respect are created by revealing your own motivation, by getting the person to talk, and by expressing sympathy and understanding. Good communication skills and a well-thought-out set of questions build rapport in in-

• You can gather information by talking directly to people who know about your topic. In order to conduct an effective interview, prepare your questions in advance. What guidelines should you follow when preparing your interview questions?

terview situations. Interviewers should always follow up the interview with a note or letter expressing their appreciation for the person's shared time and expertise.

RECORDING INFORMATION

When you find the information you've been looking for, you'll need a system for recording it. First, record the source citation completely. You'll need this information when you cite the source during your speech. Note the title of the book or article, author, and publication data including the place, publisher, and date of publication. Include the volume number if you're citing a journal article. It's helpful to record the call number or location of the source just in case you need to consult the information again.

Sometimes it's easiest to make photocopies of materials. If you take notes, you may find that notecards are easier to use than a notebook because they can be shuffled by topic area or type of support. If you do use a notebook, however, try to record each item on half of each page. There are two reasons to do this: First, since most of your information won't fill a page, you will save paper. Second, cutting the sheets in half will make it easier to sort your data or to adopt a

FIGURE 6.1
A Sample Notecard
Notecards can be effective for recording information for later use. What essential information is important to enter on each notecard?

> **general subject: Life Expectancies**
>
> **specific information:**
>
> **based on the results of a study conducted at the University of California at San Francisco, researchers reported that middle-aged men without wives were twice as likely to die as men with wives; nutritional, social, and emotional factors probably explain the difference in mortality rates**
>
> **source: "For Longer Life, Take a Wife," Newsweek, CXVI (November 1990), 73.**

classification scheme and record information in accordance with particular themes or subpoints of your speech. When preparing notecards, place the appropriate subject headings at the top of the cards and complete source citations at the bottom. This way, the cards can be classified by general subject (top right heading) and by specific information presented (top left heading). (See Figure 6.1.)

USING SOURCE MATERIAL ETHICALLY

Now that we've discussed locating and generating material for your speeches, we come to a major ethical issue—plagiarism. **Plagiarism** is defined as "the unacknowledged inclusion of someone else's words, ideas, or data as one's own."[1] One of the saddest things an instructor has to do is cite a student for plagiarism. In speech classes, students occasionally take material from a source they've read and present it as their own. Many speech teachers and members of audiences habitually scan the library periodicals section. Even if listeners have not read the article, it soon becomes apparent that something is wrong: the wording differs from the way the person usually talks, the style is more typical of written than spoken English, or the speech is a patchwork of eloquent and awkward phrasing. In addition, the organizational pattern of the speech may lack a well-formulated introduction or conclusion or be one not normally used by speakers. Often, too, the person who plagiarizes an article reads it aloud badly—another sign that something is wrong.

Plagiarism is not, however, simply undocumented verbatim quotation. It also includes (a) undocumented paraphrases of others' ideas and (b) undocumented use of others' main ideas. For example, if you paraphrase a movie review from *Newsweek* without acknowledging that staff critic David Ansen had those insights, or if you use economic predictions without giving credit to *Businessweek,* you are guilty of plagiarism.

Suppose you ran across the following idea while reading Neil Postman's *Amusing Ourselves to Death: Public Discourse in the Age of Show Business:*[2]

The television commercial is not at all about the character of products to be consumed. It is about the character of the consumers of products. Images of movie stars and famous athletes, of serene lakes and macho fishing trips, of elegant dinners and romantic interludes, of happy families packing their station wagons for a picnic in the country—these tell nothing about the products being sold. But they tell everything about the fears, fancies and dreams of those who might buy them. What the advertiser needs to know is not what is right about the product but what is wrong·about the buyer. And so, the balance of business expenditures shifts from product *research to* market *research. The television commercial has oriented business away from making products of value and toward making consumers feel valuable, which means that the business of business has now become pseudo-therapy. The consumer is a patient assured by psycho-dramas.*

Imagine that you wanted to make this point in a speech on the changing role of electronic advertising. Of course, you want to avoid plagiarism. Here are some ways you could use the ideas ethically:

1. *Verbatim quotation of a passage.* Simply read the passage aloud word for word. To avoid plagiarism, say, "Neil Postman, in his 1985 book *Amusing Ourselves to Death: Public Discourse in the Age of Show Business,* said this about the nature of television advertisements: [then quote the paragraph]."

2. *Paraphrasing of the main ideas:* Summarize the author's ideas in your own words: "We've all grown up with television advertising, and most of the time we endure it without giving it much thought. In his book *Amusing Ourselves to Death: Public Discourse in the Age of Show Business,* Neil Postman makes the point that instead of selling us on the virtues of a product, advertisers sell us our own fears and dreams. Advertisements are more about us than about the products being sold."

3. *Partial quotation of phrases:* Quote a brief passage and summarize the rest of the author's ideas in your own words: "Postman suggests that the shift from product research to market research indicates a shift in emphasis away from the product being sold and to the consumer. He says that business now focuses on making the consumer feel better through "pseudo-therapy. The consumer is a patient assured by psycho-dramas." Be sure to pause and say "quote" to indicate when you are quoting the author's words.

Plagiarism is easy to avoid if you take reasonable care. Moreover, by citing such authorities as Postman, who are well educated and experienced, you add their credibility to yours. Avoid plagiarism to keep from being expelled from the class or even from your school. Avoid it for positive reasons as well: to improve your ethos by associating your thinking with that of experts.

CHAPTER SUMMARY

1. In searching for supporting materials, you're attempting to assemble efficiently not all information but only materials relevant to your speeches, your audiences, and the occasions on which you're speaking.

2. To determine before you search the kinds of supporting materials needed, you should consider: (a) the rational requirements of the central idea, (b) the range

of available materials, (c) audience demands, and (d) the power to prove generally associated with various kinds of supporting materials.

3. In executing your searches, you'll want to know how to conduct a computerized search and how to locate printed materials (newspapers, yearbooks and encyclopedias, documents and reports, books, and biographies) as well as radio and television broadcasts. You can interview experts to obtain specific information.

4. You need to record information carefully and in a form you can use easily.

5. You must also remember to use source material ethically, avoiding plagiarism.

KEY TERMS

informational interview (p. 99)
plagiarism (p. 103)

SKILLBUILDING ACTIVITIES

1. Your instructor will divide your class into groups. Each group will locate in the library the items in the left-hand column of the following list. First, determine which of the sources listed in the right-hand column contains the material you need. Then, find each source and write down the page numbers where the material can be found. On a later day, each group will turn in its reports, comparing its list with those of other groups.

Items	**Sources**
Weekly summary of current national news	*Book Review Digest*
Brief sketch of the accomplishments of	*Congressional Record*
Lee Iacocca	*Encyclopedia Americana*
Description of a specific traffic accident	*Facts on File* local newspapers
Text of Bill Clinton's inaugural address	*The New York Times*
Daily summary of stock prices	*Oxford English Dictionary*
Origin of the word *rhetoric*	*Statistical Abstracts*
Critical commentary on A. Bloom's	*Time*
The Closing of the American Mind	*Vital Speeches of the Day*
Current status of national legislation	*The Wall Street Journal*
on educational reform	*Who's Who*

2. Select a major problem, incident, or celebration that has appeared in the news recently. Examine a story or article written about it in each of the following: *The New York Times, Christian Science Monitor, USA Today, Time, Newsweek, The New Republic,* and either *The Wall Street Journal* or *Business Week.* In a column from each source, note specifically what major facts, people, incidents, and examples or illustrations are included and what conclusions are drawn. Be prepared to discuss the differences among the sources you consulted. How are their differences related to their readership? What does this exercise teach you about the biases or viewpoints of sources?

3. Plan an interview of a celebrity or famous person. First, find out about the person by conducting a library search. Then, develop your interview questions. You might consider interviewing political leaders such as Margaret Thatcher,

Boris Yeltsin, or Nelson Mandela. Or, you could choose controversial figures like Dr. Jack Kevorkian, Yasir Arafat, Madalyn Murray O'Hair, or Oliver North.

REFERENCES

1. Louisiana State University, "Academic Honesty and Dishonesty," adapted from LSU's Code of Student Conduct, 1981.

2. Neil Postman, *Amusing Ourselves to Death: Public Discourse in the Age of Show Business* (New York: Viking Penguin, 1985), 128.

Arranging and Outlining Your Speech

*B*ob had been his company's top sales representative for the past three *years and really knew his product thoroughly. One day he was present-ing it to the board of directors of a prospective client. Before beginning his presentation, Bob decided to loosen them up with some spontaneous intro-ductory comments. He told the board about a fishing trip that he'd taken the previous summer and talked about teaching his daughter to bait a hook. After what seemed like only 5 or 10 minutes to Bob, the chair of the meeting in-terrupted to say that the board was adjourning to another meeting. Bob glanced at his watch and realized that he had rambled on for over 20 min-utes. Bob lost the account.*

Bob's decision to ad lib was disastrous. Rather than preparing formal comments and sticking to them, Bob chose instead to begin his speech by speaking in an "off-the-cuff" manner. In doing so, Bob ignored the key criteria for communicat-ing ideas to an audience:

1. *The plan of the speech must be easy for the audience to grasp and re-member.* Bob's listeners had difficulty figuring out where he was going. As a consequence, his listeners were frustrated in their attempts to untangle his re-marks. Their attention wandered, and the result was unsuccessful for both Bob and his listeners.

2. *The organizational pattern must provide for full and balanced coverage of the material.* You must use a pattern that will complement your ideas and their supporting materials—one that will clarify your central idea. Bob's lis-teners couldn't figure out his central idea because he talked about fishing in-stead of about his product.

3. *The structure of the speech should be appropriate to the occasion.* Bob's speech also failed because he underestimated the rigidity of the situation. Bob didn't satisfy his listeners' expectations, nor did he adapt to the formality of the occasion. Speakers usually are expected to observe group traditions. Board meetings have one thing in common with eulogies, speeches of introduction, and Academy Awards acceptance speeches: they normally evolve in an order that members of audiences have come to expect.

4. *The structure of the speech should be adapted to the audience's needs and level of knowledge.* When Bob rambled on about his personal life in a business meeting, he ignored his listeners' need to process information efficiently. He also insulted their intelligence by using informal language and by appearing to be unprepared. To avoid Bob's debacle, keep your audience in mind—what they know, expect, and need.

5. *The speech must move steadily forward toward a complete and satisfying finish.* Bob's listeners became increasingly frustrated because his speech didn't seem to be developing. They needed a sense of forward motion—of moving through a series of main points toward a clear destination. Backtracking slows down the momentum of the speech, giving it a stop-and-start progression rather than a smooth forward flow. You'll also enhance the sense of forward motion with internal summaries and forecasts, as well as transitions and physical movement to indicate progression.

TYPES OF ARRANGEMENT

As we use the term here, **arrangement** is the order or sequence of ideas in a pattern that suggests their relationship to each other. There are five general arrangement categories for speeches: chronological, spatial, causal, topical, and special patterns.

Chronological Patterns

Chronological patterns trace the order of events in a time sequence. This arrangement of ideas is useful when your goal is to give listeners a strong sense of development or forward motion. When using a chronological sequence, you begin at a point in time and move forward to some concluding point. Where you start and end will depend on the central idea you're working with. For example, you might describe the evolution of modern flight either from the Wright brothers or from Russia's launching of Sputnik in 1957, depending on your goal: are you trying to tell the whole story at a general level or the more specific story of space flight? Similarly, suppose you wanted to argue that we need to regulate the way presidential candidates use mass media; a chronological pattern would let you tell the story of electronic media and politics and relate the lessons to be learned as arguments for change.

> **Central Idea:** It is time for Congress to regulate the materials broadcast by presidential campaigns.

I. Review of campaign abuses, ending with the question, "How did American politics get this way?"
II. Review the stages of the electrification of presidential campaigns.
    A. The coming of radio in 1924.
    B. The first use of filmed biographies in 1924.
    C. The arrival of television in 1952.
        1. Televised political conventions.
        2. First TV advertising campaigns.
    D. The heavy use of the computer starting in 1960.
        1. Kennedy's reliance upon 1960 census data.
        2. The use of voter polls by Kennedy's consultant, Joe Napolitan.
III. What lessons can be drawn from this story?
    A. When candidates have uncontrolled access to mass media, the costs skyrocket.
    B. When candidates make electronic media their primary means of communication, voting rates decline.
    C. When Congress attempts to control spending (as it did with the Federal Campaign Spending Acts), the money gets into campaigns in other ways in order to pay for television time.
IV. The story of American mass-media presidential elections shows us the way to new reforms.[1]

Spatial Patterns

In the **spatial pattern,** the major points of the speech are organized in terms of their physical proximity to or direction from each other. A speech on the movement of weather systems from the north and south across the U.S. would fit such a pattern. Consider another example:

> **Central Idea:**   Traveling to the sites of the world's major volcanoes will let you see the creative forces of the earth at work.

I. The eruption 7,000 years ago of Mazama, a 9,900 feet high volcano in southern Oregon, covered the entire northwestern U.S. in ash and lava and created what we now call Crater Lake.
II. The sheer power and beauty of nature evident in volcanoes should motivate you to see them. Suppose you wanted to take trip to view volcanoes:
    A. Start at Mt. St. Helens in the state of Washington (1991 eruption).
    B. Journey to the Aleutian Islands off the Alaskan coast, to Mt. Akutan (1990 eruption).
    C. Cross the Pacific to Japan, to Mt. Asama (1991 eruption).
    D. Drop down to Sumatra, to find Mt. Kerinci (1987 eruption).
    E. Head west to Zaire in Africa, to Mt. Nyamuragira (1988 eruption).
    F. Then to Italy's Etna (1990 eruption), Iceland's Hekla (1991 eruption), and home again.
III. Even if the whole trip's too expensive, a visit to any of these active volcanoes could be the trip of a lifetime.[2]

Causal Patterns

Causal patterns of speech organization move either: (a) from an analysis of present causes to a prediction of future effects or (b) from present conditions to their apparent causes. Causal patterns give listeners a sense of physical coherence because ideas are developed in relationship to each other. Causal patterns assume that one event results from or causes another. When using a *cause-effect pattern,* you might first point to the increasing cost of attending college, and then argue that one of its effects is reduced enrollments. Or, using an *effect-cause pattern,* you could note that the estimated one percent decrease in college enrollments in 1992 was the result, at least in part, of the increasing costs. Compare the following outlines:

Central Idea: Acid rain [cause] is a growing problem because it threatens our health and economy [effect].

  I. Factories across the United States emit harmful acid-forming sulfur dioxide and nitrogen oxide.
 II. The effect of these emissions is to damage important ecological structures.
     A. Lakes and forests are threatened.
     B. The productivity of fertile soil is reduced.
     C. Acid particles in the air and drinking water cause 5–8 percent of all deaths in some regions of the United States.

Central Idea: Acid rain [effect] is primarily the result of modern technologies [causes].

  I. If we are going to control acid rain, we must learn about and deal with its causes.
 II. Human activities cause acid rain.
     A. One primary cause is air pollutants given off in the production of electrical energy.
     B. A second main cause is the emissions from motorized transportation.

Notice that the first outline uses a cause-effect pattern; the second uses an effect-cause pattern. Adapt your speech to the situation by beginning with ideas that are better known to audience members; then proceed to the lesser known facets of the problem. Use cause-effect if listeners are better acquainted with the cause; use effect-cause if the opposite is true.

Topical Patterns

Some speeches on familiar topics are best organized in terms of subject-matter divisions that have become standardized. Sports strategy is divided into offense and defense; kinds of courts into municipal, county, state, and federal jurisdictions; and types of trees into deciduous and evergreen categories. **Topical patterns** are most useful for speeches that enumerate aspects of persons, places, things, or

• Speaking notes
should be unobtrusive.
Think back to speaking
situations you remem-
ber. When do they be-
come distracting?

processes. Occasionally, a speaker tries to list all aspects of the topic, as in a ser-
mon on each of the seven deadly sins. More often, however, a partial listing of
the primary or most interesting aspects is sufficient. For example, suppose you
wanted to give a speech to a general audience about biases in news reporting:

Central Idea: Knowing the three basic kinds of bias in news reporting can help you guard against politicized reactions to news events.

    I. *Personalizing* the news encourages people to focus on self rather than socially-oriented views of political events.
    II. *Dramatizing* the news focuses on contests between people rather than underlying causes and effects.
    III. *Fragmenting* the news conditions people to look at particular events rather than larger patterns of social-political activity.[3]

Topical patterns are among the most popular and easiest to use. If you plan to list only certain aspects of the topic, take care to explain your choices. So, if someone asks, "Why didn't you talk about reporters who deliberately favor one side of a controversy?" you could answer, "I'm sure you're aware of that sort of bias. I wanted to deal with more deeply hidden kinds of biases that affect how we see the world."

The types of speech organization discussed so far—narrative, spatial, causal, and topical—are determined principally by the subject matter. While the audience is not ignored by the organizational pattern, it's the subject that usually suggests the pattern of organization.

Special Patterns

At times, you may decide that rather than using any of the subject-oriented speech structures, an audience-oriented, or **special pattern,** will more effectively organize your material. Special patterns often work well because they're based on the listeners' needs. We'll examine five special patterns of organization: familiarity-acceptance order, inquiry order, question-answer order, problem-solution order, and elimination order.

Familiarity-Acceptance Order

Familiarity-acceptance order begins with what the audience knows or believes (the familiar) and moves on to new or challenging ideas (the unfamiliar). In an informative speech on quarks, you can begin with what the audience already knows about molecules and then introduce the new information on the subatomic particles called *quarks.*

Persuasive speeches based on accepted audience values are very well suited to skeptical or hostile audiences, especially when your reasoning is valid and your conclusions sound. When you meet these standards, your audience can't reject your claim without denying the underlying facts or values that they already accept. Here's an outline of a persuasive speech using familiarity-acceptance order:

Central Idea: Maria Campagna embodies the values our party stands for and, therefore, should be our nominee.

    I. We all agree, I am sure, that experience, ability, and integrity are prime requisites for a holder of high public office. [*familiar and accepted values*]

II. Maria Campagna has these qualities. [*unfamiliar person to be associated with the familiar*]
   A. She has experience.
      1. She has served two terms as mayor of one of our largest cities.
      2. She has served in the state senate for 12 years.
   B. She has ability.
      1. She has successfully reorganized the cumbersome administrative machinery of our city government.
      2. She has become a recognized leader in the senate.
   C. She has integrity.
      1. She has never been suspected of any sort of corruption.
      2. Her word is as good as her bond.
III. Because Maria Campagna clearly has the qualities we demand of a holder of high public office, she deserves our support in her bid to be elected governor of this state.

Inquiry Order

Inquiry order provides a step-by-step explanation of how you acquired the information or reached the conclusion. Scientists habitually review their procedures one at a time in order to demonstrate the professionally sound techniques they used in a study. Similarly, if you want to persuade people to plant a new variety of hedge, you could recount how you studied the varieties that seemed to be dying in your neighborhood, investigated possible choices, and searched for new varieties until the kind you now advocate emerged as the best.

Inquiry order has a double advantage. First, it displays all facts and possibilities for the audience. Second, it enables listeners to judge accurately the worth of the information or policy being presented as it unfolds.

Question-Answer Order

Question-answer order raises and answers listeners' questions. First, you must determine which questions are most likely to arise in your listeners' minds. Then you need to develop your speech to answer each key question in a way that favors your conclusion. For example, when buying a new car, people often want to know about its principal features, the available options, its mileage, and its cost. When first learning about a new bond issue, listeners wonder how it will affect their taxes or government services. By structuring your speech to address these questions, you can maintain audience interest and involvement.

Problem-Solution Order

When you advocate changes in action or thought, your main points may fall naturally into a **problem-solution order** (see Figure 7.1). First, you establish that a problem exists. If your listeners are already aware of the problem, however, you might avoid describing it too extensively. For example, if your listeners walk or ride bicycles to classes, they'll be unaware that there aren't enough parking spaces on campus; but if they drive automobiles, they'll be quite familiar with the parking shortage. You also need to depict the problem in a way that will help your listeners perceive it in the same way that you do. For example, your listeners may

FIGURE 7.1
Developing the
Problem-Solution
Pattern
Notice how the
problems addressed
help the speaker
achieve the intended
purpose.

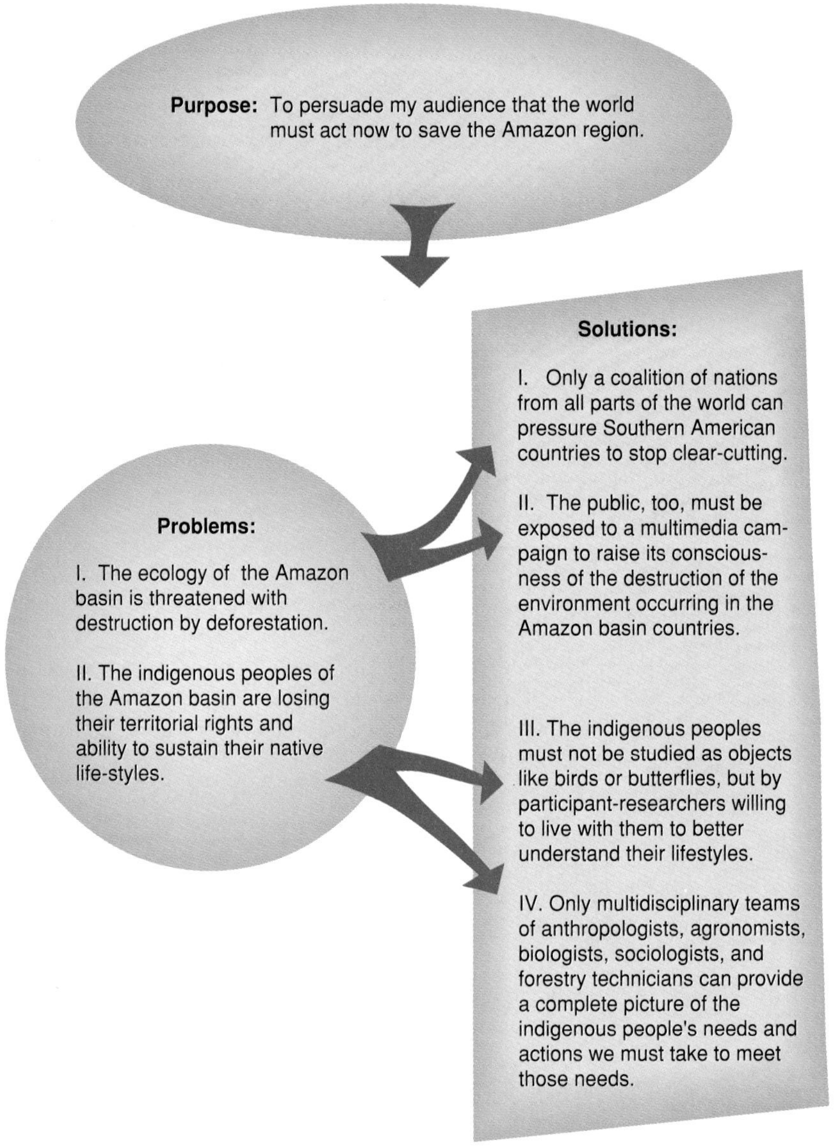

Purpose: To persuade my audience that the world must act now to save the Amazon region.

Solutions:

I. Only a coalition of nations from all parts of the world can pressure Southern American countries to stop clear-cutting.

II. The public, too, must be exposed to a multimedia campaign to raise its consciousness of the destruction of the environment occurring in the Amazon basin countries.

Problems:

I. The ecology of the Amazon basin is threatened with destruction by deforestation.

II. The indigenous peoples of the Amazon basin are losing their territorial rights and ability to sustain their native life-styles.

III. The indigenous peoples must not be studied as objects like birds or butterflies, but by participant-researchers willing to live with them to better understand their lifestyles.

IV. Only multidisciplinary teams of anthropologists, agronomists, biologists, sociologists, and forestry technicians can provide a complete picture of the indigenous people's needs and actions we must take to meet those needs.

tolerate the parking shortage as a simple inconvenience of college life. You will need to show them that there is no reason to accept a parking shortage.

Once you've established that a problem exists, you must propose a solution to it. Your solution should be workable and practical. It would be silly to suggest that a multimillion dollar parking complex be built if financing isn't available or if the parking complex still wouldn't accommodate enough automobiles. However, a car-pooling or busing system would be less expensive and would limit the number of automobiles on campus.

Elimination Order

When your cassette player doesn't work, you probably systematically search for what's wrong: are the batteries fresh? is the pause switch off? does the pickup spool turn? is the tape box jammed? Just so, with **elimination order,** you first survey all the available solutions and courses of action that can reasonably be pursued. Then, proceeding systematically, you eliminate each of the possibilities until only one remains.

Elimination order is best suited to persuasive speeches. If you want student government to bring a special performer to campus, you might show that all other suggested entertainers are booked up, too expensive, or lack widespread appeal. In this way, you lead the members of student government to agree with the choice you advocate.

To use elimination order effectively, you first must make your survey of options all-inclusive. If you overlook obvious options, your listeners won't buy your analysis. Second, you must make the options mutually exclusive; otherwise, your listeners may choose more than one. Consider this example in which the speaker makes only one alternative seem the best:

> **Central Idea:** An Isuzu Trooper is your best buy for a full-sized four-wheel drive vehicle.

    I. Three options have been proposed.
      A. Jeep Grand Cherokee
      B. Ford Explorer
      C. Isuzu Trooper
   II. The first two options should be eliminated.
      A. The Jeep Grand Cherokee is so popular that you get less for your money than you do with the others.
      B. The Ford Explorer is the newest of the three, and, feature for feature, the most expensive.
 III. The Trooper is therefore the best way to go.
      A. It has the same features as the others for less money.
      B. It's been around long enough to have a solid history of customer care and good repair.

Of course, the elimination order works only if listeners agree with the criteria you've suggested for judgment. If cost is no object, the Grand Cherokee or Explorer still will be considered. Or, someone might object that while the Explorer is a comparatively new model, Ford Motor Company has a long history in the United States. Study your listeners to make sure the criteria for elimination are acceptable to them.

CONSISTENCY OF ARRANGEMENT

You may choose one method of arrangement for the main points of your speech and another for the subordinate ideas. Just don't shift from one method to another during the presentation of the main points themselves; it will confuse your listeners and make you appear disorganized. The following outline illustrates how spatial, topical, and chronological patterns might be combined in a speech on the major cities of India.

Central Idea: The complexities of Indian culture are seen in India's cities.

    I. The major cities of western India include Bombay and Ahmadabad.
        A. Bombay
           1. Early history
           2. Development under the British
           3. Conditions today
        B. Ahmadabad
           1. (Repeat narrative sequence under A above)
   II. The major cities of central India include Delhi and Hyderabad.
        A. Delhi
           1. Early history
           2. Development under the British
           3. Conditions today
        B. Hyderabad
           1. (Repeat narrative sequence under A above)
 III. The major cities of eastern India include Calcutta and Madras.
        A. Calcutta
           1. Early history
           2. Development under the British
           3. Conditions today
        B. Madras
           1. (Repeat narrative sequence under A above)

Note that spatial sequence is used for main points I, II, and III; topical sequence for subpoints A and B; and chronological sequence for sub-subpoints 1, 2, and 3. This pattern achieves psychological closure because listeners can anticipate the pattern once they understand it.

REQUIREMENTS OF GOOD OUTLINE FORM

Outlining is a word likely to bring back terrifying visions of eight-grade English. You weren't quite sure why you had to do it; you hated it because you couldn't always think of both an A and a B to go under major heading II; and when you were all done, you were convinced it took more work than it was worth. Outlining rules seemed even more arbitrary than grammatical rules about using the words *which* and *that*.

The trick is for you to forget those nightmares from the past and concentrate on outlining's advantages for you today. The fact is, outlining is an important tool for a speaker for two reasons:

1. *Testing.* An outline allows you to see your ideas—both those present and those absent. When you actually outline a speech, you can discover what ideas you've overemphasized to the exclusion or underdevelopment of others. A speaker's outline is a testing device.

2. *Guiding.* When you're actually delivering a speech, an outline is the preferred form of notes for many, perhaps even most, speakers. A good speaking outline shows you where you've been, where you are, and where you want to get before you sit down. You even can include in your outline special speaking directions to yourself ("show map here"; "say this deliberately and emphatically").

For you to profit from both the testing and guiding aspects of outlines, you must learn to build complete, solid structures. So, we'll review the formal requirements of full outlines, discuss some strategies for phrasing the main points, and then take you through both a full speech outline (a testing device) and a speaking outline (a guiding device). We'll concentrate here on outlining the bodies of speeches; outlines of introductions and conclusions will be shown in Chapter 8.

The amount of detail that you include in an outline will depend on your subject, on the speaking situation, and on your previous experience in speech preparation. New subject matter, unique speaking contexts, and limited prior speaking experience all indicate the need for a detailed outline. Under any circumstances, a good outline should meet four basic requirements.

One Main Idea

1. Each unit in the outline should contain one main idea. If two or three ideas merge under one subpoint, your audience will lose direction and become confused. Notice the difference in clarity between the following examples.

Wrong

I. Athens, Greece, should be the permanent site for the Olympic Games because they have become more and more politicized in recent years.
  A. The U.S. decision to boycott the 1980 Summer Olympics was political.
  B. The U.S.S.R. decision to boycott the 1984 Summer Olympics was political.
  C. Also, the costs are prohibitive, and returning the games to their homeland would place renewed emphasis on their original purpose.

Notice that point C introduces two new ideas about costs and the games' purpose. Those are important ideas and deserve equal emphasis. So:

Right

I. Athens, Greece, should be the permanent site for the Summer Olympic games.
  A. The games have become more and more politicized in recent years.
    1. The U.S. decision to boycott . . .
    2. The U.S.S.R. decision to boycott . . .
  B. Costs for building new sites in new locations every four years are becoming prohibitive.
  C. Returning the games to their homeland would place renewed emphasis on their original purpose.

Subordination of Ideas

Less important ideas in the outline should be subordinate to more important ones. Subordinate ideas are indented in an outline, and they are marked with subordinate symbols. Doing a good job with subordination helps you know what to emphasize when you're speaking. Notice how proper subordination lets the main arguments stand out and the evidence cleanly relate to those arguments:

Wrong

I. The cost of medical care has skyrocketed.
   A. Operating room fees may amount to tens of thousands of dollars.
      1. Hospital charges are high.
      2. A private room may cost more than $1,500 a day.
   B. X-rays and laboratory tests are extra expenses.
   C. Complicated operations cost over $50,000.
      1. Doctors' charges constantly go up.
      2. Office calls usually cost between $25 and $100.
      3. Drugs are expensive.
      4. Most antibiotics cost $2–$3 per dose.
   D. The cost of nonprescription drugs has mounted.

This outline is a mess. A listener would feel bombarded by the numbers and general references to hospitals and doctors but probably couldn't sort it all out. The key is *fit:* what fits under what? To help the listener grasp the main ideas, notice what happens when the material is sorted by category of cost, in a topical outline:

Right

I. The cost of medical care has skyrocketed.
   A. *Hospital charges* are high.
      1. A private room may cost more than $1,500 a day.
      2. Operating room fees may amount to tens of thousands of dollars.
      3. X-rays and laboratory tests incur extra expenses.
   B. *Doctors' charges* constantly go up.
      1. Complicated operations cost several thousand dollars.
      2. Office calls usually cost between $25 and $100.
   C. *Drugs* are expensive.
      1. Most antibiotics cost $2–$3 per dose.
      2. The cost of nonprescription drugs has mounted.

Indentation

The logical relationship between units of the outline should be shown by proper indentation. Normally, you will place your main points nearest the left-hand margin of your outline because they're the most general and the most important statements. Place less important statements beneath, and indent them to the right of the main points in order of increasing specificity. In your finished outline, the most central statements will be farthest to the left; the most particular ideas and evidence will be farthest to the right. Schematically, an outline looks like this:

    I. Main point
        A. Subpoint
        B. Subpoint
            1. Sub-subpoint
            2. Sub-subpoint
    II. Main point
        A. Subpoint
            1. Sub-subpoint
            2. Sub-subpoint
        B. Subpoint

Consistency of Symbols

A consistent set of symbols should be used throughout the outline. Whatever system you use, be consistent. Items of the same importance should always be assigned the same type of symbol. Notice that throughout this book all main points are assigned roman numerals, all subpoints are assigned capital letters, and all sub-subpoints are assigned arabic numerals. Most outlines follow the system used in this book.

Good form should make clear the structure of your ideas. Once you know and understand that structure, you'll be prepared to emphasize main ideas clearly and to fit the right sorts of subordinate material under each heading.

PHRASING THE MAIN POINTS

You can help your listeners to understand your message better if you observe the rules of effective phrasing. In order to achieve maximum effectiveness in the statement of your main points, keep in mind these characteristics of good phrasing:

1. *Be concise.* State your main points as briefly as you can without distorting their meaning. Crisp, clear, straightforward statements are easier to grasp than rambling, vague, complex declarations. Say, "The Iron Curtain collapsed," not "The Iron Curtain, that symbol of postwar monolithic communism, crumbled symbolically and literally under the onslaught of democracy and capitalism."

2. *Use vivid language.* Whenever possible, state your main points in evocative words and phrases. Drab, colorless statements are easily forgotten; punchy lines grab attention. Notice how much more vivid it is to say, "The moguls and the powder of Colorado are waiting for you!" than it is to say, "Plan on spending your spring break in the Colorado Rockies."

3. *Make your statements immediate.* Phrase your main points so they'll appeal directly to the concerns of your listeners. Instead of saying, "We should take immediate action to reduce the costs of higher education," say, "Cut tuition now!"

4. *Use parallel structure.* In a speech, your listeners have only one chance to catch what you're saying; parallelism in sentence structure helps them do so. The repetition of a key phrase aids the listener in remembering this series:

Speaking of...

• • • •

Memory and Organization

If you lost your outline, would you remember the major items? Or, from the listeners' point of view, how much of your speech will they remember? If you give them 17 reasons to reject nuclear power as an energy source, how many will they remember by the end of your talk?

Structure is the key here. Research on organization and memory has shown that taking some specific outlining steps will help you and your listeners remember what you're talking about:

1. *The magic numbers.* In a classic study, Miller concluded that there is a limit to the number of items a person can easily recall—seven, plus or minus two. More recent research has suggested that a more manageable number of items is five, plus or minus two. Limit the number of points you make to from three to seven (preferably in the three-to-five range).

2. *Chunking.* But what if you actually want to get in all 17 of those reasons why the United States should quit building nuclear power plants? The answer: "chunk them." Divide the 17 points into information chunks or groups. Thus, you might treat the hazards of nuclear power under five headings: (1) flawed safety procedures, (2) mechanical failures, (3) supervisor training issues, (4) past violations of safety standards, and (5) design flaws. Five chunks are easier to remember than 17.

3. *Coordination and subordination.* As we've suggested throughout this chapter, mapping your ideas helps your listeners to follow your speech. An outline does that through its symbols: I, II, A, B, 1, 2, etc. But speakers have to do that mapping verbally, through words that signal coordinated or equally important ideas ("I have three main points") and subordinated ideas or subpoints ("There are three reasons why I believe you ought to accept my first argument"). Fitting the subpoints under the main ideas and letting an audience see, by means of your language, the coordinated or equal relationships among your main ideas will help keep listeners from getting lost.

4. *Mnemonics.* Mnemonics are devices you attach to ideas to help you remember those ideas. When you learned "Thirty days hath September, April, June, and November. . . ," you learned an easily-recalled ditty that in turn helped you to remember which months had 30 and which had 31 days. Or, you might have used the acronym FACE to memorize the treble clef notes in the spaces of the staff and EGBDF ("Every good boy does fine") to memorize the notes on the lines. Speakers, too, can sometimes find a mnemonic to help listeners remember: for example, a who-what-when-where structure for remembering the actions you want them to take, or the ABC sequence ("airwaves," "breathing," "compression") for cardiopulmonary resuscitation taught in CPR classes.

The magic number of points, the chunking of information into digestable bits, the horizontal and vertical structuring of ideas, and mnemonic devices are four important tools you can use to help you and your listeners keep track of what's going on in your speeches.

For Further Reading: G. Mandler, "Organization and Memory," in Gordon Bower, ed., *Human Memory: Basic Principles* (New York: Academic Press, 1977), 310–354. See also Mandler's articles in C. R. Puff, ed., *Memory Organization and Structure* (New York: Academic Press, 1979), 303–319. G. A. Miller, "The Magic Number Seven, Plus or Minus Two: Some Limits on Our Capacity for Processing Information." *Psychological Review* 63 (1956): 81–97.

Ineffective
   I. Weightlifters depend mainly on strength.
   II. Cardiovascular endurance is important to distance runners.
   III. When sailing, balance is a major factor.

Effective
   IV. Strength is most important to weightlifters.
   V. Cardiovascular endurance is most important to distance runners.
   VI. Balance is most important to sailors.

Notice that in the effective series the phrase *is most important to* is repeated. Such parallelism will help your listeners grasp and remember the major ideas in your speech.

PREPARING AN OUTLINE

You should develop your outline, as well as the speech it represents, gradually through a series of stages. Your outline will become increasingly complex as the ideas in your speech evolve and as you move the speech closer to its final form. But then, once you're ready to speak, the outline becomes simplified again. Your outline will go through three stages, each of which has a specific function:

1. Develop a *rough outline* that establishes the topic of your speech, clarifies your purpose, and identifies a reasonable number of subtopics.

2. Prepare a *full speech outline* of your speech in order to test the strengths and weaknesses of your prospective presentation.

3. Finally, recast your material into a *speaking outline* that compresses your full speech into key words or phrases that can be used to jog your memory when you deliver your speech.

Developing a Rough Outline

Suppose your instructor has assigned an informative speech on a subject that interests you. You decide to talk about drunk driving because a close friend was recently injured by an intoxicated driver. Your broad topic area, then, is drunk driving.

In the six to eight minutes you have to speak, you obviously can't cover such a broad topic adequately. After considering your audience and your time limit, you decide to focus your presentation on two organizations, Mothers Against Drunk Driving (MADD) and Students Against Drunk Driving (SADD).

As you think about narrowing your topic further, you jot down some possible ideas. You continue to narrow your list until your final ideas include the following:

1. Founders of MADD and SADD.
2. Accomplishments of the two organizations.
3. Reasons the organizations were deemed necessary.
4. Goals of MADD and SADD.
5. Action steps taken by MADD and SADD.
6. Ways your listeners can help.

You can help your listeners to follow your thinking by clustering similar ideas. Experiment with several possible clusters before you decide on the best way to arrange your ideas.

Your next step is to consider the best pattern of organization for these topics. A chronological pattern would enable you to organize the history of MADD and SADD, but it would not allow you to discuss ways your listeners could help. Either cause-effect or effect-cause would work well if your primary purpose were to persuade. However, this is an informative speech, and you don't want to talk about the organizations only as the causes of reducing alcohol-related accidents. In considering the special patterns, you decide that an inquiry order might work. You discard it, however, when you realize that you don't know enough about audience members' questions to use this organizational pattern effectively. After examining the alternatives, you finally settle on a topical pattern. A topical pattern allows you to present three clusters of information:

1. *Background of MADD and SADD:* information about the founders, why the organizations were founded.
2. *Description of MADD and SADD:* goals, steps in action plans, results.
3. *Local work of MADD and SADD:* the ways in which parents work with their teenagers and with local media to accomplish MADD and SADD goals

As you subdivide your three clusters of information, you develop the following general outline:

I. Background of MADD and SADD
   A. Information about the founders
   B. Reasons the organizations were founded
II. Description of the organizations
   A. Their goals
   B. The action steps they take
   C. Their accomplishments so far
III. Applications of their work on a local level
   A. "Project Graduation"
   B. Parent-student contracts
   C. Local public service announcements

A **rough outline** identifies your topic, provides a reasonable number of subtopics, and reveals a method for organizing and developing your speech. Notice that you've arranged both the main points and subpoints topically. A word of warning: *you should make sure that the speech doesn't turn into a "string of beads" that fails to differentiate between one topic and the next*. With topical outlines, always figure out a way to make the topics cohere, hold together.

The next step in preparing an outline is to phrase your main headings as precisely as possible. Then you can begin to develop each heading by adding subordinate ideas. As you develop your outline, you'll begin to see what kinds of information and supporting materials you need to find.

Developing a Full Speech Outline

A **full speech outline** is an outline built out of sentences. It offers a near-complete development of the ideas you'll be communicating to an audience in the kind of language you think is appropriate to them, to you, and to the occasion. You can use it to check on the clarity with which you've conceived the speech, explore possible gaps or weaknesses in your speech, and assess the relative amount of time you're devoting to each subtopic.

To do a full speech outline, write each item as a complete sentence. Follow the requirements of good outline form. At the end of the outline, add a bibliography of the sources you consulted, so that you or someone else can explore the topic further. Then examine the list of supporting materials: Is there adequate supporting material for each point in the speech? Is the supporting material sufficiently varied? Do you attempt to engage your listeners' attention throughout the speech? Answering these questions can help you to determine whether your speech is sound.

Developing a Speaking Outline

Of course, a full speech outline would be maddening to use when you're actually delivering your speech. It would be too detailed to manage from a lectern; you'd probably be tempted to read to your listeners because it would include so many details. If you did that, you'd lose your conversational tone.

Therefore, you need to compress your full speech outline into a more useful form. A **speaking outline** is a short, practical form to use while delivering your speech (see Figure 7.2). The actual method you use to create your speaking outline will depend on your personal preference; some people like to work with small pieces of paper, others with notecards. Whatever your choice, however, your speaking outline should serve several functions while you're addressing your audience: (a) it should provide you with reminders of the direction of your speech—main points, subordinate ideas, and so on; (b) it should record technical or detailed material such as statistics and quotations; and (c) it should be easy to read so as not to detract from the delivery of your speech.

There are four main characteristics of properly prepared speaking outlines:

1. Note most points with only a key word or phrase—a word or two should be enough to trigger your memory, especially if you've practiced the speech adequately.

2. Write down fully the ideas that must be stated precisely; for example, "Friends don't let friends drive drunk."

Sample Full Speech Outline

• • • •

If the occasion is important or if you have difficulty framing thoughts extemporaneously, you may decide to write a full speech outline. Frequently, however, you'll need to write out only the main ideas as complete sentences and state the subordinate ideas and supporting materials as key phrases. Check with your instructor if you have any doubt about how detailed to make your outline.

The speech opens with a narrative background on the founding of MADD and SADD. This orients the listeners unfamiliar with the Lightners' organizations and establishes a human-interest link between the subject matter and the audience, with its discussion of avoidable human tragedy. (See also the actual introduction in Chapter 8.)

The speaker now is ready to offer a more formal explanation of MADD and SADD. Notice that the goals—agitation, legislation, victim help, and education—are not only recited but exemplified with specific instances that make those goals more concrete. This, in turn, makes the goals easier to remember.

Friends Don't Let Friends Drive Drunk[4]

[The introduction and conclusion of this speech will be developed in detail in Chapter 8, Beginning and Ending Your Speech, pages 144–145.]

I. MADD and SADD were founded under tragic circumstances.
  A. MADD was founded in 1980 by Candy Lightner.
    1. One of her daughters was killed by a drunk driver.
    2. She wanted to protect other families from a similar tragedy.
  B. SADD was founded by Lightner's other daughter.
    1. The loss of her sister hurt her deeply.
    2. She knew the importance of peer pressure in stopping teenage drinking and driving.
II. You can understand MADD and SADD better if you know something about their goals, operations, and effectiveness.
  A. The organizations of MADD and SADD reflect the specific goals the Lightners wish to achieve.
    1. They want the general public to carry out the agitation necessary to effect changes.
      a. Members of the public can put pressure on government officials.
      b. They can write letters-to-the-editor.
      c. They can campaign for state and local task forces.
      d. They can do all this with only a minimal investment of money.
    2. They want to expose the deficiencies in current legislation and drunk driving control systems.
      a. They want to toughen the laws on operating a motor vehicle when intoxicated [offer statistics on variations in state laws].
      b. They want to pressure judges to hand down maximum instead of minimum penalties [give specific instances of light sentences].
      c. They want to see more drunk driver arrests from city, county, and state law enforcement agents [cite statistics on arrest rates].

3. They want to help the families of other victims.
   a. Most MADD and many SADD members have been victims themselves.
   b. Families are taught to put their energy into getting something done [share quotations from pamphlets] as well as into mourning.
4. And finally, MADD and SADD want to educate the general public.
   a. They want to make people conscious of the tragedies caused by drunk driving.
   b. They want to focus media attention on the problem.

Once the listeners understand something about goals, they're ready to get to the heart of this speech: a discussion of MADD and SADD's operations. It's essential that they understand and agree with these actions if they're going to answer the call to join one of the organizations in a meaningful way. A narrative is offered, leading listeners through actions in a step-by-step process and making it relatively easy for them to put themselves into the stories of MADD and SADD.

B. MADD's steps for action demonstrate the thoroughness with which the organization understands the processes of public persuasion.
1. First, a local chapter sets its goals.
2. Second, MADD educates its local organizers goal by goal so that everyone knows the reasons behind each step.
3. Third, local chapters set research priorities.
   a. One group might check on local arrest records.
   b. Another might examine drunk driving conviction rates for various judges.
   c. A third might work with local media to find out how to secure time and space for a public service announcement on drunk driving.
   d. A fourth might talk with local schools and churches about safe prom nights.
4. Fourth, once the research is complete, the local chapter can formulate its plans of action.
5. Fifth, it can "go public" with action teams and task forces.
6. This five-step process parallels the campaign model for public persuasion devised by Herbert W. Simons in his book, *Understanding Persuasion*.

Most of us want to work with winners. The speaker, therefore, carefully reviews some of the significant effects MADD and SADD actions have had upon the country. Statistical magnitudes and trends as well as specific instances are combined; in this way, listeners get "the big picture" and also concrete representations of the effects.

C. Although still young, organizations such as MADD and SADD already have had significant effects.
1. By 1984, there were 320 MADD chapters across the country.
2. About 600,000 volunteers are now working on MADD projects.
3. State laws already are changing.
   a. In 1982 alone, 25 different states enacted 30 pieces of drunk driving legislation as a result of MADD's lobbying.
   b. After the organizations submitted petitions, Congress raised the mandatory legal drinking age to 21.
   c. In Florida, convicted drunk drivers must have red bumper stickers on their cars reading, "CONVICTED DUI."
4. Fatalities from drunk driving have decreased [quote pre-1980 and post-1980 statistics].

5. MADD also takes credit for increasing the popularity of low-alcohol beer, wines, and wine coolers.

III. You can work with MADD and SADD on local projects.

    A. Set up a workshop in local high schools for parent-child contracts.

        1. In such a contract (which has no legal status), the teen agrees never to drive drunk—calling on the parent for a ride instead—while the parent agrees to ask no questions and to impose no special penalties for the teen's intoxication.

        2. The contract reinforces the importance of not driving drunk and makes the commitment to safety a mutual commitment.

    B. Set up a SADD "Project Graduation."

        1. With the cooperation of the schools and sometimes local youth organizations or churches, a community can sponsor nonalcoholic postprom parties.

        2. They allow prom-goers a chance to stay up late, have fun, and celebrate without alcohol.

    C. Work with local media to use public service announcements to halt teen and adult drunk driving.

        1. MADD chapters can order ads you may have seen on TV.

            a. Some oppose drunk driving.

            b. Some tell you to designate a nondrinking driver from among your group.

            c. Others urge hosts of parties not to let drunk guests drive.

        2. SADD chapters also can order ads and school posters, nonalcoholic party kits, and the like [show sample items].

Now the speaker is ready to move in for the sale. Get audience members involved through second-person language: YOU can set up workshops, YOU can work in Project Graduation, YOU can get public service announcements broadcast. And that's the point of the speech, of course: to involve specific listeners in specific projects. (Skip ahead to Chapter 8 to see how the conclusion flows from this call for action.)

3. Include directions for delivery such as "SHOW POSTER."

4. Indicate emphasis in any one of a number of ways: capital letters, underlining, indentation, dashes, and highlighting with colored markers. (Find methods of emphasis that will easily catch your eye, show the relationship of ideas, and jog your memory during your speech delivery.)

CHAPTER SUMMARY

1. An effective speech has five characteristics: (a) its plan is easy to grasp and remember, (b) it provides full and balanced coverage of the material, (c) it is appropriate to the occasion, (d) it is adapted to the audience's needs and level of knowledge, and (e) it moves forward toward a complete and satisfying finish.

2. Arrangement is the sequence of ideas in a pattern that suggests their relationship to each other. Five types of arrangement patterns are: chronological, spatial, causal (effect-cause and cause-effect), topical (complete or partial enu-

● Meaning is structured through patterns of organization. Which pattern best fits this situation?

meration), and special. Special arrangement patterns include familiarity-acceptance, inquiry, question-answer, problem-solution, and elimination order.

3. Be consistent when using arrangement patterns in combination. You may choose one method of arrangement for the main points of your speech and another method for the subordinate ideas. You shouldn't, however, shift from one method to another during the presentation of the main points themselves.

4. Speakers use outlines for testing their ideas and guiding their oral presentation of those ideas.

5. There are four requirements for good outline form: (a) each unit should contain only one idea, (b) less important ideas should be subordinate to more important ones, (c) the logical relationship between units should be shown by proper indentation, and (d) a consistent set of symbols should be used throughout the outline.

6. When phrasing main points, be concise, use vivid language, make your statements immediate, and use parallel structure.

7. In outlining a speech, first develop a rough outline, then prepare a full speech outline, and finally recast your material into a speaking outline.

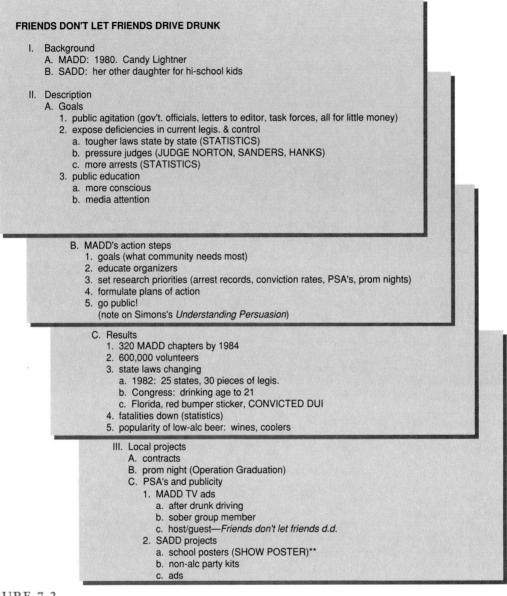

FRIENDS DON'T LET FRIENDS DRIVE DRUNK

I. Background
   A. MADD: 1980. Candy Lightner
   B. SADD: her other daughter for hi-school kids

II. Description
   A. Goals
      1. public agitation (gov't. officials, letters to editor, task forces, all for little money)
      2. expose deficiencies in current legis. & control
         a. tougher laws state by state (STATISTICS)
         b. pressure judges (JUDGE NORTON, SANDERS, HANKS)
         c. more arrests (STATISTICS)
      3. public education
         a. more conscious
         b. media attention
   B. MADD's action steps
      1. goals (what community needs most)
      2. educate organizers
      3. set research priorities (arrest records, conviction rates, PSA's, prom nights)
      4. formulate plans of action
      5. go public!
         (note on Simons's *Understanding Persuasion*)
   C. Results
      1. 320 MADD chapters by 1984
      2. 600,000 volunteers
      3. state laws changing
         a. 1982: 25 states, 30 pieces of legis.
         b. Congress: drinking age to 21
         c. Florida, red bumper sticker, CONVICTED DUI
      4. fatalities down (statistics)
      5. popularity of low-alc beer: wines, coolers

III. Local projects
   A. contracts
   B. prom night (Operation Graduation)
   C. PSA's and publicity
      1. MADD TV ads
         a. after drunk driving
         b. sober group member
         c. host/guest—*Friends don't let friends d.d.*
      2. SADD projects
         a. school posters (SHOW POSTER)**
         b. non-alc party kits
         c. ads

FIGURE 7.2
Sample Speaking Outline (on Notecards)
Notecards for a speech on MADD and SADD.

KEY TERMS

arrangement (p. 108)

causal pattern (p. 110)

chronological pattern (p. 108)

elimination order (p. 115)

familiarity-acceptance order (p. 112)

full speech outline (p. 123)

inquiry order (p. 113)

problem-solution order (p. 113)

question-answer order (p. 113)

rough outline (p. 122)

spatial pattern (p. 109)

speaking outline (p. 123)

special pattern (p. 112)

topical pattern (p. 110)

SKILLBUILDING ACTIVITIES

1. For each of the following topics, suggest two ways that materials might be organized. Discuss which of the two would be more effective:

   a. Directions for driving in snow.

   b. The evolution of stereophonic sound.

   c. A rationale for including women in combat.

   d. The effect that the influx of tourists from the West will have on Russia.

   e. A description of the proposed route for a highway bypass.

2. Bring a short magazine or newspaper article and a photocopy of it to class. Cut the photocopy into separate paragraphs or sentences. Ask a classmate to assemble the separated paragraphs or sentences into a coherent story. Compare your classmate's results to the original article.

3. For a speech entitled "The Investigator as a Resource," discussing why a lawyer may want to hire a private detective on a case-by-case basis, rearrange the following points and subpoints in proper outline form:

   a. Investigative services can save the lawyer time.

   b. Investigative reports indicate areas the lawyer should concentrate on to build a case.

   c. It is advantageous for a lawyer to employ an investigator on a case-by-case basis.

   d. The investigator performs two basic services.

   e. Known witnesses must be interviewed and other witnesses identified.

   f. The detective examines reports from the FBI and other governmental and private agencies and evaluates them for reliability and to determine what must be done.

   g. The investigator examines, collects, preserves, and analyzes physical evidence.

   h. The investigator compiles information in an effort to reconstruct an incident.

   i. Lawyers may need detective assistance only occasionally, on especially critical cases.

   j. Investigative reports can be used in out-of-court settlements.

REFERENCE

1. Information taken from Bruce E. Gronbeck, "Electric Rhetoric: The Changing Forms of American Political Discourse," *Vichiana,* 3rd series, 1st year (Napoli, Italy: Loffredo Editore, 1990), 141–61; and Herbert E. Alexander and Monica Bauer, *Financing the 1988 Election* (Boulder, Colo.: Westview Press, 1991), chap. 3.

2. The data in this outline were taken from *The World Almanac and Book of Facts 1992* (New York: World Almanac, 1991), 529–530.

3. This analysis is drawn from W. Lance Bennett, *News: The Politics of Illusion,* 2nd ed. (New York: Longman, 1988), chap. 2.

4. The material for this speech, including the statistics we have not included, was drawn from the following sources: "MADD from Hell," *Restaurant Hospitality,* April 1990; "One Less for the Road?" *Time,* 20 May 1985; "Razcal, MADD Party with High Schoolers," *Advertising Age,* 20 Nov. 1989; "Glad to be SADD," *Listen Magazine,* Oct. 1982; "War Against Drunk Drivers," *Newsweek,* 13 Sept. 1982; "They're Mad as Hell," *Time,* 3 Aug. 1981; "How to Get Alcohol Off the Highway," *Time,* 1 July 1981; "Health Report," *Prevention Magazine,* June 1984; "Water Water Everywhere," *Time,* 20 May 1985; L. B. Taylor, *Driving High* (Los Angeles: Watts, 1983); Sandy Golden, *Driving the Drunk Off the Road* (Washington, D.C.: Acropolis Books, 1983); and a pamphlet by the U. S. National Highway Traffic Safety Administration, *How to Save Lives and Reduce Injuries—A Citizen Activist Guide to Effectively Fight Drunk Driving* (Washington, D.C.: U.S. Government Printing Office, 1982).

8

Beginning and Ending Your Speech

"I'm glad I planned to wrap up my speech with a summary and a challenge," Yangsoo noted. "I didn't realize so many people would really be interested in sponsoring me in the 5K race this weekend. I kept them listening until the very last word. It's for a good cause, you know." "Yes," Yangsoo's teacher agreed. "And the concluding appeal nicely referred back to the illustration you used in your introduction. It added extra polish to your presentation. I think the whole group will get together and sponsor you in the race. If that's not an indication that you persuaded them, I don't know what is!"

Just as aerobics instructors begin with warm-ups and end with cool-downs, so must you systematically lead your audience into the environment of your speech and then take them back to their own worlds at the end. Yangsoo's success in getting sponsors for the race was partly due to how well he packaged his appeal with a strong introduction and conclusion. Well-prepared introductions and conclusions allow you to develop a relationship with your listeners by orienting them to your purposes and ideas and then reinforcing both at the end. The introduction and conclusion signal clearly when your speech starts and ends so as to prevent confusion among your listeners.

Introductions and conclusions are not trivial aspects of public speaking; they are governed by strict communication rules. If you disregard these norms, your credibility and, consequently, your effectiveness will suffer. If you meet expectations, you'll significantly improve your chances for success. In this chapter, we'll review the purposes of introductions and conclusions, examine various strategies for beginning and ending speeches, and review ways to capture and sustain listeners' attention.

BEGINNING YOUR SPEECH

The beginning of a speech must gain the listeners' attention, secure goodwill and respect for the speaker, and prepare the audience for the discussion to follow.

As a speaker, you want to engage your listeners during your entire speech; you can use the factors of attention to do this. First, however, you must gain their attention during the beginning moments of the speech. When your audience is prepared to listen, your ideas will have their greatest impact. By demonstrating the vitality of the topic and showing how important it may be for your listeners, you can turn their initial interest into sustained attention.

Your audience will probably have begun to form opinions about you and your topic even before you start to speak. Obviously, you want those opinions to be favorable. You have an opportunity to enhance them during the first few moments of your speech. Your enthusiasm for your topic and your general appearance of confidence should serve as nonverbal cues for your audience.

In many situations, your own reputation or the chairperson's introduction will help to generate goodwill. However, there may be times when your audience is opposed to you or your topic. In these instances, it's important to deal with opposition openly so that you will receive a fair hearing. By commenting on the differences between your views and those of your listeners, you can let them know that you're aware of disagreements but are seeking areas of consensus. When confronted by indifference, distrust, or skepticism, you must take steps early in the speech to change these attitudes so that your position will be received openly. Even if your listeners don't agree, you can often secure their respect for your honesty and integrity by dealing directly with them.

Finally, your introduction should engage your listeners' thinking in the subject of your speech. You must prepare the audience by stating your purpose early. Audiences that are forced to guess the purpose of a speech soon lose interest.

An introduction that secures your audience's attention and goodwill and prepares them to listen lays a solid foundation for acceptance of the central idea of your speech. You can establish attention by presenting your ideas in ways that create interest. There are a number of established means for tailoring your introduction to achieve these ends. We will examine the advantages and disadvantages of each.

Referring to the Subject or Occasion

If your audience already has a vital interest in your subject, you need only to state that subject before presenting your first main point. The speed and directness of this approach signals your eagerness to address your topic. Professor Russell J. Love used this approach when discussing rights for people with severe communication problems: "My talk tonight is concerned with the rights of the handicapped—particularly those people with severe communication disabilities. I will be presenting what I call a bill of rights for the severely communicatively disabled."[1]

Although such brevity and forthrightness may strike exactly the right note on some occasions, you should not begin all speeches this way. To a skeptical audience, a direct beginning may sound immodest or tactless; to an apathetic audience, it may sound dull or uninteresting. When listeners are receptive and friendly, however, immediate reference to the subject often produces an effective opening.

Instead of referring to your subject, you may sometimes want to refer to the occasion that has brought you and your audience together. This is especially true of a special occasion or when an important event has occurred. Franklin Delano Roosevelt began his declaration of war this way when he said: "Yesterday, December 7, 1941—a date which will live in infamy—the United States of America was suddenly and deliberately attacked by naval and air forces of the empire of Japan."[2] More recently, Ronald Reagan opened his tribute to the crew of the space shuttle *Challenger* with a reference to the occasion: "We come together to mourn the loss of seven brave Americans, to share the grief that we all feel, and perhaps in that sharing, to find the strength to bear our sorrow and the courage to look for the seeds of hope."[3] In each instance, the American people knew what had occurred; Roosevelt and Reagan could count on their concern.

Using a Personal Reference or Greeting

At times, a warm, personal greeting from a speaker or the remembrance of a previous visit to an audience or scene serves as an excellent starting point. Personal references are especially useful when a speaker is well known to the audience. In June 1990, Barbara Bush used a personal reference to a previous visit to Wellesley College as she addressed the senior class. She elaborated on her enthusiasm for the occasion when she added, "I had really looked forward to coming to Wellesley, I thought it was going to be fun; I never dreamt it would be this much fun. So thank you for that."[4]

Author Harvey MacKay combined his personal gratitude for being asked to speak to a Pennsylvania State University audience with realism. MacKay made the connection between himself and his audience with the common feelings they both shared: "I'm flattered to be here today, but not so flattered that I'm going to let it go to my head. . . . By the time you're my age ninety-nine out of a hundred will have completely forgotten who spoke at your graduation. And, I can accept that. Because I can't remember the name of my commencement speaker either. What I *do* remember from graduation day is the way I *felt:* excited, scared and challenged. I was wondering what the world was like out there, and how I would manage to make an impact."[5]

The way a personal reference introduction can be used to gain the attention of a hostile or skeptical audience is illustrated by a speech presented by Anson Mount, Manager of Public Affairs for *Playboy,* to the Christian Life Commission of the Southern Baptist Convention:

> *I am sure we are all aware of the seeming incongruity of a representative of* Playboy *magazine speaking to an assemblage of representatives of the Southern Baptist Convention. I was intrigued by the invitation when it came last fall, though I was not surprised. I am grateful for your genuine and warm hospitality, and I am flattered (though again not surprised) by the implication that I would have something to say that could have meaning to you people. Both* Playboy *and the Baptists have indeed been considering many*

of the same issues and ethical problems; and even if we have not arrived at the same conclusions, I am impressed and gratified by your openness and willingness to listen to our views.[6]

If a personal reference is sincere and appropriate, it will establish goodwill as well as gain attention. Avoid extravagant, emotional statements, however, because listeners are quick to sense a lack of genuineness. At the other extreme, avoid apologizing. Don't say, "I don't know why I was picked to talk when others could have done it so much better" or, "Unaccustomed as I am to public speaking, . . . " Apologetic beginnings suggest that your audience needn't waste time listening. Be cordial, sincere, and modest, but establish your authority and maintain control of the situation.

Asking a Question

Another way to open a speech is to ask a question or series of questions to spark thinking about your subject. For example, Nicholas Fynn of Ohio University opened a speech about free-burning of timberland as follows: "How many of you in this room have visited a National Park at one point in your life? Well, the majority of you are in good company."[7] Such a question introduces a topic gently and, with its direct reference to the audience, tends to engage the listeners.

Rhetorical questions, those for which you do not expect direct audience response, are often used to forecast the development of the speech. Shannon Dyer of Southwest Baptist University in Missouri opened her speech by wondering out loud why whistleblowers didn't prevent the *Challenger* accident and the Union Carbide plant gas leak at Bhopal, India. She moved to the body of the speech with more rhetorical questions that previewed the main points of her speech: "Thus, let's examine the dilemma of whistleblowers. First, who are whistleblowers? Then, what is the high personal price for their warnings? And finally, how can we protect these citizens—the watchdogs of our nation's safety?"[8]

Making a Startling Statement

On certain occasions, you may choose to open a speech with what is known as the *shock technique,* making a startling statement of fact or opinion. This approach is especially useful when listeners are distracted, apathetic, or smug. It rivets their attention on your topic. For example, the Executive Director of the American Association for Retired Persons (AARP), after asking some rhetorical questions about health care, caught his listeners' attention with several startling statements:

Given what we're spending on health care, we should have the best system in the world.

But the reality is that we don't.

Thirty-seven million Americans have no health insurance protection whatsoever, and millions more are underinsured.

We are twentieth—that's right, twentieth—among the nations of the world in infant mortality. The death rate for our black newborn children rivals that of Third World countries. And poor children in America, like their brothers and sisters in Third World nations, receive neither immunizations nor basic dental care.

Those statistics give us a sense of the scope of the problem. What they don't adequately portray is the human factor—the pain and the suffering.

While terminally ill patients may have their lives extended in intensive care units—at tremendous cost—middle-age minority women die of preventable and treatable cancer, hypertension and diabetes.[9]

Avoid overusing shock techniques. The technique can backfire if your listeners become angry when you threaten or disgust them.

Using a Quotation

A quotation may be an excellent means of introducing a speech, because it can prod listeners to think about something important and it often captures an appropriate emotional tone. When Agnar Pytte, President of Case Western Reserve University, spoke to the Cleveland City Club on the topic of political correctness and free speech, he opened his speech with a quotation: "As Benjamin Cardozo said: 'Freedom of expression is the indispensable condition of all our liberties.'"[10] Pytte continued by using Cardozo's statement to investigate the current debate over political correctness on college campuses. The opening quotation provided the groundwork by effectively piquing the interest of the audience and inviting listeners to further consider the impact of political correctness on free speech. Pytte could then proceed into a discussion of current examples of the political correctness debate, confident that his audience was paying attention.

Telling a Humorous Story

You can begin a speech by telling a funny story or relating a humorous experience. When doing so, however, observe the following three rules of communication:

1. Be sure that the story is at least amusing, if not funny; test it out on others before you actually deliver the speech. Be sure that you practice sufficiently so you can present the story naturally. And use the story to make a point instead of making it the center of your remarks. In other words, brevity is crucial.

2. Be sure that the story is relevant to your speech; if its subject matter or punch line is not directly related to you, your topic, or at least your next couple of sentences, the story will appear to be a mere gimmick.

3. Be sure that your story is in good taste; in a public gathering, an off-color or doubtful story violates accepted standards of social behavior and can undermine an audience's respect for you. (In general, you should avoid sexual, racist, antireligious, ageist, homophobic, and sexist humor.)

All three of these rules were observed by George V. Grune, CEO of The Reader's Digest Association, Inc., as he delivered a commencement address to the Graduate School of Business at Rollins College:

This morning I'd like to talk about global marketing and the opportunities it offers American business today—and each of you individually. I understand

• Humor can be used effectively to gain attention. However, since humor can easily backfire, what rules of communication should you observe whenever you use humor?

international marketing was a favorite subject for many of you, and I suspect earning a living is uppermost on your minds, considering the occasion we celebrate today.

There is a story about a king who once called three wise men together and posed the same problem to each: "Our island is about to be inundated by a huge tidal wave. How would you advise the people?"

The first man thought long and hard and then said, "Sire I would lead the people to the highest spot on the island and then set up an all-night prayer vigil."

The second said, "Master, I would advise the people to eat, drink and be merry for it would be their last opportunity to do so."

The third wise man said, "Your majesty, if I were you, I would immediately advise the people to do their best to learn how to live under water."

As you progress in your business career, you'll face many challenges that will test your ability to in effect "learn how to live under water." Those who adapt and find new solutions to complex issues will be the most successful. And nowhere is that more true than in the global arena.[11]

After relating his anecdote, Grune was ready to talk about the treacherous, difficult challenges facing students of international marketing.

Using an Illustration

A real-life incident, a passage from a novel or short story, or a hypothetical illustration can also get a speech off to a good start. As with a humorous story, an illustration should be not only interesting to the audience but also relevant to your central idea. Deanna Sellnow, a student at North Dakota State University, used this technique to introduce a speech on private credit-reporting bureaus:

John Pontier, of Boise, Idaho, was turned down for insurance because a reporting agency informed the company that he and his wife were addicted to narcotics, and his Taco Bell franchise had been closed down by the health board when dog food had been found mixed in with the tacos. There was only one small problem. The information was made up. His wife was a practicing Mormon who didn't touch a drink, much less drugs, and the restaurant had never been cited for a health violation.[12]

The existence of a problem with private credit-reporting bureaus is clear from this introduction. In addition, when listeners get involved with someone like John Pontier who has encountered the problem, they become more attentive. When this happens, the illustration can have a powerful impact.

Completing Your Introduction

You can use one of the approaches that we've discussed alone or you can combine two or more. You might open with a startling illustration or a humorous reference to the occasion, for example. No matter what type of introduction you use, you should have one purpose in mind: arousing the attention and winning the goodwill and respect of your listeners. Your introduction should be relevant to the purpose of your speech and should lead smoothly into the first of the major ideas that you wish to present; that is, your introduction should be an integral part of the speech. It should not be, for example, a funny story told merely to make an audience laugh; it should be thematically and tonally tied to the body of the speech.

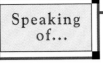

Speaking of...

Revealing Your Intentions

Consider this scenario. You are planning a speech in which you hope to persuade your listeners to donate money to your political caucus. Should you reveal your intention in your introduction?

While we generally are unaffected by the awareness that persuasion is intended, we strongly react to deception. Research suggests the worst effect on listeners will occur if you disguise your intent but it is discovered as you speak.

Other factors such as your listeners' initial attitudes also influence how they will respond to your intention. If your listeners are highly involved or strongly committed to an opposing view, they will be less inclined to listen to you if they know your goal is to persuade.

In every case, avoid the appearance of direct manipulation. You should say, "Let's investigate the options together," rather than "Today I'm going to persuade you to. . . ." Most of us like to think that we have free choice.

For further information, see: Richard Petty and John Cacioppo, "Effects of Forewarning, Cognitive Responding, and Resistance to Persuasion," *Journal of Personality and Social Psychology* 35 (1970): 645–655.

Your introduction should also forecast the speech's development by means of a preview. The preview establishes your listeners' confidence in your organization, thus enhancing your credibility. It creates listener receptivity by providing a structure for you and your listeners to follow during the speech. Here are some examples of types of previews:

1. *Announce the organizational pattern.* You might say, "I'll develop the effects of the problem of alcoholism and then examine its causes" (causal pattern). "In demonstrating how to troubleshoot minor car problems, I'll consider three topics. I'll be talking about the electrical system, the fuel system, and the mechanical system" (topical order).

2. *Use mnemonic devices.* Acronyms aid memory; for example, "I'm going to discuss the ABC's of jogging: ALWAYS wear good shoes. BABY your feet. CALL a podiatrist if problems develop."

3. *Employ alliteration.* Rely on sound similarities to create interest. For example: "My advice for finding someone to marry? Use the three A's—availability, attitude, and *amour.*"

4. *Use repetition.* Reinforce your message by repeating the main phrases. You can say, "We need to examine how tuition increases harm us, how tuition increases harm our parents, and most importantly, how tuition increases harm our state."

When effective, your introductory remarks will both establish a common ground of interest and understanding and provide a structure to guide your audience toward the conclusion that you intend to reach.

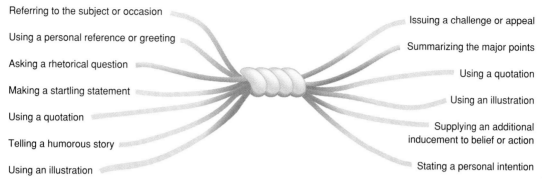

Referring to the subject or occasion

Using a personal reference or greeting

Asking a rhetorical question

Making a startling statement

Using a quotation

Telling a humorous story

Using an illustration

Issuing a challenge or appeal

Summarizing the major points

Using a quotation

Using an illustration

Supplying an additional inducement to belief or action

Stating a personal intention

FIGURE 8.1
Types of Introductions and Conclusions
You can choose among different types of introductions and conclusions for your speeches. As you choose your introduction and conclusion, ask yourself if they orient your audience to your purposes and ideas and then summarize both at the end of the speech and if they signal clearly when your speech starts and ends.

ENDING YOUR SPEECH

Just as the introduction to the speech accomplishes specific purposes, so too does the conclusion. An effective conclusion should focus the attention of your audience on your topic. It should also establish a concluding mood as it conveys a sense of finality or closure.

The principal function of the conclusion of a speech is to focus your audience's attention on your central idea. If your speech has one dominant idea, you should restate it in a clear and forceful manner. If your speech is more complex, you may summarize the key points, or you may spell out the action or belief that these points suggest.

In addition to reinforcing the central idea, your conclusion should leave the audience in the proper mood. If you want your listeners to express vigorous enthusiasm, stimulate that feeling with your closing words. If you want them to reflect thoughtfully on what you have said, encourage a calm, meditative attitude. Decide whether the response you seek is a mood of serious determination or good humor, of warm sympathy or utter disgust, of thoughtful consideration or vigorous action. Then, end your speech in a way that will create that mood.

Finally, a good ending should convey a sense of completeness and finality. Listeners grow restless and annoyed when they think the speech is finished, only to hear the speaker ramble on. Avoid false endings; tie the threads of thought together so that the pattern of your speech is brought clearly to completion.

Speakers employ many strategies to convey a sense of closure to their speeches. We will examine the conclusion techniques that are used regularly.

Issuing a Challenge

You may conclude your speech by issuing a challenge to your listeners, requesting support or action, or reminding them of their responsibilities. Allen A. Schumer, Senior Vice President for Operations of the Miller Brewing Company, urged his audience to establish employee involvement programs in their companies, and he related some of his own company's experiences with such programs. He then issued a challenge:

As I mentioned at the beginning, you are the people on the front lines of the Employee Involvement Revolution. If you win this battle of getting employee involvement accepted as a company concept, your company wins. And if your company or organization succeeds, we all succeed.

It won't happen overnight, but next week may be too late in these days of economic and corporate uncertainty. Any journey, no matter how long, must begin with a first step. I encourage you to take that first step now! Believe me, it's a step you won't regret. I promise![13]

Summarizing the Major Points or Ideas

In an informative speech, a summary allows the audience to pull together the main strands of information and to evaluate the significance of the speech. In a persuasive speech, a summary gives you a final opportunity to present, in brief form, the major points of your argument. For example, a student presented this summary of an informative speech on tornadoes:

You've seen the swirling funnel clouds on the six o'clock news. They hit sometimes without much warning, leaving in their paths death and destruction. Now you should understand the formation of funnel clouds, the classification of tornadoes on the Fujita scale, and the high cost of tornadoes worldwide in lives and property. Once you understand the savage fury of tornadoes, you can better appreciate them. Tornadoes are one of nature's temper tantrums.

If the student's purpose had been to persuade his listeners to take certain precautions during a tornado alert, the summary of the speech might have sounded like this:

The devastation left in the path of a tornado can be tremendous. To prevent you and your loved ones from becoming statistics on the six o'clock news, remember what I told you this afternoon. Seek shelter in basements, ditches, or other low areas. Stay away from glass and electric lines. And, remember the lesson of the Xenia, Ohio, disaster. Tornadoes often hit in clusters. Be sure the coast is clear before you leave your shelter. Don't be a statistic.

In each case, summarizing the main ideas of the speech gives the speaker another opportunity to reinforce the message. Information can be reiterated in the summary of an informative speech, or the major arguments or actions can be strengthened in the summary of a persuasive speech.

Using a Quotation

You can cite others' words to capture the spirit of your ideas in the conclusion of your speech. Quotations are often used to end speeches. Poetry may distill the essence of your message in uplifting language. Quoted prose, if the author is credible, may gather additional support for your central idea. Notice how Tim Dolin of West Virginia's Marshall University was able to add the credibility of Senator John Glenn to his plea for public regulation of nuclear weapons waste and disposal:

After looking at the poor management within the nuclear weapons cycle, its impact on us and how the problem can be solved, it becomes obvious something must be done. As Senator John Glenn said, "The costs of cleaning up these sites will be extraordinarily high, but the costs of doing nothing will be higher. After all, what good does it do to protect ourselves from the Soviets by building nuclear weapons if we poison ourselves in the process?" [14]

Using an Illustration

Illustrations engage your listeners emotionally. If you use a concluding illustration, it can set the tone and direction of your final words. Your illustration should be both inclusive and conclusive—inclusive of the main focus or thrust of your speech and conclusive in tone and impact. Sometimes the same illustration can be used to tie together a whole speech. This is what Michael Twitchell, a student in a speaking contest, did when talking about the causes and effects of depression. Here's his opening:

Have you ever felt like you were the little Dutch boy who stuck his finger in the leaking dike? You waited and waited but the help never came. The leak became worse and the water rushed around you and swept you away. As you fought the flood, gasping and choking for air, you realized that the flood was inside yourself. You were drowning and dying in your own mind. According to the American Journal of Psychiatry, *as many as half the people in this room will be carried away by this devastating flood. What is this disaster? Mental depression.*

Notice how Twitchell's concluding words reinforce the illustration used in his introduction:

Let's go back to my illustration of the little Dutch boy. He was wise to take action and put his finger in the dike, preventing the flood. In the case of depression, each one of us must be like the little Dutch boy—willing to get involved and control the harmful effects of depression. [15]

Supplying an Additional Inducement to Belief or Action

Sometimes you may conclude a speech by quickly reviewing the principal ideas presented in the body and then supplying one or more additional reasons for endorsing the belief or taking the proposed action. In his speech, Michael Twitchell spoke at length about the devastating effects of depression. After proposing numerous reasons for people to get involved in the battle, Twitchell offered, in the conclusion to his speech, an additional inducement:

Why should you really care? Why is it important? The depressed person may be someone you know—it could be you. If you know what is happening, you can always help. I wish I had known what depression was in March of 1978. You see, when I said David Twitchell could be my father, I was making a statement of fact. David is my father. I am his son. My family wasn't saved; perhaps now yours can be. [16]

• Speakers sometimes indicate their personal intentions to take action. This is especially effective when the speaker is highly regarded by listeners or when immediate actions are urged. Can you think of specific situations when stating a personal intention would work well to conclude a speech?

Stating a Personal Intention

Stating your own intention to adopt the action or attitude you recommend in your speech is particularly effective when your prestige with the audience is high or when you have presented a concrete proposal requiring immediate action. By professing your intention to take immediate action, you and your ideas gain credibility. In the following example, a speaker sets himself up as a model for the actions he wants his listeners to take:

> *Today I have illustrated how important healthy blood is to human survival and how blood banks work to ensure the possibility and availability of blood for each of us. It is not a coincidence that I speak on this vital topic on the same day that the local Red Cross Bloodmobile is visiting campus. I want to urge each of you to ensure your future and mine by stopping at the Student Center today or tomorrow to make your donation. The few minutes that it takes may add up to a lifetime for a person in need. To illustrate how firmly I believe in this opportunity to help, I'm going to the Student Center to give my donation as soon as this class is over. I invite any of you who feel this strongly to join me.*

Speaking of...

How Long Should It Be?

According to a classic study, the average speaker spends about 10 percent of the total speech on the introduction and 5 percent on the conclusion. The introduction may increase to 13 percent in speeches designed to stimulate or inspire, such as sermons, dedications, or memorials. In practical terms, this means that you will probably take 1 minute to introduce a 10-minute speech and 30 seconds to conclude it.

Can you think of circumstances when you'd spend more time introducing or concluding your remarks? less time?

For the original study, see: Edd Miller, "Speech Introductions and Conclusions," *The Quarterly Journal of Speech* 32 (1946): 181–183.

Regardless of the means you choose for closing your speech, remember that your conclusion should focus the attention of your listeners on the central theme you've developed. In addition, a good conclusion should be consistent with the mood or tenor of your speech and should convey a sense of completeness and finality.

CAPTURING AND HOLDING ATTENTION

Watch an audience, and you'll quickly realize that listeners' attention can drift away from the message. No matter how captivating your introduction or how well-planned the body of your speech, attention ebbs and flows as listeners think about last night, the 90-degree heat, or paying the rent on time. Unless you maintain listeners' attention beyond the introduction, your message will be lost.

Attention is the ability to focus on one element in a given perceptual field. When attention is secured, competing elements in the perceptual field fade and, for all practical purposes, cease to exist. For example, when you listen to your favorite album, you can block out the rest of the world. Sometimes, you can pay attention so completely that it seems like only minutes instead of hours have passed.

How can you capture and hold the attention of your listeners when giving a speech? Your ideas can be presented in nine ways that have high attention value. The **factors of attention** are: activity, reality, proximity, familiarity, novelty, suspense, conflict, humor, and the vital (see Figure 8.2). These factors of attention can be used anywhere in your speech. It's a good idea to distribute them throughout the body of your speech to stimulate your listeners to follow your ideas closely.

Activity

Suppose you've got two TV sets side by side. On one set, two Senate aides discuss American policy in Somalia. On the other, there's a high-speed cops-and-

Sample Outline for an Introduction and a Conclusion

• • • • An introduction and conclusion for the classroom speech on MADD and SADD might take the following form. Notice that the speaker uses suspense in combination with startling statements to lead the audience into the subject. The conclusion combines a summary with a final illustration and a statement of personal intention.

Friends Don't Let Friends Drive Drunk

Introduction

I. Many of you have seen the "Black Gash," the Vietnam War memorial in Washington, D.C.
   A. It contains the names of more than 40,000 Americans who gave their lives in Southeast Asia between 1961 and 1973.
   B. We averaged over 3,000 war dead a year during that painful period.

II. Today, another enemy stalks Americans.
   A. The enemy kills, not 3,000, but over 20,000 citizens every 12 months.
   B. The enemy is not hiding in jungles but can be found in every community in the country.
   C. The enemy kills, not with bayonets and bullets, but with bottles and bumpers.

III. Two organizations are trying to contain and finally destroy the killer.
   A. Every TV station in this town carries a public service ad that says "Friends Don't Let Friends Drive Drunk."
   B. In response to the menace of the drunk driver, two national organizations—Mothers Against Drunk Driving and Students Against Drunk Driving—have been formed and are working even in this community to make the streets safe for you and me.
   C. [Central idea] MADD and SADD are achieving their goals with your help.
   D. To help you understand what these familiar organizations do, first I'll tell you something about the founders of MADD and SADD; then, I'll describe their operations; finally, I'll mention some of the ways community members get involved with them.

[Body]

Conclusion

I. Today, I've talked briefly about the Lightners and their goals for MADD and SADD, their organizational techniques, and ways in which you can get involved.

II. The work of MADD and SADD volunteers—even on our campus, where I'm sure you've seen their posters in the Student Center—is being carried out to keep you alive.
   A. You may not think you need to be involved; but remember: After midnight, one in every five or fewer drivers on the road is probably drunk: You could be involved whether you want to be or not.
   B. That certainly was the case with Julie Smeiser, a member of our sophomore class, who just last Friday was hit by a drunk driver when going home for the weekend.
III. If people don't take action, we could build a new "Black Gash"—this time for victims of drunks—every two years, and soon fill Washington, D.C., with monuments to needless suffering.
   A. Such monuments would be grim reminders of our unwillingness to respond to enemies at home with the same intensity with which we attacked enemies abroad.
   B. A better response would be to support actively groups such as MADD and SADD, who are attacking the enemy on several fronts at once in a war on motorized murder.
IV. If you're interested in learning more about SADD and MADD, stop by Room 324 in the Student Center tonight at 7:30 to hear the president of the local chapter of SADD talk about this year's activities. I'll be there; please join me.

robbers car chase, replete with flying debris, collisions, and a fiery conclusion. Which set are you likely to watch? Similarly, a speaker can heighten activity by being sure to:

- *Choose active verbs. Raced, tore, shot through, slammed, ripped, slashed, catapulted, flew, flashed*—most of these are simple verbs, but they depict activity.
- *Select dynamic stories.* Use illustrations that depict action, that tell fast-moving stories. Propel your story forward, and your audience will stay with you.
- *Use short segments.* Keep your speech moving—it will seem to drag if one point is expanded while other points are skimmed over. Speeches of instruction and demonstration, particularly if visual aids are used, demand systematic and lively progress.

Reality

The earliest words you learned were names for tangible objects such as *mommy, cookie,* and *truck.* While the ability to abstract—to generalize—is one of the marks of human intelligence, don't lose your audience by becoming too abstract.

FIGURE 8.2
The Factors of
Attention
Speakers can use the
factors of attention
to capture and hold
the interest of their
listeners. Which can
you use in your next
speech?

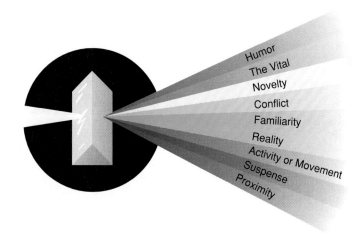

Refer to specific events, persons, and places. For example, when we referred to "tangible objects," an abstract phrase, we gave you three real examples: *mommy, cookie,* and *truck.* Concrete words have more force than general references.

Proximity

Proximity means *nearness;* we usually notice things that closely surround us. A direct reference to a person in the audience, a nearby object or place, an incident that has just occurred, or the immediate occasion helps you to command attention. The following introduction uses proximity to engage the listeners:

> *Do you realize how much fast food students consume? Within four blocks of this classroom are nine restaurants, including McDonald's, Wendy's, Cracker Barrel, Domino's Pizza, Kentucky Fried Chicken, and Best Steak House. Two of the others are local submarine shops. Even the student union runs a fast-food counter. Should we start wondering what our lunch habits are doing to our nutrition—to our bodies and our minds?*

Familiarity

References to the familiar are attention-sustaining, especially in the face of new or strange ideas. The familiar is comfortable. People drive the same route to work, children sing the same songs over and over, and you've probably watched your favorite movie more than once. Stories about George Washington, Abraham Lincoln, and Martin Luther King, Jr., get repeated on occasions when cultural memories are used to guide decisions. How many times have you heard speakers repeat John F. Kennedy's famous phrase, "Ask not what your country can do for you; ask what you can do for your country"? We like the reassurance that such familiarity provides.

Novelty

Novel happenings, dramatic incidents, or unusual developments attract attention. Look at the tabloid newspaper headlines next time you're in the grocery checkout line: "Grandmother Gives Birth to Quadruplets," "Princess Di to Marry Martian," "Elvis Sighted at Amusement Park." These bizarre stories catch our attention. References to size and contrast work well to create novelty. In an address at the University of Virginia, nineteenth-century journalist Henry W. Grady used novel and startling contrasts to focus attention on the gap between the rich and the poor:

> *A home that cost three million dollars and a breakfast that cost five thousand are disquieting facts to the millions who live in a hut and dine on a crust. The fact that a man . . . has an income of twenty million dollars falls strangely on the ears of those who hear it as they sit empty-handed with children crying for bread.[17]*

When using novelty, blending the familiar and the novel, the old and the new, often yields the best results. Otherwise, you risk stretching the credulity of your listeners, as do those supermarket tabloids. To stimulate interest in the evolving nature of the self-defense plea in criminal courts, you might cite recent, highly publicized trials in which alleged victims claim self-defense in response to years of physical or mental abuse. Citing specific cases, such as the Menendez brothers' murder of their parents, provides novelty; linking this case with more common cases will reassure your listeners that the self-defense plea is a conventional defense.

Suspense

Much of the appeal in mystery stories arises because we don't know how they will end. Films such as *The Silence of the Lambs* and *The Crying Game* have enough unusual twists to hold audiences spellbound. You, too, can use uncertainty in your speeches by pointing to puzzling relationships or unpredictable forces. Introduce suspense into the stories you tell, building up to a surprising climax. Hint that you'll divulge valuable information later: "Stay with me through this speech, because by the end you'll learn how to cut your book bill in half every semester."

Conflict

Controversy grabs attention. Soap operas are fraught with love, hate, violence, passion, and power struggles. Conflict, like suspense, suggests uncertainty; like activity, it's dynamic. The next time you hear the news, listen for conflict. Newscasters often portray natural phenomena, such as floods, as nature's assaults on human beings. Sportscasters describe athletes as "battling the odds." And even weather forecasters talk about "surviving Arctic blasts of frigid air." The concept of struggle brings the sense of urgency to the day's events.

In your speeches, you can create conflict among ideas, such as the competing theories regarding the extinction of dinosaurs. You can present opposing viewpoints among experts. You can emphasize, for example, the conflicts inherent in the struggles of individuals fighting the system, confronting the forces of nature, or facing the ravages of disease. When your ideas are cast as controversies or conflicts, they become dramatic and engaging.

Humor

Listeners usually pay attention when they're enjoying themselves. Humor can unite you and your audience by relaxing everyone and providing a change of pace. When using humor to capture and hold attention, remember to stick close to your central idea by choosing humor that is relevant. Be sure to use only humorous stories that are in good taste, and so avoid offending members of your audience. Comedian Bill Cosby met both of these requirements when he poked fun at a University of South Carolina graduating class. In his commencement speech, Cosby reminded his listeners: "All across the United States of America, people are graduating. And they are hearing so many guest speakers tell them that they are going forth. As a parent I am concerned as to whether or not you know where 'Forth' is. Let me put it to you this way: We have paved a road—the one to the house was already paved. 'Forth' is not back home."[18]

The Vital

The phrase, *the vital,* was coined by Alan Monroe, the original author of this textbook, to reflect our tendency to be concerned with things that immediately benefit us. We pay attention to matters that affect our health, reputation, property, or employment. When a speaker says, "Students who take internships while in college find jobs after graduation three times as fast as those who don't," you're likely to pay attention—getting a job is vital to you. Appealing to *the vital,* therefore, is a matter of personalizing the speech for a particular audience—making it as relevant to their concrete circumstances as possible. When Bill Clinton introduced health care reform to Americans, he linked it to their vital interests: their health, their security, and their well-being.

Use these nine attention-getters to maintain your listeners' attention throughout your speech. They give your speech sparkle and spunk, they reach out to your listeners, and they help your listeners follow and remember your speech.

CHAPTER SUMMARY

1. Introductions should seize attention, secure goodwill, and prepare an audience for what you will be saying.
2. Types of introductions include referring to the subject or occasion, using a personal reference or greeting, asking a rhetorical question, making a startling statement of fact or opinion, using a quotation, telling a humorous story, and using an illustration.
3. In concluding your speech, you should attempt to focus the thoughts of your audience on your central theme, maintain the tenor of your speech, and convey a sense of finality.

4. Techniques for ending a speech include issuing a challenge or appeal, summarizing the major points or ideas, using a quotation, using an illustration, supplying an additional inducement to belief or action, and stating a personal intention.

5. You can capture and sustain your listeners' attention by using one or more of the nine factors of attention: activity, reality, proximity, familiarity, novelty, suspense, conflict, humor, and the vital.

KEY TERMS

attention (p. 143)
factors of attention (p. 143)

SKILLBUILDING ACTIVITIES

1. In class groups, devise two excellent introductory strategies for the following speakers to use in the situations noted:

Speaker	Situation
Marilyn Quayle	A pro-life conference
Steven Spielberg	A radio broadcaster's conference
Roger Staubach	A banquet sponsored by the Fellowship of Christian Athletes
Janet Reno	A meeting of the Fraternal Order of Police
Hillary Clinton	The American Medical Association

2. Consult an almanac to find out what famous events occurred on this date in history. Then, write an introduction for an informative speech to your classmates referring to the occasion. Use past events in your introduction to create listener interest. Rewrite your introduction for a persuasive speech to an alumni reunion.

3. Participate in a chain of introductions and conclusions. One student will begin by suggesting a topic for a speech. A second student will suggest an appropriate introduction and conclusion and justify those choices. A third student will challenge those selections and propose alternative introductions and/or conclusions. Continue this discussion until everyone proposes and defends introductions and conclusions that could be appropriate to the speech topics discussed.

REFERENCES

1. Russell J. Love, "The Barriers Come Tumbling Down," Harris-Hillman School Commencement, Nashville, Tenn. (21 May 1981). Reprinted by permission.

2. Franklin Delano Roosevelt, "War Message," in James Andrews and David Zarefsky, eds. *American Voices: Significant Speeches in American History 1640–1945* (New York: Longman, 1989), 476.

3. Ronald Reagan, "Memorial Service for the Crew of the Space Shuttle *Challenger*," Remarks at the Johnson Space Center in Houston, Tex., 31 Jan. 1986,

Weekly Compilation of Presidential Documents 22 (3 Feb. 1986): 117–119.

4. Barbara Bush, "Choice and Change," Wellesley College, 1 June 1990, manuscript available from the author.

5. Harvey MacKay, "How to Get a Job," *Vital Speeches of the Day* 57 (19 Aug. 1991).

6. Anson Mount, Manager of Public Affairs for *Playboy* magazine, from a speech presented to the Christian Life Commission of the Southern Baptist Convention, in *Contemporary American Speeches*, 5th ed., edited by Wil A. Linkugel et al. (Dubuque, Ia.: Kendall/Hunt, 1982).

7. Nicholas Fynn, "The Free Burn Fallacy," *Winning Orations 1989*. Reprinted by permission of Larry Schnoor, Executive Secretary, Interstate Oratorical Association, Mankato State University, Mankato, Minn.

8. Shannon Dyer, "The Dilemma of Whistleblowers," *Winning Orations 1989*. Reprinted by permission of Larry Schnoor, Executive Secretary, Interstate Oratorical Association, Mankato State University, Mankato, Minn.

9. Horace B. Deets, "Health Care for a Caring America: We Must Develop a Better System," *Vital Speeches of the Day* 55 (1 Aug. 1989).

10. Agnar Pytte, "Political Correctness and Free Speech: Let the Ideas Come Forth," *Vital Speeches of the Day* 57 (1 Sept. 1991).

11. George V. Grune, "Global Marketing: Global Opportunities," *Vital Speeches of the Day* 55 (15 July 1989).

12. Deanna Sellnow, "Have You Checked Lately?" *Winning Orations*. Reprinted by permission of Larry Schnoor, Executive Secretary, Interstate Oratorical Association, Mankato State University, Mankato, Minn.

13. Allen A. Schumer, "Employee Involvement," *Vital Speeches of the Day,* 54 (1 July 1988).

14. Tim Dolin, "The Hidden Legacy of the Arms Race," *Winning Orations 1989*. Reprinted by permission of Larry Schnoor, Executive Secretary, Interstate Oratorical Association, Mankato State University, Mankato, Minn.

15. Michael A. Twitchell, "The Flood Gates of the Mind," *Winning Orations*. Reprinted by permission of Larry Schnoor, Executive Secretary, Interstate Oratorical Association, Mankato State University, Mankato, Minn.

16. Twitchell, "The Flood Gates of the Mind."

17. From an address by Henry W. Grady, presented to the Literary Societies of the University of Virginia, 25 June 1889.

18. Bill Cosby, "University of South Carolina Commencement Address," 1990, unpublished manuscript available from the author.

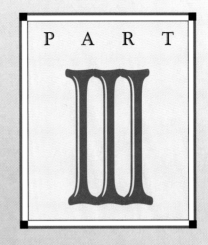

PART

III

. . . .

Presenting
Your
Speech

Wording Your Speech

*E*rnesto was asked to come to his daughter Contessa's high school career *day to speak about the skills needed to run your own business. He worked hard on the speech. He wanted to speak to the seniors on their own level, in their language. He did the best he could. Afterwards, he asked Contessa what she thought. "You had many good ideas," she said. "You probably got several kids thinking about businesses they could open after college." Ernesto responded, "Great, but I noticed some were laughing while I talked—why?" "Well, Dad," she replied, "you sometimes talked funny. We're not used to hearing our parents say 'chill out,' 'rad,' or 'awesome.' That kind of language doesn't sound right coming out of your mouth."*

As Ernesto discovered, language functions on multiple levels. Language is a *referential, relational,* and *symbolic* medium of communication. Through its pointing abilities, language refers to aspects of the world: "dog," "tree," "cupcake." Through its relational powers, it suggests associations between people; "Give me that cupcake" not only points to cupcakes but also indicates that one person has the power or authority to command another person. And as we saw, different generations—father's idioms versus daughter's idioms, for example—develop their own special languages that don't sound right when spoken by someone from another generation. And, because our symbol systems can be abstracted from the concrete world and even focus our attention on nonreal (unicorns) and nonconcrete (democracy) entities, whole empires of thought can be constructed out of language. So, it's not enough to know the words; you must also understand how language reflects human relationships and shared senses of reality—your culture and thinking.

In the next three chapters, we'll turn our attention to the encoding or deciphering of messages. **Encoding** occurs when you put ideas into words and actions. This includes your choice of language, use of visual aids, and even bodily and vocal behaviors. In this chapter, we'll focus on making effective word choices, using language strategically, and giving an overall tone and force to your speeches by thinking about their style.

MAKING EFFECTIVE WORD CHOICES

Before you can think strategically about language, you must be able to use it in understandable ways. You can clarify your messages if you keep in mind five features of effective word choice: accuracy, simplicity, coherence, language intensity, and appropriateness.

Accuracy

Careful word choice is an essential ingredient to effectively transmitting your meaning to an audience. If you tell a hardware store clerk, "I broke the dohickey on my hootenanny and I need a thingamajig to fix it," you'd better have the hootenanny in your hand or the clerk won't understand. When you speak, one goal is precision. You should leave no doubt about your meaning.

Words are symbols that represent concepts or objects. Your listener may attach a meaning to your words that's quite different from the one you intended. This misinterpretation becomes more likely as your words become more abstract. *Democracy,* for example, doesn't mean the same thing to a citizen in the suburbs as it does to a citizen in the ghetto. *Democracy* will elicit different meanings from Americans who belong to the Moral Majority than it will from those who belong to the American Socialist Party.

Students of General Semantics, the study of words or symbols and their relationships to reality, continually warn us that many errors in thinking and communication arise from treating words as if they were the actual conditions, processes, or objects. Words are not fixed and timeless in meaning, nor does everyone use them in exactly the same way.

To avoid vagueness, choose words that express the exact shade of meaning you wish to communicate. You might say that an object *shines,* but the object might also *glow, glitter, glisten, gleam, flare, blaze, glare, shimmer, glimmer, flicker, sparkle, flash,* and *beam.* Which word allows you to describe the object more precisely?

Simplicity

"Speak," said Lincoln, "so that the most lowly can understand you, and the rest will have no difficulty." Because electronic media reach audiences more varied than Lincoln could have imagined, you have even more reason to follow his advice today. Say *learn* rather than *ascertain, try* rather than *endeavor, use* rather than *utilize, help* rather than *facilitate.* Don't use a longer or less familiar word when a simple one is just as clear. Evangelist Billy Sunday illustrated the effectiveness of familiar words in this example:

> *If a man were to take a piece of meat and smell it and look disgusted, and his little boy were to say, "What's the matter with it, Pop?" and he were to say,*

"It is undergoing a process of decomposition in the formation of new chemical compounds," the boy would be all in. But if the father were to say, "It's rotten," then the boy would understand and hold his nose. "Rotten" is a good Anglo-Saxon word, and you do not have to go to the dictionary to find out what it means.[1]

Simplicity doesn't mean *simplistic;* never talk down to your audience. Just remember that short, direct words convey precise, concrete meanings.

Coherence

People listening to you speak don't have the luxury of reviewing the points you have made as they do when they are reading a written essay. Nor are they able to perceive punctuation marks that might help them distinguish one idea from another as you speak. In order to be understood, oral communication requires **coherence,** or the logical connection of ideas. To achieve coherence, you must use **signposts,** or words or phrases such as *first, next,* or *as a result,* that help listeners follow the movement of your ideas. Signposts such as "the history of this invention begins in. . . " also provide clues to the overall message structure.

Summaries, like signposts, provide clues to the overall speech structure. Preliminary and final summaries are especially helpful in outlining the major topics of the speech. **Preliminary summaries** (also called *forecasts* or *previews*) precede the development of the body of the speech, usually forming part of the introduction; **final summaries** follow the body of the speech, usually forming part of the conclusion. Consider the following examples:

Preliminary Summaries	**Final Summaries**
Today I am going to talk about three aspects of. . . .	I have talked about three aspects of. . . .
There are four major points to be covered in. . . .	These four major points—[restate them]—are. . . .
The history of the issue can be divided into two periods. . . .	The two periods just covered—[restate them]—represent. . . .

In addition to these summarizing strategies, signposts may be **connectives,** or transitions—linking phrases that move an audience from one idea to another. The following are useful connective statements:

- *In the first place. . . . The second point is. . . .*
- *In addition to. . . . notice that. . . .*
- *Now look at it from a different angle:. . .*
- *You must keep these three things in mind in order to understand the importance of the fourth:. . .*
- *What was the result?*
- *Turning now to. . . .*

The preceding signposts are neutral: they tell an audience that another idea is coming but don't indicate whether it's similar, different, or more important. You can improve the coherence of your speeches by indicating the precise relationships among ideas. Those relationships include parallel/hierarchical, similar/different, and coordinate/subordinate relationships. Here are some examples:

- *Parallel:* Not only . . . but also. . . .
- *Hierarchical:* More important than these. . . .
- *Different:* In contrast. . . .
- *Similar:* Similar to this. . . .
- *Coordinated:* One must consider X, Y, and Z. . . .
- *Subordinated:* On the next level is. . . .

Preliminary or final summaries and signposts are important to your audience. The summaries give listeners an overall sense of your entire message; if listeners can easily see the structure, they'll better understand and remember your speech. The signposts lead your listeners step by step through the speech, signaling specific relationships between and among ideas.

Intensity

You can communicate your feelings about ideas and objects through word choices. You can communicate your *attitude* toward your subject by choosing words that show how you feel. For example, consider these attitudinally weighted terms:

Highly Positive	Relatively Neutral	Highly Negative
Savior	G.I.	Enemy
Patriot	Soldier	Baby-killer
Freedom fighter	Combatant	Foreign devil

Those nine terms are organized by their intensity, ranging from the highly positive *savior* to the highly negative *foreign devil*. Notice the religious connotations present in the extreme examples of language intensity.

How intense should your language be? Communication scholar John Waite Bowers suggested a useful rule of thumb: let your language be, roughly, one step more intense than the position or attitude held by your audience.[2] For example, if your audience is already committed to your negative position on tax reform, then you can choose intensely negative words, such as *regressive* and *stifling*. If your audience is uncommitted, you should opt for comparatively neutral words, such as *burdensome*. And, if your audience is in favor of tax changes, you can use still less negative words, such as *unfair,* so as to avoid turning them off and to encourage them to keep an open mind. Intense language can generate intense reactions, but only if you match your word choices to your listeners' attitudes.

Appropriateness

Your language should be appropriate to the speech topic and situation. Solemn occasions call for restrained and dignified language; joyful occasions call for informal and lively word choices. The language used at the christening of a baby wouldn't work at a pep rally, and vice versa. Suit your language to the tone of the occasion.

Make sure that your language is appropriate to your audience. Before you use

• Getting someone to see your point of view often depends on strategic rhetorical decisions. What choices could be involved here?

informal language, check to see who's listening. Informal language, including slang, quickly goes out of style. *Gee whiz, wow, good grief, far out, awesome,* and *radical* became popular at different times. *Far out* would sound silly in a speech to your peers, and *radical* would sound ridiculous to an audience of senior citizens.

In summary, as you work through your speech, be sure your vocabulary is as accurate as possible, simple without being simplistic, held together with words

Ethical Moments

Doublespeak

Advertisers and politicians are often accused of using words that deceive or mislead. Think of any recent advertising or political campaign. *Liberal,* for instance, was once a positive label. In the 1988 national presidential campaign, the word became associated with negative attributes. *Liberal* then connoted the big spender—someone who wasted public energy and tax dollars on unrealistic schemes.

You can probably identify hundreds of words or phrases used to disguise facts. The Reagan and Clinton administrations didn't want to raise taxes but pursued *revenue enhancement* through *user fees.* People below the poverty line are *fiscal underachievers.* Nuclear weapons are labeled *radiation enhancement devices* and *peacekeepers.* And the 1984 invasion of Grenada was officially a *predawn vertical insertion.* Some language usage makes the unpleasant seem good and the positive appear negative. Language can shield us from the reality it represents.

Such name calling is by no means limited to politicians. Advertisers market *new and improved* products. We're tantalized with *real faux pearls* and *genuine imitation leather.* Advertisers exploit our health consciousness with *low-cholesterol* and *high-fiber* ingredients. Take a few moments to think about the following uses of language:

1. Suppose that you notice biased language in an article you're reading to research a speech topic. Should you cite the article as supporting material in your speech?

2. You genuinely believe in your recommendations for solving the problems you outline in a speech and you want to convince your listeners to sign a petition for change. Is it fair to use scare tactics or to tell them that they've got only one day left to act when in fact there's more time?

3. Should you ever use racy, obscene, or questionable language during a speech? Does it affect the relationship you establish with your listeners?

4. Is it ever fair to call people who aren't present *crooks* or attach similar labels to them?

5. Do you think language can obscure our understanding of reality? Under what circumstances do you think this happens? Should anything be done to make language more honest? What can you do to accomplish this?

that produce coherence, at a useful level of intensity, and appropriate to the audience and occasion.

USING LANGUAGE STRATEGICALLY

Effective word choice is your first linguistic battle; it helps your speeches to be understood. You will also, however, want to tap more directly into the powers of language—the powers of language to alter people's minds and move them to action. To accomplish those goals, you need to use oral language strategically, rhetorically. We will focus on four of the most common language strategies: definitions, restatement, imagery, and metaphor.

Defintions

Audience members need to understand the fundamental concepts of your speech. You can't expect them to understand your ideas if your language is unfamiliar. As a speaker, you have several options when working to define unfamiliar or difficult concepts.

You're most familiar with a **dictionary definition,** which categorizes an object or concept and specifies its characteristics: "An orange is a *fruit* (category) that is *round, orange* in color, and a member of the *citrus family* (characteristics)." Dictionary definitions sometimes help you to learn unfamiliar words, but they don't help an audience very much. If you do use dictionary definitions, go to specialized dictionaries. You certainly wouldn't depend on *Webster's Third International Dictionary* to define *foreclosure* or *liability* for a presentation on real estate law. For this technical application, sources such as *Black's Law Dictionary* and *Guide to American Law* are more highly respected.

Occasionally, a word has so many meanings that you have to choose one. If that's the case, use a **stipulative definition** to orient your listeners to your subject matter. A stipulative definition designates the way a word will be used in a certain context. You might say, "By *rich* I mean. . . ." or you might use an expert's stipulative definition such as this one from former President Jimmy Carter:

> *Who is rich? I'm not talking about bank accounts. But I would say that everyone here is rich. And we don't deliberately discriminate. A rich person is someone with a home and a modicum of education and a chance for at least a job and who believes that if you make a decision that it'll have some effect at least in your own life, and who believes that the police and the judges are on your side. These are the rich people.[3]*

You can further clarify a term or concept by telling your audience how you are *not* going to use the concept—by using a **negative definition.** So, Chicago police Sergeant Bruce Talbot defined "gateway drug" in this manner: "[F]or adolescents, cigarette smoking is a gateway drug to illicit drugs such as marijuana and crack cocaine. By gateway drug I do not mean just that cigarettes are the first drug young people encounter, alcohol is. But unlike alcohol, which is first experienced in a social ritual such as church or an important family event, cigarettes are the first drug minors buy themselves and use secretly outside the family and social institutions."[4] Defining negatively can clear away possible misconceptions. Using a negative definition along with a stipulative definition, as did Sergeant Talbot, allows you to treat a commonplace phenomenon in a different way.

Sometimes you can reinforce an idea by telling your listeners where a word came from. One way to do this is by using an **etymological definition.** An etymological definition is the derivation of a single word; we offered one in Chapter 1, tracing the word *communication* back to its Latin origins.

One of the best ways to define is by an **exemplar definition,** especially if the concept is unfamiliar or technical. Exemplar definitions are familiar examples.

• Definitions help you to grasp concepts. What kinds of definitions are being probably used in this situation?

You might tell your listeners, "Each day, most of you stroll past the Old Capitol on your way to classes. That building is a perfect example of what I want to talk about today—Georgian architecture." Be careful to use in your definition only those examples that are familiar to your audience members.

A **contextual definition** tells listeners how a word is used in a specific context. So, Professor Jonathan Mann was arguing that AIDS and other new diseases are changing our understanding of health—not as individuals but as a society. He captures that change by defining the word *solidarity* in terms of health:

> [S]olidarity describes a central concept in this emerging perspective on health, individuals, and society. The AIDS pandemic has taught us a great deal about tolerance and non-discrimination, a refusal to separate the condition of the few from the fate of the many. Solidarity arises when people realize that excessive differences among people make the entire system unstable. Charity is individual; solidarity is inherently social, concerned with social justice, and therefore also economic and political.[5]

Still another means of making technical or abstract notions easier to understand is the **analogical definition.** An analogy compares a process or event that is unknown with known ones, as in, "Hospitals and labs use cryogenic tanks, which work much like large thermos bottles, to freeze tissue samples, blood, and other organic matter." By referring to what is familiar, the analogical definition can make the unfamiliar much easier to grasp. But the speaker must be sure that the analogy fits.

The points here are simple but important: (1) You have many different kinds of definitions to choose from when working with unfamiliar or difficult concepts. (2) Select definitional strategies that make sense for your subject matter, your audience, and your purposes.

Restatement

If accuracy and simplicity were your only criteria as a speaker, your messages might resemble a famous World War II bulletin: "Sighted sub, sank same." But, because words literally disappear into the atmosphere as soon as they're spoken, you don't have the writer's advantage when transmitting ideas to others. Instead, you must rely heavily on restatement. **Restatement** is the repetition of words, phrases, and ideas so as to clarify and reinforce them. The key here is not simply to repeat yourself, but to repeat or rephrase in order to advance the listeners' understanding or acceptance of an idea.

Restating an idea from a number of perspectives usually involves listing its components or redefining the basic concept. You can see this principle of reiteration at work in the following excerpt from Bill Clinton's speech to Georgetown University students in 1991:

> *To turn America around, we need a new approach founded on our most sacred principles as a nation, with a vision for the future. We need a New Covenant, a solemn agreement between the people and their government, to provide opportunity for everybody, inspire responsibility throughout our society, and restore a sense of community to this great nation. A New Covenant to take government back from the powerful interests and the bureaucracy, and give this country back to ordinary people.*
>
> *More than 200 years ago, the founders outlined our first social compact between government and the people, not just between lords and kings. More than a century ago, Abraham Lincoln gave his life to maintain the Union the compact created. Sixty years ago, Franklin Roosevelt renewed that promise with a New Deal that offered opportunity in return for hard work.*
>
> *Today we need to forge a New Covenant that will repair the damaged bond between the people and their government and restore our basic values—the notion that our country has a responsibility to help people get ahead, that citizens have not only the right but a responsibility to rise as far and as high as their talents and determination can take them, and that we're all in this together.*[6]

Notice Clinton's tactics here: first, he justifies the need for the concept. Then, he formally defines it ("a solemn agreement. . ."). Next, he indicates its functions. He then offers examples of previous convenants from American history, finally getting to "Today we need to forge. . . ," which allows him to offer more detail on what he sees as the functions of the New Covenant. These varied restatements thus serve as a structure for his developmental materials.

Restatement can help your listeners remember your ideas more readily.

However, be careful of mindless repetition; too many restatements, especially of simple ideas, can be boring.

Imagery

People grasp their world through the senses of sight, smell, hearing, taste, and touch. To intensify listeners' experiences, you can appeal to these senses. The senses through which you reach your listeners *directly* are the visual and the auditory. Listeners can see you, your facial expressions, your movements, and your visual aids, and they can hear what you say (see Figure 9.1).

You can stimulate your listeners' senses *indirectly* by using language to recall images they have previously experienced. **Imagery** consists of sets of sensory pictures evoked in the imagination through language. The language of imagery is divided into seven types, each related to the particular sensation that it seeks to evoke: visual (sight), auditory (hearing), gustatory (taste), olfactory (smell), tactile (touch), kinesthetic (muscle strain), and organic (internal sensations).

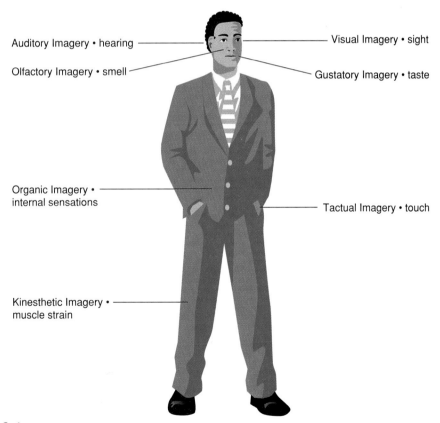

Auditory Imagery • hearing

Olfactory Imagery • smell

Visual Imagery • sight

Gustatory Imagery • taste

Organic Imagery •
internal sensations

Tactual Imagery • touch

Kinesthetic Imagery •
muscle strain

FIGURE 9.1
The Types of Imagery
Speakers can stimulate their listeners' senses indirectly through language which triggers sensations.

Visual Imagery

Visual imagery describes optical stimuli. Try to make your audience see the objects or situations that you're describing. Mention size, shape, color, and movement. Recount events in vivid visual language. Consider the conclusion from a speech by former Federal Communications Commissioner Newton N. Minow to the Gannett Foundation Media Center in 1991. He envisioned a past event, a look at primitive TV in 1938, to reintroduce some timeless problems. He played off the "vision" of television as well as the imagery of light (or dark, in the case of the Gulf War of 1991). *Vision* became a wonderfully ambiguous word referring both to light and to what we learn to see in the world:

> *I commend some extraordinary words to the new generation. E. B. White sat in a darkened room in 1938 to see the beginning of television, an experimental electronic box that projected images in the room. Once he saw it, Mr. White wrote:*
>
> > *"We shall stand or fall by television, of that I am sure. I believe television is going to be the test of the modern world, and that in this new opportunity to see beyond the range of our vision, we shall discover either a new and unbearable disturbance to the general peace, or a saving radiance in the sky."*
> >
> > *That radiance falls unevenly today. It is still a dim light in education. It has not fulfilled its potential for children. It has neglected the needs of public television. And in the electoral process it has cast a dark shadow.*
> >
> > *This year, television has enabled us to see Patriot missiles destroy Scud missiles above the Persian Gulf. Will television in the next thirty years be a Scud or a Patriot? A new generation now has the chance to put the vision back into television, to travel from the wasteland to the promised land, and to make television a saving radiance in the sky.*[7]

Auditory Imagery

To create auditory imagery, use words that help your listeners hear what you're describing. Auditory imagery can project an audience into a scene. Author Tom Wolfe described a demolition derby by recounting the chant of the crowd as it joined in the countdown, the explosion of sound as two dozen cars started off in second gear, and finally "the unmistakable tympany of automobiles colliding and cheap-gauge sheet metal buckling."[8]

Gustatory Imagery

Gustatory imagery depicts sensations of taste. Sometimes you may even be able to help your audience taste what you're describing. Mention its saltiness, sweetness, sourness, or spiciness. Remember that foods have texture as well as taste. While demonstrating how to make popcorn, you might mention the crispness of the kernels, the oily sweetness of melted butter, and the grittiness of salt. Such descriptions allow your listeners to participate in the experience through their imaginations.

Olfactory Imagery

Olfactory imagery describes sensations of smell. Help your audience smell the odors connected with the situation you describe. Smell is a powerful sense because it normally triggers a flood of associated images. You can stimulate this process by describing the odor or by comparing the odor with more familiar ones. Elspeth Huxley remembered her childhood trek to Kenya at the turn of the century by recalling its smells:

> *It was the smell of travel in those days, in fact the smell of Africa—dry, peppery yet rich and deep, with an undertone of native body smeared with fat and red ochre and giving out a ripe, partly rancid odour which nauseated some Europeans when they first encountered it but which I, for one, grew to enjoy. This was the smell of the Kikuyu, who were mainly vegetarian. The smell of tribes from the Victoria Nyanza basin, who were meat-eaters and sometimes cannibals, was quite different; much stronger and more musky, almost acrid, and, to me, much less pleasant. No doubt we smelt just as strong and odd to Africans, but of course we were fewer in numbers, and more spread out.*[9]

Tactile Imagery

Tactile imagery is based on the sensations that come to us through physical contact with external objects. In particular, tactile imagery gives sensations of texture and shape, pressure, and heat or cold. Let your audience feel how rough or smooth, dry or wet, or slimy or sticky modeling clay is (texture and shape). Let them sense the pressure of physical force on their bodies, the weight of a heavy laundry bag, the pinch of jogging shoes, the blast of a high wind on their faces (pressure).

Sensations of heat or cold are aroused by thermal imagery. General Douglas MacArthur's great speech to the Cadets of West Point on "duty, honor, and country" used vivid examples of tactile imagery as he described soldiers of the past, "bending under soggy pack on many a weary march, from dripping dusk to drizzly dawn, slogging ankle deep through mire of shell-pocked roads; to form grimly for the attack, blue-lipped, covered with sludge and mud, chilled by the wind and rain, driving home to their objective, and for many, to the judgment seat of God."[10]

Kinesthetic Imagery

Kinesthetic imagery describes the sensations associated with muscle strain and neuromuscular movement. Let your listeners experience for themselves the agonies and joys of marathon racing—the muscle cramps, the constricted chest, the struggle for air—and the magical serenity of getting a second wind and gliding effortlessly toward the finish line.

Organic Imagery

Hunger, dizziness, nausea—these are organic images. Organic imagery captures internal feelings or sensations. There are times when an experience is not complete without the description of inner feelings. The sensation of dizziness as a mountain climber struggles through the rarified mountain air to reach the summit is one example. Another is the way the bottom drops out of your stomach when

● You can recreate experiences for others through image-evoking language. How would you describe this scene to someone?

a small plane tips sharply, then rights itself. Since such imagery is powerful, you shouldn't offend your audience by overdoing it. Develop the rhetorical sensitivity required to create vividness without making the resultant image gruesome, disgusting, or grotesque.

The seven types of imagery we have considered—visual, auditory, gustatory, olfactory, tactile, kinesthetic, and organic—may be referred to as "doorways to the mind."[11] They open new levels of awareness that help listeners experience your message. Different people respond to different kinds of imagery, so you should insert several types of perceptual "doorways."

In the following example, note how the speaker combines various sensory appeals to arouse listener interest and reaction:

The strangler struck in Donora, Pennsylvania, in October of 1948. A thick fog billowed through the streets enveloping everything in thick sheets of dirty moisture and a greasy black coating. As Tuesday faded into Saturday, the fumes from the big steel mills shrouded the outlines of the landscape. One could barely see across the narrow streets. Traffic stopped. Men lost their way returning from the mills. Walking through the streets, even for a few moments, caused eyes to water and burn. The thick fumes grabbed at the throat and created a choking sensation. The air acquired a sickening bittersweet smell, nearly a taste. Death was in the air.[12]

In this example, college student Charles Schaillol uses vivid, descriptive phrases to affect the senses of his listeners—visual: "thick sheets of dirty moisture"; organic: "eyes to water and burn"; and olfactory, gustatory: "sickening bittersweet smell, nearly a taste."

To be effective, such illustrations must appear plausible. The language must convey a realistic impression that the situation described could happen. The speaker who describes the strangler that struck Donora offers a plausible account of the event. More important, he does so in a fashion that arouses feelings. His listeners wouldn't have shared the experience if he had simply said, "Air pollution was the cause of death in Donora."

Metaphor

Images created by appealing to the senses are often the result of metaphors. A **metaphor** is the comparison of two dissimilar things. Charles Schaillol's description of fog as "thick sheets of dirty moisture" is one example. Scholar Michael Osborn notes that the metaphor should "result in an intuitive flash of recognition that surprises or fascinates the hearer."[13] Furthermore, good metaphors extend our knowledge or increase our awareness of a person, object, or event. When they're fresh or vivid, they can be powerful aids in evoking feelings. For example, referring to a table's "legs" is a metaphor, but it's boring. It's much more interesting to say, "Balanced on four toothpicks, the antique table swayed under its heavy burden."

Metaphors drawn from everyday experiences provide wide audience appeal. In the following speech, Martin Luther King, Jr., relied on our experiences of light and darkness:

> *With this faith in the future, with this determined struggle, we will be able to emerge from the bleak and desolate midnight of man's inhumanity to man, into the bright and glittering daybreak of freedom and justice.*[14]

This basic light-dark metaphor allowed King to suggest (a) sharp contrasts between inhumanity and freedom and (b) the inevitability of social progress (as "daybreak" follows "midnight"). The metaphor communicated King's beliefs about justice and injustice and urged others to action.

Words are not neutral pipelines for thought. Words not only reflect the world outside your mind, but also, as critic Kenneth Burke suggests, help *shape* our perceptions of people, events, and social contexts. Language has a potent effect on people's willingness to believe, to feel, and to act.

Sample Speech

• • • •

William Faulkner (1897–1962) presented the following speech on 10 December 1950 as he accepted the Nobel Prize for Literature. His listeners might have expected a speech filled with the kind of pessimism so characteristic of his novels. Instead, he greeted them with a stirring challenge to improve humankind.

Notice in particular Faulkner's use of language. Although known for the tortured sentences in his novels, he expresses his ideas clearly and simply in his speech. His style suggests a written speech yet his use of organic imagery and powerful metaphors keep the speech alive. The atmosphere is generally serious, befitting the occasion. You might expect a Nobel Prize winner to talk about himself, but Faulkner did just the opposite. He stressed his craft, writing, and the commitment necessary to practice that craft; this material emphasis led naturally to an essentially propositional rather than narrative form. More than 40 years ago, William Faulkner offered a speech that is as relevant today as it was in 1950.

Even though he's accepting one of the most prestigous awards a human being can receive, Faulkner immediately tries to deflect attention from himself to his work. This he does through a series of contrasts built around a "not this . . . but this" construction. The contrasts sharpen the points he'll make throughout the speech: it's the art, not the artist, that counts; creating art is extraordinarily hard work; we can't write out of fear but out of the need to elevate the soul and spirit of humanity.

Because those are his central ideas, he frames his whole speech as an address to young writers. The language of the whole speech is forecast in the first paragraph: agony, sweat, profit, anguish, and travail versus spirit, glory, acclaim, pinnacle comprise his vocabulary. Metaphors of struggle and childbirth are contrasted with images of soul and achievement.

Faulkner is speaking at the dawn of the atomic age, and hence feels compelled to address the issue of the bomb and our fear of it. He attacks that fear immediately. First, he suggests the presence of the fear and then via restatement comes back to it in the next three sentences. Second, he continues the linguistic contrasts between fear *and* spirit,

On Accepting the Nobel Prize for Literature
William Faulkner[15]

I feel that this award was not made to me as a man, but to my work—a life's work in the agony and sweat of the human spirit, not for glory and least of all for profit, but to create out of the materials of the human spirit something which did not exist before. So this award is only mine in trust. It will not be difficult to find a dedication for the money part of it commensurate with the purpose and significance of its origin. But I would like to do the same with the acclaim too, by using this moment as a pinnacle from which I might be listened to by the young men and women already dedicated to the same anguish and travail, among whom is already that one who will some day stand here where I am standing./1

Our tragedy today is a general and universal physical fear so long sustained by now that we can even bear it. There are no longer problems of the spirit. There is only the question: When will I be blown up? Because of this, the young man or woman writing today has forgotten the problems of the human heart in conflict with itself which alone can make human heart in conflict *and* the agony and the sweat.

Faulkner's now ready to expand his central ideas via a series of literal and metaphorical contrasts. These sentences really need to be read aloud to capture the pounding rhythm that guides them: love *versus* lust, defeats *versus* victories, value *and* hope *versus* pity *and* compassion. *Body metaphors complete the paragraph:* bones, scars, heart *versus* glands. *Faulkner also achieves a sense of forward motion through a series of words connected with* ands: *"love and honor and pity and pride and compassion and sacrifice." That series sets up the more specific metaphorical and literal contrasts that comprise the rest of the paragraph.*

Having presented young writers with a series of sharply differentiated contrasts, Faulkner now is ready to conclude with his own optimistic vision of the future of literary writing. A flood of imagery washes over the listeners: images are auditory ("the last ding-dong of doom," "his puny inexhaustible voice," and "the poet's voice"); visual ("the last worthless rock hanging tideless in the last red and dying evening"); tactile ("the pillars" that provide support for people to "endure and prevail"); and organic ("lifting his heart"). Together with those images, the main vocabulary of great writing— soul, spirit, compassion, sacrifice, endurance, courage, honor, hope, pride, pity, *and* glory—*is recited again. The constant restatement of that vocabulary, the interwining of images and exhortations, the affirmation of life in the face of atomic devastation, and, of course, the sheer presence of Faulkner himself combine to make this one of the two or three greatest Nobel Prize speeches ever given.*

good writing because only that is worth writing about, worth the agony and the sweat./2

He must learn them again. He must teach himself that the basest of all things is to be afraid; and, teaching himself that, forget it forever, leaving no room in his workshop for anything but the old verities and truths of the heart, the old universal truths lacking which any story is ephemeral and doomed—love and honor and pity and pride and compassion and sacrifice. Until he does so, he labors under a curse. He writes not of love but of lust, of defeats in which nobody loses anything of value, of victories without hope and, worst of all, without pity or compassion. His griefs grieve on no universal bones, leaving no scars. He writes not of the heart but of the glands./3

Until he relearns these things, he will write as though he stood among and watched the end of man. I decline to accept the end of man. It is easy enough to say that man is immortal simply because he will endure: that when the last ding-dong of doom has clanged and faded from the last worthless rock hanging tideless in the last red and dying evening, that even then there will still be one more sound: that of his puny inexhaustible voice, still talking. I refuse to accept this. I believe that man will not merely endure: he will prevail. He is immortal, not because he alone among creatures has an inexhaustible voice, but because he has a soul, a spirit capable of compassion and sacrifice and endurance. The poet's, the writer's, duty is to write about these things. It is his privilege to help man endure by lifting his heart, by reminding him of the courage and honor and hope and pride and compassion and pity and sacrifice which have been the glory of his past. The poet's voice need not merely be the record of man, it can be one of the props, the pillars to help him endure and prevail./4

SELECTING AN APPROPRIATE STYLE: STRATEGIC DECISIONS

Finally, let's consider the aspects of speaking style that control audience members' overall impressions of you as a person, the nature of your message, and even the occasion itself. The combination of these aspects of oral communication is generally called *tone*. **Tone** is the predominant effect or character of the speech.

While tone is an elusive quality of speech, you may, nevertheless, identify some of its primary features. We'll pay special attention to three dimensions of tone: written vs. oral style, serious vs. humorous atmosphere, and gendered vs. gender-neutral language.

Written Versus Oral Style

Generally, spoken language is uncomplicated; it has to be since we use it every day—at the grocery store, over the back fence, around the supper table, and in the street. But some spoken language is complicated and formal; this is the type of language many people use when giving a speech. There are two types of language: oral style and written style. While **oral style** is informal and imprecise (typical of conversation), **written style** is formal and precise (typical of written works). Consider the following examples of written and oral style:

Written Style	**Oral Style**
Remit the requested amount forthwith.	Hand over the cash.
Will you be having anything else?	Whutkinahgitcha?

Most of us compose speeches in a written, rather than an oral, style. This is more likely if we write out the whole speech before giving it. The result is stilted and stiff and may sound like this:

> *I am most pleased that you could come this morning. I would like to use this opportunity to discuss with you a subject of inestimable importance to us all—the impact of inflationary spirals on students enrolled in institutions of higher education.*

Translated into an oral style, this speech would start as follows:

> *Thanks for coming. I'd like to talk today about a problem for all of us—the rising cost of going to college.*

Notice how much more natural the second version sounds. The first is wordy—filled with prepositional phrases, complex words, and formal sentences. The second contains shorter sentences and simpler vocabulary, and it addresses the audience directly.

For most speech occasions, you should cultivate an oral style. On rare, highly ceremonial occasions, you may decide to read from a prepared text. However, even then, you should strive for oral style.[16]

Serious Versus Humorous Atmosphere

You cultivate the atmosphere of the speaking occasion largely through your speaking style. In a graduation speech or an awards banquet address, you want to encourage the personal reflection of your listeners; but at a fraternity gathering or holiday celebration, you want to create a social, interactive atmosphere.

Sometimes the atmosphere of the occasion dictates what speaking style should be used. You don't expect a light, humorous speaking style during a funeral. Even so, sometimes a minister, priest, or rabbi will tell a funny story about the deceased. Yet the overall tone of a funeral eulogy should be somber. In contrast, a speech after a football victory, election win, or successful fund drive is seldom solemn. Victory speeches are times for celebration and unity.

Humorous speeches can have serious goals. As we'll see in Chapter 15, even speeches designed to entertain have worthy purposes. These speeches can be given in grave earnestness. The political satirist who throws humorous but barbed comments at pompous, silly, or corrupt politicians aims to amuse the audience as well as urge political reform.

The speaking **atmosphere** is the mind-set or mental attitude that you attempt to create in your audience. A serious speaker urging future profesors to remember the most important things in life might say, "Rank your values and live by them." That same idea expressed by actor Alan Alda sounded more humorous:

> *We live in a time that seems to be split about its values. In fact it seems to be schizophrenic.*
>
> *For instance, if you pick up a magazine like* Psychology Today, *you're liable to see an article like "White Collar Crime: It's More Widespread than You Think." Then in the back of the magazine they'll print an advertisement that says, "We'll write your doctoral thesis for 25 bucks." You see how values are eroding? I mean, a doctoral thesis ought to go for at least a C-note.*[17]

Which atmosphere is preferable? The answer depends on the speaking situation, your speech purpose, and your listeners' expectations.

Gendered Versus Gender-Neutral Nouns and Pronouns

While words themselves are not intrinsically good or bad, as we noted at the beginning of this chapter, they can communicate values or attitudes to your listeners and they suggest relationships between you and your audience. Gender-linked words, particularly nouns and pronouns, require special attention. **Gender-linked words** are those that directly or indirectly identify males or females—*policeman, washerwoman, poet,* and *poetess.* Pronouns such as *he* and *she* and adjectives such as *his* and *her* are also obviously gender-linked words. **Gender-neutral words** do not directly or indirectly denote males or females—*chairperson, police officer,* or *firefighter.*

Since the 1960s and the advent of the women's movement, consciousness of gendered language has gradually surfaced. The question of whether language use affects culture and socialization still is being debated. However, as a speaker you must be careful not to alienate your audience or to propagate stereotypes unconsciously through your use of language. In addition to avoiding most gender-linked words, you've got to handle two more problems:

1. *Inaccurately excluding members of one sex.* Some uses of gendered pronouns inaccurately reflect social-occupational conditions in the world: "A nurse sees *her* patients eight hours a day, but a doctor sees *his* for only ten minutes." Many women are doctors, and many men are nurses. Most audience members are aware of this and may be displeased if they feel that you're stereotyping roles in the medical profession.

2. *Stereotyping male and female psychological or social characteristics.* "Real men never cry." "A woman's place is in the home." "The Marines are looking for a few good men." "Sugar 'n spice 'n everything nice—that's what little girls are made of." Falling back on these stereotypes gets speakers into trouble with audiences, both male and female. In these days of raised consciousness, audiences are insulted to hear such misinformed assertions. In addition, these stereotypes conceal the potential in individuals whose talents are not limited by their gender.

These problem areas demand your attention. A speaker who habitually uses sexist language is guilty of ignoring important speaking conventions that have taken shape over the last several decades. How can you avoid sexist language? Here are four easy ways:

1. *Speak in the plural.* Say, "Bankers are often. . . . They face. . . ." This tactic is often sufficient to make your language gender-neutral.

2. *Say "he or she" when you must use a singular subject.* Say, "A student majoring in business is required to sign up for an internship. He or she can. . . ." This strategy works well as long as you don't overdo it. If you find yourself cluttering sentences with "he or she," switch to the plural.

3. *Remove gender inflections.* It's painless to say *firefighter* instead of *fireman, chair* or *chairperson* instead of *chairman,* and *tailor* instead of *seamstress.* Gender inflections can usually be removed without affecting your speech.

4. *Use gender-specific pronouns for gender-specific processes, people, or activities.* It is acceptable to talk about a mother as *her* or a current or former president of the United States as *him.* Men do not naturally bear children, and a woman has not yet been elected to the White House.

Ultimately, the search for gender-neutral idioms is an affirmation of mutual respect and a recognition of equal worth and the essential dignity of individuals. Gender differences are important in many aspects of life, but when they dominate public talk, they're ideologically oppressive. Be gender neutral in public talk to remove barriers to effective communication.[18]

Selecting an appropriate style is a matter of assessing yourself, your audience, the situation or context, and your speaking purposes. A thorough assessment of these variables will help you to select an appropriate style—written or oral, serious or humorous, gendered or gender-neutral.

In summary, wording your speech demands careful thought about the clarity of your language use, the persuasive force lying behind words, and the overall sense of tone or style that results from choosing language with particular characteristics. In the world of international diplomacy, a wrong word can cause a breakdown in negotiations. In your world, it can produce confusion, misunderstanding, or even disgust. Take time to shape your oral language as carefully as you shape your ideas.

CHAPTER SUMMARY

1. Successful speeches generally are characterized by accurate, simple, coherent, properly intense, and appropriate language choices.

2. Rhetorical strategies are word and phrase choices intended to control the impact of the speech. Four of the most common are definition, restatement, imagery, and metaphor.

3. Speakers can define unfamiliar or difficult concepts in multiple ways, via dictionary, stipulative, negative, etymological, exemplar, contextual, and analogical definitions.

4. Restatement is the intentional repetition of ideas or concepts to clarify or add force to ideas.

5. Imagery consists of word pictures created in the imagination through language. There are seven types of images: visual, auditory, gustatory, olfactory, tactile, kinesthetic, and organic sensations.

6. In selecting an appropriate speaking style, you must make decisions about written versus oral language, a serious versus humorous atmosphere, and gendered versus gender-neutral language.

KEY TERMS

analogical definition (p. 159)
atmosphere (p. 169)
coherence (p. 154)
connectives (p. 154)
contextual definition (p. 159)
dictionary definition (p. 158)
encoding (p. 152)
etymological definition (p. 158)
exemplar definition (p. 158)
final summaries (p. 154)
gender-linked words (p. 169)

gender-neutral words (p. 169)
imagery (p. 161)
metaphor (p. 165)
negative definition (p. 158)
oral style (p. 168)
preliminary summaries (p. 154)
restatement (p. 160)
signposts (p. 154)
stipulative definition (p. 158)
tone (p. 168)
written style (p. 168)

SKILLBUILDING ACTIVITIES

1. Choose one of the items listed below and describe it, using the seven kinds of imagery to create an involving portrait for your listeners.
   One of the creatures in *Jurassic Park*.
   A tropical plant.
   A breakfast food.
   A complicated machine.
   The oldest building on campus.

2. As a take-home assignment, rewrite a complicated message (e.g., an insurance policy, an agreement for a credit card or a loan, income tax instructions, or a

difficult passage from a book) in simple yet still accurate language. Present the material as a short speech in your class. Submit it for your instructor's comments.

3. Read one of the sample speeches in this textbook. Identify the methods the speaker uses to make the language effective. Were the speaker's word choices effective? Did the speaker choose an appropriate style? What rhetorical strategies can you discover in the speech?

REFERENCES

1. Quoted in John R. Pelsma, *Essentials of Speech* (New York: Crowell, Collier, and Macmillan, 1934), 193.

2. John Waite Bowers, "Language and Argument," in *Perspectives on Argumentation,* edited by G. R. Miller and T. R. Nilsen (Glenview, Ill.: Scott, Foresman, 1966), 168–172.

3. James E. Carter, "Excellence Comes from a Repository That Doesn't Change," *Vital Speeches of the Day* 59 (1 July 1993), 548.

4. Bruce Talbot, "Statement," Hearings before Senate Committee on Commerce, Science, and Transportation, *Tobacco Product Education and Health Promotion Act of 1991, S. 1088,* 14 Nov. 1991, 102nd Congress (Washington, D.C.: U.S. Government Printing Office, 1991), 77.

5. Jonathan Mann, "Global AIDS: Revolution, Paradigm, and Solidarity," *Representative American Speeches, 1990–1991,* edited by Owen Peterson (New York: H. W. Wilson Co., 1991), 88.

6. William J. Clinton, "The New Covenant," in *Representative American Speeches, 1991–1992,* edited by Owen Peterson (New York: H. W. Wilson Co., 1992), 52–53.

7. Newton N. Minow, "How Vast the Wasteland Now?" in *Representative American Speeches, 1991–1992,* edited by Owen Peterson (New York: H. W. Wilson Co., 1992), 169.

8. A selection from Tom Wolfe, *The Kandy-Kolored Tangerine-Flake Streamline Baby* (Thomas K. Wolfe, Jr., 1965). Reprinted by permission of Farrar, Straus and Giroux, Inc. and International Creative Management.

9. Elspeth Huxley, *The Flame Trees of Thika: Memories of an African Childhood* (London: Chatto & Windus, 1959), 4.

10. Excerpt from Douglas MacArthur, "Duty, Honor and Country," *The Dolphin Book of Speeches,* edited by George W. Hibbit (George W. Hibbit, 1965). Reprinted by permission of Doubleday & Company, Inc.

11. Victor Alvin Ketcham, "The Seven Doorways to the Mind," *Business Speeches by Business Men,* edited by William P. Sanford and W. Hayes Yeager (New York: McGraw-Hill, 1930).

12. From Charles Schaillol, "The Strangler," *Winning Orations.* Reprinted by permission of Larry Schnoor, Executive Secretary, Interstate Oratorical Association, Concordia College, Moorhead, Minn.

13. Michael Osborn, *Orientations to Rhetorical Style* (Chicago: Science Research Associates, 1976), 10.

14 From Martin Luther King, Jr., "Love, Law and Civil Disobedience" (Martin Luther King, Jr., 1963). Reprinted by permission of Joan Daves.

15. William Faulkner, "On Accepting the Nobel Prize for Literature," *The Faulkner Reader* (New York: Random House, 1954).

16. For a summary of several technical studies distinguishing between oral and written styles, and for a discussion of sixteen characteristics of oral style, see John F. Wilson and Carroll C. Arnold, *Public Speaking as a Liberal Art,* 5th ed. (Boston: Allyn and Bacon, 1983), 227–229.

17. Alan Alda, "A Reel Doctor's Advice to Some Real Doctors," in Stephen E. Lucas, *The Art of Public Speaking* (New York: Random House, 1983), 364.

18. Studies of gender and communication have flooded the academic marketplace. For overviews, see H. M. Hacker, "Blabbermouths and Claims: Sex Differences in Self-Disclosure in Same-Sex and Cross-Sex Friendship Dyads," *Pscyhology of Women Quarterly* 5 (1981): 385–401; Judith C. Pearson, *Gender and Communication* (Dubuque, Ia.: Wm. C. Brown, 1985); Barbara Bate, *Communication and the Sexes* (New York: Harper & Row, 1987); Lea P. Stewart, Pamela J. Cooper, and Sheryl A. Friedly, *Communication Between the Sexes: Sex Differences and Sex-Role Stereotypes* (Scottsdale, Ariz.: Gorsuch Scarisbrick, 1986); and Carole Spitzack and Kathryn Carter, "Women in Communication Studies: A Typology of Revision," *Quarterly Journal of Speech* 73 (1987): 401–423.

Delivering Your Speech

Norman moaned, "I just don't understand why I blanked out like that. I'm really embarrassed. How can I ever give another speech?" Professor Ramirez smiled and asked, "Why do you think you had memory lapses during your speech?" "Oh, I don't know," replied Norman. "I just couldn't remember which words came next." "How did you prepare to give this speech?" Norman's professor asked. "Did you write it out?" "Sure," he answered, "I always write them out, then memorize them. Then I make note-cards and my outline to hand in. But I never had trouble remembering a speech before." "Norm, maybe you've been using the wrong approach. What do you think would happen if you made a detailed outline first and didn't write out the speech word for word at all?" Norman considered his professor's suggestion. "Well, I suppose I could, but what if I couldn't remember the exact words I wanted to use?" Professor Ramirez responded, "That's where the outline would be helpful. It would jog your memory, and you wouldn't be tied to your notes as much. I'll bet your eye contact and responsiveness to your audience would improve, too."

Like Norman, you may be struggling with the physical aspects of delivering your speeches. You're in good company: many famous speakers had to overcome severe delivery problems before becoming effective speakers. Abraham Lincoln suffered from extreme speech fright; Eleanor Roosevelt was awkward and clumsy; John F. Kennedy had a strong dialect and repetitive gestures. These speakers realized that success depends not only on careful planning before the speech but also on effective presentation. The oral delivery of the speech can heighten or reduce the impact of your ideas.

You must be aware that you communicate with your entire body—your face, your gestures, your voice, and your posture. Your voice and bodily movements—

the *aural and visual channels of communication*—help to transmit your feelings and attitudes about yourself, your audience, and your topic. You may see speakers who approach the lectern dragging their feet and fussing with their notes. Their attitudes are abundantly clear even before they utter their first words. Unwittingly, these speakers establish audience predispositions that work against them. Even if their ideas are important, they're overshadowed by their distracting nonverbal communication.

If you've heard a recording or seen a video of Martin Luther King, Jr., giving his "I Have a Dream" speech, you can appreciate the dramatic difference between hearing him speak and merely reading a copy of the speech. The same is true of Jesse Jackson, Camille Paglia, Rush Limbaugh, and Boris Yeltsin. Oral presentation can add fire to the message. Orality's great strength—its edge—comes from your voice's person-sharing qualities and from your physical presence.

Your speech will gain strength and vitality if it's presented well. To help you achieve this objective, we'll discuss three important aspects of presentation: selecting the method of presentation, using your voice to communicate, and using your body to communicate.

SELECTING THE METHOD OF PRESENTATION

How should you present your speech? Your choice will be based on several criteria, including the type of speaking occasion, the purpose of your speech, your audience analysis, and your own strengths and weaknesses as a speaker. Attention to these considerations will help you to decide whether your method of presentation should be impromptu, memorized, read from a manuscript, or extemporized.

The Impromptu Speech

An **impromptu speech** is a delivered on the spur of the moment without preparation. The ability to speak off the cuff is useful in an emergency, but you should avoid impromptu speeches whenever possible, because they produce unpredictable outcomes. In an impromptu speech, you must rely entirely on previous knowledge and skill. You might be asked in the middle of a sorority meeting, for example, to give a progress report on your pledge committee. For best results when speaking on an impromptu basis, try to focus on a single idea—such as plans for the annual pledge-week open house—carefully relating all details connected to that idea. This strategy will keep you from rambling incoherently.

The Memorized Speech

On rare occasions, you may write out your speech and commit it to memory. When notecards or a TelePrompTer cannot be used, it may be acceptable for you to give a **memorized speech.** When making a toast at your parents' twenty-fifth wedding anniversary, for example, you probably wouldn't want to speak from notecards. Some speakers, such as comedians, deliver their remarks from memory to free their hands for character-related gesturing.

Speakers who use memorized presentations are usually most effective when they write their speeches to sound like informal and conversational speech rather

• Speakers must choose among several methods of presentation. Which method is used here? What are other options?

than formal, written essays. Remember that with a memorized speech, you'll have difficulty responding to audience feedback. Since the words of the speech are predetermined, you can't easily adjust them as the speech progresses.

The Manuscript Speech

A **manuscript speech** is written out beforehand and then read from a manuscript or TelePrompTer. By using TelePrompTers, speakers can appear to be looking at television viewers while they're really reading their manuscripts projected onto clear sheets of Plexiglas. When extremely careful wording is required, the manuscript speech is appropriate. When the president addresses Congress, for example, a slip of the tongue could misdirect domestic or foreign policies. Many radio and television speeches are read from manuscripts because of the strict time limits imposed by broadcasting schedules.

The Extemporaneous Speech

Most speeches that you'll deliver will be extemporaneous. An **extemporaneous speech** is one that is prepared in advance and presented from abbreviated notes.

Speaking of...	**Lecture Fees of the Rich and Famous**	

Speaker	**Fee per Speaking Engagement**
CNN's Ted Turner	$ 35,000
Feminist writer, Gloria Steinem	15,000
Novelist Stephen King	20,000
Actress Diana Rigg	12,500
Comic writer Dave Barry	10,000
TV interviewer Barbara Walters	25,000
Conservative Jeane Kirkpatrick	20,000
Comedian Bob Hope	100,000
Former First Lady Rosalynn Carter	20,000
Football commentator John Madden	35,000
TV interviewer Jane Pauley	25,000

So, all you need to do is brush your teeth, get a good night's sleep, and practice your speechmaking skills day after day. Who says that talk is cheap?

From Matthew Connor, "Lecture Fees of the Rich and Famous," *Forbes FYI* (1992): 74–77.

Most of the advice in this textbook pertains to extemporaneous speaking. Extemporaneous speeches are nearly as polished as memorized ones, but they are more vigorous, flexible, and spontaneous.

Before giving an extemporaneous speech, you must plan and prepare a detailed outline and speaking notecards. Then, working from the notecards, you practice the speech aloud, using your own words to communicate the ideas. Your expressions differ somewhat each time you deliver the speech. Your notes, however, regulate the order of ideas. With this approach, you gain control of the material and also preserve your spontaneity of expression. Good preparation is the key to extemporaneous speaking. Otherwise, your speech may resemble an impromptu speech; in fact, the terms *impromptu* and *extemporaneous* are often confused.

You'll use all four types of speech presentation for different occasions during your lifetime, but extemporaneous speaking is the most important.

USING YOUR VOICE TO COMMUNICATE

Your voice is an instrument that helps convey the meaning of language. Since prehistoric (preliterate) times, when all cultures were oral, voice has been the primary connector between people. Sounds flow from a mouth to many ears; sounds integrate people, creating a sense of identification, of community.[1] Although you've been speaking for years, you've probably not tapped the potential of your voice—its power to connect you with others. You'll need to take time to practice in order to achieve your vocal potential, just as you would to master any instrument. The suggestions in this section will help you to get started.

• The most successful speakers of our time possess the quality of conversationality. What is conversationality?

You communicate your enthusiasm to your listeners through your voice. By learning about the characteristics of vocal quality, you can make your ideas more interesting. Listen to a stock market reporter rattle off the daily industrial averages. Every word might be intelligible, but the reporter's vocal expression may be so repetitive and monotonous that the ideas seem unexciting. Then, listen to Al Michael doing a play-by-play of a football game or Dick Vitale covering a basketball game. The excitement of their broadcasts depends largely on their use of voice.

Our society prizes one essential vocal quality above all others—a sense of "conversationality."[2] The conversational speaker creates a sense of two-way, interpersonal relationship, even when behind a lectern. The best hosts of afternoon talk shows or evening newscasts speak as though they're engaging each listener in a personal conversation. Speakers who've developed a conversational quality— Geraldo Rivera, Oprah Winfrey, Dick Cavett, Joan Lunden, and Regis Filbin, for example—have recognized that they're talking *with,* not *at,* an audience.

The Effective Speaking Voice

Successful speakers use their voices to shape their ideas and emotionally color their messages. A flexible speaking voice has intelligibility, variety, and understandable stress patterns.

Intelligibility

Intelligibility refers to the ease with which a listener can understand what you're saying and is dependent upon loudness, rate, enunciation, and pronunciation. Most of the time, inadequate articulation, a rapid speaking rate, or soft volume is acceptable because you know the people you're talking with and because you're probably only 3–5 feet from them. In public speaking, however, you may be addressing people you don't know, often from 25 feet or more away. When speaking in public, you have to work on making yourself intelligible:

1. *Adjust your volume.* Probably the most important single factor in intelligibility is how loudly you speak. Volume is related to the *distance* between you and your listeners and the amount of *noise* that is present. You must realize that your own voice sounds louder to you than it does to your listeners. Obviously, you need to project your voice by increasing your volume if you're speaking in an auditorium filled with several hundred people. However, you shouldn't forget that a corresponding reduction in volume is also required when your listeners are only a few feet away. The amount of surrounding noise with which you must compete also has an effect on your volume. (See Figure 10.1.)

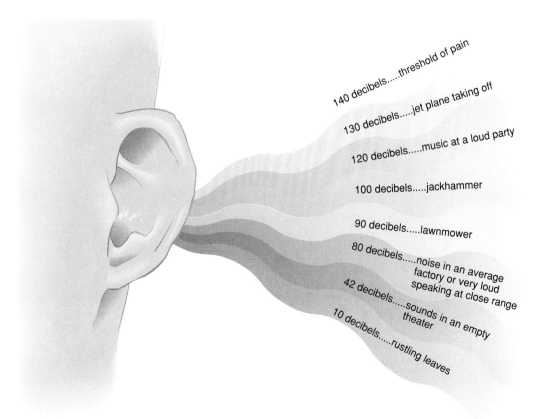

140 decibels.....threshold of pain

130 decibels.....jet plane taking off

120 decibels.....music at a loud party

100 decibels.....jackhammer

90 decibels.....lawnmower

80 decibels.....noise in an average factory or very loud speaking at close range

42 decibels.....sounds in an empty theater

10 decibels.....rustling leaves

FIGURE 10.1 Loudness Levels   As you can see, noise varies considerably. How could you adjust your volume if you were speaking to a "quiet" audience? What if you were competing with a lawnmower outside the building?

2. *Control your rate.* **Rate** is the number of words spoken per minute. In animated conversation, you may jabber along at 200–250 words per minute. This rate is typical of people raised in the North, Midwest, or West. As words tumble out of your mouth in informal conversations, they're usually intelligible because they don't have to travel far. In large auditoriums or outdoors, though, rapid delivery can impede intelligibility. Echoes sometimes distort or destroy sounds in rooms; ventilation fans interfere with sound. In the outdoors, words seem to vanish into the open air.

When addressing larger audiences, cut your rate by a third or more. Obviously you don't go around timing your speaking rate, but you can remind yourself of potential rate problems as you prepare to speak. Get feedback from your instructors and classmates regarding your speaking rate.

3. *Enunciate clearly.* **Enunciation** refers to the crispness and precision with which you form words. Good enunciation is the clear and distinct utterance of syllables and words. Most of us are "lip lazy" in normal conversation. We slur sounds, drop syllables, and skip over the beginnings and endings of words. This laziness may not inhibit communication between friends, but it can seriously undermine a speaker's intelligibility.

When speaking publicly, force yourself to say *going* instead of *go-in, just* instead of *jist,* and *government* instead of *guvment.* You will need to open your mouth wider and force your lips and tongue to form the consonants firmly. If you're having trouble enunciating clearly, ask your instructor for some exercises to improve your performance. (See "Speaking of . . . Vocal Exercises.")

4. *Meet standards of pronunciation.* To be intelligible, you must form sounds carefully and meet audience expectations regarding acceptable pronunciation. Even if your words aren't garbled, any peculiarity of pronunciation is sure to be noticed by some listeners. Your different pronunciation may distract your listeners and undermine your credibility as a speaker.

A **dialect** is language use—including vocabulary, grammar, and pronunciation—unique to a particular group or region. Your pronunciation and grammatical or syntactical arrangement of words determine your dialect. You may have a foreign accent, a white southern or black northern dialect, a New England twang, or a Hispanic trill. A clash of dialects can result in confusion and frustration for both speaker and listener. Audiences can make negative judgments about the speaker's credibility—that is, the speaker's education, reliability, responsibility, and capacity for leadership—based solely on dialect.[3] Paralinguists call these judgments *vocal stereotypes.*[4] Wary of vocal stereotypes, many news anchors have adopted a midwestern American dialect, a manner of speaking that is widely accepted across the country. Many speakers become bilingual, using their own dialects when facing local audiences but switching to midwestern American when addressing more varied audiences. When you speak, you'll have to decide whether you should use the grammar, vocabulary, and vocal patterns of middle America. The language of your audience is the primary factor to consider.

Variety

As you move from conversations with friends to the enlarged context of public speaking, you may discover that listeners accuse you of monotony of pitch or rate. When speaking in a large public setting, you should compensate for the greater distance that sounds have to travel by varying certain characteristics of your voice. Variety is produced by changes in rate, pitch, stress, and pauses.

1. *Vary your rate.* Earlier, we discussed the rate at which we normally speak. Alter your speaking rate to match your ideas. Slow down to emphasize your own thoughtfulness or quicken the pace when your ideas are emotionally charged. Observe, for example, how Larry King varies his speaking rate from caller to caller or how an evangelist changes pace regularly. A varied rate keeps an audience's attention riveted to the speech.

2. *Change your pitch.* **Pitch** is the frequency of sound waves in a particular sound. Three aspects of pitch—level, range, and variation—are relevant to effective vocal communication. Your everyday or **optimum pitch level**— whether it is habitually in the soprano, alto, tenor, baritone, or bass range— is adequate for most of your daily communication needs.

The key to successful control of pitch depends on understanding the importance of **pitch variation.** As a general rule, use higher pitches to communicate excitement and lower pitches to create a sense of control or solemnity. Adjust the pitch to fit the emotion.

Stress

A third aspect of vocal behavior is stress. **Stress** is the way in which sounds, syllables, and words are accented. Without vocal stress, you'd sound like a computer. Vocal stress is achieved in two ways—through vocal emphasis and through the judicious use of pauses.

Use Vocal Emphasis. Emphasis is the way that you accent or attack words. You create emphasis principally through increased volume, changes in pitch, or variations in rate. Emphasis can affect the meanings of your sentences. Notice how the meaning of "Tom's taking Jane out for pizza tonight" varies with changes in word emphasis:

1. "TOM's taking Jane out for pizza tonight." (Tom, and not John or Bob, is taking Jane out.)

2. "Tom's taking JANE out for pizza tonight." (He's not taking out Sue.)

3. "Tom's taking Jane OUT for pizza tonight." (They're not staying home as usual.)

4. "Tom's taking Jane out for PIZZA tonight." (They're not having seafood or hamburgers.)

5. "Tom's taking Jane out for pizza TONIGHT." (They're going out tonight, not tomorrow or next weekend.)

A lack of vocal stress not only gives the impression that you are bored but also causes misunderstandings of your meaning. Changes in rate can also be used to add emphasis. Relatively simple changes can emphasize where you are in an outline: "My s-e-c-o-n-d point is. . . ." Several changes in rate can indicate the relationship among ideas. Consider the following example:

> *We are a country faced with . . . [moderate rate] financial deficits, racial tensions, an energy crunch, a crisis of morality, environmental depletion, government waste . . . [fast rate], and - a- stif - ling - na - tion - al - debt [slow rate].*

The ideas pick up speed through the accelerating list of problems but then come to an emphatic halt with the speaker's main concern, the national debt. Such variations in rate emphasize for an audience what is and what isn't especially important to the speech.

Use Helpful Pauses. Pauses are the intervals of silence between or within words, phrases, or sentences. When placed immediately before a key idea or before the climax of a story, they can create suspense: "And the winner is [pause]!" When placed after a major point, pauses can add emphasis, as in: "And who on this campus earns more than the president of the university? The football coach [pause]!" Inserted at the proper moment, a dramatic pause can express feelings more forcefully than words. Clearly, silence can be a highly effective communicative tool if used intelligently and sparingly and if not embarrassingly prolonged.

Sometimes, speakers fill silences in their discourse with sounds: *um, ah, er, well-ah, you-know,* and other meaningless fillers. Undoubtedly, you've heard speakers say, "Today, ah, er, I would like, you know, to speak to you, um, about a pressing, well-uh, like, a pressing problem facing this, uh, campus." Such vocal intrusions convey feelings of hesitancy and a lack of confidence. Make a concerted effort to remove these intrusions from your speech. Also avoid too many pauses and those that seem artificial, because they can make you appear manipulative or overrehearsed.

On the other hand, don't be afraid of silences. Pauses allow you to stress important ideas, such as the punch line in a story or argument. Pauses also intensify the involvement of listeners in emotional situations, such as when Barbara Walters or William F. Buckley, Jr., pause for reflection during an interview.

Controlling the Emotional Quality

A listener's judgment of a speaker's personality and emotional commitment often centers on that speaker's vocal quality—the fullness or thinness of the tones and whether the sound is harsh, husky, mellow, nasal, breathy, or resonant. Depending on your vocal quality, an audience may judge you as being angry, happy, confident, fearful, sincere, or sad.

Fundamental to a listener's reaction to vocal quality are **emotional characterizers,** cues about a speaker's emotional state. These cues include laughing, crying, whispering, inhaling, or exhaling.[5] Emotional characterizers combine with your words to communicate subtle shades of meaning. Consider for a moment, a few of the many ways you can say, "I can't believe I ate the whole thing." You might say it as though you were reporting a fact, as if you can't believe you ate it *all,* or as though eating the entire thing were an impossible achievement; or

• Effective vocal de-
livery can be impor-
tant in many contexts.
Can you think of other
ways to employ the
characteristics of ef-
fective vocal delivery?

you might say it as though you were expressing doubts about whether you actually did eat the whole thing. As you say the sentence to express these different
meanings, you might laugh or inhale sharply, altering your emotional characterizers. Such changes are important cues to meaning for listeners.

Your vocal qualities are of prime importance in determining the impression
you make on an audience. While you can't completely control your vocal qualities, you can be alert to their effects on your listeners. Keep your repertoire of
vocal qualities in mind as you decide how to express key ideas for an audience.

Vocal Exercises

The instructor's manual that accompanies this textbook has several exercises for voice improvement; your instructor can get it from HarperCollins Publishers. If you or others are concerned about the way you use your voice, those exercises can be most useful. Here's a sample of what you can do:

Breath control. Say the entire alphabet, using only one breath. As you practice, try saying it more and more slowly so as to improve your control of exhalation.

Control of pitch. Sing "low, low, low, low," dropping one note of the musical scale each time you sing the word until you reach the lowest tone you can produce. Then sing your way back up the scale. Now sing "high, high, high, high," going up the scale to the highest note you can reach. Sing your way back down. Go up and down, trying to sense the notes you're most comfortable with—your so-called optimum pitch. Give most of your speeches around your optimum pitch.

Articulatory control. Pronounce each of the following word groups, making sure that each word can be distinguished from the others. Have someone check your accuracy: jest, gist, just; thin, think, thing; roost, roosts, ghost, ghosts; began, begun, begin; wish, which, witch; affect, effect; twin, twain, twine. Or try the following tongue twisters:

- The sixth sheik's sixth sheep's sick.
- Three gray geese in the green grass grazing; gray were the geese and green was the grazing.
- Barry, the baby bunny's born by the blue box bearing rubber baby buggy bumpers.

Practicing Vocal Control

Don't assume that you'll be able to master in a day all of the vocal skills we have described. Take your time to review and digest the ideas presented. Above all, *practice aloud.* Record yourself on tape and then listen to the way you're conveying ideas. Ask your instructor to provide exercises designed to make your vocal instrument more flexible. When you're able to control your voice and make it respond to your desires, you'll have a great deal more control over your effect on listeners. Before any vocal skill can sound natural and be effective with listeners, it must become so automatic that it will work with little conscious effort. Once your voice responds flexibly in the enlarged context of public speaking, you'll be able to achieve the sense of conversationality so highly valued in our society.

USING YOUR BODY TO COMMUNICATE

Just as your voice communicates and shapes meanings through the aural channel, your physical behavior carries messages through the visual channel. You can use both the aural and visual channels to create a better understanding of your presentation. To help you explore the ways of enhancing your use of the visual channel, we'll examine the speaker's physical behavior.

Dimensions of Nonverbal Communication

While some use the phrase *nonverbal communication* to refer to all aspects of interpersonal interaction that are nonlinguistic, we'll focus the discussion here on physical behavior in communication settings. In recent years, research has reemphasized the important role of physical behavior in effective oral communication.[6] Basically, three generalizations about nonverbal communication should guide your speechmaking:

1. *Speakers reveal and reflect their emotional states through their nonverbal behaviors.* Your listeners read your feelings toward yourself, your topic, and your audience from your facial expressions. Consider the contrast between a speaker who walks briskly to the front of the room, head held high, and one who shuffles, head bowed and arms hanging limply. Communication scholar Dale G. Leathers summarized a good deal of research on nonverbal communication processes: "Feelings and emotions are more accurately exchanged by nonverbal than verbal means. . . . The nonverbal portion of communication conveys meanings and intentions that are relatively free from deception, distortion, and confusion."[7]

2. *The speaker's nonverbal cues enrich or elaborate the message that comes through words.* A solemn face reinforces the dignity of a wedding. The words "We must do either *this* or *that*" can be illustrated with appropriate arm-and-hand gestures. Taking a few steps to one side tells an audience that you're moving from one argument to another. A smile enhances your comment on how happy you are to be there.

3. *Nonverbal messages form a reciprocal interaction between speaker and listener.* Listeners frown, smile, shift nervously in their seats, and engage in many types of nonverbal behavior. The physical presence of listeners and the natural tendency of human beings to mirror each other when they're close together mean that nonverbal behavior is a social bonding mechanism. For this chapter, though, we'll concentrate on the speaker's control of physical behavior in four areas: *proxemics, movement and stance, facial expressions,* and *gestures.*

Proxemics

Proxemics is the use of space by human beings. Two components of proxemics, physical arrangement and distance, are especially relevant to public speakers:

Physical arrangements. The layout of the room in which you're speaking, including the presence or absence of a lectern; the seating plan; the location of chalkboards and similar aids; and any physical barriers between you and your audience.

Distance. The extent or degree of separation between you and your audience.[8]

Both of these components have a bearing on the message you communicate publicly. Typical speaking situations involve a speaker facing a seated audience. Objects in the physical space—the lectern, a table, several flags—tend to set the speaker apart from the listeners. This setting apart is both *physical* and *psychological.* Literally as well as figuratively, objects can stand in the way of open communication. If you're trying to create a more informal atmosphere, you should reduce the physical barriers in the setting. You might stand beside or in front of the lectern instead of behind it. In very informal settings, you might even sit on the front edge of a table while talking.

So, what influences your use of physical space?

1. *The formality of the occasion.* The more solemn or formal the occasion, the more barriers will be used; on highly formal occasions, speakers may even speak from an elevated platform or stage.

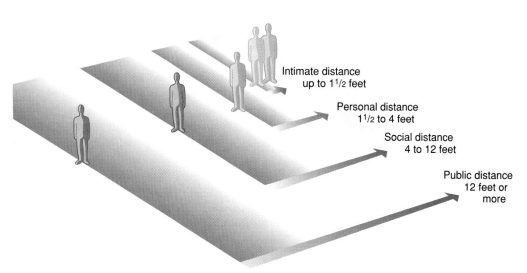

FIGURE 10.2   Classification of Interhuman Distance   Anthropologist Edward T. Hall has identified typical distances for various human interactions. Can you provide an example of communication that might occur at each of the four distances?

2. *The nature of the material.* Extensive quoted material or statistical evidence may require you to use a lectern; the use of visual aids often demands such equipment as an easel, a VCR, or an overhead projector.

3. *Your personal preference.* You may feel more at ease speaking from behind rather than in front of the lectern.

The distance component of proxemics adds a second set of considerations. In most situations, you'll be talking at what anthropologist Edward T. Hall has termed a "public distance"—12 feet or more from your listeners.[9] (See Figure 10.2.) To communicate with people at that distance, you obviously can't rely on your normal speaking voice or subtle changes in posture or movement. Instead, you must compensate for the distance by using larger gestures, broader shifts of your body, and increased vocal energy. By contrast, you should lower your vocal volume and restrict the breadth of your gestures when addressing a few individuals at a closer distance.

Movement and Stance

The ways you move and stand provide a second set of bodily cues for your audience. **Movement** includes physical shifts from place to place; **posture** refers to the relative relaxation or rigidity and vertical position of the body. Movements and posture can communicate ideas about yourself to an audience. The speaker who stands stiffly and erectly may, without uttering a word, be saying, "This is a formal occasion" or "I'm tense, even afraid, of this audience." The speaker who leans forward, physically reaching out to the audience, often is saying silently, "I'm interested in you. I want you to understand and accept my ideas." The speaker who sits casually on the front edge of a table and assumes a relaxed posture may suggest informality and readiness to engage in a dialogue with listeners.

Movements and postural adjustments regulate communication. As a public speaker, you can, for instance, move from one end of a table to the other to indicate a change in topic; or you can accomplish the same purpose by changing your posture. At other times, you can move toward your audience when making an especially important point. In each case, you're using your body to reinforce transitions in your subject or to emphasize a matter of special concern.

But keep in mind that your posture and movements can also work against you. Aimless and continuous pacing is distracting. Nervous bouncing or swaying makes listeners seasick, and an excessively erect stance increases tension in listeners. Your movements should be purposeful and enhance the meaning of your words. Stance and movement can help your communicative effort and produce the impressions of self-assurance and control that you want to exhibit.

Facial Expressions

When you speak, your facial expressions function in a number of ways. First, they communicate much about yourself and your feelings. What researchers Paul Ekman and Wallace V. Friesen call *affect displays* are communicated to an audience through the face. **Affect displays** are facial signals of emotion that an audience perceives when scanning your face to see how you feel about yourself and how you feel about them.[10]

Second, facial changes provide listeners with cues that help them interpret the contents of your message. Are you being ironic or satirical? Are you sure of your conclusions? Is this a harsh or pleasant message? Researchers tell us that a high percentage of the information conveyed in a typical message is communicated nonverbally. Psychologist Albert Mehrabian has devised a formula to account for the emotional impact of the different components of a speaker's message. Words, he says, contribute 7 percent, vocal elements 38 percent, and facial expression 55 percent.[11]

Third, the "display" elements of your face—your eyes, especially—establish a visual bond between you and your listeners. Our culture values eye contact. The speaker who looks people square in the eye is likely to be perceived as earnest, sincere, forthright, and self-assured. In other words, regular eye contact with your listeners helps establish your credibility. Speakers who look at the floor, who read from notes, or who deliver speeches to the back wall sever the visual bond with their audiences and lose credibility.

Of course, you can't control your face completely, which is probably why listeners search it so carefully for clues to your feelings. You can, however, make sure that your facial messages don't belie your verbal ones: when you're uttering angry words, your face should be communicating anger; when you're pleading with your listeners, your eyes should be engaging them intently. In short, let your face mirror your feelings. That's one of the reasons it's there!

Gestures

Gestures are purposeful movements of the head, shoulders, arms, hands, and other areas of the body that support and illustrate the ideas you're expressing. Fidgeting with your clothing and notecards and playing with your hair aren't purposeful gestures. They distract from the ideas you're communicating. The effective public speaker commonly uses three kinds of gestures:

1. *Conventional gestures* are physical movements that are symbols with specific meanings assigned by custom or convention. These gestures *condense* ideas: they are shorthand expressions of things or ideas that would require many words to describe fully. A speaker can use the raised-hand "stop" gesture to interrupt listeners who are drawing premature conclusions or the "V for victory" sign when congratulating them for jobs well done.

2. *Descriptive gestures* are physical movements that describe the idea to be communicated. Speakers often depict the size, shape, or location of an object by movements of the hands and arms; that is, they draw pictures for listeners. You might indicate the size of a box by drawing it in the air with a finger or raise an arm to indicate someone's height.

3. *Indicators* are movements of the hands, arms, or other parts of the body that express feelings. Speakers throw up their arms when disgusted, pound the lectern when angry, shrug their shoulders when puzzled, or point a threatening finger when issuing a warning. Such gestures communicate emotions to your listeners and encourage similar responses in them. Your facial expressions and other body cues usually reinforce such gestures.[12]

You can improve your gestures through practice. As you practice, you'll obtain better results by keeping in mind three factors that influence the effectiveness of gestures: relaxation, vigor and definiteness, and proper timing.

First, if your muscles are tense, your movements will be stiff and your gestures awkward. You should make a conscious effort to relax your muscles before you start to speak. You might warm up by taking a few steps, shrugging your shoulders, flexing your muscles, or breathing deeply.

Second, good gestures are natural and animated. They communicate the dynamism associated with speaker credibility. You should put enough force into your gestures to show your conviction and enthusiasm. Avoid exaggerated or repetitive gestures such as pounding the table or chopping the air to emphasize minor ideas in your speech. Vary the nature of your gestures as the ideas in your speech demand.

Third, timing is crucial to effective gestures. The *stroke* of a gesture—that is, the shake of a fist or the movement of a finger—should fall *on* or slightly before the point the gesture emphasizes. Just try making a gesture after the word or phrase it was intended to reinforce has already been spoken and notice how ridiculous it appears. Practice making gestures until they're habitual, and then use them spontaneously as the impulse arises.

Adapting Nonverbal Behavior to Your Presentations

Although you'll never completely control your physical behavior, you can gain skill in orchestrating your gestures and other movements. You can make some conscious decisions about how you will use your body together with the other channels of communication to communicate effectively.

1. *Plan a proxemic relationship with your audience that reflects your own needs and attitudes toward your subject and your listeners.* If you're comfortable behind a lectern, use it; however, keep in mind that it's a potential barrier between you and your listeners. If you want your whole body to be visible to the audience but you feel the need to have your notes at eye level, stand beside the lectern and arrange your notecards on it. If you want to relax your body, sit behind a table or desk; but compensate for the resulting loss of action by increasing your volume. If you feel relaxed and want to be open to your audience, stand in front of a table or desk. Learn to be yourself while speaking publicly.

Consider your listeners' needs as well. The farther you are from them, the more important it is for them to have a clear view of you, the harder you must work to project your words, and the broader your physical movements must be. The speaker who crouches behind a lectern in an auditorium of 300 people soon loses contact. Think of large lecture classes you've attended or outdoor political rallies you've witnessed. Recall the delivery patterns that worked effectively in such situations. Put them to work for you.

2. *Adapt the physical setting to your communicative needs.* If you're going to use visual aids—such as a chalkboard, flipchart, or working model—remove the tables, chairs, and other objects that might obstruct your audience's view. Increase intimacy by arranging chairs in a small circle or stress formality by using a lectern.

3. *Adapt the size of your gestures and amount of your movement to the size of the audience.* Keeping in mind what Hall noted about public distance in communication, you should realize that subtle changes of facial expression or small hand movements can't be seen clearly in large rooms or auditoriums. Although many auditoriums have a raised platform and a slanted floor to make you more visible, you should adjust to the distance between yourself and your audience by making your movements and gestures larger.

4. *Continuously scan your audience from side to side and from front to back, looking specific individuals in the eye.* Your head should not be in constant motion; *continuously* does not imply rhythmic, nonstop bobbing. Rather, take all your listeners into your field of vision periodically; establish firm vi-

sual bonds with individuals occasionally. Such bonds enhance your credibility and keep your auditors' attention riveted on you.

Some speakers identify three audience members—one to the left, one in the middle, and one to the right—and make sure they regularly move from one to the other of them. For those who don't have trouble moving from side to side, another technique is to do the same thing from front to back, especially if the audience isn't too big. Making sure that you are achieving even momentary eye contact with specific listeners in different parts of the audience creates the sense of visual bonding that you want.

5. *Use your body to communicate your feelings about what you're saying.* When you're angry, don't be afraid to gesture vigorously. When you're expressing tenderness, let that message come across your relaxed face. In other words, when you communicate publicly, use the same emotional indicators as you do when you talk to individuals on a one-to-one basis.

6. *Use your body to regulate the pace of your presentation and to control transitions.* Shift your weight as your speech moves from one idea to another. Move more when you're speaking more rapidly. Reduce bodily action and gestures accordingly when you're slowing down to emphasize particular ideas.

7. *Finally, use your full repertoire of gestures while talking publicly.* You probably do this in everyday conversation without even thinking about it; recreate that behavior when addressing an audience. Physical readiness is the key. Keep your hands and arms free and loose so that you can call them into action easily, quickly, and naturally. Let your hands rest comfortably at your sides, relaxed but ready. Then, as you unfold the ideas of your speech, use descriptive gestures to indicate size, shape, or relationships, making sure the movements are large enough to be seen in the back row. Use conventional gestures also to give visual dimension to your spoken ideas. Keep in mind that there is no right number of gestures to use. However, as you practice, think of the kinds of bodily and gestural actions that complement your message and purpose.

To see someone who adapted his nonverbal behavior to the requirements of the situation, secure a videotape of the second—the so-called Richmond—presidential debate of 1992, which included President George Bush and candidates H. Ross Perot and Bill Clinton. Watch Clinton in particular: he physically moved in on his audience when making his most important and personal points; his gestures were larger when he was seated on a stool than when he was wading into the audience; he visually took in the whole audience and focused intently on the people who asked him questions; his feelings were reflected in his stance; he shifted body positions to indicate shifts in topics. Through much of the 1992 campaign, and in the Richmond debate particularly, President Clinton demonstrated near-perfect coordination of the verbal and nonverbal channels of oral communication.

Selecting the appropriate method of presentation and using your voice and body productively will enhance your chances of gaining support for your ideas. *Practice* is the key to the effective use of these nonverbal elements. Through practice, you'll have an opportunity to see how your voice and body complement or detract from your ideas. The more you prepare and practice, the more confident you'll feel about presenting the speech and the more comfortable you'll be. Remember that the nonverbal channel of communication creates meaning for your audience.

CHAPTER SUMMARY

1. Every speaker should effectively use the aural and visual channels of communication.

2. Begin with an appropriate method of presentation—impromptu, memorized, manuscript, or extemporaneous delivery. Your choice will be based on the type of speaking occasion, the seriousness and purpose of your speech, your audience analysis, and your own strengths and weaknesses as a speaker.

3. Regardless of the method of presentation, a good voice enables a speaker to make a message clearer. A flexible speaking voice has intelligibility, variety, and understandable stress patterns.

4. Volume, rate, enunciation, and pronunciation interact to affect intelligibility.

5. Different standards of pronunciation create regional differences known as *dialects*.

6. Changes in rate, pitch, and stress and pauses create variety in presentation and help eliminate monotonous delivery.

7. Emotional characterizers communicate subtle shades of meaning to listeners.

8. Three generalizations about nonverbal communication are significant: (a) speakers reveal and reflect their emotional states through their nonverbal behaviors; (b) nonverbal cues enrich or elaborate the speaker's message; and (c) nonverbal messages form an interaction between speaker and listener.

9. Speakers knowledgeable about the effects of proxemics can use space to create physical and psychological intimacy or distance. A speaker's movement and posture regulate communication.

10. Facial expressions communicate feelings, provide important cues to meaning, establish a visual bond with listeners, and establish speaker credibility.

11. Gestures enhance listener response to messages if the gestures are relaxed, definite, and properly timed.

12. Speakers commonly use conventional gestures, descriptive gestures, and indicators.

KEY TERMS

affect displays (p. 187)
dialect (p. 180)
emotional characterizers (p. 182)
emphasis (p. 181)
enunciation (p. 180)
extemporaneous speech (p. 176)
gesture (p. 188)
impromptu speech (p. 175)
manuscript speech (p. 176)

memorized speech (p. 175)
movement (p. 187)
optimum pitch level (p. 181)
pitch (p. 181)
pitch variation (p. 181)
posture (p. 187)
proxemics (p. 185)
rate (p. 180)
stress (p. 181)

SKILLBUILDING ACTIVITIES

1. Divide the class into teams and play charades. For rules, see David Jauner, "Charades as a Teaching Device," *Speech Teacher* 20 (1971): 302. A game of charades not only will loosen you up psychologically but should help sensitize you to the variety of small but perceptible cues you read when interpreting messages.

2. Form small task groups. Appoint a member of the group to record ideas and then think of as many situations as possible in which each of the four methods of speaking would be used. Choose a reporter to convey the group's examples to the class.

3. Choose a selection from a poetry anthology and practice reading it aloud. As you read, change your volume, rate, pitch and emphasis, and use pauses. Practice reading the poem in several ways to heighten different emotions or to emphasize different interpretations. Record your reading of the poem on tape and play it back to evaluate it, or ask a friend to listen and offer suggestions.

REFERENCES

1. For a fascinating discussion of oral speech's communal powers—of its "psychodynamics"—see Chapter 3 of Walter J. Ong, *Orality and Literacy: The Technologizing of the Word* (London: Methuen, 1982).

2. Thomas Frentz, "Rhetorical Conversation, Time, and Moral Action," *Quarterly Journal of Speech* 71 (1985): 1–18.

3. Mark Knapp, *Essentials of Nonverbal Communication* (New York: Holt, Rinehart & Winston, 1980).

4. Klaus R. Scherer, H. London, and Garret Wolf, "The Voice of Competence: Paralinguistic Cues and Audience Evaluation," *Journal of Research in Personality* 7 (1973): 31–44; Jitendra Thakerer and Howard Giles, "They Are—So They Spoke: Noncontent Speech Stereotypes," *Language and Communication* 1 (1981): 255–261; Peter A. Andersen, Myron W. Lustig, and Janis F. Andersen, "Regional Patterns of Communication in the United States: A Theoretical Perspective," *Communication Monographs* 54 (1987): 128–144.

5. Bruce L. Brown, William J. Strong, and Alvin C. Rencher, "Perceptions of Personality from Speech: Effects of Manipulations of Acoustical Parameters," *Journal of the Acoustical Society of America* 54 (1973): 29–35.

6. Much of the foundational research is summarized in Mark L. Knapp, *Nonverbal Communication in Human Interaction,* 2nd ed. (New York: Holt, Rinehart & Winston, 1978).

7. Dale G. Leathers, *Nonverbal Communication Systems* (Boston: Allyn & Bacon, 1975), 4–5.

8. For a fuller discussion, see Leathers, 52–59.

9. Hall divides interhuman communication distances into four segments: *intimate distance,* up to 1½ feet apart; *personal distance,* 1½ to 4 feet; *social distance,* 4 to 12 feet; and *public distance,* 12 feet or more. With these distinctions, he has carefully noted how people's eye contact, tone of voice, and ability to touch and observe change from one distance to another. See Edward T. Hall, *The*

Hidden Dimension (New York: Doubleday, 1969), Chapter 10.

10. Paul Ekman, *Emotion in the Human Face,* 2nd ed. (Cambridge: Cambridge Univ. Press, 1982).

11. Robert Rivlin and Karen Gravelle, *Deciphering the Senses: The Expanding World of Human Perception* (New York: Simon & Schuster, 1984), 98. Such numbers, of course, are only formulaic estimates and are important only as proportions of each other.

12. For a more complete system of classifying gestures, see Paul Ekman and Wallace V. Friesen, "Hand Movements," *Journal of Communication* 22 (1972): 360.

Using Visual Aids

The first time he used visual aids in a speech, Chris decided to save a little time and money on visual aids by ordering an opaque projector, which projects pages of a book directly onto a screen. His problems began almost as soon as he arrived in the classroom. First, he nearly gave himself a hernia carrying the projector into the room; he had no idea how heavy it would be. Then, when he turned the projector on, he could barely make himself heard over its noisy cooling fan. Worse yet, as he showed the first graphic, his classmates broke into laughter—the image was upside down. Chris next discovered a more serious problem, that the magnification of an opaque projector is insufficient for the people in the back row to read the graph. After that experience, Chris decided to create computer-generated graphs for his next speech. He transferred the graphs to transparencies and practiced using the overhead projector before his speech. As a result, his presentation was much better. Everyone could see the graphs and hear Chris's explanations. Preparing and practicing ahead of time prevented Chris from making embarrassing mistakes.

From the time you participated in "show and tell" in elementary school to the times when you and your family watched the slides of your vacation, you've included **visual aids** in your communication efforts. Like Chris, you still are communicating visually as a public speaker. Your physical presence in front of an audience makes a powerful visual statement, and your use of visual aids can make visual communication an essential part of the speech transaction. For these reasons, it's important for you to learn more about visual aids.

Your world is filled with visual communication. Television, film, transparencies, VCRs and videotape, overhead projections, billboards, banners trailing from airplanes, and sidewalk tables with store bargains surround you and demand your attention. You live in one of the most visually-oriented societies in the world today. Thousands of companies, from major television and film studios to small-town graphics-production shops in neighborhood basements, thrive on the attention that superior visual communication demands in our society.

Research on visual media, learning, and attitude change has given us a lot of information about the impact of visual aids on audiences.[1] Experienced speakers have offered additional advice. In this chapter, we'll combine what we've learned from social-scientific research with wisdom from the professionals. First, we'll focus on the functions of visual aids; then we'll examine the various types of visual aids and explore ways to use them effectively.

THE FUNCTIONS OF VISUAL AIDS

Visual aids are those materials that rely primarily upon sight. Visual materials enhance your presentation in two ways: (a) they aid listener comprehension and memory and (b) they add persuasive impact to your message.

Comprehension and Memory

The old saying "A picture's worth a thousand words" seems especially true if the picture adds information that's easily understood visually. We understand ideas better and remember them longer if we see them as well as hear them. Research has demonstrated that bar graphs are especially effective at making statistical information more accessible to listeners. Charts and human-interest visuals, such as photographs, have proven to help listeners process and retain data.[2] Even simple pictures have had significant effects on children's recall and comprehension during storytelling.[3] Visuals can be immensely valuable if your purpose is to inform or teach an audience. Visuals make information easier to understand, retain, and recall.

Persuasion

In addition to enhancing comprehension and memory, visuals can heighten the persuasive impact of your ideas because they engage listeners actively in the communicative exchange. Lawyers, for example, aware of the dramatic persuasive effects of visuals, often include visual evidence such as photographs of injuries or diagrams of crime scenes in their cases in order to sway the opinions of juries. Some lawyers even have experimented with the use of video technology to create dramatic portrayals of events in order to influence jury decisions; for example, by showing the dangerous traffic flow of an intersection in a vehicular homicide case.

Undeniably, your credibility and your persuasiveness are enhanced by good visuals.[4] By satisfying the "show-me" attitude prevalent among listeners, visual materials provide a crucial means of meeting listener expectations.[5]

TYPES OF VISUAL SUPPORT

There are many different types of visual materials. Depending upon your speech topic and purpose, you may choose one or several types of visual support. We will discuss each type and examine specific approaches to using it to supplement your oral presentations.

Actual Objects

You can often bring to a presentation the actual objects you're discussing. Live animals or plants can, under some circumstances, be used to enhance your speeches. If your speech explores the care and feeding of laboratory mice, you can reinforce your ideas by bringing to the speech one or two mice in a properly equipped cage. Describing the differences between two varieties of plants may be easier if you demonstrate the differences with real plants. Discretion and common sense will help make such visuals work *for* you rather than *against* you. You might be stretching your luck, for example, by bringing a real horse into the classroom to demonstrate saddling techniques or by bringing an untrained puppy to accomplish paper training.

Using the **actual object** should focus audience attention on your speech, not serve as a distraction. A speech about scuba diving is enhanced by a display of the essential equipment. A speech about the best way to repair rust holes in an automobile fender is clarified by samples of the work in stages. Cooking or house remodeling demonstrations are enlivened with samples prepared before the presentation, since the presenter usually doesn't have time to perform the actual work during the presentation.

You can use your own body to add concreteness and vitality to your presentation. You might, for example, demonstrate yoga positions, warm-up exercises, ballet steps, or tennis strokes during your speech. Remember to control the experience. Make sure that everyone, even people in the back rows, can see you. Demonstrate a yoga position on a sturdy tabletop rather than on the floor. Slow the tempo of a tennis stroke so that the audience can see any intricate action and subtle movements. One advantage of properly controlled visual action is that with it you can control the audience's attention to your demonstration. You also should dress appropriately. A senior nursing major might add credibility by wearing a uniform when demonstrating CPR, and an aerobics instructor can wear a leotard and tights. Of course, the clothing should not substitute for a clearly visible demonstration of CPR or aerobics.

Photographs and Slides

Sometimes, when you can't bring the actual object to the location of your speech, you can still show your audience what it's like by using photographs. Photographs can give the audience a visual sense of your topic. For example, photos can illustrate flood damage to ravaged homes or depict the beauty of a wooded area threatened by a new shopping mall. Make sure that your audience is able to see details from a distance. You can enlarge photos or use slides so that people can see them more easily. Avoid passing small photos through the audience, because such activity is disruptive. The purpose of a visual aid is to draw the attention of all members of the audience simultaneously.

Like photographs, slides (35mm transparencies) allow you to depict color, shape, texture, and relationships. It is also easier to show many slides than many photographs. If you're presenting a travelogue, you may use slides to show your audience the buildings and landscape of the region. If you're giving a speech on the history of the steam engine, you can use slides to show various steam engines in operation. If you're speaking against the construction of a dam, you can enhance your persuasiveness by showing slides of the whitewater that will be disrupted by the dam. If you're discussing stylistic differences among famous artists, you may wish to show slides of art works from the Baroque and Neoclassical periods.

Using slides requires familiarity with projection equipment. It also requires some forethought about the setup of the presentation. Have you loaded the slides in the cartridge correctly? Will you speak from the front of the room or from next to the projector? Will your voice carry over the noise of the projector? Do you know how to change the projection lamp? Did you bring along a spare bulb just in case? Will you need an extension cord? Do you know how to remove a jammed slide? Attention to small, seemingly inconsequential details like these will make a major difference in how smoothly the presentation goes. If you operate on the assumption that whatever can go wrong will, you'll be prepared to solve most problems.

Videotapes and Films

Videotapes and films also can be useful in illustrating your points. Videotaped segments from several current soap operas can dramatically reinforce your claim that minorities are underrepresented in daytime television. Two or three video-taped political ads can help you illustrate methods for packaging a candidate. As with all projection equipment, familiarity with the operation of a videocassette recorder or film projector ensures a smooth presentation. Make sure that you can operate the equipment properly and quickly. Delays increase your nervousness and detract from your presentation.

Chalkboard Drawings

Chalkboard drawings are especially valuable when you want to present an idea step by step. By drawing each step as you discuss it, you can center the audience's attention on your major points. Coaches often use this approach when showing players how to execute particular plays. Timelines and size comparison diagrams also can be sketched on a chalkboard. To visually represent the history of the civil rights movement in the United States, you can create a timeline that illustrates key events, such as the arrival of the first slaves in Jamestown, the Emancipation Proclamation, and the 1965 Voting Rights Act.

Whether or not you use drawings will depend on the formality of the situation. If you're brainstorming ideas for building renovation with a prospective client, quick sketches may suffice. However, if you're meeting with the client's board of directors, the same rough drawings will be inadequate. The board will expect a polished presentation, complete with a professionally prepared prospectus. Similarly, chalkboard drawings may be sufficient to explain cell division to a group of classmates, but when presenting the same information as part of a science fair project, you need refined visual support materials. The care with which you prepare these visuals will convey to your audience an attitude of either indifference or concern.

• Photographs and models provide realistic and colorful details of objects. Diagrams focus attention on specific parts of the object. Which of these visual aids would you use in a speech on sailboats? What advantages does each offer?

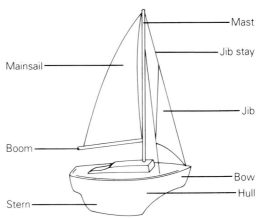

Overhead Projections

You can use an overhead projector just as you would use a chalkboard, to illustrate points as you talk. However, an overhead projector offers some advantages over a chalkboard: you can turn it off when you've made your point, thus removing any distraction from your message. Another advantage is that you can uncover one part of a transparency at a time, keeping the remainder covered so as to control the flow of information. Finally, you can prepare transparencies before the speech, giving them a more professional appearance than chalkboard drawings. During the speech you can point to the transparency or add to it to emphasize your claims.

Ethical Moments

. . . .

Video in the Courtroom

The use of videotaped materials in the courtroom has become increasingly frequent since it was first used to record witness depositions or testimony more than 20 years ago. Recently, videotape played a crucial role in the Rodney King trial. It also created strong public debate following the beating of truck driver Reginald Denny during the Los Angeles riots. In both cases, jurors carefully examined videotaped evidence.

We now know that videotape affects how we comprehend information. For example, jurors who view black-and-white videotaped recordings retain more information than jurors who see color videotape or a live witness; witnesses videotaped in color are judged more credible by jurors than witnesses taped in black and white; and jurors who view videotape remember the information they see longer than jurors who watch a live trial.

Considering this, do you think videotape can change the outcome of a trial? Should regulations be placed on the use of videotape in legal settings? Can you think of other ways videotape could influence communication?

For more research results, see: G. R. Miller and N. Fontes, *Videotape on Trial* (Beverly Hills, Calif.: Sage, 1979) and Jarice Hanson, *Understanding Video: Applications, Impact, and Theory* (Newbury Park, Calif.: Sage, 1987.)

When you're using either a chalkboard or an overhead projector, be aware of your technique. First, make your drawings large enough so that the audience can see them. Second, continue to talk to the audience as you draw. Your audience's attention may wander if you ignore them while drawing. They may also get bored if you talk to the chalkboard or to the light source. Third, be sure to stand where you do not block the audience's view of your visuals. Fourth, when you're through talking about the illustration, erase it or turn off the projector.

Graphs

Graphs show relationships among various parts of a whole or between variables across time. Graphs are especially effective for representing numerical data. There are several types of graphs:

1. **Bar graphs** show the relationships between two or more sets of figures (see Figure 11.1). Research has demonstrated that plain bar graphs are the most effective method for displaying statistical comparisons,[6] perhaps because bar graphs represent numbers in a visual form. If you were illustrating the difference between lawyers' and doctors' incomes or between male lawyers' and female lawyers' incomes, you would probably use a bar graph.

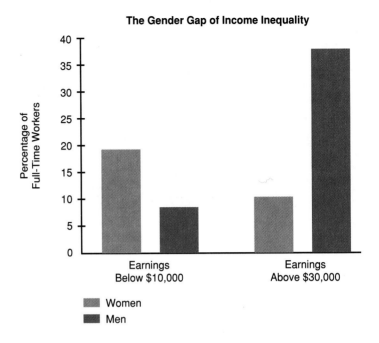

FIGURE 11.1
Bar Graph
Bar graphs illustrate
relationships.

2. **Line graphs** show relationships between two or more variables, usually over time (see Figure 11.2). If you were trying to explain a complex economic correlation between supply and demand, you would use a line graph.

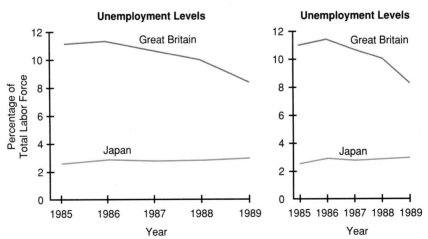

FIGURE 11.2   Line Graph   Line graphs can reveal relationships, but they can also deceive the unwary. These graphs show the same data but use different spacing along the axes to change the visual image.

3. **Pie graphs** show percentages by dividing a circle into the proportions being represented (see Figure 11.3). A speaker raising funds for a charitable organization could use a pie graph to show how much of its income was spent on administration, research, and aid to the needy. Mayors use pie graphs to show citizens what proportion of their tax dollars go to municipal services, administration, education, recreation, and law enforcement.

FIGURE 11.3
Pie Graph
Pie graphs dramatize relationships among a limited number of segments. Ideally, a pie graph should have from two to five segments. A pie graph should never have more than eight segments.

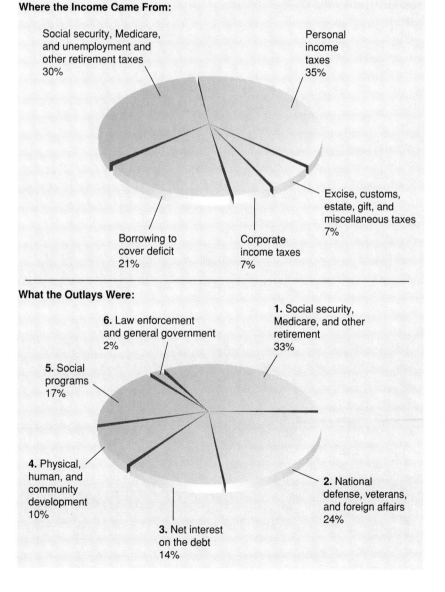

Federal Government Income and Expenditures

Where the Income Came From:

Social security, Medicare, and unemployment and other retirement taxes 30%

Personal income taxes 35%

Excise, customs, estate, gift, and miscellaneous taxes 7%

Borrowing to cover deficit 21%

Corporate income taxes 7%

What the Outlays Were:

6. Law enforcement and general government 2%

1. Social security, Medicare, and other retirement 33%

5. Social programs 17%

4. Physical, human, and community development 10%

3. Net interest on the debt 14%

2. National defense, veterans, and foreign affairs 24%

4. **Pictographs** function like bar graphs but use symbols instead of bars to represent size and numbers (see Figure 11.4). A representation of U.S. and Russian grain exports might use a miniature drawing of a wheat shock or an ear of corn to represent 100,000 bushels; this representation would allow a viewer to see at a glance the disparity between the exports of two countries. You can easily create pictographs with computer clip art.

FIGURE 11.4
Pictograph
Speakers with artistic skills can create interesting visual aids, such as this graphic representation of U.S. wine exports.

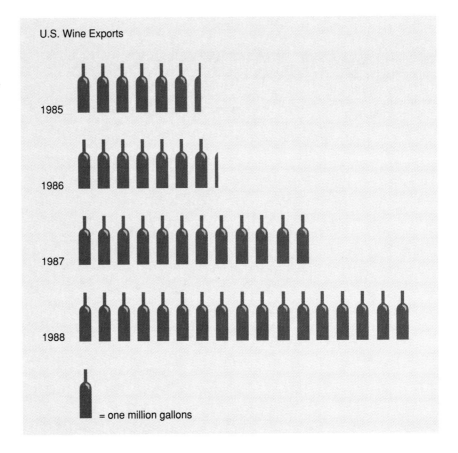

U.S. Wine Exports

1985

1986

1987

1988

= one million gallons

Your choice of bar, line, pie, or pictorial graphs will depend on the subject and the nature of the relationship you wish to convey. A pie graph, for example, can neither easily illustrate discrepancies between two groups nor show change over time. Bar and line graphs do not show the total amount being represented.

Regardless of the type of graph you choose, when you are preparing a graph, you must be very careful not to distort your information. A bar graph can create a misleading impression of the difference between two items if one bar is short and wide while the other is long and narrow. Line graphs can portray very different trends if the units of measurement are not the same for each time period. You can avoid misrepresenting information by using consistent measurements in your graphs and by using a computer to generate your graphs.

Charts and Tables

Charts and tables condense large blocks of information into a single representation. **Tables** present information in parallel columns while **charts** can take a number of varied forms. The Periodical Table of Elements and the E test chart in your optometrist's office are two common charts you've probably seen. Most wage-earners are familiar with the tax tables that accompany the Internal Revenue Service 1040 tax forms. Charts can be used effectively in speeches. For example, if you want to discuss Japan's international trade, you can break down imports and exports on a table. If you want to show a large company's channels of communication or lines of authority, your presentation will be much easier to follow if your listeners have an organizational chart for reference.

There are two special types of charts: **flipcharts** unveil ideas one at a time on separate sheets; **flowcharts** show relationships among ideas or facts on a single sheet. Both flipcharts and flowcharts may include drawings or photos. If you present successive ideas with a flipchart, you'll focus audience attention on specific parts of your speech. In a speech on the Civil War battle at Gettysburg, you could use a separate chart for each day of the battle. If you presented the entire three days on one chart, the chart would become cluttered and your audience might stray from your explanation to read the entire chart. You could also use separate charts to focus on specific assaults in the battle.

You can use a flowchart to indicate the chronological stages of a process; for example, a flowchart will allow audiences to visualize the stages of a fund-raising campaign or the process of smelting iron. You can also use a flowchart to show relationships among ideas or interdependent actions, such as the reactions when a catalyst is added to otherwise stable chemicals. And, of course, you're familiar with organizational flowcharts used by groups to show the relationships among members of the group. In a speech on the passage of a legislative bill, a flowchart would clarify each step of the process.

As long as the information is not too complex or lengthy, tables and charts may be used to indicate changes over time and to rank or list items and their costs, frequency of use, or relative importance. Tables and charts should be designed so that they can be seen and so that they convey data simply and clearly. Too much information will force the audience to concentrate more on the visual support than on your oral explanation. For example, a dense chart, showing all the major and minor offices of a company, may simply overwhelm listeners as they try to follow your explanation. If the organization is too complex, you may want to develop a series of charts, each one focusing on a smaller unit of information.

Models

Models can dramatize your explanations. **Models** are reduced or enlarged scale replicas of real objects. Architects construct models of new projects to show clients. Developers of shopping malls, condominiums, and business offices use models when persuading zoning boards to grant needed rights-of-way or variances. You can use models of genes to accompany your explanation of gene splicing. As with other visual aids, models need to be manageable and visible to the audience. You can increase listener interest if you use a model that comes apart so that different pieces can be examined. Be sure to practice removing and replacing the parts before your speech.

STRATEGIES FOR SELECTING AND USING VISUAL AIDS

Your decision about which visual aids will work best for you should be based on four considerations: (a) the characteristics of the audience and occasion, (b) the communicative potential of various visual materials, (c) your ability to integrate verbal and visual materials effectively, and (d) the potential of computer-generated visual materials.

Consider the Audience and Occasion

Before you choose your visual aids, common sense will tell you to consider what your listeners already know about your subject. Do you need to bring a map of the United States to an audience of college students when discussing the westward movement of the population in this country? If you're going to discuss a football team's offensive and defensive formations, should you provide diagrams of the formations for your listeners? Can you expect an audience to understand the administrative structure of the federal bureaucracy without providing an organizational chart?

How readily an audience can comprehend aurally what you have to say is another more difficult question to consider. It may be quite difficult, for example, to decide what your classmates know about governmental structures or what Rotary Club members know about football plays. Probably the best thing you can do is to check out your speculations by speaking with several of your potential listeners well ahead of your speech. In other words, before making any final decisions about visual supporting materials, do as much audience research as you possibly can.

As part of your preparation for using visuals, take into account the nature of the speaking occasion. Certain occasions demand certain types of visual support materials. The corporate executive who presents a report of projected future profits to the board of directors without a printed handout or diagram will probably find his or her credibility questioned. The military adviser who calls for governmental expenditures for new weapons without offering pictures or drawings of the proposed weapons and printed technical data on their operation is not likely to be a convincing advocate. An athletic coach without a chalkboard may succeed only in confusing team members at half-time. Plan ahead to supply the visual media demanded by the situation. If the speaking occasion doesn't appear to require certain visual supports, analyze the occasion further for different visual possibilities. Use your imagination. Be innovative. Don't overlook opportunities to make your speech more meaningful, more exciting, and more interesting for your listeners.

Consider the Communicative Potential of Various Visual Aids

Keep in mind that each type of visual aid is best at communicating a particular kind of information. Each visual also must blend with your spoken presentation as well as with your audience. In general, pictorial or photographic visuals can make an audience *feel* the way you do. For example, you can use slides, movies,

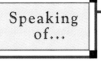

Speaking of...

Using Visual Aids in Business

It's wise to use visual aids when developing a professional presentation for a client or business meeting. Research has shown that visual aids are effective tools for three reasons. First, visual aids can make your presentation more persuasive. Second, they enhance your audience's estimate of your credibility and appearance of professionalism. Third, presenters using visual aids require less meeting time to achieve their results. Overall, it makes good sense to incorporate visual aids in your presentations.

sketches, or photographs of your travels in Indonesia to accompany a travelogue. Such visual aids stimulate your audience to share in the awe that you experienced at the beauty of the landscape. If you show slides of hospitalized victims in war-torn Bosnia, you are likely to gain an emotional response. Such a response can maximize your efforts to persuade your listeners.

Visuals containing descriptive or written materials, on the other hand, can help an audience *think* the way you do. For example, models, diagrams, charts, and graphs about the population and economy of Indonesia may persuade your listeners to conclude that the United States should send more foreign aid to Indonesia. A timeline representing ethnic conflicts in Eastern Europe can help your listeners understand the historial context of modern fighting in the region. Such visual aids encourage understanding and thought rather than emotional responses.

Integrate Verbal and Visual Materials Effectively

To be effective, your visual aids should complement your spoken message. Visuals should save time, enhance the impact of your speech, clarify complex relations, and generally enliven your presentation. Consider the following suggestions for getting the maximum benefit from your visuals:

1. *Use color to create interest.* Use contrasting colors (red on white, black on yellow) to highlight information in an organizational chart or to differentiate segments of a pie graph or bars in a bar graph. As a rule, color commands attention better than black and white.

2. *Keep visual aids clear and simple.* This is especially important for charts and other graphic devices. Make essential information stand out clearly from the background. Let simplicity guide your preparation.

3. *Make your visuals large enough to be seen easily.* Listeners get frustrated when they must lean forward and squint in order to see detail in a visual aid. Make your figures and lettering large enough so that everyone can see them. Follow the example of John Hancock who, when signing the Declaration of

Independence in 1776, wrote his name large enough to "be seen by the King of England without his glasses."

4. *Make your visuals neat.* Draw neatly, spell correctly, make lines proportional, and make letters symmetrical. Such advice may seem unnecessary, but too often beginning speakers throw together visual materials at the last minute. They forget that their visual aids also contribute to audiences' assessment of their credibility. Misspelled words and sloppy graphs will lower listeners' estimation of your competence.

5. *Decide how to handle your visual aids in advance.* Decide on a visual aid and practice with it well in advance, especially for demonstration speeches. Suppose you want to demonstrate tombstone dabbing or making paper casts of old tombstone faces. Tombstones are heavy. Should you bring one to class? How can you hold it up while you talk? Tombstone dabbing is very messy. Should you actually use the chemicals to clean the stone's surface? Should you actually show your classmates the various dabbing techniques? How can you demonstrate dabbing so that everyone can see it? How much of the process should you show? Unless you think through such questions in advance, you may find yourself making poor decisions during the speech.

6. *Compensate orally for any distraction your visual aid may create.* Remember that you must compete with your visual aid for your listeners' attention. Listeners may find the visual aid so intriguing that they miss part of your message. You can partially compensate for any potential distraction by building reiteration into your speech. By repeating your main ideas you can be reasonably certain that your listeners will follow your thoughts. As added insurance, you also might keep your visual aid out of sight until you need to use it.

7. *Coordinate slides, films, overhead projections, or videotapes with your verbal message.* Mechanical or electronic messages can easily distract your listeners. You need to talk louder and move move vigorously when using a machine to communicate, or you need to show the film or slides either *before* or *after* you comment on their content. Whatever strategy you choose, make sure that your visual materials are well integrated into your oral presentation. That is, use transitions that integrate your visual aids with the speech. If you are using a chart, you might say, "This chart shows you what I've been saying about the lines of communication in organizations. . . ." Also indicate where you obtained the information represented on the chart and summarize the information before you go on to your next idea.

8. *Hand your listeners a copy of the materials you wish them to reflect on after your speech.* If you're making recommendations to a student council, you should provide copies of your proposal for the council's subsequent action. Or if you're reporting the results of a survey, your listeners will better digest the most pertinent statistics if you give each audience member a copy of them. Few people can recall the seven warning signs of cancer, but they might keep a wallet-sized list handy if you provide it. Of course, you would not duplicate your entire speech, you would select only those items with lasting value.

Ethical Moments

Can Pictures Lie?

Can pictures lie? Aren't they each worth a thousand words? Isn't seeing believing? Isn't showing better than telling? Not necessarily—especially in today's visually centered world. Consider:

- Hopes of finding American soldiers missing in action in Vietnam (MIAs) were briefly inspired by photos that seemed to show the Americans holding signs that displayed current dates. Those pictures turned out to have been faked.

- During the 1992 campaign, political action committees (PACs) ran ads that showed Bill Clinton holding hands in victory with Ted Kennedy on the Democratic Convention stage. What the PAC had done was put a picture of Kennedy's head on Vice President Al Gore's body.

- During the 1988 campaign, another PAC ran an ad whose text included these words: "As governor, Michael Dukakis vetoed mandatory sentences for drug dealers. He vetoed the death penalty. His revolving-door prison policy gave weekend furloughs to first-degree murderers not eligible for parole. While out, many committed other crimes like kidnapping and rape. And many are still at large. Now Michael Dukakis says he wants to do for America what he's done for Massachusetts." The pictures accompanying those statements showed: (1) the sun setting over a prison with guards in the watchtowers; (2) a revolving gate where prisoners, many representing minorities, presumably were being let out as quickly as they were being put in; and, (3) guards standing watch over empty prisons at night—when crime increases.

Thanks to digital editing, you now can easily add to or subtract from pictures, printing the altered photos so cleanly that the forgery is almost impossible to detect. Pictures can be altered to "say" something that isn't true. Or, they can add images that transform the meanings of words. The visual dimension can be helpful to both speaker and audience when it is used in morally defensible ways. It can be destructive of the truth when it's not.

These suggestions should enable you to take advantage of the communicative potential of visual media. Good visual aids don't detract from your message. Instead, they fit your ideas and leave the audience with a feeling of completeness.

Evaluate Computer-Generated Visual Materials

You can tap into the expanding world of computer graphics when you prepare your visual aids. While you may not be able to produce results similar to those on the latest televised football game, you can still use readily available computer-generated visual materials. Computers are very effective when processing numerical data and converting them into bar, line, and pie graphs. As with other types of visual aids, you should choose the computer graphics that fit your pur-

● Computer-generated visual aids can enhance your credibility by giving your presentation a professional quality. What should you do to ensure well-prepared computer-generated visual aids?

pose, physical setting, and audience needs. Here are some suggestions for ways to use such materials:

1. *Use computer graphics to create an atmosphere.* It's easy to make computer banners with block lettering and pictures. Hang a banner in the front of the room to set a mood or establish a theme. For example, a student urging her classmates to get involved in a United Way fund-raising drive created a banner with the campaign slogan, "Thanks to you, it works for all of us." Initially, the banner captured attention; during the speech the banner reinforced the theme.

2. *Enlarge small computer-generated diagrams.* Most computer diagrams are too small to be seen easily by an audience. You can use a photo duplicating machine that enlarges images to make a more visible diagram. Computer diagrams can also be transferred to overhead transparencies or slides.

3. *Enhance the computer-generated image in other ways.* Use markers to color pie graphs or to darken the lines of a line graph. Use press-on letters to make headings for your graphs. Convert computer-generated images into slide transparencies for projection during your speech. Mixing media in such ways can give your presentations a professional look. If you have access to

the right technology, you can create three-dimensional images of buildings, machines, or the human body.

CHAPTER SUMMARY

1. Visual aids as a discrete mode, or channel, of communication can aid listener comprehension and memory and add persuasive impact to a speech.
2. There are many types of visual aids: actual objects, photographs and slides, videotapes and films, chalkboard drawings, graphs, charts, and models.
3. Types of graphs include bar, line, pie, and pictographs.
4. Flipcharts unveil ideas one at a time; flowcharts show the entire process on a single sheet.
5. In selecting and using visual aids, consider the audience and the occasion, examine the communicative potential of various visual aids, and find ways to integrate verbal and visual materials effectively.

KEY TERMS

actual objects (p. 196)	line graphs (p. 200)
bar graphs (p. 199)	models (p. 203)
charts (p. 203)	pictographs (p. 202)
flipcharts (p. 203)	pie graphs (p. 201)
flowcharts (p. 203)	tables (p. 203)
graphs (p. 199)	visual aids (p. 194)

SKILLBUILDING ACTIVITIES

1. Plan a short speech explaining or demonstrating a complex process. Choose two different types of visual aids and ask the class to evaluate their effectiveness. You might consider the following processes:
   a. The procedure for gene splicing.
   b. The legislative process for getting a bill signed into law.
   c. The genetic inheritance of color traits in flowers.
   d. The procedure for rotating automobile tires.
   e. The pattern of jet stream movements.
   f. The composition of photographs.
2. Work in small groups to develop at least three different types of visual aids for three of the following topics. A representative of each group will report to the class as a whole, telling about or showing the proposed visual aids.
   a. How to play a musical instrument.
   b. How to splint a broken arm or leg.
   c. How to assemble a windmill from Legos.
   d. How to do the Australian crawl.
   e. How to cut your utility bill.
   f. How to put in a contact lens.

3. Videotape a television demonstration show and play the videotape in class. Evaluate the use of visual aids in the show. Were they easily seen? Did they demand attention? Did the speaker use the visual aids effectively? What would have made the use of visual aids more effective?

4. Evaluate the effectiveness of the visual aids used in your textbooks. What types are they? How are they used: to reinforce information, to clarify ideas, or to support theories? Which subjects seem to require the most visual support?

REFERENCES

1. The general theories of Gestalt psychology are reviewed in Ernest R. Hilgard, *Theories of Learning* (New York: Appleton-Century-Crofts, 1956). Their applications in areas of visual communication can be found in Rudolph Arnheim, *Visual Thinking* (Berkeley: Univ. of California Press, 1969); John M. Kennedy, *A Psychology of Picture Perception* (San Francisco: Jossey-Bass, 1974); Sol Worth, "Pictures Can't Say Ain't," *Versus* 12 (Dec. 1975): 85–108; Leonard Zusne, *Visual Perception of Form* (New York: Academic Press, 1976); and John Morgan and Peter Welton, *See What I Mean: An Introduction to Visual Communication* (London: Edward Arnold, Publishers, 1986). For discussions of research on media and learning, see G. Salomon, *Interaction of Media, Cognition, and Learning* (San Francisco: Jossey-Bass, 1979) and E. Heidt, *Instructional Media and the Individual Learner* (New York: Nichols, 1976).

2. William J. Seiler, "The Effects of Visual Materials on Attitudes, Credibility, and Retention," *Speech Monographs* 38 (Nov. 1971): 331–334.

3. Joel R. Levin and Alan M. Lesgold, "On Pictures in Prose," *Educational Communication and Technology Journal* 26 (1978): 233–244. See Marilyn J. Haring and Maurine A. Fry, "Effect of Pictures on Children's Comprehension of Written Text," *Educational Communication and Technology Journal* 27 (1979): 185–190.

4. For more specific conclusions about the effects of various sorts of visual materials, see Virginia Johnson, "Picture-Perfect Presentations," *Training & Development Journal* 43 (1989): 45; F. M. Dwyer, "Exploratory Studies in the Effectiveness of Visual Illustrations," *AV Communication Review* 18 (1970): 235–244; G. D. Feliciano, R. D. Powers, and B. E. Kearle, "The Presentation of Statistical Information," *AV Communication Review* 11 (1963): 32–39; M. D. Vernon, "Presenting Information in Diagrams," *AV Communication Review* 1 (1953): 147–158; and L. V. Peterson and Wilbur Schramm, "How Accurately Are Different Kinds of Graphs Read?" *AV Communication Review* 2 (1955): 178–189.

5. For a clear exploration of the relationships between ideas and visuals, see Edgar B. Wycoff, "Why Visuals?" *AV Communications* 11 (1977): 39, 59.

6. See Feliciano et al., "The Presentation of Statistical Information"; Vernon, "Presenting Information in Diagrams"; and Peterson and Schramm, "How Accurately Are Different Kinds of Graphs Read?"

P A R T

IV

. . . .

Types
of
Public
Speaking

Speeches to Inform

"How on earth can I make this speech interesting and relevant to my class?" Bob asked his instructor, Ms. McGee. He knew a great deal about the Vietnam War, and he wanted his class to know more about its causes and its effects on American life. "Well," his instructor replied, "first think about what really interests your classmates."

"Bar hopping, sports, movies, dances, and television," replied Bob. "Then that's your key," Ms. McGee answered. "Bar hopping's my key?" "No, no," she said, "mass media are the keys! Think of all the television programs and films focusing on Vietnam. For movies, we've had Coming Home, Apocalypse Now, The Deer Hunter, Full Metal Jacket, Platoon, Born on the Fourth of July, Heaven and Earth, *and all the Rambo movies. On television we've had docudramas such as HBO's "Vietnam War Stories" as well as prime time TV series such as "Magnum P.I.," "Hill Street Blues," "Tour of Duty," and "China Beach." Some have touched on Vietnam, and others have featured it. Use those movies and TV programs as ways to reach your audience."*

Our society almost worships facts. A staggering amount of information is available to us, particularly because of such technological developments as electronic media, photostatic printing, miniaturized circuitry, fax machines, and computerized data storage and retrieval systems. By itself, mere information tells us nothing. Information is simply there until human beings shape, interpret, and act on it. Public speakers often serve as interpreters of information. They are called upon to assemble, package, and present information to other human beings.

One theme will be sounded again and again in this chapter: "mere information" is useless until you put it together in ways that make it clear and relevant to others. Informative speeches clarify facts and ideas for audiences. Without clarification or interpretation, information is meaningless. The informative speaker's job is to adapt data and ideas to human needs. In this chapter, we'll discuss various types of informative speeches, outline the essential features of informative talks, and then review some ways of structuring each type of informative speech.

TYPES OF INFORMATIVE SPEECHES

Informative speeches take many forms depending on the situation, the level of knowledge possessed by listeners, and your own abilities as a presenter of data. Four of these forms—speeches of definition, instructions and demonstrations, oral reports, and lectures—occur so frequently, however, that they merit special attention. They represent four common ways in which people package or integrate information to meet the needs of others.

Speeches of Definition

"Mommy, what's a 'tattletale'?" "Professor Martinez, what's the difference between RAM and ROM?" "Joanne, before we can decide whether to buy this house, you're going to have to answer a dumb question for us—what are 'covenants'?" You've been asking questions like these all of your life. A speech of definition doesn't just offer a dictionary definition. Rather, a **speech of definition** seeks to define concepts or processes in ways that make them relevant to listeners. Once 5-year-old Sarah knows what a tattletale is, she'll know she has a human relations problem; once you know the differences between RAM and ROM, you'll make a great leap forward in your introduction to computing class; and once you know that covenants are binding agreements that may restrict land use, you'll explore them very carefully before purchasing property. You may find yourself defining who you are for a potential employer or defining an organization for others. Speakers are sometimes called upon to give speeches of definition for special occasions. For example, they might consider what "liberty" is on Independence Day or what "peace" is on Armistice Day.

Instructions and Demonstrations

Throughout your life, you've heard classroom instructions, job instructions, and instructions for the performance of special tasks. Not only have you gone through many "tell" sessions but you've also had people "show" you how to execute actions—how to sort various kinds of plastic for recycling, how to manage a voter registration table, how to operate a cash register, and how to put together a fast-food order. Generally, **instructions** are verbal communications that explain processes, while **demonstrations** are verbal and nonverbal messages explaining and illustrating those processes. Both involve the serial presentation of information, usually in steps or phases. Both require clarity because your listeners are expected to learn or reproduce these steps themselves.

Oral Reports

An **oral report** is a speech that arranges and interprets information gathered in response to a request made by a group. Academic reports, committee reports, and

• You encounter many forms of informative speaking every day, including lectures, television demonstrations, and weather reports. What are the characteristics of effective informative speeches?

executive reports are examples of oral reports. Scientists and other scholars announce their research findings in oral reports at professional conventions. Committees in business, industry, and government carry out special tasks and then present oral reports to their parent organizations or constituencies. Board chairpersons present annual oral reports to the stockholders on the past year's activities. You may have been asked to present a treasurer's report to an organization of which you are a member.

Lectures

Lectures increase the audience's understanding of a particular field of knowledge or activity. They usually involve explanations and definitions. For instance, a business executive might define *management by objectives* and go on to show how such management can modernize a small business; an historian might tell a group of students what sociocultural forces converged to create the American Revolution; and a social worker could lecture an audience of government officials on the local impact of federal deficit-reduction plans. Characteristic types of lectures include talks on travel and public affairs; classroom lectures; and talks at club meetings, study conferences, and institutes.

Choosing a Topic

If you're searching for informative speech topics, you can develop possible topics by brainstorming (see Chapter 2) or you can develop your ideas from standard subject areas. Consider these subject areas as you generate your own informative speech topics:

1. *People.* We're all curious about the lives of others. Build on this curiosity by focusing on someone you know, someone you admire, or someone unique. You might investigate the lives of the Wright brothers or Blanche Scott, the first American woman to fly. Or what about famous people like Bill Cosby or Clara Barton? Perhaps villians like Rasputin or John Dillinger fascinate you.

2. *Places.* This might be an opportunity to talk about a place you've visited or would like to visit—a city, museum, park, or another country. Cities like Rome or your hometown, museums like the Louvre or the local football hall of fame, parks like the Everglades or your favorite state park, and countries like Tanzania or Argentina can be intriguing speech topics.

3. *Things.* The possibilities are endless. Begin with what you already know. You could talk about your baseball card collection, the architectural style of your neighbor's house, or your uncle's antique automobile.

4. *Events.* Famous occurrences make good speech topics. There are recent events like political elections, the bombing of the World Trade Center, the floods caused by the Mississippi River, or the conflict in Bosnia-Herzegovina. In addition, you might talk about historical events such as famous battles, unusual discoveries, natural disasters, or memorable celebrations.

5. *Ideas.* Theories, principles, concepts, theologies, and traditions can make excellent informative speeches. You could explain the traditions of Taoism, the theory of relativity, the principles of capitalism, the concept of aging, or the doctrines of Catholicism.

6. *Procedures.* Descriptions of processes can be fascinating. Your listeners may have wondered how watches work, what enables microwave ovens to cook food, or how ballets are choreographed.

ESSENTIAL QUALITIES OF INFORMATIVE SPEECHES

Your goal as an informative speaker is to make it easy for your listeners to retain new information. There are four things you can do to ensure that your listeners remember what you say. You should strive for clarity, the association of new ideas with familiar ones, packaging or clustering of ideas, and motivational appeal.

Clarity

Informative speeches achieve maximum clarity when listeners can follow and understand what the speaker is saying. Clarity is largely the result of two factors: effective organization and the careful selection of words.

Achieving Clarity through Effective Organization

Limit Your Points.   Confine your speech to three or four principal ideas, grouping whatever facts or ideas you wish to consider under these main headings. Even if you know a tremendous amount about your subject matter, remember that you can't make everyone an expert with a single speech.

Use Transitions to Show Relationships Among Ideas.   Word your transitions carefully. Make sure to indicate the relationship of the upcoming point to the rest of your ideas. You might say, "Second, you must prepare the chair for caning by cleaning out the groove and cane holes"; "The Stamp Act Crisis was followed by an even more important event—The Townshend Duties"; "To test these hypotheses, we set up the following experiment." Such transitions allow listeners to follow you from point to point.

Keep Your Speech Moving Forward.   Rather than jumping back and forth between ideas, charging ahead, and then backtracking, develop a positive forward direction. Move from basic ideas to more complex ones, from background data to current research, or from historical incidents to current events.

Achieving Clarity through Word Choice

The second factor in achieving clarity is being understood. You can develop understanding through careful selection of your words. For a fuller development of the use of language, see Chapter 9. For now, think about the following ways to achieve clarity.

Keep Your Vocabulary Precise, Accurate —Not Too Technical.   In telling someone how to finish off a basement room, you might be tempted to say, "Next, take one of these long sticks and cut it off in this funny-looking gizmo with a saw in it and try to make the corners match." An accurate vocabulary will help your listeners remember what supplies and tools to get when they approach the same project: "This is a ceiling molding; it goes around the room between the wall and the ceiling to cover the seams between the paneling and the ceiling tiles. You make the corners of the molding match by using a mitre box, which has grooves that allow you to cut 45-degree angles. Here's how you do it."

Simplify When Possible.   If your speech on the operation of a two-cycle internal combustion engine sounds like it came out of the documentation for computer software, then it's too technical. An audience bogged down in unnecessary detail and complex vocabulary can become confused and bored. Include only as much technical vocabulary as you need.

Use Reiteration to Clarify Complex Ideas.   Rephrasing helps to solidify ideas for those who didn't get them the first time. You might say, for example, "Unlike a terrestrial telescope, a celestial telescope is used for looking at moons, planets, and stars; that is, its mirrors and lens are ground and arranged in such a way that it focuses on objects thousands of miles—not hundreds of feet—away from the observer." In this case, the idea is rephrased; the words aren't simply repeated.

FIGURE 12.1
Association of
New Ideas with
Familiar Ones
Audiences grasp new
concepts more quickly
when those concepts
are compared to
things they already
know. What familiar
concepts could you
use to explain
molecules? gene
splicing? inflation?

Associating New Ideas with Familiar Ones

Audiences grasp new facts and ideas more readily when they can associate them with what they already know. In a speech to inform, try to connect the new with the old (see Figure 12.1). To do this, you need to know enough about your audience to choose relevant experiences, images, analogies, and metaphors to use in your speech.

Sometimes the associations you ought to make are obvious. A college dean talking to an audience of manufacturers on the problems of higher education presented his ideas under the headings of raw material, casting, machining, polishing, and assembling. He translated his central ideas into an analogy that his audience, given their vocations, would understand. If you cannot think of any obvious associations, you may have to rely on common experiences or images. For instance, you might explain the operation of the pupil in a human eye by comparing it to the operation of a camera lens aperture, or you could explain a cryogenic storage tank by comparing it to a thermos bottle.

Clustering Ideas

You can help listeners make sense out of your speech by providing them with a well-organized package of tightly clustered ideas. Research on memory and organization has demonstrated that the "magic number" of items we can remember is seven, plus or minus two; more recent research has suggested that the number is probably five, again plus or minus two.[1] This research suggests that you ought to group items of information under three, five, or seven headings or in three, five, or seven clusters. You might, for example, organize a lecture on the history of the Vietnam War into three clusters—the 1950s, the 1960s, and the 1970s—rather than breaking it down year by year. College registration may be presented to freshmen as a five-step process: (a) secure registration materials, (b) review course offerings, (c) see an advisor, (d) fill out the registration materials, and (e) enter the information into the computer. The American Cancer Society has organized the most common symptoms of cancer into seven categories to help you remember them.

Speaking
of...

· · · ·

Using Psychological Principles for Clarity

Clustering items of information is often useful for speakers because it makes information much easier for listeners to grasp and retain. Psychologists throughout this century have been interested in discovering why things appear the way they do to us. Four principles of perception and cognition are still current in the literature:

1. *Proximity* suggests that elements close together seem to organize into units of perception; you see pairs made up of a ball and a block, not sets of blocks and sets of balls.

2. *Similarity* suggests that like objects are usually grouped together; you see three columns rather than three rows of items.

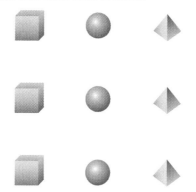

3. *Closure* is the tendency to complete suggested shapes; you see the figure of a tiger even though the lines are not joined.

4. *Symmetry* suggests that balanced objects are more pleasing to perceive than unbalanced ones.

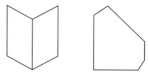

These four principles suggest ways in which you can cluster ideas in your speeches: (1) Put your most important ideas close together so they can play off each other; (2) construct your main points in similar grammatical ways to make the structure stand out; (3) offer enough typical examples to allow for closure; and (4) balance your treatments of the main ideas to give a sense of symmetry—for example, use parallel sentences.

These principles can help you organize your speeches to take advantage of your listeners' natural perceptions.

For more information, see John R. Anderson, *Cognitive Psychology and Its Implications* (New York: W. H. Freeman, 1980), 53–56; Ronald H. Forgus and Lawrence E. Melamed, *Perception: A Cognitive-Stage Approach,* 2nd ed. (New York: McGraw-Hill, 1976), 177–182; and Michael Kobovy and James R. Pomerantz, eds., *Perceptual Organization* (Hillsdale, N.J.: Lawrence Erlbaum Associates, 1980).

Mnemonic devices in your outline also can provide memory triggers. CPR instructors teach the ABC of cardiopulmonary resuscitation: (a) clear the *airwaves,* (b) check the *breathing,* and (c) initiate chest *compressions.* A speaker giving a talk on the Great Lakes can show listeners how to remember the names of the lakes by thinking of HOMES: Huron, Ontario, Michigan, Erie, and Superior. These memory devices also help you to remember the main points in your outline. Information forgotten is information lost; package your data and ideas in memorable clusters.

Motivating Your Audience

Finally, and perhaps most important, you must be able to motivate your audience to listen. Unfortunately, many people ignore this essential feature of good informative speeches. Many of us blithely assume that because we are interested in something, our audience also will want to hear about it. You may be fascinated by collecting American commemorative stamps, but your listeners may yawn through your entire speech unless you motivate them. You need to give them a reason to listen. To get them enthused, you might explain how stamps reflect our heritage or you might tell them how competitions are held for stamp art.

Keep in mind what we've said about attention in Chapter 8. You can use the factors of attention to engage the members of your audience and to draw them into your speech.

STRUCTURING INFORMATIVE SPEECHES

Now that we've described the various types of informative speeches and examined their essential features, it's time to examine ways to structure each of those types. Of course, it's possible to use any of the organizational patterns we've described earlier, but some patterns are better suited to particular types than others. Let's look at some examples.

Speeches of Definition

Because one of your primary jobs in speeches of definition is to bring coherence and focus to information or concepts, structuring such speeches is a crucial activity.

Introduction

Because speeches of definition treat either unfamiliar or familiar concepts in a new light, their introductions must create curiosity and establish need in listeners. Creating curiosity is a special challenge in speeches on unfamiliar concepts since we're all tempted to say, "Well, if I've made it this far in life without knowing anything about black holes or carcinogens or trap blocking, why should I bother with learning more about these ideas now?" You need to make people wonder about the unknown. Use new information to attract attention and arouse curiosity.

Speeches of definition must also be attentive to the needs or wants of the audience. In other words, their introductions should include explicit statements that indicate how the information can affect the listeners, such as, "Understanding the dynamics of trap blocking will help you better appreciate line play in football and thereby increase your enjoyment of the game every Saturday afternoon in our stadium."

Body

Most speeches of definition use a topical pattern because such speeches usually describe various aspects of an object or idea. It seems natural, for example, to use a topical pattern for a speech on computer programming careers, organizing the body of the speech around such topics as "the duties of a computer programmer," "skills needed by a computer programmer," and "training you will need to become a computer programmer."

There are occasions when other patterns may serve your specific purpose even better than topical patterns. You might use an effect-cause pattern, for example, when preparing an informative speech on the laws of supply and demand. You could enumerate a series of effects with which people are already familiar—changing prices at the gas pumps—and then discuss the laws of supply and demand that account for such changes.

Conclusion

Conclusions for speeches of definition have two characteristics: (a) they usually include a summary of the main points, and (b) they often stress the ways in which people can apply the ideas that have been presented. For example, the speaker discussing diabetes could conclude by offering listeners the titles of books containing more information, the phone number of the American Diabetes Association, the local address of a clinic, or the meeting time and place of a diabetics support group.

A speech defining diabetes could be outlined in a topical pattern as follows:

Sample Outline for a Speech of Definition

• • • •

What Is Diabetes?[2]

The speaker uses a vividly developed personal example to gain attention.

Introduction

I. I never knew my grandmother. She was a talented artist; she raised six kids without all the modern conveniences like microwave ovens and electric clothes dryers; and my dad still talks about the time she foiled a would-be burglar by locking him in a broom closet until the police came. My grandmother had diabetes. It finally took her life. Now my sister has it. So do 13 million other Americans.

The scope of the problem is explained.

II. Diabetes threatens millions of lives, and it's one of nature's stealthiest diseases.

A motivation for listening is provided.

III. It's important to understand this disease because, more than likely, you or someone you know will eventually have to deal with it.

Supporting testimony shows the severity of the disease.

A. Diabetes is the third leading cause of death behind heart disease and cancer, according to the American Diabetes Association.

Listeners are warned that ignorance of the disease makes the problem worse.

B. Over one-third of those suffering from the disease don't even know they have it. That simple knowledge could make the difference between a happy productive life and an early death.

The scope of the problem is expanded by pointing out that other medical conditions are complicated by diabetes.

C. Furthermore, diabetes is implicated in many other medical problems: it contributes to coronary heart disease; it accounts for 40 percent of all amputations and most cases of new blindness.

The three main ideas of the speech are previewed.

D. In the next few minutes, let's look at three things you should know about "the silent killer," diabetes—what it is, how it affects people and how it can be controlled.

The first main point is stated.

Body

I. What diabetes is.

Diabetes is defined in medical terms.

A. Diabetes is a chronic disease of the endocrine system that affects your body's ability to deliver glucose to its cells.

The symptoms of diabetes are explained.

B. The symptoms of diabetes, according to Dr. Charles Kilo, are weight loss in spite of eating and drinking, constant hunger and thirst, frequent urination, and fatigue.

The second main point is provided.

II. How diabetes affects people.

Type I diabetes is operationally defined.

A. Type I diabetes occurs when your body cannot produce insulin, a substance that delivers glucose to your cells.

Supporting statistics show the scope of this type.

1. Only 5 to 10 percent of all diabetics are Type I.

Who is affected by Type I is further explained.

2. This type, also known as *juvenile diabetes,* usually shows up in the first 20 years of life.

The genetic and environmental triggers are described.

3. Type I diabetes can be passed on genetically but is also thought to be triggered by environmental agents such as viruses.

The treatment is revealed.

4. Type I diabetics must take insulin injections to treat the disease.

Type II diabetes is operationally defined. Notice how this section of the speech parallels the preceding section in development.

Supporting statistics show the scope of this type.

Who is affected by Type II is further explained.

Other demographic facts are provided.

The treatment is revealed.

The third main point is provided.

The treatments for Type I are explained.

Insulin injections are one treatment option.

Blood sugar must be monitored.

Supporting testimony is offered for new treatments.

Near-infrared beams determine blood sugar levels.

New methods of delivering insulin are outlined.

The treatments for Type II are explained.

Testimony supports the value of weight loss.

Dietary changes are developed.

Insulin-stimulating medications are explained.

Insulin injections replace unsuccessful behavior modifications.

Listeners are reminded of the definition of diabetes.

The three main ideas of the speech are reiterated.

The speech reaches closure by referring to the introductory personal example.

Listeners are warned that diabetes could affect them.

B. Type II diabetes occurs when your body produces insulin but fails to use it effectively.
   1. Of all diabetes 90 to 95 percent are Type II.
   2. This type usually shows up after a person turns 40.
   3. It often affects people who are overweight; more women are affected than men.
   4. Insulin injections are sometimes used to treat the disease.

III. How to control diabetes.
   A. Type I diabetes cannot be cured, but it can be controlled.
      1. Patients must take insulin injections, usually several times a day.
      2. Patients need to monitor their blood sugar levels by pricking a finger and testing a drop of blood.
      3. According to *Science News,* several new treatments are available:
         a. One new device uses near-infrared beams to determine blood sugar level.
         b. Insulin can be taken through the nose or in pill form.
         c. Pancreatic transplants have been performed with limited success.
   B. Type II diabetes can be controlled through life-style modifications.
      1. Usually these diabetics are required to lose weight by exercising, according to Dr. JoAnn Manson.
      2. Changes in diet are also required.
      3. Some people take oral hypoglycemic medications that stimulate the release of insulin and foster insulin activity.
      4. If these modifications fail, Type II diabetics must take insulin injections.

Conclusion

   I. Diabetes is a serious disease in which the body can no longer produce or use insulin effectively.
   II. The two types of diabetes occur at different stages in life and require different measures for control of the disease.
   III. My grandmother lived with her diabetes for years but eventually lost her life to it. My sister has the advantages of new treatments and future research in her fight with diabetes.
   IV. As we age, many of us will be among the 600,000 new diabetics each year. Through awareness, we can cope effectively with this silent killer.

Notice several features of this speech:

1. The speaker attempts early to engage listeners' curiosity and review listeners' personal needs to draw the audience into the topic. The use of a personal example is particularly good for this kind of speech.

2. The speaker offers statistics on diabetes early so that the audience knows that the disease is widespread and serious.

3. Three topics are previewed, then developed in the body of the speech to engage three aspects of listeners' thinking.

4. After offering a summary of the central idea, the speaker returns to the personal example, adding closure to the speech.

Instructions and Demonstrations

Flip through your television channels and you'll come across cooking demonstrations, home-improvement shows, sewing instructions, and painting lessons. Each presents the steps required to complete a project. Like successful educational television shows, instructions and demonstrations should break down a process or procedure into a series of steps. Each step should be easy to understand and to visualize.

Introduction

In some speaking situations, such as presentations in speech communication classrooms, listener attendance may not be voluntary. On these occasions, you'll have to pay attention to motivational matters. If your audience has invited you to speak or is attending your talk voluntarily, you can assume listener interest. When giving instructions or offering a demonstration, you'll usually need to spend only a little time generating curiosity or motivating people to listen. After all, if you're instructing listeners in a new office procedure or giving a workshop on how to build an ice boat, they already have the prerequisite interest and motivation; otherwise they wouldn't have come. When your audience is already motivated to listen, you can concentrate your introduction on two other tasks.

1. *Preview your speech.* If you're going to take your listeners through the steps involved in making a good tombstone rubbing, give them an overall picture of the process before you start detailing each operation.

2. *Encourage listeners to follow along.* Even through some of the steps may be difficult, urge everyone to listen. A process such as tombstone rubbing, for example, looks easier than it is: many people are tempted to quit listening and give up somewhere along the way. If, however, you forewarn them and promise them special help with the difficult techniques, they will be more likely to bear with you.

Body

As we suggested earlier, most speeches of demonstration and instruction follow a natural chronological or spatial pattern. Consequently, you usually will have little trouble organizing the body of a speech of demonstration or instruction. Your

It is important to coordinate verbal and visual materials during instructions or demonstrations. What suggestions do you have to create effective integration of verbal and visual materials?

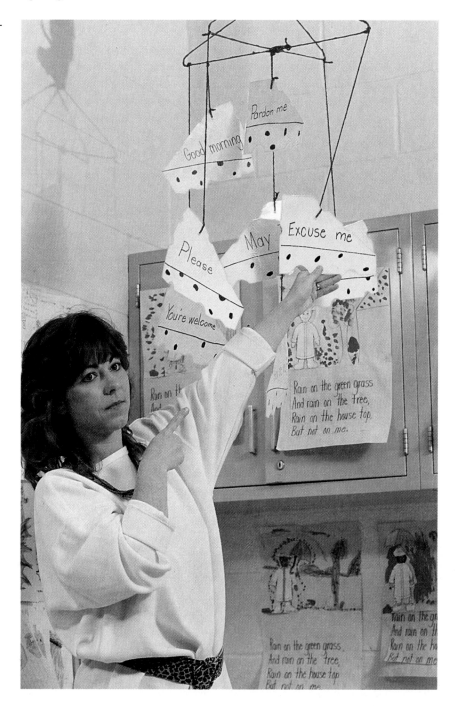

problems are more likely to be technical and may include the following:

1. *The problem of rate.* If the glue on a project needs to set before you can go on to the next step, what do you do? You can't just stand there and wait for it to dry. Instead, you could have a second object, already dried, ready for

the next step. You also need to preplan some material for filling the time—perhaps additional background or a brief discussion of what problems can arise at this stage. Preplan your remarks carefully for those junctures so you can maintain your audience's attention.

2. *The problem of scale.* How can you show various embroidery stitches to an audience of 25? When dealing with minute operations, you often must increase the scale of operation. In this example, you could use a large piece of poster board or even a 3- by 4-foot piece of cloth stretched over a wooden frame. By using an oversized needle, yarn instead of thread, and stitches measured in inches instead of millimeters, you could easily make your techniques visible to all audience members. At the other extreme, in a speech on how to make a homemade solar heat collector, you should work with a scaled-down model.

3. *The coordination of verbal and visual methods.* Both instructions and demonstrations usually demand that speakers "show" while "telling." To keep yourself from becoming flustered or confused, be sure to practice *doing* while *talking*—demonstrating your material while explaining aloud what you're doing. Decide where you'll stand when showing a slide so that the audience can see both you and the image; practice talking about your aerobic exercise positions while you're actually doing them; work a dough press in practice sessions as you tell your mythical audience how to form professional-looking cookies. If you don't, you'll inevitably get yourself into trouble in front of your real audience.

Conclusion

Conclusions for demonstration speeches usually have three parts:

1. *Summary.* Most audiences need this review, which reminds them to question procedures or ideas they don't understand.

2. *Encouragement.* People trying new processes or procedures usually get in trouble the first few times and need to be reassured that such trouble is predictable and can be overcome.

3. *Offer of help.* What sounded so simple in your talk may be much more complicated in execution. If possible, make yourself available for assistance: "As you fill out your registration form, just raise your hand if you're unsure of anything and I'll be happy to help you." Or point to other sources of further information and assistance: "Here's the address of the U.S. Government Printing Office, whose pamphlet X1234 is available for only a dollar; it will give you more details"; "If you run into a filing problem I haven't covered in this short orientation to your job, just go over to Mary McFerson's desk, right over here. Mary's experienced in these matters and is always willing to help." Such statements not only offer help but assure your listeners that they won't be labeled as dim-witted if they actually have to ask for it.

Thinking through requirements of speeches of instruction and demonstration might result in a speaking outline like the one on page 226.

Sample Outline for a Speech of Demonstration

• • • •   How to Plant Tomatoes

Introduction

Listeners' interest is aroused by using questions and gustatory imagery.

I. Have you ever picked a luscious red tomato from the vine and bitten into it? Can you imagine the taste—juicy and sweet? What if I told you that you could have your very own tomatoes anytime you wanted them? And at a fraction of the cost of store-bought tomatoes?

Four steps for growing tomatoes are previewed.

II. Well, you can. With a little time and patience, you can grow your very own delicious tomatoes. In four easy steps, you can have your own tomatoes ready to eat in 65 days. Here's how.

Body

The first step is stated and a chart is displayed, showing varieties of tomatoes in columns along with their characteristics. Soil requirements are developed. Notice how parallel development of characteristics rounds out this section of the speech. Sunlight requirements are developed. Growing season requirements are developed. Disease resistance is developed.

I. First, you must select a variety of tomato seed that's suited to various geographical, climatological, agricultural, and personal factors.
   A. Some tomatoes grow better in hard soils; some in loose soils.
   B. Some varieties handle shade well; some need direct sunlight.
   C. Some are well suited to short growing seasons; others to long seasons.
   D. Each variety tends to resist certain diseases, such as blight, better than others.

The second step is stated. Explanation of mixture is provided, and mixture is prepared, indicating proportions. Germination trays are filled. Half-grown and fully grown seedlings are brought out to demonstrate growth. Technique of thinning seedlings is demonstrated. Six-inch plants are shown. Plants of different strengths are shown.

II. Once you have selected a variety (or maybe even two, so that they mature at different times), you must start the seeds.
   A. Prepare a mixture of black dirt, peat moss, and vermiculite as I am doing.
   B. Fill germination trays, pots, or cut-off milk cartons with the germination soil, and insert seeds.
   C. With water, sunlight, and patience, your plants will grow. I can't show you that growth here today, but I can use these seedlings to illustrate their care along the way.
      1. When the seedlings are about an inch or two tall, thin them.
      2. At about 6 inches [show them], you can transplant them safely.
      3. But, you'll know more about which plants are strong if you wait until they are 10 to 12 inches tall.

The third step is stated. Unpotting of seedlings is demonstrated. Enlarged drawing that illustrates proper hole preparation and spacing of plants is shown. Packing soil is demonstrated. Amount of water per plant is shown.

   D. Now you are ready to transplant the seedlings to your garden.
      1. Carefully unpot the seedlings, being sure not to damage the root network.
      2. Put each seedling in an already-prepared hole in your plot; this diagram shows you how to do that.
      3. Pack the garden soil firmly but not so hard as to crush the roots.
      4. Water it almost every day for the first week.
      5. Put some sort of mulching material—grass clippings, hay,

Black plastic and mulching materials are shown and explained.

Sketches of various styles of cages are shown.

black sheets of plastic—between the rows if weeds are a problem.

E. Once you know that your plants are growing, cage or stake each plant.

Conclusion

The four steps of the process are summarized.

I. Growing tomatoes is a four-step process. First, you select the appropriate variety for your needs; next, you start the seeds in a special soil mixture; then, you transplant the seedlings; and, finally, you stake the plants.

The speaker's personal testimony is provided.

II. I used to settle for tough, dry, over-priced tomatoes in the supermarket until I discovered that I could grow them myself.

A final offer is made for the audience to sample garden tomatoes.

III. You can too! If my simple four-step process isn't enough to convince you, stop by my garden and pick a vine-ripened tomato. You'll never settle for less again.

Speaking of...

• • • •

Choosing Sources

The difference between getting lost in a hopeless tangle of information and locating exactly what you need to know is having a plan of attack. The basic principle is to build your knowledge base by first reading nontechnical sources and then proceeding to use more technical, expert sources. For example, if you plan a speech on radial keratotomy—surgery for nearsightedness—begin your topic development by reading general periodicals on the subject. You might find several articles in *Health* magazine, for instance. After locating these basic sources and developing an understanding of the procedure, obtain more technical sources. You might schedule an interview with an opthomologist, consult specialty journals, and read summaries of scientific research. Finally, having an advanced understanding of the topic area, you can begin to sort the information you have gathered and prepare it for presentation to an audience.

Also see: Robert Berkman, *Find It Fast* (New York: Harper & Row, 1990).

Oral Reports

Your principal strategy in an oral report must be to meet the audience's expectations with the information and the recommendations you present.

Introduction

An oral report is requested by a group, committee, or class; the audience, therefore, generally knows what it expects and why. As a result, in introducing oral reports, you need not spend much time motivating your listeners. Instead, you should concentrate on describing how you gathered and organized your information and pointing ahead to any action that your listeners are expected to take in light of your information. The key to a good introduction for an oral report is orientation—reviewing the past (your listeners' expectations and your preparations), the present (your goal now), and the future (your listeners' responsibilities once you are done). Remember that you're giving your report to your audience for a *purpose*.

Body

The principle for organizing the body of an oral report can be stated simply: select the organizational pattern best suited to your audience's needs. Have you been asked to provide your listeners with a history of a group or a problem? Use a chronological pattern. Do they want to know how a particular state of affairs came to be? Try a cause-effect format. Have you been asked to discuss an organizational structure for the group? A topical pattern will allow you to review the constitutional responsibilities of each officer.

Conclusion

Most oral reports end with a conclusion that mirrors the introduction. Mention again your report's purpose; review its main points; publicly thank committee members; and then either offer a motion to accept the committee recommendations, or—in the case of informative reports—request questions from the audience. Conclusions to reports, when done well, are quick, firm, efficient, and pointed.

The example on page 229 examines the pros and cons of various proposals and recommends one to the group.

Lectures

You'll find it's often difficult to engage an audience fully in a lecture—to get them interested in the topic and tuned in to the point of view you're taking. This problem should guide the way you structure the introductions, bodies, and conclusions of lectures.

Introduction

Introductions and conclusions can provide your greatest challenges when structuring lectures. It is particularly important in lectures to raise curiosity. How many of your classmates are wondering about the causes of the Vietnam War at ten o'clock in the morning? Who cares how the geography of the countryside shaped Bosnian guerilla strategies? How many of us want to know why the American experience in Vietnam still affects domestic politics? As was suggested in this chapter's opening vignette, you can earn your listeners' attention by relating your topic to something they are familiar with or interested in—in the case of the speech on Vietnam, the mass media. You should also include in your introduction a forecast of the lecture's structure.

Body

Most lectures fit well into causal or topical organizational patterns. The body of your Vietnam War lecture could be divided into causes and effects; or it could be

Sample Outline for an Oral Report

• • • •

Report from the Final Examination Committee

The charge of the committee is stated.

I. My committee was asked to compare and contrast various ways of structuring a final examination in this speech class and to recommend a procedure to you.

Step 1 is reviewed.

A. First, we interviewed each one of you.

Step 2 is explained.

B. Then, we discussed the pedagogical virtues of various exam procedures with our instructor.

Step 3 is summarized, introducing the committee's conclusions. Notice that the introduction orients the listener to the committee's charge and the procedures for reaching its conclusions.

C. Next, we deliberated as a group, coming to the following conclusions.

The first option is offered.

II. At first we agreed with many students that we should recommend a take-home essay examination as the "easiest" way out.

The disadvantages to the first option are summarized.

A. But we decided that our wonderful textbook is filled with so much detailed and scattered advice that it would be almost impossible for any of us to answer essay-type questions without many, many hours of worry, work, and sweat.

An additional problem with the first option is explained.

B. We also wondered why a course that stresses oral performance should test our abilities to write essays.

The second option is offered.
The primary disadvantage of this option is presented.

III. So we reviewed the option of a standard, short-answer, in-class final.

A. Although such a test would allow us to concentrate on the main ideas and central vocabulary—which have been developed in lectures, readings, and discussion—it would require a fair amount of memorization.

A further limitation is developed.

B. We also came to the realization that merely understanding communication concepts will not be enough when we start giving speeches outside this classroom.

The final, recommended option is stated.
The option is explained.

IV. Our recommendation is an oral examination over the course materials.

A. Each of us could be given an impromptu speech topic, some resource material, and ten minutes to prepare a speech.

The grading and goals of the option are developed.

B. We could be graded on both substantive and communicative decisions we make in preparing and delivering the speech.

The most important feature of the option is stated.

C. Most important, such a test would be consistent with this course's primary goal and could be completed quickly and almost painlessly.

The purpose of the committee is restated.

V. My committee was charged with finding a format for a final examination.

The main points are reviewed.

A. We compared various options for our final examination including take-home and in-class written examinations and opted for an oral examination.

Final recommendations for action are provided.

B. The next step is to present our recommendation to our instructor.

FIGURE 12.2
Checklist for
Introductions and
Conclusions to
Informative Speeches

Speeches of Definition

_____ 1. Does my introduction create curiosity or entice my audience to listen?
_____ 2. Does my introduction include an explicit statement that shows my listeners how the information in my speech will affect them?
_____ 3. Does my conclusion summarize my main ideas?
_____ 4. Does my conclusion stress ways my listeners can apply the ideas I've discussed?

Instructions and Demonstrations

_____ 1. Does my introduction encourage everyone to listen?
_____ 2. Does my introduction pique listener curiosity?
_____ 3. Do I preview my main points in my introduction?
_____ 4. Do I summarize my main points in my conclusion?
_____ 5. Do I encourage listeners to try new procedures even though they may experience initial difficulty?
_____ 6. Do I tell my listeners where they can find help or information in the future?

Oral Reports

_____ 1. Do I remind my listeners of their request for information?
_____ 2. Do I describe the procedures I used for gathering information for this report?
_____ 3. Does my introduction include a forecast of subtopics?
_____ 4. Does my introduction suggest the action which will be recommended in the report?
_____ 5. Does my conclusion mention the main purpose of the report?
_____ 6. Does my conclusion review the main points of the report?
_____ 7. Do I recognize and thank committee members for their contributions?
_____ 8. Do I call for action on a motion or questions from my listeners?

Lectures

_____ 1. Does my introduction raise listeners' curiosity?
_____ 2. Do I forecast my main topics in my introduction?
_____ 3. Does my conclusion suggest implications of the information listeners have received or call for listeners' action?

set up topically to discuss the social, economic, political, and moral dimensions of the war. A straightforward problem-solution format also works well with the right subject matter; for example, a speech on the problem of bringing the North and South Vietnamese to the negotiating table could be built around the military, political, and sociocultural steps the United States took to force direct negotiation between the warring parties.

Conclusion

Typically, the conclusion of a good lecture suggests additional implications or calls for particular actions. (See Figure 12.2.) For example, if you have explained in a lecture how contagious diseases spread through geographical areas, you

Sample Speech

• • • •

The following speech, "The Geisha," was delivered by Joyce Chapman when she was a freshman at Loop College, Chicago. It illustrates most of the virtues of a good informative speech: (1) it provides enough detail and explanations to be clear; (2) it works from familiar images of geishas, adding new ideas and information in such a way as to enlarge listeners' frames of reference; (3) its topical organization pattern is easy to follow; (4) and, it gives listeners reasons for listening.

The Geisha[3]
Joyce Chapman

A personal reference establishes an immediate tie between Ms. Chapman and her topic.

Ms. Chapman works hard to bring the listeners—with their stereotyped views of Geishas—into the speech through comments many might have made and references to familiar films.

As you may have already noticed from my facial features, I have Oriental blood in me and, as such, I am greatly interested in my Japanese heritage. One aspect of my heritage that fascinates me the most is the beautiful and adoring Geisha./1

I recently asked some of my friends what they thought a Geisha was, and the comments I received were quite astonishing. For example, one friend said, "She is a woman who walks around in a hut." A second friend was certain that a Geisha was, "A woman who massages men for money and it involves her in other physical activities." Finally, I received this response, "She gives baths to men and walks on their backs." Well, needless to say, I was rather surprised and offended by their comments. I soon discovered that the majority of my friends perceived the Geisha with similar attitudes. One of them argued, "It's not my fault, because that is the way I've seen them on TV." In many ways my friend was correct. His misconception of the Geisha was not his fault, for she is often portrayed by American film producers and directors as: a prostitute, as in the movie, *The Barbarian and the Geisha,* a streetwalker, as seen in the TV series, "Kung Fu," or as a showgirl with a gimmick, as performed in the play, *Flower Drum Song./2*

The central idea is stated clearly.

A Geisha is neither a prostitute, streetwalker, or showgirl with a gimmick. She is a lovely Japanese woman who is a professional entertainer and hostess. She is cultivated with exquisite manners, truly a bird of a very different plumage./3

A transition moves the listeners easily from the introduction to the body of the speech via a forecast.

The first section of the body of the speech is devoted to an orienting history which cleverly wipes away most of the negative stereotypes of the Geisha.

I would like to provide you with some insight to the Geisha, and, in the process perhaps, correct any misconception you may have. I will do this by discussing her history, training, and development./4

The Geisha has been in existence since 600 A.D., during the archaic time of the Yakamoto period. At that time the Japanese ruling class was very powerful and economically rich. The impoverished majority, however, had to struggle to survive. Starving fathers and their families had to sell their young daughters to the teahouses in order to get a few yen. The families hoped that the girls would have a better life in the teahouse than they would have had in their own miserable homes./5

During ancient times only high society could utilize the Geisha's talents because she was regarded as a status symbol, exclusively for the elite. As the Geisha became more popular, the common people developed their own imitations. These imitations were often crude and base, lacking sophistication and taste. When American GIs came home from World War II, they related descriptive accounts of their wild escapades with the Japanese Geisha. In essence, the GIs were only soliciting with common prostitutes. These bizarre stories helped create the wrong image of the Geisha./6

Today, it is extremely difficult to become a Geisha. A Japanese woman couldn't wake up one morning and decide, "I think I'll become a Geisha today." It's not that simple. It takes sixteen years to qualify./7

A nice transition moves Chapman to her second point on the rigors of Geisha training. She discusses the training in language technical enough to make listeners feel that they're learning interesting information but not so detailed as to be suffocating.

At the age of six a young girl would enter the Geisha training school and become a Jo-chu, which means housekeeper. The Jo-chu does not have any specific type of clothing, hairstyle, or make-up. Her duties basically consist of keeping the teahouse immaculately clean (for cleanliness is like a religion to the Japanese). She would also be responsible for making certain that the more advanced women would have everything available at their fingertips. It is not until the girl is sixteen and enters the Maiko stage that she concentrates less on domestic duties and channels more of her energies on creative and artistic endeavors./8

The Maiko girl, for example, is taught the classical Japanese dance, Kabuki. At first, the dance consists of tiny, timid steps to the left, to the right, backward and forward. As the years progress, she is taught the more difficult steps requiring syncopated movements to a fan./9

The Maiko is also introduced to the highly regarded art of floral arrangement. The Japanese take full advantage of the simplicity and gracefulness that can be achieved with a few flowers in a vase, or with a single flowering twig. There are three main styles: Seika, Moribana, and Nagerie. It takes at least three years to master this beautiful art./10

During the same three years, the Maiko is taught the ceremonious art of serving tea. The roots of these rituals go back to the thirteen century, when Zen Buddhist monks in China drank tea during their devotions. These rituals were raised to a fine art by the Japanese tea masters, who set the standards for patterns of behavior throughout Japanese society. The tea ceremony is so intricate that it often takes four hours to perform and requires the use of over seventeen different utensils. The tea ceremony is far more than the social occasion it appears to be. To the Japanese, it serves as an island of serenity where one can refresh the senses and nourish the soul./11

One of the most important arts taught to the Geisha is that of conversation. She must master an elegant circuitous vocabulary flavored in Karyuki, the world of flowers and willows, of which she will be a part. Consequently, she must be capable of stimulating her client's mind as well as his esthetic pleasures./12

The third point of the speech—how a Geisha develops her skills in her actual work—is clearly introduced and then developed with specific instances and explanations.

Having completed her sixteen years of thorough training, at the age of twenty-two, she becomes a full-fledged Geisha. She can now serve her clients with duty, loyalty, and most important, a sense of dignity./13

The Geisha would be dressed in the ceremonial kimono, made of brocade and silk thread. It would be fastened with an obi, which is a sash around the waist and hung down the back. The length of the obi would indicate the girl's degree of development. For instance, in the Maiko stage the obi is longer and is shortened when she becomes a Geisha. Unlike the Maiko, who wears a gay, bright, and cheerful kimono, the Geisha is dressed in more subdued colors. Her make-up is the traditional white base, which gives her the look of white porcelain. The hair is shortened and adorned with beautiful, delicate ornaments./14

The conclusion is short and quick. Little more is needed in a speech that has offered clear explanations, though some speakers might want to refer back to the initial overview of negative stereotypes in order to remind the listeners how wrong such views are.

As a full-fledged Geisha, she would probably acquire a rich patron who would assume her sizable debt to the Okiya, or training residence. This patron would help pay for her wardrobe, for each kimono can cost up to $12,000. The patron would generally provide her with financial security./15

The Geisha serves as a combination entertainer and companion. She may dance, sing, recite poetry, play musical instruments, or draw pictures for her guest. She might converse with them or listen sympathetically to their troubles. Amorous advances, however, are against the rules./16

So, as you can see the Geisha is a far cry from the back-rubbing, street-walking, slick entertainer that was described by my friends. She is a beautiful, cultivated, sensitive, and refined woman./17

probably should conclude by discussing actions that listeners can take to break the contagion cycle. Or if you have explained the concept of children's rights to a parent-teacher organization, you might close by asking your listeners to consider what these rights should mean to them—how they should change their thinking and their behavior toward six-year-olds.

CHAPTER SUMMARY

1. Speeches to inform include talks that seek to assemble, package, and interpret raw data, information, or ideas.

2. The four types of informative speeches are speeches of definition, instructions and demonstrations, oral reports, and lectures.

3. No matter what type of informative speech you're preparing, you should strive for four qualities: clarity; associating new ideas with familiar ones; clustering ideas to aid memory and comprehension; and motivating your audience.

4. Each type of informative speech can be structured into introductions, bodies, and conclusions that maximize your ability to reach your audiences.

KEY TERMS

demonstrations (p. 213)

instructions (p. 213)

lectures (p. 214)

oral report (p. 213)

speech of definition (p. 213)

SKILLBUILDING ACTIVITIES

1. In a concise written report, indicate and defend the type of arrangement (chronological sequence, spatial sequence, and so on) you think would be most suitable for an informative speech on the following subjects:

    a. The status of minority studies on campus.

    b Recent developments in genetic engineering.

    c. Mayan excavations in Central America.

    d. Saving for retirement.

    e. How the stock market works.

    f. Censorship of video games.

    g. Diet fads of the 1980s and 1990s.

    h The fraternity tradition.

    i. Buying your first house.

    j. What life will be like in the year 2500.

2. Plan a two- to four-minute speech in which you will give instructions. For instance, you might explain how to calculate your life insurance needs, how to canvass for a political candidate, or how to make a group flight reservation. This exercise is basically descriptive, so limit yourself to using a single visual aid.

3. Describe an unusual place you have visited on a vacation—for example, a church in a foreign city or a historical site. Deliver a four- or five-minute speech to the class, in which you describe this place as accurately and vividly as possible. Then ask the class to take a moment to envision this place. If possible, show them a picture of what you have described. How accurately were they able to picture the place? How might you have ensured a more accurate description? What restrictions did you feel without the use of visual aids?

REFERENCES

1. For background on information packaging, see G. Mandler, "Organization and Memory," in *Human Memory: Basic Processes,* Gordon Bower, ed. (New York: Academic Press, 1977), 310–354; Mandler's articles in C. R. Puff, ed., *Memory Organization and Structure* (New York: Academic Press, 1976); and G. A. Miller, "The Magic Number Seven, Plus or Minus Two: Some Limits on Our Capacity for Processing Information," *Psychological Review* 63 (1956): 81–97.

2. Information for this outline was taken from Phyllis Barrier, "Diabetes: It Never Lets Up," *Nation's Business* (Nov. 1992): 77; David Bradley, "Is a Pill on the Way for Diabetics?" *New Scientist* (27 June 1992): 17; C. Ezzell, "New Clues to Diabetes' Cause and Treatment," *Science News* (21 Dec. 1991): 406; Charles Kilo and Joseph R. Williamson, *Diabetes* (New York: John Wiley & Sons, 1987): Mark Schapiro, "A Shock to the System," *Health* (July–Aug. 1991): 75–82; Carrie Smith, "Exercise Reduces Risk of Diabetes," *The Physician and Sportsmedicine* (Nov. 1992): 19; John Travis, "Helping Diabetics Shed Pins and Needles," *Science News* (6 July 1991): 4.

3. Joyce Chapman, "The Geisha," in Roselyn Schiff et al., *Communication Strategy: A Guide to Speech Preparation* (Glenview, Ill.: Scott, Foresman, 1981). Used with the permission of HarperCollins Publishers.

Speeches to Persuade

For as long as she can remember, Tia has been a baseball fan. As a child, she played in Little League, and now she attends major league games in Tiger Stadium. Sitting in the bleachers, she sometimes notices the billboards along the outfield fences for Detroit National Bank, the United Auto Workers, Little Caesar's Pizza, and Thorn Apple Valley hotdogs. Some of her favorite players endorse soft drinks and sports equipment on television. No game is complete without a bag of peanuts from a roving vendor. Tia and her co-workers disagree about what players are the most valuable and about coaching decisions.

The actions Tia takes—buying season tickets, consuming the soft drinks endorsed by players and products pitched by vendors, patronizing merchants who advertise at the park, squabbling over players' abilities and coaching strategies—are the results of effective persuasion. Tia thinks she's just going out for entertainment; in reality, she's being immersed in a symbolic environment filled with persuasive messages.

Most of us, too, are subject to persuasion every day, even when we don't realize it. Billboards confront you on your way to school, posters call for your attention, teachers urge you to see their points of view, campus signs plead with you not to litter, and Burger King wants you to "Have It Your Way"—as long as it's a Whopper. Speaking publicly in order to persuade shares many features with other kinds of persuasion that we experience all the time.

The general purpose of persuasion is to change or reinforce attitudes or behaviors. The speaker who persuades makes a very different demand on the audience than does the speaker who informs. The informative speaker is satisfied when listeners understand what has been said. The persuader, however, attempts to influence the listener's thoughts or actions. The persuader may even plead with the audience to agree with or act on the speech. Occasionally, persuaders seek to reinforce ideas or actions that already exist in listeners. They may defend the status quo, urging rejection of proposed changes. Whatever the specific purpose, the general purpose of persuasion is to convince audiences.

Think back to our discussion of specific speaking purposes. Your goals help you to determine what kind of speech you need to give. If your purpose is to help your audience understand the American two-party political system, you can offer an informative speech tracing the development of that system through various periods of American history. However, if you'd like to convince people that one party is better than the other, that a particular election has been misinterpreted by some historians, or that voting is a fundamental democratic right, you seek to change your audience's attitudes with a persuasive speech.

• We are bombarded with competing persuasive messages every day. What messages vie for your attention here?

To persuade audiences successfully, you must make them *want* to believe or act. When people are forced to accept beliefs, they may soon abandon them. So, two subsidiary purposes of persuasive speaking must be kept in mind: (a) to provide the audience with motives for believing, by appealing to their basic needs or desires and (b) to convince them that your recommendation will satisfy these desires.

We'll begin this chapter with a discussion of motive needs and the motivational appeals that speakers can use to tap those needs. Then, we'll examine the motivated sequence, an organizational pattern that helps you to incorporate motivational appeals successfully into your speeches.

ANALYZING THE NEEDS AND DESIRES OF LISTENERS

As we've said, a speech must appeal to listeners' needs and desires. It's helpful to think of these needs and desires as *motive needs.*

Motive Needs

A **motive need** is an impulse to satisfy a psychological-social want or a biological urge. Such needs may arise from physiological considerations—pain, lack of food, or surroundings that are too hot or cold—or they may come about for sociocultural reasons, such as when you feel left out of a group or wonder whether your peers like you. If you feel the need deeply, your feelings may compel you to do something about your situation. You might eat, adjust the thermostat, or join a group. In each situation, you will have been motivated to act.

Translating Motive Needs into Motivational Appeals

Once you recognize the power of motive needs to propel human action, you may ask, "How can I identify and satisfy these needs in a speech? How can I use these basic needs, wants, and desires as the basis for effective public communication?" The answer to both of these questions is, "With the use of motivational appeals." A **motivational appeal** is either (a) a visualization of a desire and a method for satisfying it or (b) an assertion that an entity, idea, or course of action holds the key to fulfilling a particular motive need.

Suppose that you want to borrow a friend's car. How do you prepare to ask? Usually, you create scenarios in your mind. In these scenarios, you try out various motivation appeals: "Should I mention how far it is to walk? [*appeal to sympathy*] What about a reminder of the time I loaned my friend something? [*appeal to previous affiliation*] Should I ease my friend's fears by stressing my safe driving record?" [*appeal to previous success*] By examining the alternatives, you assemble a group of motivational appeals and organize them into narratives that serve as prods to action.

At other times, you may create motivational appeals through verbal labeling or **attribution.**[1] Suppose that you avoid going to church because you think of churches as conformist, authoritarian, dominating, repressive, and destructive institutions. One night, however, you attend a religious meeting where the preacher talks about the adventure of living a God-based life, the beauty of God's creation, the reverence one feels in living a spiritual life, and the endurance one must call upon to overcome doubts. On reflection, you decide that you have misconstrued the church's motivation. You become a devout churchgoer.

What happened? You changed the attributes of *church* in your own mind. Instead of attributing negative terms, such as *conformity, authority,* and *dominance,* to *church,* you began to attribute to it positive terms, such as *adventure, beauty,* and *reverence.* Your behavior eventually changed because you had begun to use different terms to label things. Motivational appeals may use language to activate desires in people.

FIGURE 13.1
Maslow's Hierarchy
of Needs
Abraham Maslow
arranged fundamental
human needs in a
hierarchy in which
lower-level needs
must be met before
higher-level needs
operate. Can you
think of several
examples of each
need?

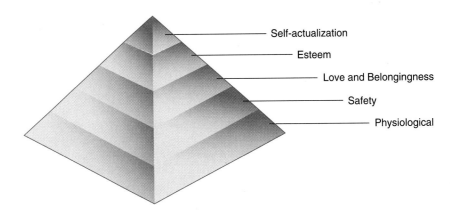

- Self-actualization
- Esteem
- Love and Belongingness
- Safety
- Physiological

Some Common Motivational Appeals

If you attempted to list the potential motivational appeals for every audience, you might never finish. The task is endless. Rather than trying to list each individual appeal, consider the general thrust of each motive cluster. A **motive cluster** is a group of individual appeals that are grounded in the same fundamental human motivation. Table 13.1 shows the three motive clusters—affiliation, achievement, and power—as well as the motivational appeals within each cluster.[2] **Affiliation motives** include the desire to belong to a group or to be well liked or accepted. This cluster also includes love, conformity, dependence upon others, sympathy toward others, and loyalty. **Achievement motives** are related to the intrinsic or extrinsic desire for success, adventure, creativity, and personal enjoyment. **Power motives** concern primarily the desire to exert influence over others.[3]

If you begin with this list, you'll be in a better position to choose those motivational appeals with the greatest relevance to your topic and audience. Remember this guideline as you make your choices: *motivational appeals work best when they have value for your listeners.* Analyze your audience and then choose your motivation appeals based on what you've learned about it.

TABLE 13.1 Motive Clusters   Individual motivational appeals fall into clusters that share a common theme. Think of a current television advertisement and identify the motive clusters in it.

Affiliation	Achievement	Power
Companionship	Acquisition/saving	Aggression
Conformity	Success/display	Authority/dominance
Deference/dependence	Prestige	Defense
Sympathy/generosity	Pride	Fear
Loyalty	Adventure/change	Autonomy/independence
Tradition	Perseverance	
Reverence/worship	Creativity	
Sexual attraction	Curiosity	
	Personal enjoyment	

The Affiliation Cluster

Affiliation motives are dominated by a desire for acceptance or approval. They refer to a greater concern for promoting interpersonal bonds than for achieving personal success or individual power. A social desire to be part of a group is an affiliation motive. What follows are some examples of appeals to listeners' affiliation desires:

1. *Companionship and affiliation.* "Birds of a feather flock together." We all need others—their presence, their touch, and their acceptance of who we are. That's why we respond to appeals such as, "We care about you," "Join our group and find fellowship with kindred souls," and "You're one of a select group to receive this special offer."

2. *Conformity.* "You've got the right one, ba-by." Ads for soft drinks work to convince you that "your kind of person" drinks Coke, Mountain Dew, or Pepsi. "The Pepsi Generation" explicitly stressed conformity, and the "You've got the right one, ba-by" campaign always shows groups of people approving Ray Charles's endorsement of that cola. At times, people's need to belong becomes so strong that they feel psychological pressure to be "one of the crowd." Commercials stressing what "the prudent homeowner does," what "the successful businesswoman wears," and what "all Americans believe" contain appeals to conformity.

3. *Deference/dependence.* "Nine out of ten doctors recommend. . . ." We defer to wisdom, experience, or expertise that surpasses our own. Testimony of experts to whom listeners might defer is a successful form of supporting material.

4. *Sympathy/generosity.* "You could be the parent this child has never known for a dollar a day." Such appeals appear in magazine ads asking you to support efforts to save children around the world through financial foster-parenting. All charitable appeals to give and appeals to self-sacrifice in the name of the "common good" assume that your social self—the part of you that bonds with others—will overcome your private self, the self-centered part of you. "Reach out and touch someone," "Give that others might live," and "There but for the grace of God go I" are appeals that form the heart of many actuative speeches.

5. *Loyalty.* "The camaraderie becomes something that you carry the rest of your life with those individuals. Sometimes you never get a chance to see those individuals again, but in your heart you know you'd do anything for them because they did that for you in a situation which could have gotten them killed."[4] With these words, Vietnam veteran Ron Mitscher tried to describe the loyalty he felt to his fellow soliders—to other members of "the Brotherhood." Speakers often ask listeners to be loyal to family, friends, organizations, states, geographical regions, or their nation.

6. *Tradition.* "Always for them: duty, honor, country. Always their blood, and sweat and tears, as they saw the way and the light."[5] When Gen. Douglas MacArthur wanted to symbolically unite West Point cadets to yesterday's soldiers, he appealed to tradition—the values that mark the entrance arch to the Academy. The past is stationary, stable; we use it to guide us into the unknown future—hence its great rhetorical strength.

7. *Reverence or worship.* "But in a larger sense we cannot dedicate, we cannot consecrate, we cannot hallow this ground. The brave men, living and dead, who struggled here, have consecrated it far above our power to add or detract."[6] With these words, President Abraham Lincoln invoked a sense of reverence for the dead of both the North and South after the bloody battle of Gettysburg, Pennsylvania. In doing so, he recognized our inferiority to others, to institutions, to nature, and to deities who humble us in their magnitude and eternity. Reverence can take three forms: hero worship, reverence for institutions, and divine worship. As a speaker, you have relatively little power to make your listeners revere you or your words; however, you can appeal to their reverence for ideas, people, or institutions.

8. *Sexual attraction.* "Nothing gets between me and my Calvin's." With that campaign, Calvin Klein jeans used an appeal that has sold you deodorant, hair rinse and spray, beer and liquor, automobiles—and blue jeans. Sex sells. As your consciousness of gender roles is raised, you may find blatantly sexual appeals objectionable. However, few sexual appeals are blatant; you'll notice that at the core they most often are appealing to people's desire to be attractive. Most of us respond positively to messages that promise to enhance our personal physical and psychological attractiveness to others.

The Achievement Cluster

Achievement motives concern an individual's desire to attain goals, to excel in certain behaviors or activities, or to obtain prestige or success. The following appeals to achievement motives can pull a person toward the accomplishment of a particular goal:

1. *Acquisition/saving.* "Earn good money now in our new Checking-Plus accounts!" We live in an era of investment clubs, Supplemental Retirement Accounts (SRAs), and more financial advisers than bankers. *Reward* is the name of the game, and its lure is strong. By describing material rewards in social, spiritual, or personal terms, you can also appeal to other motives at the same time as you appeal to achievement motives. So, appeals to buy U.S.

Saving Bonds not only promise reward but visualize you as part of a great American tradition—an affiliative appeal.

2. *Success/display.* "Successful executives carry the Connerton electronic organizers." "To make maximum use of your talents, act today. . . ." Appeals such as these depend on people's interest in making a mark and in developing or actualizing themselves.

3. *Prestige.* "L'Oreal—Because you're worth it!" Ads for luxury automobiles, designer clothes, and expensive personal grooming products make use of this appeal to your sense of worth—to your place in a community or within a power structure. Ownership of material goods carries with it status. An appeal to listeners' desire for prestige should take into account their desire for affiliation. For example, driving an expensive foreign car identifies one as a member of an elite group.

4. *Pride.* "Be proud of America. Support the troops." So far as appeals to pride are concerned, the 1991 Gulf War was a high point for many Americans. Over 80 percent of them supported President Bush's conduct of that operation; the appeal was strong. Such appeals tighten our loyalties to groups and—when coupled with appeals to adventure, creativity, or independence—move us to greater personal exertion.

5. *Adventure/change.* "Taste the High Country!" says the beer advertiser. "Join the Navy and see the world," says the local recruiter. The human soul yearns for release; the human body tingles at the prospect of risk. Participating in adventure is a way that people validate their own worth.

6. *Perseverance.* "If at first you don't succeed, try, try again." Pieces of conventional wisdom like this saying recognize that change does not come easily and that individuals must be taught to be patient as they seek a better life. Change is often slow but certainly worth the wait. Visualizing what the future will bring is an effective strategy in motivating people to persevere. "We shall overcome" and "For a better tomorrow" appeal to perseverance.

7. *Creativity.* "Draw me." Ads that say "Draw me," urging you to draw a duck to earn a scholarship for a correspondence art course, and cookbooks that promise you'll become a gourmet chef appeal to your need to be creative.

8. *Curiosity.* "Have you ever wondered what a well-trained American student can do to make an African tribal village a better place to live?" Children open alarm clocks to find out where the tick is, and adults crowd the sidewalks to gaze at a celebrity. Appeals to curiosity launch exploration, scholarship, and experimentation—and enrollment in the Peace Corps.

9. *Personal enjoyment.* "Let the good times roll!" Perhaps the most totally self-centered appeal is the appeal to pleasure. As many times as we act as group members, we act as individuals, responding to the promise of personal comfort and luxury, aesthetic enjoyment, recreation and rest, relief from home and work restraints, and just plain fun.

The Power Cluster

Humans seek to dominate and control others, either physically or symbolically. Appeals to power motives are often the most potent of all appeals. Although people can use power to manipulate others, not all uses of power are negative. By appealing to people's sense of social and moral responsibility, as well as to the power motives described below, you can urge people to use power in positive ways:

1. *Aggression.* "We have not raised armies with ambitious designs of separating from Great Britain and establishing independent States. We fight not for glory or for conquest. We exhibit to mankind the remarkable spectacle of a people attacked by unprovoked enemies, without any imputation or even suspicion of offense."[7] Thus did John Dickinson, the "Pennsylvania Farmer" as he called himself, urge the colonists to fight back against the British in the spring of 1775. Humans tend to form territorial or hierarchical groups and societies. The human urge to claim rights and territory is the foundation for appeals to personal and social competition. No one wants to lose. That's why advertisers tell you to "get ahead of the crowd" or "beat your competition to the punch."

2. *Authority/dominance.* "If the FDA [Food and Drug Administration] will not protect us, we must protect ourselves."[8] When Samantha Hubbard built that argument in a speech attacking the irradiation of food, she was appealing to our natural design to dominate our environment before it dominates us. Aggressive people can win in competition. Even McGruff, the crime-fighting dog featured in public service announcements who says, "Take a bite out of crime," appeals to the desire to dominate.

3. *Defense.* "If I were an American, as I am an Englishman, while a foreign troop was landed in my country, I never would lay down my arms—never—never—never."[9] In encouraging England to get out of America in 1777, former prime minister William Pitt recognized the power of an appeal to a defensive position. The line between attack and self-defense may seem a thin one at times, yet it's important to maintain it. It's seldom socially acceptable to attack someone else. A socially acceptable way to raise people's fighting spirit for a public cause is to appeal to the need for defense; President Bush worked hard in 1991 to portray the U.S. role in the Persian Gulf as one of defense rather than offense. The appeal is linked to power in terms of listeners' ability to exert authority over their collective needs through the defense of vital interests.

4. *Fear.* "Friends don't let friends drive drunk." This slogan of the Mothers Against Drunk Driving (MADD) campaign makes double use of fear appeal: it appeals to your fear of not being a true friend as well as to your fear of accidents involving drunk drivers. People have many fears—of failure, of death, of speechmaking, of inadequacy. Look at the ads: "Speed kills," "Ring around the collar!" "American Express: don't leave home without it." Fear can drive people to achievement and bravery or to hatred and butchery. Use fear appeals cautiously.

5. *Autonomy/independence.* "Free should the scholar be—free and brave. Free even to the definition of freedom, 'without any hindrance that does not arise out of his own constitution.'"[10] When Ralph Waldo Emerson spoke these words a century and a half ago, he was working hard to convince American intellectuals to separate themselves from European thinkers. You also hear this appeal: "Be your own person; don't follow the crowd." Ap-

peals to "be yourself" and "stand on your own two feet" draw their force from our struggles to stand apart from one another.

You may have noticed that some of the appeals we've just described seem to contradict each other. For example, fear seems to oppose adventure; sympathy and generosity seem to work against independence. Remember that human beings are rather changeable creatures, who at different times may pursue quite different goals.

There is a limitless number of human wants, needs, and motives, and of combinations of the three. We have, however, discussed some of the basic motives to which expert speakers often appeal in order to motivate their listeners.[11]

• Product advertisers rely on motivational appeals to influence the buying behaviors of target audiences. Which motivational appeals can you identify in these advertisements?

LEVI'S STREETLIGHTS. THE HOTTEST JEANS ON TWO

Be picky. We are.

How to Use Motivational Appeals

In practice, motivational appeals are seldom used alone; speakers usually combine them. Suppose you were selecting a new car. What factors would influence your decision? One would be price (*saving*); another would be comfort and appearance (*personal enjoyment*); a third might be European styling (*prestige*) or uniqueness (*independence*). These factors combined would add up to *pride* of ownership. Some of these influences, of course, would be stronger than others; some might conflict. But all of them probably would affect your choice. You would base your decision to buy the car on the strongest of the appeals.

Because motivational appeals are interdependent, it's a good idea to coordinate them. You should select three or four appeals that are related and that target segments of your audience. When you cluster appeals, you tap multiple dimensions of your listeners' lives.

Review your appeals for their pertinence and consistency. After all, you don't want to describe the *adventure* of spelunking (cave exploration) so vividly that you create a sense of *fear*. Conflicting appeals are counterproductive. Examine the following series of main headings for a speech given by a tourist agency representative urging students to take a summer trip to Europe:

I. The three-week tour is being offered for the low price of $2,000 (*acquisition and savings*).
II. There will be a minimum of supervision and regimentation (*independence*).
III. You'll be traveling with friends and fellow students (*companionship*).

In the complete presentation, this representative also emphasized the educational value of the experience (*self-advancement*) and said that a special mountain-climbing expedition would be arranged (*adventure*). Notice how the speaker targeted student audiences.

One final piece of general advice: inconspicuous appeals work best. Avoid saying, "I want you to *imitate* Jones, the successful banker" or "If you give to the anti-apartheid fund, we'll print your name in the newspapers so that your *reputation* as a caring person will be known to everybody." People rarely admit, even to themselves, that they act on the basis of self-centered motivations—greed, imitation, personal pride, and fear. Be subtle when using these appeals. For example, you might encourage listeners to imitate the actions of well-known people by saying, "Habitat for Humanity counts among its volunteers the former president and First Lady, Jimmy and Rosalyn Carter."

ORGANIZING THE SPEECH: THE MOTIVATED SEQUENCE

Now it's time to think about organizing your appeals. As we've suggested, an important consideration in structuring appeals is your listeners' psychological tendencies—ways in which individuals' own motivations and circumstances favor certain ways of structuring ideas. You must learn to sequence supporting materials and motivational appeals to form a useful organizational pattern for speeches as a whole. Since 1935, the most popular such pattern has been called **Monroe's**

Ethical Moments

Using Fear Appeals

Among the most potent appeals to audiences are fear appeals. Research suggests that fear appeals are so powerful that they actually can interfere with a listener's ability to process information critically. However, research indicates that fear appeals retain their effectiveness over extended periods of time.

Sometimes fear appeals are used for laudable goals, such as the Juvenile Awareness program at New Jersey's Rahway State Prison (the basis of the 1977 television special "Scared Straight"). In this program, deliquent youths are introduced to convicts who descibe the horrors of prison life. Results suggest that the program helps deter young people from further delinquent activity.

However, fear appeals are always accompanied by the potential for misuse. The possibility of misuse raises a number of ethical considerations. Think about the following applications of your classroom speaking. Evaluate the ethics of each situation. What would you do if you were the speaker? Why?

1. You are planning a persuasive speech to convince your audience that war is morally wrong. You are totally commited to peace and believe that anything you can do to maintain peace in this world is your moral obligation; therefore, you exaggerate some of the facts about recent world conflicts to frighten your audience about the results of war.

2. You give a speech on the increase of date rape on college campuses. In order to convince your audience that date rape is wrong and extremely common, you create scenarios that appeal to the fears of your listeners. Your scenarios are so vivid that several of your listeners, who are rape survivors, are visibly overcome with emotion. One of the listeners is so upset that she must leave the classroom during your speech. Everyone in the audience sees her leave.

3. Knowing that fear impedes the ability to think critically, you decide to arouse fears in your listeners so that they will fail to perceive your argument is unsound. You feel that it is your listeners' responsibility to listen critically and that if they are willing to accept unsound arguments, they're fools.

4. You feel very strongly that the college president is wrong to continue investing college money in countries where tortue and imprisonment without trial are legal. You present a very persuasive speech in which you appeal to your audience's fears by suggesting that the college president is actually propagating torture and corrupting the values of U.S. citizens to the point that someday torture and imprisonment without trial might be legal in the United States. Your listeners become so incensed, as a result of your speech, that they march to the president's house and set his car on fire.

5. You are preparing to give a speech on hate crimes in the United States and you want to make sure that you have your audience's attention before you begin. Therefore, you decide to present the details of a series of grisly murders committed in your town by a psychopath—even though these murders were not motivated by hate but by mental illness and so they aren't examples of hate crimes.

motivated sequence (see Figure 13.2).[12] We will devote the rest of this chapter to it.

The motivated sequence ties problems and solutions to human motives. The motivated sequence for the presentation of verbal materials is composed of five basic steps:

1. *Attention.* Create interest and desire.
2. *Need.* Develop the problem by analyzing wrongs in the world and by relating them to the individual's interests, wants, or desires.
3. *Satisfaction.* Propose a plan of action that will alleviate the problem and satisfy the individual's interests, wants, or desires.
4. *Visualization.* Depict the world as it will look if the plan is put into action.
5. *Action.* Call for personal commitments and deeds.

Using the Motivated Sequence to Structure Actuative Speeches

The motivated sequence provides an ideal blueprint for urging an audience to take action. That's what it was designed for—since it was used originally as the basis for sales presentations. Let's look first at some ways that you might use Monroe's sequence to structure actuative speeches.

Step 1: Getting Attention

You must challenge audience disengagement or apathy at the very beginning of your speech if you hope to persuade your listeners to adopt a belief or to act. A review will remind you how startling statements, illustrations, questions, and other supporting materials can focus attention on your message. You can't persuade an audience unless you have its attention.

Step 2: Showing the Need: Describing the Problem

Once you've captured the attention of your listeners, you're ready to explain why your policy is needed. To do this, you must show that a definite problem exists. You must point out, through facts and figures, just how bad the present situation is: "Last month our Littleton plant produced only 200 carburetors rather than the 300 scheduled. If we don't increase production, we'll have to shut down our main assembly line at Denver. That will cost the company over $800,000 and put 150 people out of work."

In its full form, a need or problem step has four parts:

1. *Statement.* Give a definite, concise statement of the problem.
2. *Illustration.* Give one or more examples explaining and clarifying the problem.
3. *Ramification.* Offer additional examples, statistical data, testimony, and other forms of support showing the extent and seriousness of the problem.
4. *Pointing.* Offer an explanation of how the problem directly affects the listener.

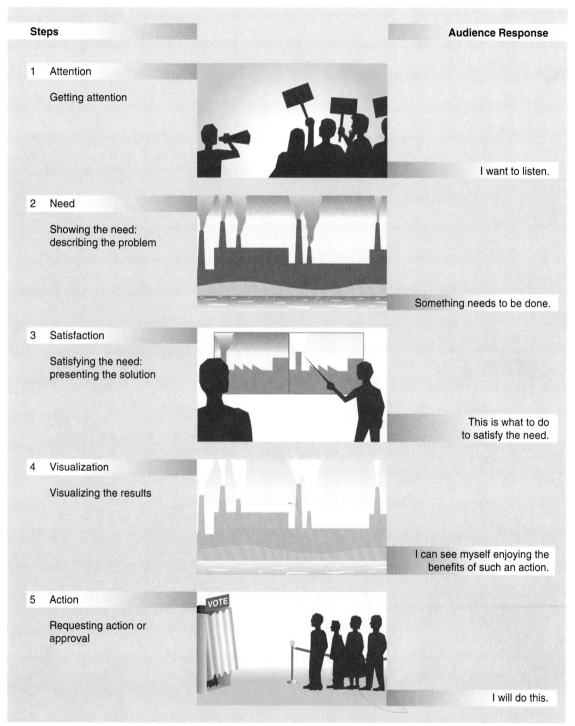

FIGURE 13.2 The Motivated Sequence   Notice how the audience will respond to each step of the motivated sequence.

Sample Outline for a Persuasive Speech

• • • •   Each of the five steps of the motivated sequence is illustrated in the following speech outline

Are Lotteries the Answer?[13]

Specific Purpose: To persuade listeners to reject the hidden costs of state lotteries.

Attention step: The speaker uses a typical, hypothetical illustration to set out the problem clearly.

I. Yesterday, thousands of men and women in our state stepped up to the cashier at their local convenience stores and purchased lottery tickets. Many of these men and women, such as Eldon Washington and Carmen Ruiz, went home with a chance on a dream instead of the basic necessities of life. Tomorrow, they'll go back to purchase another lottery ticket. It's time we reconsidered this form of institutionalized gambling—our state lottery.

Need step: The speaker identifies two needs—one appealing to a fear of addiction and the other to sympathy for others—to force listeners to think about something other than their own interests and desires. The fear appeal is aimed at personal concerns, and the sympathy appeal at the plight of others.

II. The costs of the state lottery must be addressed.
 A. The state lottery has two hidden costs.
  1. It encourages gambling.
   a. The percentage of people playing the lottery has risen dramatically in states such as California and Ohio.
   b. The number of people being treated for compulsive gambling disorders has risen in the same proportions.
   c. With few exceptions, states lack sufficient treatment programs for compulsive gamblers.
  2. The lottery is a regressive tax on the poor.
   a. People earning under $10,000 per year are more likely to buy lottery tickets than any other group.
   b. Poor people spend a higher percentage of their incomes on lottery tickets.
 B. Unless we reconsider the hidden costs of our state lotteries, they will continue to encourage gambling and exploit the poor.

Satisfaction step: Knowing that a move to abolish lotteries would be unsuccessful in these times, the speaker proposes measures of help and control—aid for addicts and limits on advertising and purchases. These measures do not seem radical but rather temperate and sensible. They're well suited for an audience that probably buys lottery tickets now and then.

III. What can be done to offset the negative impacts of the state lottery?
 A. More states should be encouraged to follow the example of New Jersey, one of the few states to fund a program to help compulsive gamblers.
  1. New Jersey spends less than .0007 percent of total lottery revenues for its treatment program.
  2. Studies indicate that treatment of compulsive gambling is highly successful.
 B. Limits should be placed on advertising for lottery ticket sales.
  1. Total advertising budgets should be fixed.
  2. Advertisements should be discontinued during the peak family television viewing hours.

Visualization step: *Here, the lines of analysis offered by the speaker can be turned into word pictures of treatment programs, reduced advertising, and not-unreasonable limitations on individual purchases (details not provided here). The audience must be made to see the solution in positive ways—even to picture its own activities when the solution is in effect.*

Action step: *Specific actions aren't called for in a straightforward persuasive speech—only potential actions. The speaker thus is arming listeners to act in response to the central idea when they get a chance; the speaker is trying to prepare the audience for action when the time comes.*

C. Limits should be placed on the number of tickets purchased by one individual.

IV. If government were to act more responsibly in its promotion of the state lottery, imagine the benefits that would accrue.

    A. An increased number of compulsive gamblers could be identified and treated.

        1. Treatment programs could be established and staffed, using only a minimal amount of lottery revenue.

        2. The focus on treatment probably would encourage further research into addictive behaviors.

    B. The media mania accompanying large jackpots could be curbed.

    C. The propensity of some individuals to spend beyond their means would be stopped.

    D. The revenue produced by the lottery would remain relatively unaffected.

V. We need to understand the true costs of our state lotteries.

    A. Consider those who are most affected by lottery ticket purchases—compulsive gamblers and the poor.

    B. When given the opportunity, voice your opinion for treatment programs and limiting advertisements—we need responsible government.

Statement and *pointing* should always be present, but the inclusion of *illustration* and *ramification* will depend on the amount of detail required to convince the audience. Whether you use the complete development or only part of it, the *need* step is critical in your speech. Here your subject is first tied to the needs and desires of your listeners.

Step 3: Satisfying the Need: Presenting the Solution

The solution or satisfaction step urges the adoption of a policy. Its goal is to get your listeners to agree that the program you propose is the correct one. Therefore, this step consists of presenting your proposed solution to the problem and proving that this solution is practical and desirable.

Five items are usually contained in a fully developed satisfaction step:

1. *Statement.* State the attitude, belief, or action you wish the audience to adopt. This is a statement of action: "We need to adopt an incentive system for our Littleton carburetor plant."

2. *Explanation.* Make sure that your proposal is understood. Visual aids such as charts and diagrams can be very useful here. In our example, you would define the incentive system: "By *incentive system,* I mean that workers at the Littleton plant should be paid by the actual number of carburetors completed rather than the hours worked."

3. *Theoretical demonstration.* Show how your proposed solution meets the need. For example, you could say, "Worker productivity will rise because workers are paid not just for putting in time but for completing carburetors."

4. *Reference to practical experience.* Supply examples to prove that the proposal has worked effectively where it has been tried. Facts, figures, and the testimony of experts support your contention: "Production at our New Albany plant increased by 50 percent after we instituted this compensation schedule."

5. *Meeting objections.* Forestall opposition by answering any objections that might be raised against the proposal. You might counter the objections of the labor union by arguing, "Increased plant productivity will allow us to expand the medical benefits for plant workers."

Just as certain phases can sometimes be omitted from the need step, one or more of these phases can be left out of the satisfaction step. Also, the foregoing order does not always have to be followed exactly. Occasionally, you can best meet objections by answering them as they arise. In other situations, the theoretical demonstration and reference to practical experience can be combined. If the satisfaction step is developed properly, at its conclusion the audience will say, "Yes, you're right; this is a practical and desirable solution to the problem you identified."

Step 4: Visualizing the Results

The function of the visualization step is to intensify desire. It should picture for the audience future conditions if your proposal (a) is adopted or (b) is not adopted. Because it projects the audience into the future, this step might also be called the *projection step.* This projection can be accomplished in one of three ways: by (1) the *positive method,* (2) the *negative method,* or (3) the *method of contrast.*

1. *The positive method.* Describe how conditions will improve under your proposal. Make such a description vivid and concrete. Select a situation that you are quite sure will arise. Then picture your listeners actually enjoying the conditions your proposal will produce. For example, if plant productivity allows better medical benefits, describe the advantages for everyone—lower deductibles, dental care, free eye examinations, and hospice services.

2. *The negative method.* Describe conditions as they will be in the future if your proposal is *not* carried out. Picture for your audience the evils that will arise from failure to follow your advice. Select the most undesirable conditions and show how they will be aggravated if your proposal is rejected. You might describe plant employees being laid off, losing their pension plan, and experiencing the trauma of finding new jobs in a tight job market.

3. *The method of contrast.* Combine the two preceding methods. Use the negative approach first and then use the positive approach. In this way, the benefits of the proposal are contrasted with the disadvantages of the present system. The following illustration shows how a speaker, urging you to carefully plan all four years of college before starting your freshman year, might develop a visualization step by the method of contrast.

Suppose that you enter the university, as nearly a quarter of our students do, with little sense of educational interests and goals. In your first two semesters, you simply take a few required courses and pass your writing and speaking skills tests. In your second year, you start experimenting with some electives on the basis of friends' recommendations: "Take Speech 101 because it's easy"; "Take Photography 102 because it's cool"; "Take Art 103 because it's pretty"; "Take History 104 because I'm taking it"; "Take Astronomy 105 because the professor is neat." Now comes your junior year—you're nowhere near a major, and you're getting close to the three-quarter mark in your education. Your adviser nags you, your parents nag you, your friends nag you—you even get down on yourself. In your senior year, you sample some social work courses, finally discovering something you really like. Only then do you realize it will take three or four more semesters—if you're lucky—to complete a B.S.W. degree.

In contrast, suppose you—like another quarter of our entering students— seek career and personal advising early. You enroll for the no-credit "Careers and Vocational Choices" seminar in your first semester. While meeting your liberal arts requirements, you take classes in as many different departments as possible so as to get a broad sampling. Near the end of your sophomore year, you talk with people in both career planning and personal counseling, all the while trying courses in areas of possible interest. By your junior year, you get departmental advisers in two majors, find out you don't really like one as much as you thought, and then go only to the second after midyear. You then complete that major, taking a correspondence class to catch up because you were a little behind; but still you graduate with other freshman who entered the year you did.

*Careful planning, reasoning through choices, and rigorously analyzing your own interests and talents—these are the actions that separate the com-*pleters *from the* complainers *at the end of your years here. So. . . . [Move into the action step at this point.]*

Whichever method you use—positive, negative, or contrast—remember that the visualization step must stand the test of reality. The conditions you picture must be realistic and vivid. Let your listeners actually see themselves enjoying the advantages or suffering the evils you describe. The more realistically you depict the situation, the more strongly your listeners will react.

Step 5: Requesting Action

The function of the action step is to call for explicit action. You can do this by offering a challenge or appeal, a special inducement, or a statement of personal intention. For examples, review the conclusions discussed in Chapter 8. Your request for action should be short, to take advantage of your audience's motivational intensity. Finish your speech firmly and sit down.

Remember that the motivated sequence is flexible. You can adapt it to various situations once you are familiar with its basic pattern. Like cooks who alter good recipes to their personal tastes, you can adjust the formula for particular occasions— changing the number of main points from section to section, sometimes omitting restatement from the attention step, sometimes omitting the positive or negative projections from the visualization step. *Like any recipe, the motivated sequence is designed to give you a formula that fits many different situations.*[14] It gives you an excellent pattern but does not remove the human element; you still must think about your choices. Consider the choices made in the following example.

Sample Outline for an Actuative Speech

• • • •

Numbers That Can Save Your Life[15]

Specific Purpose: To urge students to begin checking their blood pressure even while in school.

Attention step: The speaker opens with common, everyday numbers to ease the audience into the speech; of course, the speaker also wants listeners by the end of the speech to see their blood pressure numbers in as commonplace a framework as they see their ID, telephone, and social security numbers.

I. Americans live in a maze of numbers:
   A. Your student ID number identifies you on the campus.
   B. Your telephone number lets others reach you.
   C. Your social security number follows you from near birth to death and after.

II. A number most of you ignore, however, could kill you—your blood pressure.
   A. According to the Department of Health and Human Services, this year 310,000 Americans will die from illnesses where the major factor is hypertension.
   B. Two million will suffer strokes, heart attacks, and kidney failure as a direct result of hypertension.
   C. According to Dr. Theodore Cooper, Director of the Heart and Lung Institute, "Hypertension can be brought under control through proven treatment which is neither unduly hazardous, complicated or expensive."
   D. Before this will sink in, you must understand what high blood pressure does to your body.

Need step: The speaker decides to attack the problem of hypertension by using multiple devices: statistics to quantify the enormity of the problem, expert testimony to add some emotional power to the numbers, and a good explanation of what happens to people with high blood pressure to make the problem seem real. A final piece of testimony is added to stir in a little more fear.

   1. When your blood pressure becomes too great for the arterial walls, it can tear a muscle; and if the artery breaks, you can die.
   2. High blood pressure can also result from fatty tissues, salts, and fluid build-ups that cause the arteries to narrow and the heart to work harder, until it stops.
   E. Even worse, according to the National High Blood Pressure Council, "Half of those who have high blood pressure don't even know that they do. Of those who do, only half are being treated; only half again of those have their blood pressure under control. Patients and physicians alike just don't seem to take this condition seriously."

Satisfaction step: The speaker puts forward a three-layered solution: a national mass-media assault, a community-based solution, and personal steps listeners can take. Listeners thus can feel a comprehensive solution has been offered.

III. Thus, the public needs to be aware of these problems, health care must be improved, and hypertensives must learn that self-control is life.
   A. Public service ads can keep the issue before the public.
   B. Community- and business-supported hypertension clinics must be established at little or no cost to clients.
   C. Individuals simply must monitor their own blood pressure regularly.

Visualization step: The speaker goes with both negative and positive visualization. The negative visualization of more heart attacks is fueled by fear and is complemented nicely by a positive visualization arising from specific instances of successful programs.

IV. The future of a significant proportion of our population depends on these programs.

    A. Given the American diet, general lack of exercise, and tense life-styles, heart attacks will claim more and more victims annually without these programs.

    B. With such programs, our collective health will improve measurably.

       1. Drs. Andrea Foote and John Erfurt have established a Worker Health Program, which was tested at four different sites and which allowed 92 percent of the hypertensives at those job sites to control their blood pressure.

       2. The Hypertensive Education Program in Michigan and Connecticut is cutting the insurance rates in those states.

       3. In 1970, Savannah, Georgia, had the infamous title, "Stroke Capital of the World"; but today, with 14 permanent blood pressure reading stations and special clinics, the stroke rate has been cut in half.

Action step: Listeners in a speech class can't do much to affect the national and community programs, but they certainly can implement the personal aspects of the solution. That's what the speaker stresses, telling what range to look for and where to get a blood pressure check free of charge.

V. Even now, in your prime, it's time for you to develop good health maintenance habits.

    A. You could be one of America's 11 million people with high blood pressure and not even know it.

    B. Even if you're not, you should monitor yourself to remain safe in the knowledge that your pressure is in the normal—90/70 to 140/90—range.

    C. Get your blood pressure checked today, free of charge, at the Student Health Center and save a life—your own.

Sample Speech to Actuate Using the Motivated Sequence

• • • •

The following speech, delivered to a joint session of Congress on December 8, 1941, by President Franklin Delano Roosevelt, requested a declaration of war against Japan. Round-the-clock negotiations with Japan suddenly had been disrupted when, on Sunday morning, December 7, the Japanese launched a massive surprise attack on Pearl Harbor, Hawaii, sinking eight American battleships and other smaller craft and leveling planes and airfields.

The nation was numbed, Congress was indignant, and the president moved quickly. The joint session was held in the House chamber. The galleries were overflowing, and the speech was broadcast worldwide. Notice that this message contains only a short attention step because the surprise attack created all of the necessary attention, a longer need step (paragraphs 2 through 10) that details the situation in the Pacific, and a short satisfaction step (paragraph 11) that only hints at American military strategy. The visualization step (paragraphs 12 through 16) attempts to steel the nation for war, and it is followed by a concise, sharply drawn action step. The president's strategies seem clear. The fact that the need and visualization steps receive detailed development shows his concern for (a) providing an informational base for the action and (b) offering a psychological orientation to wartime thinking.

For A Declaration of War Against Japan[16]
Franklin Delano Roosevelt

Attention step: The attention of the world already is focused on the Pearl Harbor incident; little is needed to gain attention.

Need step: National and international audiences are still shocked and confused. Therefore, President Roosevelt offers background information in paragraphs 2 and 3 as well as descriptions of the attacks in paragraphs 4 through 9, summarizing the need for American action in paragraph 10.

TO THE CONGRESS OF THE UNITED STATES: Yesterday, December 7, 1941—a date which will live in infamy—the United States of America was suddenly and deliberately attacked by naval and air forces of the Empire of Japan./1

The United States was at peace with that nation and, at the solicitation of Japan, was still in conversation with its government and its Emperor, looking toward the maintenance of peace in the Pacific. Indeed, one hour after Japanese air squadrons had commenced bombing in Oahu, the Japanese Ambassador to the United States and his colleague delivered to the Secretary of State a formal reply to a recent American message. While this reply stated that it seemed useless to continue the existing diplomatic negotiations, it contained no threat or hint of war or armed attack./2

It will be recorded that the distance of Hawaii from Japan makes it obvious that the attack was deliberately planned many days or even weeks ago. During the intervening time the Japanese government had deliberately sought to deceive the United States by false statements and expressions of hope for continued peace./3

The attack yesterday on the Hawaiian Islands has caused severe damage to American naval and military forces. Very many American lives have been lost. In addition, American ships have been reported torpedoed on the high

Satisfaction step: *The United States now is preparing for war and the secrecy that surrounds it; hence the president does not detail the actions taken.*

Visualization step: *The president must gather in the American people and get them behind his war effort. Visualization is important for him to accomplish those goals, so he invokes history or memory (paragraph 12), the righteousness of the cause (paragraph 13), the treachery of the opponents (paragraph 14), the reality of warfare (paragraph 15), and optimism for a successful completion of hostile actions (paragraph 16).*

Action step: *The action needed is obvious: President Roosevelt calls directly upon the joint session of Congress to pass the resolution declaring war on the Japanese Empire.*

seas between San Francisco and Honolulu./4

Last night Japanese forces attacked Hong Kong./5

Last night Japanese forces attacked Guam./6

Last night Japanese forces attacked the Philippine Islands./7

Last night the Japanese attacked Wake Island./8

This morning the Japanese attacked Midway Island./9

Japan has, therefore, undertaken a surprise offensive extending throughout the Pacific area. The facts of yesterday speak for themselves. The people of the United States have already formed their opinions and well understand the implications to the very life and safety of our nation./10

As Commander-in-Chief of the Army and Navy I have directed that all measures be taken for our defense./11

Always will we remember the character of the onslaught against us./12

No matter how long it may take us to overcome this premeditated invasion, the American people in their righteous might will win through to absolute victory./13

I believe I interpret the will of the Congress and of the people when I assert that we will not only defend ourselves to the uttermost but will make very certain that this form of treachery shall never endanger us again./14

Hostilities exist. There is no blinking at the fact that our people, our territory, and our interests are in grave danger./15

With confidence in our armed forces—with the unbounded determination of our people—we will gain the inevitable triumph—so help us God./16

I ask that the Congress declare that since the unprovoked and dastardly attack by Japan on Sunday, December 7, a state of war has existed between the United States and the Japanese Empire./17

CHAPTER SUMMARY

1. Speeches to persuade and actuate have psychological or behavioral change as their primary goal.

2. Because need satisfaction is important to all human beings, the concept of motive need is central to an understanding of persuasion and actuation.

3. Keys to the achievement of persuasion are motivational appeals, which are verbally created visualizations that link an idea, entity, or course of action to a motive.

4. Occasionally motivational appeals are attached directly to other concepts in a verbal process known as attribution.

5. Commonly used motivational appeals can be grouped into three clusters: affiliation, achievement, and power.

6. Monroe's motivated sequence is an organizational pattern for actuative and persuasive speeches based on people's natural psychological tendencies.

7. The five steps in the motivated sequence are attention, need, satisfaction, visualization, and action. Each step can be developed by using appropriate rhetorical devices.

KEY TERMS

achievement motives (p. 238)
affiliation motives (p. 238)
attribution (p. 237)
Monroe's motivated sequence (pp. 244, 246)
motivational appeal (p. 237)
motive cluster (p. 238)
motive need (p. 237)
power motives (p. 238)

SKILLBUILDING ACTIVITIES

1. Present a five- to eight-minute actuative speech in which your primary goal is to get class members to actually *do* something: sign a petition, write a letter to an official, attend a meeting, give blood, or take some other personal action. Use the motivated sequence to create attention, lay out needs, propose a solution, visualize the results, and call for action. On a future "Actuative Speech Check-Up Day," find out how many took the actions you suggested. How successful were you? Why?

2. In a brief persuasive speech, attempt to alter your classmates' impression or understanding of a particular concept. Analyze their current attitudes toward it and then prepare a speech reversing those attitudes. Sample topics might include: pesticides, recycling, United Nations peacekeeping operations, in vitro fertilization, animal rights, or genetic counseling for prospective parents.

3. What relevant motivational appeals might you use in addressing each of the following audiences? Be ready to discuss your choices in class.

   a. A group of farmers protesting federal agricultural policy.

   b. A meeting of pre-business majors concerned about jobs.

   c. Women at a seminar on nontraditional employment opportunities.

   d. A meeting of local elementary and secondary classroom teachers seeking smaller classes.

   e. A group gathered for an old-fashioned Fourth of July picnic.

REFERENCES

1. For a fuller discussion of attribution, see Philip G. Zimbardo, *Psychology and Life,* 12th ed. (New York: HarperCollins, 1990).

2. For a fuller discussion of motivational appeals, see Bruce E. Gronbeck, Ray E. McKerrow, Douglas Ehninger, and Alan H. Monroe, *Principles and Types of Speech Communication,* 12th ed. (New York: HarperCollins, 1994), Chap. 6.

3. Katharine Blick Hoyenga and Hermit T. Hoyenga, *Motivational Explanations of Behavior: Evolutionary, Physiological, and Cognitive Ideas* (Monterey, Calif.: Brooks/Cole Publishing, 1984), Chap. 1; Joseph Veroff, "Contextualism and Human Motives," *Frontiers of Motivational Psychology: Essays in Honor of John W. Atkinson,* edited by Donald R. Brown and Joseph Veroff (New York: Springer-Verlag, 1986), 132–145; Abigail J. Stewart, ed., *Motivation and Society: A Volume in Honor of David C. McClelland* (San Francisco: Jossey-Bass, 1982); Janet T. Spence, ed., *Achievement and Achievement Motives* (San Francisco: W. H. Freeman, 1983).

4. From an interview with Ron Mitscher, Vietnam veteran, for *Parallels: The Soldiers' Knowledge and the Oral History of Contemporary Warfare,* edited by J. T. Hansen, A. Susan Owen, and Michael Patrick Madden (New York: Aldine de Gruyter, 1992), 137.

5. From Douglas MacArthur, "Duty, Honor and Country," in *The Dolphin Book of Speeches,* edited by George W. Hibbitt (New York: Doubleday, 1965).

6. Abraham Lincoln, "Gettysburg Address," speech delivered in 1863, reprinted in *Lincoln at Gettysburg: The Words That Remade America,* edited by Garry Wills (New York: Simon & Schuster, 1992), 261.

7. John Dickinson, "The Declaration on Taking Up Arms," speech delivered 6 July 1775, reprinted in *The World's Best Orations,* edited by David J. Brewer (St. Louis: Ferd. P. Kaiser, 1899), 5:1855.

8. Samantha L. Hubbard, "Irradiation of Food," speech reprinted in Bruce E. Gronbeck et al., *Principles of Speech Communication,* 11th brief ed. (New York: HarperCollins, 1992), 354.

9. William Pitt [the Elder], "The Attempt to Subjugate America," speech delivered in 1777, reprinted in Brewer, 3:1070.

10. Ralph Waldo Emerson, "The American Scholar," speech delivered in 1837, reprinted in Brewer, 10:2005.

11. See David C. McClelland, *Power: The Inner Experience* (New York: Irvington, 1975); David C. McClelland, *Human Motivation* (Glenview, Ill.: Scott, Foresman, 1985).

12. To see how Monroe originally conceived of the motivated sequence, see especially the Foreword to Alan H. Monroe, *Principles and Types of Speech* (Chicago: Scott, Foresman, 1935), vii–x.

13. We've omitted most supporting materials, but they can be found in Tim Schreiner, "The West: Who Plays California's Lottery?" *American Demographics* 8 (1986): 526; John Mikesell and Maureen A. Pirog-Good, "State Lotteries and Crime: The Regressive Revenue Producer Is Linked with a Crime Rate Higher by 3 Percent," *American Journal of Economics and Sociology* 49 (1990): 7, 13; William H. Willemen, "Lottery Losers," *The Christian Century* 107 (Jan. 1990): 48.

14. We're not suggesting here that the other organizational patterns discussed in Chapter 7 should be discarded; as we noted there, they're useful in specific circumstances. Here, we're noting that the motivated sequence is particularly useful for motivationally oriented persuasive speeches, especially actuative speeches.

15. This outline is based on Todd Ambs, "The Silent Killer," *Winning Orations;*

his materials were formed into an outline by special arrangement with Larry Schnoor, Executive Director, Interstate Oratorical Association, Concordia College, Moorhead, Minn.

16. Originally published in the *Congressional Record,* 77th Congress, 1st Sess., vol. 87, pt. 9 (8 Dec. 1941), 9504–9505.

Argumentation and Critical Thinking

"*Turrell Baker for President! We need a strong class president, and, through his active participation in school sports, Turrell has proven he can lead. Turrell holds the school record for passes completed, and he was instrumental in winning our last two home games this year. Turrell's versatile, too. He participated in track and field as a middle-distance runner and was a key player on an intramural volleyball team. We need effective decision makers in student government. Turrell's just the person to do the job right!"* Ms. Caligari looked up from the flyer she had been reading. "So," she asked her public speaking class, "would this message convince you to vote for Turrell?" The students murmured, but no one said much. Ms. Caligari smiled. "You're having trouble making up your minds here because of relevance: are Turrell's athletic experiences and achievements relevant to the claim that he'd make a great class president? If the reasons don't fit the claim, the argument's dead."

The ability to think critically is central to your participation in the social world. You're constantly bombarded with requests, appeals, and pleas to change your beliefs or adopt new ways of doing things. Sorting through all those appeals to determine which are justified and whether you should alter your thoughts or actions requires analysis and evaluation skills. Before committing yourself, you've got to be able to analyze appeals, such as those given for Turrell Baker, to determine if the reasons fit the claim being made. If you don't do that, you'll follow every new piper who comes along playing catchy tunes, regardless of where that person is leading you.

You need to develop what's called a *critical spirit*—the ability to analyze others' ideas and requests.[1] Criticism is a process of careful assessment, evalua-

• Public advocates use argumentation to convince others. Can you think of situations such as this one where argumentation is critical?

tion, and judgment of ideas and motives. It's also a matter of supporting your assessment, evaluation, and judgment with reasons. As you engage in evaluation—assessing reasons or offering counterreasons—you become a critical thinker. You also develop critical skills when you advance a claim and then offer reasons why others ought to accept it. The critical spirit should be cultivated by both speakers and listeners.

Argumentation is a process of advancing claims supported by good reasons and allowing others to test those claims and reasons or to offer counterarguments. Through argumentation, people hope to come to reasonable conclusions about factual, valuative, and policy matters. The act of arguing does not consist merely of offering an opinion or stating information; it commits you to communicating by using good reasons.

You probably engage in argument in many ways. In public forums such as city council meetings, you might provide reasons your community should erect an incinerator for burning solid waste or you might advocate better community regulation of local day-care facilities. You might write a letter to the editor of a newspaper providing your solution for the welfare crisis or urging other readers to vote for your candidate on election day. In conversations with friends, you

FIGURE 14.1
The Elements
of Argument
Why are all three
elements necessary
for an argument?

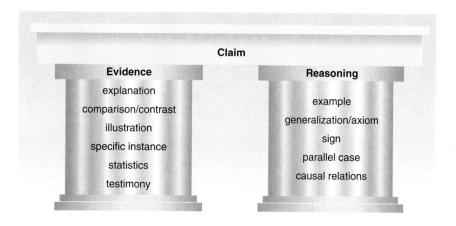

probably stick up for your sports team. In each of these cases, you'll be more effective if your arguments are sound. In this chapter, we'll examine the structure of arguments, then offer ways for you to critically evaluate the arguments of others, and we'll finish with some tips to help you argue effectively.

THE MACHINERY OF ARGUMENTATION

Every argumentative unit is like a piece of machinery, and all of its parts must work together for the argument to win agreement from an audience. Just as a machine is built with belts and pulleys that transform power into production, so an argument is built with three essential elements that must work together to compel belief in another person: (a) the claim or proposition you are defending, (b) the relevant evidence that you provide in support of that claim, and (c) the reasoning pattern that you use to connect the evidence with the claim. (See Figure 14.1.) Our next task is to examine these building blocks of argument.

Types of Claims

Most argumentative speeches assert that: (a) something is or is not the case; (b) something is desirable or undesirable; or (c) something should or should not be done. Such judgments or assessments are the speaker's **claims** or propositions. Your first task as an arguer or listener is to determine the type of claim being argued.

Claims of Fact

A **claim of fact** asserts that something is or is not the case. If you're trying to convince listeners that "Price controls on raw agricultural products result in food shortages," you're presenting a factual claim—asserting that a given state of affairs exists. When confronted with this sort of claim, two questions can occur to the critically aware listener:

1. *By what criteria, or standards of judgment, should the truth or accuracy of the claim be measured?* If you're asked to determine someone's height,

you immediately look for a yardstick or other measuring tool. Similarly, listeners look for a standard by which to measure the accuracy of a factual claim. Before agreeing that price controls result in shortages, discriminating listeners will want to know what you mean by *shortages*. Would you define *shortages* as "the disappearance, for all practical purposes, of a given kind of food" or merely as "less of that food than everyone might desire?" Against what standard, precisely, is the accuracy of the claim to be judged? As a speaker, you need to build those judgments into your speeches.

2. *Do the facts of the situation fit the criteria?* Does the actual amount of produce currently on supermarket shelves fall within the limits set by your definition of *shortages?* First, get listeners to agree to certain standards of judgment, and then present evidence that a given state of affairs meets those standards. In these ways, you work to gain the assent of listeners to your factual claims.

Claims of Value

When your claim asserts that something is good or bad, desirable or undesirable, justified or unjustified, you're advancing a **claim of value**—a claim about the intrinsic worth of the belief or action in question. Here, too, it is always appropriate to ask: (a) by what standards is something to be judged? and (b) how well does the item in question measure up to the standards specified?

For example, you can measure the quality of a college by the distinction of its faculty (intellectual value), the excellence of its physical plant (material value), the success of its graduates (practical value), the size of its endowment (monetary value), or the reputation that it enjoys according to surveys of educational excellence (educational value). You then can assess the worth of a particular college by each of these criteria to come up with the sorts of scores you find in books that rate colleges. In other words, value judgments are not mere assertions of personal preference—"I like Miami or Ohio." Rather, they must be argued for, as if someone else is going to examine or challenge them.

Claims of Policy

A **claim of policy** recommends a course of action that you want the audience to approve. Typical examples are: "Federal standards for air quality *should be* substantially strengthened"; "The student senate *should have* the authority to expel students who cheat." In both instances, you're asking your audience to endorse a proposed policy or course of action. When analyzing a policy claim, four questions are relevant:

1. *Is there a need for such a policy or course of action?* If your listeners don't believe that a change is called for, they're not likely to approve your proposal.

2. *Is the proposal practical?* Can we afford the expense it would entail? Would it really solve the problem or remove the evil it is designed to correct? Does such a policy stand a reasonable chance of being adopted? If you can't show that your proposal meets these and similar tests, you can hardly expect it to be endorsed.

3. *Are the benefits your proposal will bring greater than its disadvantages?* People are reluctant to approve a proposal that promises to create conditions worse than the ones it is designed to correct. Burning a barn to the ground may be an effective way to get rid of rats, but it's hardly a desirable one. The benefits and disadvantages that will result from a plan of action must always be carefully weighed along with considerations of its basic workability.

4. *Is the proposal superior to any other plan or policy?* Listeners are hesitant to approve a policy if they have reason to believe that an alternative course of action is more practical or more beneficial.

As you've seen, then, different types of claims make varying demands on you as an arguer. (See Table 14.1.) And, too, arguers must tell audiences how to assess their claims. Articulating criteria or standards for judgment is essential for the person who tries to win an argument. If you think tuition increases should be tied to the Consumer Price Index while your opponent believes tuition should be tied to rises and falls in state tax revenue, you have a serious disagreement over what standards to apply. Rather than haggling about increases and decreases in tuition, you and your opponent have to stop and see whose standard for judgment will be accepted by your listeners. When you agree upon the criteria, you can conduct a meaningful debate.

Unless there are sound reasons for delay, you should announce your claim early in your speech. If listeners don't see precisely where you're going in your argument, your strongest arguments may be lost on them. Take time to say something such as, "Today, I want to convince you that increases and decreases in student tuition should be coupled with the Consumer Price Index. If the Board of Regents takes this action, the cost of education will be more fairly distributed between the state and the students."[2]

TABLE 14.1   Types of Claims   Notice how each type of claim can be analyzed.

Claim	Description	Analysis
Claim of fact	Assertion of truth or that something exists	1. By what criteria is the truth or accuracy of the claim measured? 2. Do the facts of the situation fit the criteria?
Claim of value	Assertion that something is good or bad; desirable or undesirable; justified or unjustified	1. By what standards is something to be judged? 2. How well does the thing measure up?
Claim of policy	Recommendation of a course of action	1. Is there a need for this policy or course of action? 2. Is the proposal practicable? 3. Are the benefits of the proposal greater than its disadvantages? 4. Is the proposal better than other courses of action?

• Careful audience analysis will help you to determine what kind of evidence will work best for your listeners. In order to choose the best evidence, what questions should you ask about your listeners?

Types of Evidence

As you discovered in Chapter 5, supporting materials clarify, amplify, and strengthen the ideas in your speech. They provide evidence for the acceptance of your central idea and its supporting points. Evidence is a crucial part of developing a clear, compelling argument. It can be presented in any of the forms of supporting materials with which you are already familiar: explanations, comparisons and contrasts, illustrations, specific instances, statistics, and testimony.

You've already engaged in the process of research required to find the supporting materials necessary to reinforce your ideas. The selection of relevant evidence is particularly important in constructing good arguments. There is no single or easy rule for selecting relevant evidence. Supporting material that is relevant to one claim may not be relevant to another, or it may provide logical proof but not compelling reasons for action. You should consider both the rational and the motivational characteristics of evidence as you select it.

Rationally Relevant Evidence

The type of evidence you choose should reflect the type of claim you advocate. For example, if you're defending the claim that censorship violates the First Amendment guarantee of freedom of speech, you'll probably choose testimony by noted authorities or definitions of terms to advance your claim. On the other hand, examples, illustrations, and statistics work better for showing that a problem exists or a change is needed. For example, if your public library has removed adult literature from its shelves and you present statistics showing that nine out of ten Americans believe that this is a violation of their rights, you'll be showing that there is popular support for a change. As you can see, the claim you present requires a logically relevant type of evidence. As you plan your arguments, you should ask yourself, "What type of evidence is logically relevant in support of my claim?"

Motivationally Relevant Evidence

If you hope to convince listeners to adopt your attitudes or actions, your claim must be supported by more than logically relevant evidence. Your evidence must also create in listeners a desire to become involved. That is, it must be motivationally relevant to them. In order to best determine what evidence works for specific audiences, you should ask the two questions presented below.

What Type of Evidence Will This Audience Demand? Whenever a government proposes higher taxes, taxpayers usually demand explanations of underlying financial needs, statistical evidence, financial reports, testimony from experts in economics, examples of how higher taxes will affect them, and comparisons and contrasts with other sources of revenue. Mere examples or illustrations are not compelling enough to garner public support for higher taxes. On the other hand, if you're reviewing a recent film for a group of friends, an example from the plot, a figurative analogy, or an illustration of dialogue would be more forceful as proof than statistical word counts, box office receipts, or testimony from published movie critics. Careful audience analysis will help you determine what type of evidence is needed to move your particular group of listeners psychologically.

What Specific Evidence Will Generate the Best Response? You should pose this question once you've determined the type of evidence required by your argument. For example, if you've decided to use expert testimony to support your argument, whom should you quote? Or if you're using an illustration, should you use a factual example or develop one of your own? Will listeners be more moved by a personalized story or a general illustration?

To answer these and similar questions about your listeners, you need to analyze them. A homogeneous audience may be suspicious of outsiders. It might react best to local experts or illustrations from the local community or common range of experience. A heterogeneous audience, on the other hand, will require more generally recognized authorities and geographically varied examples because it does not share experience and background. You should consider your listeners' demographic or psychological characteristics in order to choose the most effective evidence for them.

Ethical Moments

· · · · ·

Using Evidence in Argumentation

As we noted in the Ethical Moments feature in Chapter 2, many ethical decisions confront you when you engage in public debate. Some of these decisions have to do with how you treat your opponent, how you use the time you're sharing with another speaker, and how you play to the audience. Some decisions center on how you use evidence. Consider the following ethical dilemmas:

1. Should you suppress evidence that contradicts a point you're making? If your opponent doesn't know about it, should you bring it up?

2. Should you leave in all of the *maybe's* and *perhaps'* when you read a quotation? After all, you can always use ellipses (those three little dots that indicate something's been left out) to honestly report what you did. Consider the following sentence: "One of the least promising avenues of research in the quest for a cure for cancer is herbal therapy." Now, read the sentence omitting several words: "One . . . promising avenue(s) of research in the quest for a cure for cancer is herbal therapy."

3. Does it make any difference if you overqualify a source? Perhaps you interview a Congressional page or speak to a receptionist. Will it hurt if you quote "a source close to the White House"?

4. What difference does it make if a poll was conducted by the National Right-to-Life Committee or Planned Parenthood's Pro-Choice Committee? What if each organization asks polling questions in such a way as to encourage a particular response? Can you just say that "a recent national poll found that 75 percent of our citizens favor abortion rights?" You haven't really *lied* in suppressing the polling agency or the actual questions, have you? Is this acceptable?

Overall, it's one thing to accidentally *discover* supporting materials in the library but quite another to purposefully *search* for supporting material. In selecting evidence, keep in mind both your claim and its requirements as well as your listeners and their needs.

Forms of Reasoning

Reasoning or *inference* is a process of connecting something that is known or believed (evidence) to a concept or idea (claim) that you wish others to accept. **Patterns of reasoning** are habitual ways in which a culture or society uses inferences to connect what is accepted to what it is being urged to accept. In our culture, there are five reasoning patterns: from examples, from generalization or axiom, from sign, from parallel case, and from causal relation.

Reasoning from Examples

Often called *inductive reasoning,* **reasoning from examples** involves examining a series of examples of known occurrences (evidence) and drawing a general conclusion (claim). The inference of this reasoning pattern is, "What is true of particular cases is true of the whole class." This inference represents a kind of mental inductive leap from specifics to generalities. For example, the National Cancer Institute has studied hundreds of individual case histories and discovered that people with high-fiber diets are less prone to develop cancers of the digestive tract. With an inductive leap, the Institute then moved to the factual claim, "High-fiber diets prevent certain types of cancer." Commuters use a similar pattern of reasoning every time they drive during rush hour. After trial and error, they decide that a residential street is the best route to take home between 5:00 and 5:30 P.M. and the expressway between 5:30 and 6:00 P.M. In other words, after experiencing enough instances, they arrive at a generalization and act on it.

Reasoning from Generalization

Reasoning from generalization (sometimes called *deduction*) means applying a general truth to a specific situation. It is essentially the reverse of reasoning from examples or induction. In high school consumer education class, you may have learned that buying goods in large quantities saves money (the generalization). Now, you may shop at discount stores because they purchase goods in quantity, thereby saving money and passing that savings on to you (the claim deduced from the evidence). Or, you may believe that getting a college education is the key to a better future (the generalization). Therefore, if you get a college degree, you will get a better job (claim). This inference gathers power because of experience (you learned it through observation) or by definition (one of the characteristics of education is self-improvement). You ultimately accept this inference because of the uniformities you believe exist in the world.

Reasoning from Sign

Reasoning from sign uses an observable mark, or *sign,* as proof of the existence of a state of affairs. You reason from sign when you notice cracked, itching skin between your toes (the evidence) and decide you have athlete's foot (the claim). The cracked, itching skin does not cause the condition; rather, it's a sign of the fungus that does cause it. Detectives, of course, are experts at reasoning from sign. When they discover that a particular suspect had motive, means, and opportunity (the signs), they make the claim that he or she might be the murderer. Your doctor works the same way every time he or she examines your tongue and your throat for signs of disease. Reasoning from sign works well with natural occurrences (ice on the pond is always a sign that the temperature has been below 32°F). However, reasoning from sign can be troublesome in the world of human beings (as when some people take body weight as a sign of laziness or skin color as a sign of dishonesty). Signs, of course, are circumstantial evidence—and could be wrong. Just ask detectives and doctors. The inference that evidence is a sign of a particular conclusion is not always true. Yet, we often must use signs as indicators; otherwise, we couldn't project our economy, predict our weather, or forecast the rise and fall of political candidates.

TABLE 14.2   Kinds of Reasoning   Try to think of additional examples of each kind of reasoning.

Reasoning	Description	Examples
Reasoning from examples (inductive reasoning)	Drawing a general conclusion from instances or examples	I enjoy the music of Bach, Beethoven, and Brahms. I like classical music.
Reasoning from generalization or axiom (deductive reasoning)	Applying a general conclusion to a specific example	Irish Setters are friendly dogs. I think I'll get an Irish Setter puppy for my niece.
Reasoning from sign	Using an observable mark or symptom as proof of a state of affairs	The petunias are all dead. Someone forgot to water them.
Reasoning from parallel case	Asserting that two things or events share similar characteristics or patterns	North Korea is developing nuclear technology; South Korea won't be far behind.
Reasoning from causal relation	Concluding that an event that occurs first is responsible for a later event	The engine won't start because the carburetor is flooded with gasoline.

Reasoning from Parallel Case

Another common reasoning pattern, **reasoning from parallel case,** involves thinking solely in terms of similar things and events. Your college or university, for example, probably designed its curriculum by examining the curricula of similar colleges or universities. These curricula functioned as evidence; the claim was that similar courses should be offered at your university. The inference that linked the evidence and the claim was probably something such as, "What worked at Eastern University will work here at Western University because they are similar institutions." Your instructors might use parallel reasoning every time they tell you, "Study hard for this exam. The last exam was difficult; this one will be, too." Obviously this is not a generalization, since every exam will probably not be the same. However, your instructors are asserting that the upcoming examinations and past examinations are similar cases—they have enough features in common to increase the likelihood that careful study habits will benefit you.

Reasoning from Cause

Finally, **reasoning from cause** is an important vehicle for reaching conclusions. The underlying assumption of causal reasoning is that events occur in a predictable, routine manner, with causes that account for occurrences. Reasoning from cause involves associating events that come before with events that follow. (See Table 14.2.) When substance abuse appears to be increasing across the coun-

Minority Opinions

Minority opinion may be one of the best things for strengthening decision making and public debate. People make better decisions when challenged by minority views because they are stimulated to think more creatively. Even clearly erroneous minority views are valuable in creating better decision making.

In one study, groups of students were observed as they tried to reach a consensus about the colors and brightness of 20 slides. In some of the groups, confederates were planted to disagree with majority decisions. In those groups, more creative associations and language choices were made to describe colors. In addition, more unusual arguments were offered to convince the confederates.

In this study and others like it, people exposed to minority opinions may be unlikely to adopt those views. But the exposure to minority opinions is vital since it stimulates the formulation of more strategies to solve problems and more creative decision making. The value of minority views "lies not so much in the correctness of its position but rather in the attention and thought processes it induces."*

Considering this, should you seek out views opposed to your own? Will you develop better speeches if you read arguments on both sides of issues? Does public debate result in a healthier society?

*Elizabeth Stark, "Influence: The Nays Have It," *Psychology Today* (June 1986): 18.

try, people scramble to identify causes: the existence of international drug cartels, corrupt foreign governments, organized crime inside our own borders, lower moral standards, the break-up of the nuclear family, and lax school discipline. The trick for the arguer is to assert causes that might reasonably be expected to produce the effects—to point to material connections between, for example, foreign governments' actual policies and the presence of drugs in Chicago or other American cities. Overall, the inference in causal reasoning is simple and constant: every effect has a cause.

EVALUATING ARGUMENTS

The reasoning process is the pulley around which the machine of argument runs. You must test reasoning in order to protect yourself, both as a speaker and as a critical listener, from embarrassment when you're arguing and from faulty decisions when you're listening to others. For each kind of reasoning, there are special tests or questions that help you determine the soundness of arguments. Consider the following questions as you construct arguments and evaluate those of others:

Reasoning from Examples

1. Have you looked at enough instances to warrant generalizing? If you live in Montana, you don't assume spring has arrived after experiencing one warm day in February.

2. Are the instances fairly chosen? You certainly hope that your neighbors don't think you have "a rotten kid" just because she picked one of their flowers; you want them to judge your daughter only after seeing her in many different situations.

3. Are there important exceptions to the generalization or claim that must be considered? While presidential elections show that, generally, "As Maine goes, so goes the nation," there have been enough exceptions to this rule to keep presidential candidates who lose in Maine campaigning hard.

Reasoning from Generalization

1. Is the generalization true? Men are better drivers than women; people who marry young are more likely to divorce; public schools provide inadequate education. Each of these statements is a generalization. You need to determine if sufficient evidence exists to support the truth of the statement.

2. Does the generalization apply to this particular case? Usually, discount stores have lower prices, but if a small neighborhood store has a sale, it may offer better prices than a discount house. While the old saying, "Birds of a feather flock together" certainly applies to birds, it may not apply to human beings.

Reasoning from Sign

1. Is the sign fallible? As we have noted, many signs are merely circumstantial. Be extremely careful not to confuse sign reasoning with causal reasoning. If sign reasoning were infallible, your weather forecaster would never be wrong.

2. Is the observation accurate? Star witnesses sometimes testify to things that later prove to be wrong; children see ghosts at night; and jealous lovers assume the worst. Be sure that the observation is reliable.

Reasoning from Parallel Case

1. Are there more similarities than differences between the two cases? City A and City B may have many features in common—size, location, and so on—yet they probably also have many different features, perhaps in the subgroups that make up their populations and in their degree of industrial development. Too many differences between two cases rationally destroy the parallel.

2. Are the similarities you have pointed out the relevant and important ones? There are two children in your neighborhood who are the same age, go to the same school, and wear the same kinds of clothes; are you there-fore able to assume that one is well-behaved simply because the other is? Probably not, because more relevant similarities than their clothing and age would include their home lives, their relationships with siblings, and so forth. Comparisons must be based on relevant and important simi-larities.

Reasoning from Cause

1. *Can you separate causes and effects?* We often have a difficult time doing this. Do higher wages cause higher prices, or is the reverse true? Does a strained home life make a child misbehave, or is it the other way around?

2. *Are the causes strong enough to have produced the effect?* Did Bill Clin-ton's ability to play the saxophone really win the election for him, or was that an insufficient cause? There probably were much stronger and more impor-tant causes.

3. *Did intervening events or persons prevent a cause from having its normal effect?* If a gun is not loaded, you can't shoot anything, no matter how hard you pull the trigger. Even if droughts normally drive up food prices, that might not happen if food has been stockpiled, if spring rains have left enough moisture in the soil, or if plenty of cheap imported food is available.

4. *Could any other cause have produced the effect?* Although crime often in-creases when neighborhoods deteriorate, increased crime rates can be caused by any number of other changes—alterations in crime reporting methods, in-creased reporting of crimes that have been going on for years, or closings of major industries. We rationally must sort through all of the possible causes before championing one.

DETECTING FALLACIES IN REASONING

As we've been stressing, your primary job as a critical listener and arguer is to evaluate the claims, evidence, and reasoning of others. On one level, you're looking for ways that the ideas and reasoning of others are important to your own thinking; and, on another level, you're examining the logical soundness of others' thinking. A **fallacy** is a flaw in the rational properties of an argument or inference. There are many different fallacies. Let's look at eight common ones.

1. *Hasty generalization.* A **hasty generalization** is a claim made on the basis of too little evidence. You should ask, "Has the arguer really examined enough typical cases to make a claim?" If the answer is *no,* then a flaw in reasoning has occurred. Urging a ban on aspirin because several people have died of allergic reactions to it and the closure of a highway because of a traf-fic fatality are examples of hasty generalization.

2. *Genetic fallacy.* A **genetic fallacy** occurs when someone assumes that the only "true" understanding of some idea, practice, or event is to be found in its origins—in its "genes," literally or metaphorically. People sometimes as-sume that if an idea has been around for a long time, it must be true. Many

Speaking
of...

• • • •

Evaluating Arguments

Undoubtedly you'll participate in disputes or arguments many times as an advocate or a bystander. Often, you'll have to determine if your arguments or those of others were effective. Here are four questions you can ask to help discover the effectiveness of an argument:

1. *What was its effect?* Did the argument convince people to vote? to boycott? to donate canned goods? Clearly, if your argument results in a desired response, it was effective; However, this is only one way of judging the effectiveness of arguments. You must also ask the next three questions.

2. *Was the argument valid?* Did the arguer follow a logical order of development? Did he or she use supporting materials to prove the points? Were those supporting materials relevant to the claim advanced? If the argument was sound, it can be judged valid.

3. *Was the argument truthful?* Did it meet the test of reality? If an argument doesn't correspond to the way things really are, then it fails the truthfulness test.

4. *Was the argument ethical?* Did it advocate what is morally good? Did the arguer use ethical means to achieve results? This is an especially important test in this age of ethical malaise.

For additional development of these ideas, see J. Michael Sproule, *Argument: Language and Its Influence* (New York: McGraw-Hill, 1980), 22–24.

people who defended slavery in the nineteenth century referred to the biblical practices of slavery to support their claim. Genetic study can help us understand a concept, but it's hardly proof of present correctness or justice.

3. *Appeal to ignorance.* People sometimes **appeal to ignorance** by arguing with double negatives: "You can't prove it won't work!" They may even attack an idea because information about it is incomplete. "We can't use radio beams to signal UFOs and extraterrestrials because we don't know what languages they speak." Both of these are illogical claims because they depend upon what we don't know. Sometimes we must simply act on the basis of the knowledge we have, despite the gaps in it. In countering such claims, you can cite parallel cases and examples.

4. *Bandwagon Fallacy.* A frequent strategy is to appeal to popular opinion or to urge people to "jump on the bandwagon." The **bandwagon fallacy** assumes that if everyone else is doing something, you should too: "But Christopher, everyone knows the world is flat!" or "But Dad, everyone else is going!" While these appeals may be useful in stating valuative claims, they're not the basis for factual claims. Even if most people believe or think something, it still may not be true. The world has witnessed hundreds of widely believed but false ideas, from the belief that night air causes tuberculosis to panic over an invasion by Martians.

5. *Sequential fallacy.* The **sequential fallacy** is often present in arguments based on evidence from causal relations. The fallacy arises from the assumption that if one event follows another, the first must be the cause. Thunder and lightning do not cause rain, although they often occur sequentially; and, even if you usually catch colds in the spring, the two are not causally related. That is, the season of the year does not cause your cold—a virus does.

6. *Begging the question.* **Begging the question** is rephrasing an idea and then offering it as its own reason. This kind of reasoning is circular thought. If someone asserts, "Abortion is murder because it is taking the life of the unborn," he or she has committed a fallacy by rephrasing the *claim* (it is murder) to constitute the *reason* (it is taking life). Sometimes questions can be fallacious, such as "Have you quit cheating on tests yet?" The claim, phrased as a question, assumes that you've cheated on tests in the past. Whatever your answer to the question, therefore, you're guilty. Claims of value are especially prone to begging the question.

7. *Appeal to authority.* **Appeal to authority** occurs when someone who is popular but not an expert urges the acceptance of an idea or a product. Television advertisers frequently ask consumers to purchase products because movie stars or sports heroes endorse them. Celebrities promote everything from blue jeans to beer. The familiar figure provides name recognition but not expertise. You can detect this fallacy by asking, "Is he or she an expert on this topic?"

8. *Name calling.* **Name calling** is the general label for attacks on people instead of on their arguments. Name calling may take the form of an attack on the special interests of a person: "Of course, you're defending her. You voted for her." Or it may be an attack on a personal characteristic rather than on ideas: "You're just a dweeb" (or yuppie or chauvinist). Even dweebs, yuppies, and chauvinists sometimes offer solid claims. Claims ought to be judged on their own features, not on the characteristics of the person who makes them.

These are some of the fallacies that creep into argumentation. A good basic logic book can point out additional fallacies.[3] Armed with knowledge of such fallacies, you should be able to protect yourself against unscrupulous demagogues, sales personnel, and advertisers.

TIPS FOR DEVELOPING ARGUMENTATIVE SPEECHES

As you get ready to pull all of your claims, kinds of evidence, and reasoning patterns together into coherent argumentative speeches, consider the following pieces of advice:

1. *Place your strongest arguments first or last.* This strategy takes advantage of the *primacy-recency effects.* Arguments presented first set the agenda for what is to follow, and a strong opening argument often impresses an audience with its power, thereby heightening the credibility of the arguer (the primacy effect). We also know that listeners tend to retain the most recently presented

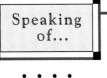

Organizing Your Arguments

Your audience will often determine how you organize your arguments. In particular, whether you present just one side of the issue or reveal both sides can depend upon your listeners. Research results confirm that you should present one side when your listeners:

1. Already favor your position on the issue.
2. Are not well educated, either on the issue or in general.
3. Will be required to make a public commitment.

On the other hand, you should present both sides of the issue when your listeners:

1. Initially disagree with your position on the issue.
2. Are generally well educated.
3. Will be exposed to counterpersuasion.

idea (the recency effect), so you might put your strongest argument at the end of your speech so that listeners will remember your best shot.[4]

2. *Vary your evidence.* Different listeners are likely to prefer different kinds of evidence, and most listeners want supporting materials that are both logically relevant and psychologically motivating. For example, if you're arguing in favor of capital punishment, you can use statistical trends to signal the widespread problem of premeditated violence. To clinch this argument, though, more than sanitized facts are necessary. You'd be wise to provide descriptions of victims of premeditated crime in order to involve your audience in the human drama of the problem.

3. *Avoid personal attacks on opponents.* Maintain arguments on an appropriate intellectual level. This tactic enhances your credibility. If you can argue well without becoming vicious, you'll earn the respect—and perhaps the agreement—of your listeners; most know that the more someone screams, the weaker his or her arguments are. Work from strong, not loud, arguments.

4. *Know the potential arguments of your opponents.* The best advocates know their opponents' arguments better than their opponents do; they have thought about those arguments and ways of responding to them ahead of time. Having thought through opposing positions early allows you to prepare a response and feel confident about your own position.

5. *Practice constructing logical arguments and detecting fallacious ones.* Ultimately, successful argument demands skill in performing the techniques of public reasoning. You need to practice routinely constructing arguments with solid relationships between and among claims, evidence, and reasoning

patterns; and you need to practice regularly detecting the fallacies in other people's proposals. Critically examine product advertisements, political claims, and arguments that your neighbors make in order to improve your communication skills—as both a sender and a receiver of argumentative messages.

Sample Argumentative Speech

• • • •

Policies are supported by particular factual assertions as well as values. The advisability of a policy is based on the truth-value of the facts offered in its support and on the audience's willingness to accept the value judgments being made. In many cases, it's necessary to attack conclusions drawn on the basis of factual data in order to argue for a reconsideration of a policy. Jenny Clanton of Southeastern Illinois College faced this problem in her analysis of NASA's continued willingness to use Plutonium 238 as its "fuel of choice" in launching space flights.

The Challenger Disaster That Didn't Happen[5]
Jenny Clanton

Speaker stimulates audience motivation to listen with a startling observation that the Challenger disaster saved future lives.

On January 28, 1986, the American Space Program suffered the worst disaster in its more than 30 year history. The entire world was shocked when the space shuttle Challenger exploded seconds after lift-off, claiming the lives of seven brave astronauts and crippling our entire space agenda. I suppose the oldest cliché in our culture, spoken on battlegrounds and indeed virtually anywhere Americans die, is "We must press forward so we can say they did not die in vain." Rest assured. They didn't. The deaths of our seven astronauts probably saved the lives of untold thousands of Americans./1

The danger of the next shuttle launch is developed with expert testimony.

For, you see, if the O-rings had not failed on January 28, 1986, but rather on May 20, 1987, the next scheduled shuttle launch, in the words of Dr. John Gofman, Professor Emeritus at the University of California at Berkeley, you could have "kissed Florida good-bye."/2

Additional expert testimony is used in the explanation of why failure of the next scheduled launch would have been disastrous.

Because the next shuttle, the one that was to have explored the atmosphere of Jupiter, was to carry 47 pounds of Plutonium 238, which is, again according to Dr. Gofman, the most toxic substance on the face of the earth. Dr. Helen Caldicott corroborates Dr. Gofman's claim in her book, *Nuclear Madness,* when she cites studies estimating one ounce of widely dispersed Plutonium 238 particles as having the toxicity to induce lung cancer in every person on earth./3

Today, when you leave this room, I want you to fully understand just what impact NASA's plans could have on this planet. I want you to become cynical.

The speaker forecasts the impact of the speech on the audience.

The three main points of the speech are previewed.

I want you to be a little scared. I want you to become angry. But most of all, I want you to begin to demand some answers./4

To move you in this direction I would first like to explore with you just what plutonium is and what could happen if it were released in our atmosphere. Second, let's consider NASA's argument for the safety of the plutonium as used in the shuttle program. And finally, I want to convince you that NASA's conclusions are flawed./5

The first point is stated. Plutonium is defined and its effects are explained.

So now, let's turn our attention to the nature of plutonium. Plutonium is a man-made radioactive element, which is produced in large quantities in nuclear reactors from uranium. Plutonium is a chemically reactive metal, which, if exposed to air, ignites spontaneously and produces fine particles of plutonium dioxide. These particles, when dispersed by wind and inhaled by living organisms, lodge in the lungs. Lung cancer will follow—sooner or later. Once inside the human body, plutonium rests in bone tissue, causing bone cancer. Plutonium 238 is so poisonous that less than one millionth of a gram is a carcinogenic dose./6

Expert testimony further establishes the dangers of Plutonium.

Last July, *Common Cause* magazine contacted Dr. Gofman at Berkeley and asked him to place Plutonium 238 in perspective. Before I share Dr. Gofman's assessment, please understand he's no poster-carrying "anti-nuke." Dr. Gofman was co-discoverer of Uranium 233, and he isolated the isotope first used in nuclear bombs. Dr. Gofman told Karl Grossman, author of the article "Redtape and Radio-activity," that Plutonium 238 is 300 times more radioactive than Plutonium 239, which is the isotope used in atomic bombs./7

Additional expert testimony compares Plutonium to nuclear reactors.

Dr. Richard Webb, a nuclear physicist and author of *The Accident Hazards of Nuclear Power Plants,* said in a similar interview that sending 46.7 pounds of Plutonium 238 into space would be the equivalent of sending five nuclear reactors up—and then hoping they wouldn't crash or explode./8

The first point is summarized.

Dr. Gofman's final assessment? It's a crazy idea, unless shuttle launches are 100 percent perfect. Which is just about what NASA would have liked us to believe, and at first glance NASA's guarantees are pretty convincing./9

NASA's argument for the safety of Plutonium is explained. Government officials' explanations are paraphrased.

NASA estimates the chance of releasing Plutonium into the environment, because of the possibility of a malfunction of the space shuttle, at .002 percent—that's not quite 100 percent perfect, but it's awfully close. NASA and the Department of Energy base their reliability figures on three factors: (1) the Titan 34D launch vehicle and its high success rate; (2) Energy Department officials in the March 10th *Aviation Week and Space Technology* magazine explain that the Plutonium would be safely contained in an unbreakable, quarter-inch-thick iridium canister, which would withstand pressures of over 2,000 pounds per square inch; and (3) in that same article, NASA explains there is "little public danger" because the Plutonium on board would be in the form of oxide pellets, each one inch in diameter. If you'll remember, the danger of Plutonium is in fine particles./10

Statistics and a baseball analogy are provided to show another perspective.

Now, let's take a second glance. One month later, the April 28th issue of *Aviation Week and Space Technology* reported that two of the last nine Titans launched have blown up. Two failures in nine trips is great in baseball, but not when we're dealing with nuclear payloads. That same article estimates loss of orbiter and crew, not at .002 percent but at 1 in 25./11

Two questions about the safety of Pluto-nium are posed.

With odds on the launch vehicle reduced to 1 in 25, the dual questions arise: just how breach-proof is that canister and, in a worst case scenario, what could happen if the pellets of 238 were released? For the answers to those questions, we go to Dr. Gary Bennett, former Director of Safety and Nuclear Operations, who not only answers those questions, but also explains why NASA is so insistent on using Plutonium./12

Expert testimony is used to explain the dangers.

Last July, Dr. Bennett told *Common Cause* that there is concern within NASA and the Department of Energy that an explosion aboard the Galileo spacecraft, a Titan or other rocket, would, in turn, set off an explosion of the booster rockets. Bennett admitted that government tests in 1984 and 1985 determined that if the shuttle exploded, and then the booster rockets exploded, there would be a likelihood of breaching the iridium canister. The Plutonium would then be vaporized and released into the environment; and there goes Florida./13

NASA's reasons for taking safety risks are explained. The magnitude of the risk is elaborated.

But why would NASA take such a risk? It's really quite simple. On the one hand, Plutonium 238 is the one fuel that would enable space exploration beyond the limit of Mars. Without it, distant space exploration must wait for research to develop an equally effective, safe fuel. On the other hand, a worst case scenario would create the worst nuclear accident in history. In short, NASA weighed exploration now against the chances for disaster and opted to take the risk. The only problem is, I really don't like the idea of someone risking my life without consulting me—and I hope you don't either. By the way, there is evidence that NASA and the Department of Energy have projected some pretty horrible figures. Under the Freedom of Information Act rules, Karl Grossman was able to obtain agencies' estimates for the number of lives lost in a major accident. The only problem is that every reference to the number of people affected is blanked out with Liquid Paper and the term Exempt #1 is written over the deletion. James Lombardo of the Energy Department explains the whiteouts were necessary for—you've got it—national security reasons. I would contend that national security would be threatened by mass anger over the callousness of the Energy Department, and justifiably so. Representative Edward Markey agrees, and when he was head of the House Subcommittee on Energy, Conservation and Power, he uncovered most of the information I share with you today./14

The speaker reviews the questions asked in her interview with Congressman Markey.
Markey explains congressional involvement with the nuclear power industry rather than NASA.

In a telephone interview last August, I asked Congressman Markey three questions. Why hasn't Congress done anything? What should be done? What can we do to help?/15

His answer to the first question was quite interesting. You may remember that shortly after the shuttle exploded and just when Congress was showing some interest in a thorough investigation of the space program, another larger, even more dramatic accident occurred—Chernobyl. The attention to Chernobyl as it related to our own power industry captured not only the attention of most Americans, but of Congress as well. Consequently, most of our nuclear experts are involved in working with Congress and the nuclear power industry./16

The reasons for Space Watch are mentioned.

And while Congress is focusing on one facet of the nuclear question, NASA and the Department of Energy are receiving much less attention. Which is why Congressman Markey helped found Space Watch./17

Actions necessary to make space flight safe are listed.

Representative Markey is of the opinion that hysteria accomplishes nothing, but that all space flight should be halted until either Plutonium 238 can be made safe, which is highly unlikely, or until an alternative fuel can be found. The burden of proof should be on NASA and not on the public./18

Specific steps the audience can take to make space flight safe are provided.

This is where you and I come in. First, if by now you are sufficiently scared or angry, contact Space Watch through Representative Markey's office.Then, keep abreast of developments and exert pressure through your elected officials if Congress does nothing to interfere with NASA's plans. Send your objections not only to your own legislators, but to Representative Markey as well. Allow him to walk into the House with mailbag after mailbag of letters in opposition to NASA's unbridled desire to go to Jupiter. We have a friend in Congress who solicits help. The least we can do is give it to him./19

The speaker summarizes the main idea of the speech and concludes with a quotation.

One last thought; as of November, Plutonium 238 is still NASA's and the Department of Energy's fuel of choice. Dr. Bennett's last words in that July interview were, "I think you should understand there's a degree of risk with any kind of launch vehicle." But isn't that the point?/20

CHAPTER SUMMARY

1. Argumentation is a process of advancing propositions or claims supported by good reasons and allowing others to examine those claims and reasons in order to test them or to offer counterarguments.

2. Criticism is a process of careful assessment, evaluation, and judgment of ideas and motives. Both listeners and speakers should engage in critical thinking.

3. Arguments are built from three elements—the claim, the evidence, and the reasoning pattern.

4. The types of claims common to arguments are claims of fact, claims of value, and claims of policy.

5. Evidence for arguments can be chosen to reflect the rational quality of the claim (rationally relevant evidence) or to stimulate audience involvement (motivationally relevant evidence).

6. Five forms of reasoning connect evidence and claims—reasoning from examples, reasoning from generalization, reasoning from sign, reasoning from parallel case, and reasoning from cause.

7. A fallacy is a flaw in the rational properties of an argument or inference. There are many kinds of fallacies; the most common fallacies are hasty generalization, genetic fallacy, appeal to ignorance, bandwagon fallacy, sequential fallacy, begging the question, appeal to authority, and name calling.

8. In developing argumentative speeches: (a) organize your arguments by putting the strongest first or last, (b) vary the evidence, (c) avoid personal attacks on

opponents, (d) know the potential arguments of your opponents, and (e) practice constructing logical arguments and detecting fallacious ones.

KEY TERMS

appeal to authority (p. 273)	genetic fallacy (p. 271)
appeal to ignorance (p. 272)	hasty generalization (p. 271)
argumentation (p. 260)	name calling (p. 273)
bandwagon fallacy (p. 272)	patterns of reasoning (p. 266)
begging the question (p. 273)	reasoning (p. 266)
claim (p. 261)	reasoning from cause (p. 268)
claim of fact (p. 261)	reasoning from examples (p. 267)
claim of policy (p. 262)	reasoning from generalization (p. 267)
claim of value (p. 262)	reasoning from parallel case (p. 268)
fallacy (p. 271)	reasoning from sign (p. 267)
	sequential fallacy (p. 273)

SKILLBUILDING ACTIVITIES

1. Choose a controversial topic and phrase it as a question of policy, such as, "Should the federal government abolish Social Security?" or "Should all 18-year-olds be required to complete two years of military service?" As a class, think of arguments for and against the policy. Then, determine what rationally and motivationally relevant evidence would be required to develop each argument.

2. Prepare a ten-minute argumentative exchange on a topic involving you and another member of your class. Dividing the time equally, one of you will advocate a claim and the other will oppose it. Adopt one of the following formats: (a) a Lincoln-Douglas format—the first person speaks for four minutes, the second speaks for five, and then the first person returns for a one-minute rejoinder; (b) an issue format—both parties agree on a number of key issues and then each speaks for two-and-a-half minutes on each issue; (c) a debate format—each speaker presents a constructive speech for three minutes, and then each speaker gives a two-minute rebuttal; (d) a heckling format—each speaker has five minutes to speak; but, during the presentation of each speech, the audience or opponent may ask questions which the speaker must answer.

3. Turn the class into a deliberative assembly, decide on a motion or resolution to be argued, and then schedule a day or two for a full debate. Class members should assume argumentative roles: advocates, witnesses, direct examiners, cross-examiners, and summarizers. The deliberative assembly allows each speaker to be part of a team. To read about the use of this format, see John D. Day, ed., *American Problems: What Should Be Done? Debates from "The Advocates"* (Palo Alto, Calif.: National Press Books, 1973).

REFERENCES

1. Harvey Siegel, *Educating Reason: Rationality, Critical Thinking, and Education* (New York: Routledge, 1988), 1–47. The importance of critical thinking has

been underscored in two national reports on higher education: The National Institute on Education, *Involvement in Learning: Realizing the Potential of American Higher Education,* 1984; and the American Association of Colleges, *Integrity in the College Curriculum: A Report to the Academic Community,* 1985. For a summary of research on critical thinking in the college setting, see James H. McMillan, "Enhancing College Students' Critical Thinking: A Review of Studies," *Research in Higher Education* 26 (1987): 3–29.

2. A full discussion of the logical grounding of claims in evidence and reasoning is presented in the classic book on argumentation: Douglas Ehninger and Wayne Brockriede, *Decision by Debate,* 2nd ed. (New York: Harper & Row, 1978).

3. See: Irving M. Copi, *Introduction to Logic,* 7th ed. (New York: Macmillan, 1986).

4. Most students of persuasion believe that the primacy and recency effects are equally potent; see Stephen W. Littlejohn and David M. Jabusch, *Persuasive Transactions* (Glenview, Ill.: Scott Foresman, 1987), 235–236. Others, however, believe that because the primacy effect can color listeners' reactions to everything you say, your best argument should almost always come first; see Gary C. Woodward and Robert E. Denton, Jr., *Persuasion and Influence in American Life* (Prospect Heights, Ill.: Waveland Press, 1988), 299–300.

5. Jenny Clanton, "The Challenger Disaster That Didn't Happen," *Winning Orations* (1988). Reprinted by permission of Larry Schnoor, Executive Secretary, Interstate Oratorical Association, Mankato State Univ., Mankato, Minn.

Speaking on Special Occasions

A kira was anxious, almost shaking, as she walked to the lectern. She'd given several speeches that semester and was quite confident of her speech skills. She'd even overcome her fear of speaking publicly in English. But this time it was different. She'd been named the most improved speaker by the class Awards Committee and was about to get a certificate. She realized that she would be judged not just by her speaking skills but by her ability to say something memorable or profound. She now knew what was meant by the phrase special occasion. *So that's how she started her speech: "When I read Chapter 15 of our textbook, I thought it was odd to call it 'Speaking on Special Occasions.' But when I tried to think of what to say today, I came to understand that title: a 'special occasion' like this one is when your own* invention *of speech material runs into the* convention *of audience expectations. What's special in this case is not the person doing the speaking but the occasion that creates those expectations in your listeners."*

Special occasions seem to have lives of their own. They even have considerable authority over us. They can regulate our behavior because, after all, they're bigger and often older than we are. Social groups and institutions control special occasions and seem to force us to conform to their rules—including their rules for public speaking.

In this chapter, we'll look at several kinds of speeches that you may give in the presence of, or as a representative of, some of those groups and institutions. Our focus will be on speeches that are given to or for *communities,* a word etymologically related to the idea of *communication.* How can we feel a part of communities when our differences divide us? The answer to this question will form the deep backdrop for this chapter. First, we'll consider an individual's relationships to communities and then we'll examine types of speeches for special occasions—speeches used to mark occasions that are particularly important to communities.

CEREMONY AND RITUAL IN THE COMMUNITY

The word *community* comes from the Latin *communis,* meaning *common,* or, more literally, *commonality.* A community is not simply the physical presence of people who live in the same town (their "local community") or who worship in the same place (although that place of worship is sometimes called "a religious community"). Physical presence is not the key to community membership, but psychological state is. A **community** is a group of people who think of themselves as bonded together—whether by blood, locale, nationality, race, occupation, gender, or other shared experience or attributes.

The phrase *who think of themselves* is key here. Really, of course, you draw from the same genetic pool as the others in your family, but why is that important to your concept of kinship? Why not eye color or hair shade or shoe size instead? Of course there really are biological differences between males and females, but is one's gender important in determining who gets paid more, who draws combat duty in time of war, or who's generally expected to raise the kids? College professors and lawyers both go to school about the same amount of time, yet we pay experienced lawyers about twice as much as experienced professors—how come? Yes, skin comes in many different colors, but why have we made so much of that fact?

• We tend to think of ourselves in terms of social groups and roles. How would you answer the question "What am I?"

The point here is simple but absolutely important: *While physiological, psychological, and social differences between people are real, the importance attached to those differences is socially constructed in arbitrary ways.*

A **social construction** is a linguistic mechanism used by group members to understand, interpret, and evaluate the world around them. Words store our experience of the world; just uttering *pit bull* brings to mind for most people stories of their own or other people's experiences with vicious dogs. Words encode our common attitudes; we have positive or negative words for people because our feelings vary. The difference between *student-athlete* and *jock* reflects a difference in how we value what the person does while at school. Saying that "we socially construct our world" isn't to say that we create it in some brute way—the physicality of the world is real, solid, and it hurts when you bump your toe into a desk. Rather, it's to say that *human beings orient themselves to the world via language.*

It follows, then, that, at one level or another, communication always is the attempt to get others to see, interpret, and evaluate the world as we do. The language you share with your culturemates helps you to get others to see as you do. But, of course, people change and meanings aren't stable. *Democracy* means one thing in the United States and another in the Russian republics because of differing traditions, governmental institutions, and personal experiences. When U.S. and Russian citizens talk to each other about democratic institutions, they must be careful to indicate concretely how each is seeing, interpreting, and evaluating the world when using that term. Because we all change and have differing relationships with each other, finding common definitions of key words or concepts is crucial to human understanding.

And that is the point of this chapter: periodically, communities must stop to define themselves, their beliefs, attitudes, and values, their place in the world. We do this on special occasions—and hence this chapter. However, as we've seen throughout this book, arriving at definitions shared by everyone is very, very difficult: *In an age of diversity, there is a tendency to fragment society rather than to share beliefs, attitudes, and values as a community.* The great challenge of special-occasion speaking, therefore, is to get a society to live the motto stamped on American money: *E pluribus unum,* "Out of many, one."

So far, we've been talking in social-psychological terms—in terms of group-individual relationships understood psychologically and linguistically. We now need to extend the discussion into the realm of speechmaking. That extension is easy: your sense of community is created in large part through public address. Social communities—family and friends—take shape through interpersonal, or one-on-one, talk; but most of the groups you value influence your life through public talk. You may have memorized and recited in a group the Boy Scout Law and oath, with each recitation reinforcing the scouts' beliefs and values. Many religious groups have ceremonies involving group confession of sins and profession of faith, and most depend upon speechmaking—preaching—to instill and reinforce doctrine and morals.

Speeches for special occasions not only draw their themes and force from the beliefs, attitudes, and values of the groups to whom they are addressed, but also are *ritualized,* structured in patterns standardized by that group. "Ritual action," to political scientist David Kertzer, "has a formal quality to it. It follows highly structured, standardized sequences and is often enacted at certain places and times that are themselves endowed with special symbolic meaning. . . . I have defined **ritual** as action wrapped in a web of symbolism."[1] If introductions of speakers often seem trite, it's because introducing someone into your community is a ritualized activity. If nomination speeches sound the same from campaign to campaign, it's because few of us want surprises in our campaign processes. Surprise can lead to change; and change, in turn, could upset our political system. In speeches for special occasions (except, as we shall see, speeches to entertain), the emphasis is on ritualized tradition rather than revolutionary change.

This brings us, then, to the great challenge of special-occasion speechmaking. *In an age of diversity, when each of us has been socialized into any number of specific ethnic, social, political, and religious groups—each of which makes demands upon our beliefs, attitudes, and values—how can we create a sense of shared community?* Is it possible to share community when people are divided into two genders, innumerable religions, young and elderly people, multiple ethnic groups, a growing number of political parties, and Mac versus IBM users? How can public speakers reach across differences to create a sense of mutual identity among listeners? Or, if people do feel a sense of community, what can we do ritualistically and rhetorically to make them sensitive to the demands of community upon them?

Let's now look at three types of special-occasion talk: speeches of introduction, speeches of courtesy, and speeches to entertain. How do we live out *E pluribus unum?*

SPEECHES OF INTRODUCTION

Speeches of introduction are usually given by members of the group that will hear the speech. They're designed to prepare the community (the audience) to accept the featured speaker and his or her message. In a way, a speech of introduction asks permission for an outsider to speak. The decision to grant that permission is based upon what the nonmember can contribute to the group: the group must *want* to hear the outsider before the featured speaker can be successful. Or if the speaker is a member of the group, the introduction may serve as a reminder of his or her role and accomplishments within the community or organization.

Purpose

If you're invited to give a speech of introduction, remember that your main objective is to create a desire in others to hear the speaker you're introducing. Everything else should be subordinate to this aim. Don't bore your audience with a long recital of the speaker's biography or with a series of anecdotes about your acquaintance with the person. Above all, don't air your own views on the subject of the speaker's message. You're only the speaker's advance agent; your job is to sell that person to the audience. Your goals should be: (1) to arouse curiosity about the speaker and the subject in the minds of the listeners so that it will be easy to capture their attention and (2) to motivate the audience to like and respect the speaker so they'll tend to respond favorably to the forthcoming information or proposal.

Ethical Moments

Waving the Bloody Shirt

The phrase *waving the bloody shirt* dates from the year 1868, when tax collector and school superintendent A.P. Huggins was roused from his bed, ordered to leave the state, and given 75 lashes by members of the Ku Klux Klan. Huggins reported the incident to the military authorities, and an officer took his bloodied shirt to Washington and gave it to Radical Republican Congressman Benjamin Butler of Massachusetts. Later, when giving a speech in support of a bill permitting the president to enforce Reconstruction laws with military force, Butler waved Huggins's shirt. From then on, Republican orators regularly "waved the bloody shirt," blaming the South for starting the Civil War and accusing it of disloyalty to the Union and to its flag.

Similarly, in the late 1980s and early 1990s people have burned the U.S. flag to protest hypernationalism and to call attention to threats to freedom of speech and the Bill of Rights. In reaction, many people have "waved the burning flag," denouncing flag burning as unpatriotic and as a symbol of anti-American sentiment. "Waving the bloody shirt" and "waving the burning flag" represent particular persuasive strategies in special-occasion speaking: protest and counterprotest rallies, political and organizational conventions, news conferences called on Flag Day or the Fourth of July. In special-occasion speeches, you're likely to hear patriotic recitals of the lives of martyrs who died that we might enjoy freedom; of traditional values and their symbols; and of the United States as the democratic bulwark, impervious to the assaults of all other political systems around the world.

Buried in this kind of public speaking are difficult ethical moments. Certainly, as Americans, we should know our history and who our martyrs were; we should be able to openly discuss values and the topics of patriotism and allegiance; and the United States—for better or worse—is expected to play a significant role in the international scene.

1. But what if our definition of *patriotism* begins to preclude discussion of alternative viewpoints?

2. What if references to *traditional American values* halt the examination of values of other people's cultures?

3. When does the defense of democracy become cultural imperialism—an attack on all other cultures, economies, and political systems?

Special-occasion speaking *is* a time for reflecting upon one's own culture and belief systems, but such situations can easily be used to batter someone else's culture and thoughts. What the Greeks called *epideictic* oratory, the oratory of praise and blame, is talk filled with ethical minefields. At what point does waving the bloody shirt or the burning flag stop, rather than encourage, dialogue?

Formulating the Content

Usually, the better-known or more respected a speaker is, the shorter your introduction needs to be; the less well-known the person is, the more you'll need to arouse interest in the speaker's subject and to build up the person's prestige. When presenting a speech of introduction:

1. *Be brief.* To say too much is often worse than to say nothing at all. For example, if you were to introduce the president, you might simply say, "Ladies and gentlemen, the president of the United States." The prestige of the person you introduce won't always be great enough for you to be so brief, but it's always better to say too little than to speak too long.

2. *Talk about the speaker.* Anticipate the audience's questions: "Who are you? What's your position in business, education, sports, or government? What experiences have you had that qualify you to speak on the announced subject?" Build up speakers' identities, tell what they know or have done, but do not praise their abilities as speakers. Let them demonstrate their own skills.

3. *Emphasize the importance of the speaker's subject.* For example, in introducing a speaker who'll talk about the oil industry, you might say, "In one way or another, the oil industry is in the news every day—Middle East concerns, the ups and downs of the cost of heating oil, gasohol research, tanker spills, our energy needs for the twenty-first century. To help us make sense of the industry and the ways it impacts our daily lives, today's speaker. . . ."

4. *Stress the appropriateness of the subject or the speaker.* If your town is considering a program to rebuild its Main Street area, a speech by a city planner is likely to be timely and appreciated. References to relevant aspects of a speaker's background or the topic can tie speaker and speech to the audience's interests.

5. *Use humor if it suits the occasion.* Nothing puts an audience at ease better than laughter. Take care, however, that the humor is in good taste and doesn't negatively affect the speaker's credibility. The best stories are usually those shared by the introducer and speaker and told so as to illustrate a positive character trait of the speaker.

SPEECHES OF COURTESY: WELCOMES, RESPONSES, ACCEPTANCES, AND TOASTS

Speeches of courtesy explicitly acknowledge the presence or qualities of the audience or of a member of the audience. When you extend a welcome to a political candidate who's visiting your class or when you accept an award like Akira did, for example, you are giving speeches of courtesy.

Typical Situations

Speeches of courtesy fulfill social obligations such as welcoming visitors, responding to welcomes or greetings, accepting awards from groups, and toasting individuals with short speeches recognizing achievements.

Sample Speech of Introduction

• • • •   Under all circumstances, the four primary virtues of a speech of introduction are (1) tact, (2) brevity, (3) sincerity, and (4) enthusiasm. These virtues are illustrated in the following introduction.

Introducing a Classmate
Angela Vangelisti

A popular sport in the student union cafeteria is reading through lists of ingredients in prepared foods and candies, especially the chemical additives. One of the best players of this sport I've seen is our next speaker, Angela Vangelisti. Angela is amazing. Even with products like coffee whitener, which contains only one or two things I've even heard of, Angela can identify most of the emulsifiers, stabilizers, and flavor enhancers that make up fake food./1

While identifying chemical food additives passes the time in the cafeteria, there's also a serious side to the game. As Angela knows, there's a difference between blue dye nos. 1 and 2, and between good old yellow no. 5 and yellow no. 6; the cancer risk varies from one to the other. For example, the red dye no. 3 that you'll find in maraschino cherries is related to thyroid tumors. These are some of the reasons I was gratified to learn that Angela would share some of her technical knowledge as a nutrition major in a speech entitled, "How to Read Labels and Live Longer."/2

Welcoming Visitors

When guests or visiting groups are present, someone extends a public greeting to them. For example, your basketball announcer might greet the opposing team or a fraternity chapter president might greet the representative from the national office who's visiting your campus. The speech of welcome is a way of introducing strangers into a group or organization, giving them group approval, and making them feel more comfortable.

Responding to a Welcome or Greeting

Responses are ways for outsiders to recognize their status as visitors and to express appreciation for acceptance by the group or organization. Thus, the representative from the national office who's visiting a fraternity might respond to a greeting, in turn, by thanking the group for its welcome or by recognizing its importance and accomplishments.

Accepting Awards

An individual who has received an award usually acknowledges the honor. Sometimes the award is made to an organization rather than to an individual, in which case someone is selected to respond for the group. In all cases, the acceptance of

• Speeches of courtesy are given to welcome visitors, to respond to greetings, to accept awards, and to recognize an individual's achievements. In each case, the speaker acknowledges the group that makes up the audience. What principles should guide a speaker on these occasions?

awards via a speech is a way of thanking the group and acknowledging the importance of the activity being recognized; for example, people who receive Academy Awards (if they do more than blubber) thank the American Academy of Motion Picture Arts and Sciences for the Oscar and often recognize the importance of making serious films on significant subjects.

Offering Toasts

While toasts offered to bridegrooms or others being roasted can become silly, the act of toasting is usually an important ritual. Toasts are acts of tribute; through them, a group recognizes the achievements of an individual and expresses the hope that the person will continue to achieve distinction. After negotiations, heads of state usually toast each other's positive personal qualities, accomplishments, and desire for future good relations. Ceremonially, toasts can unite separated peoples.

Purpose

The speech of courtesy has a double purpose. The speaker not only expresses a sentiment of gratitude or hospitality but also tries to create an aura of good feel-

A Sample Toast

• • • •
What follows is a short toast offered to a retiring professor by those attending a spring dinner in his honor. Notice its conciseness, the qualities of the person that form the basis for the tribute, and the use of illustrations (the honoree's values) not only to celebrate the person but to suggest to those assembled the nature of the community standards for accomplishment.

A Toast to Leo Brecker

As we prepare to leave the dinner table, I'd like to offer a toast to the man we honor this evening—retiring Professor Leo Brecker./1

Leo, you've been a part of this university for 50 years: as an undergraduate before and after World War II; as a graduate student; and as a professor of speech education, broadcasting, and mass communication. Your life is indistinguishable from the life of this university. You embody the values everyone else reaches for. You constantly pose what you call the "interesting questions" that are the essence of the scholar's life. You often say that no matter how crazy our students are, they're still the reason we come to work every day. You remind us weekly that we are not only *in* the world but are *of* the world; just as the world gives us the opportunity to study and teach, so do we owe it not only our thanks but our attention and good works./2

In living out the values that justify the very existence of the state university, Leo, you've been the flesh-and-blood example of all that is good in higher education. For that, I toast you—your vision, your daily life, and your ideals that will guide our future. In you, Professor Brecker, we see the best that we can be. I toast you in the hope that the best is indeed yet to come for all of us./3

ing in the audience. Usually the success of such a speech depends on satisfying the listeners that the appropriate thing has been said.

Formulating the Content

The scope and content of a speech of courtesy should be guided by the following principles:

1. *Indicate for whom you're speaking.* When you act on behalf of a group, make clear that the greeting or acknowledgment comes from everyone and not from you alone.

2. *Present complimentary facts about the person or persons to whom you are extending the courtesy.* Review the accomplishments or qualities of the person or group you're greeting or whose gift or welcome you're acknowledging.

3. *Illustrate; don't argue.* Present incidents and facts that make clear the importance of the occasion, but don't be contentious. Avoid areas of disagree-

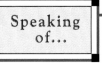

• • • •

Rhetoric and Memory

What people learn from their elders, their teachers, their public media, their clergy, is fully as important to invention as knowledge learned by means of sensory experience. . . . Memory and rhetoric thrive in cultures that celebrate community and plentitude.

Memory is called the "lost canon" of rhetorical study because, it seems, in a day of writing and electronic communication, the human being has little need to remember anything. Not so, says rhetorician Sharon Crowley. While you can learn much about the physical aspects of the world without a good memory, you learn about the most important aspects of life—what is good or bad, useful or useless, just or unjust, beautiful or ugly—only through others' memories. Some of that is written down; but, since the beginning of time, most wisdom has been passed on from generation to generation orally, by word of mouth. Ceremonial speaking is central to the transmission of wisdom in society.

Source: From Sharon Crowley, "Modern Rhetoric and Memory," in *Rhetorical Memory and Delivery: Classical Concepts for Contemporary Composition and Communication,* edited by John Frederick Reynolds (Hillsdale, N.J.: Lawrence Erlbaum Associates, 1993), 43.

ment. Don't use a speech for courtesy as an opportunity to air your own views on controversial subjects or to advance your own policies. Express concretely and vividly the thoughts that are already in the minds of your listeners.

These virtues are illustrated in William Faulkner's "On Accepting the Nobel Prize for Literature," reprinted in Chapter 9, pages 166–167. Faulkner clearly indicates he's speaking *as* a writer *to* future writers. He honors those young writers by taking their compositional problems seriously; his own difficulties as a writer, which come out in the flood of metaphors and images that make up the bulk of his speech, stand not as arguments but as illustrations of the struggle he finds at the core of all good writing.

Speeches of courtesy are more than merely polite talk. The courtesies extended in welcoming someone into your midst or in thanking someone for work done are statements of your group's rules for living—its guiding principles. In extending courtesies to others, you're acknowledging the culture you share with them.

SPEECHES TO ENTERTAIN

Speeches to entertain present special challenges to speakers. As you may recall, we identified the speech to entertain as a type embodying an independent general purpose in Chapter 2. Discounting slapstick of the slipping-on-a-banana-peel type, most humor depends primarily upon a listener's sensitivities to the routines and morals of his or her own society. This is obvious if you've ever listened to someone tell jokes from a foreign country. Often, humor cannot be translated, in

FIGURE 15.1
Checklist for Using Humor

These questions will help you determine the most effective way to use humor.

Purpose

_____ 1. Is my humor in good taste or will it damage my credibility as a speaker?

_____ 2. Does my humorous story have a point?

_____ 3. Has the story been overused? Is it a cliché?

_____ 4. Does the point of my humor relate to the point I'm making in my speech?

_____ 5. Am I using the humor simply for its own sake, or does it have a purpose in my speech?

_____ 6. Does the humor increase group cohesion?

_____ 7. Does the story depend upon potentially offensive ethnic, religious, or gender stereotypes? If so, can I rework the story to avoid offensiveness?

_____ 8. Is the story brief enough not to sidetrack me?

_____ 9. Where is the humor used in my speech? Can I keep it from getting in the way of the idea I'm clarifying?

Delivery

_____ 1. Does the use of humor make me self-conscious?

_____ 2. Can I communicate a humorous story well? If not, what can I do to improve my delivery?

_____ 3. Is the punch line clear?

_____ 4. What will I do if my listeners don't respond appropriately to my humor?

_____ 5. Have I tested my stories on others?

_____ 6. Can I avoid copying the delivery style of someone else and use my own speaking style?

part because of language differences (puns, for example, don't translate well) and, in larger measure, because of cultural differences.

Purpose

Like most humor in general, speeches to entertain usually work within the cultural frameworks of a particular group or society. Such speeches may be "merely funny," as in comic monologues, but most are serious in their force or demand on audiences. After-dinner speeches, for example, are usually more than dessert; their topics are normally relevant to the group at hand, and the anecdotes they contain usually are offered to make a point. That point may be as simple as deflecting an audience's antipathy toward the speaker or making the people in the audience feel more like a group, or it may be as serious as offering a critique of society.

Speakers seeking to deflect an audience's antipathy often use humor to ingratiate themselves. For example, Henry W. Grady, editor of the _Atlanta Constitution,_ expected a good deal of distrust and hostility when he journeyed to New York City in 1886 to tell the New England Society about "The New South." He opened the speech not only by thanking the society for the invitation, but also by telling stories about farmers, husbands and wives, and preachers. He praised Abraham Lincoln, a northerner, as "the first typical American" of the new age; told another humorous story about shopkeepers and their advertising; poked fun at the great Union General Sherman—"who is considered an able man in our hearts, though some people think he is a kind of careless man about fire"; and as-

sured his audience that a New South, one very much like the old North, was arising from the ashes.[2] Through the use of humor, Henry Grady had his audience
cheering every point he made about the New South that evening.

Group cohesiveness can also be created through humor. (See Figure 15.1.)
Especially when campaigning, politicians spend much time telling humorous stories about their opponents, hitting them with stinging remarks. In part, of course,
biting political humor detracts from the opposition candidates and party; however, such humor also can make one's own party feel more cohesive. For example, Democrats collected Richard Nixon's 1972 bumper stickers that said, "Nixon
Now," cut off the *w,* and put them on their own autos. Democrats did endless turns
on the names Bush and Quayle in 1988. Similarly, Republicans poked fun at
Michael Dukakis, laughing at a picture of him awkwardly driving a tank. Such
zingers allow political party members to laugh at their opponents and to celebrate
their membership in the "better" party.

Finally, speeches to entertain can be used not merely to poke fun at outsiders
and to celebrate membership but even to critique one's society. Humor can be
used to urge general changes and reform of social practices.

Formulating the Content

When arranging materials for speeches to entertain, develop a series of illustrations,
short quotations or quips, and stories, each following another in fairly rapid suc-
cession. Most important, make sure that each touches on a central theme or point.
An entertaining speech must be more than a comic monologue; it must be cohesive
and pointed. The following sequence works well for speeches to entertain:

1. Relate a story or anecdote, present an illustration, or quote an appropriate
passage.
2. State the main idea or point of view implied by your opening.
3. Follow with a series of additional stories, anecdotes, quips, or illustrations that amplify or illuminate your central idea; arrange those supporting
materials so they're thematically coherent.
4. Close with restatement of the central point you have developed; as in step
1, you can use a quotation or one final story that clinches and epitomizes
your speech as a whole.

Sample Speech to Entertain

• • • •

By organizing your speech materials in the pattern just suggested, you'll not only provide your listeners with entertainment but help them remember your central idea. The speech that follows illustrates the four steps.

A Case for Optimism[3]
Douglas Martini

Most of you probably have heard some version of this poem:

Twixt the optimist and pessimist

The difference is droll:

The optimist sees the doughnut,

The pessimist, the hole.

The longer I live, the more I'm convinced of the truth of that poem. Like a doughnut, life may seem full, rich, and enjoyable, or it can seem as empty as that hole in the middle. To the pessimist, the optimist seems foolish. But I'm here today to tell you it's the pessimist who's the foolish one./1

Another way of seeing the difference between an optimist and a pessimist is this way: an optimist looks at an oyster and expects a pearl; a pessimist looks at an oyster and expects ptomaine poisoning. Even if the pessimist is right—which is not very often—he probably won't enjoy himself either before or after he proves it. But the optimist is happy because he always has that expectation of future reward./2

Pessimists are easy to recognize. They're the ones who go around asking "What's good about it?" when someone says "Good morning." If they looked around, they undoubtedly could find *something* good, as did the storekeeper after she was robbed. The day after the robbery she was asked about the loss. "Lose much?" her friend wanted to know. "Some," she said, "but then it would have been worse if the robbers had got in the night before. You see, yesterday I just finished marking everything down 20 percent."/3

There's another story about a happy-go-lucky shoemaker who left the gas heater in his shop turned on overnight, and upon arriving in the morning he struck a match to light it. There was a terrific explosion, and the shoemaker was blown out through the door to the middle of the street. A passerby rushed to help and asked if he were injured. The shoemaker got up slowly, jiggled his arms and legs, looked back at the burning shop, and said, "No, I'm not hurt, but I sure got out just in time, didn't I?"/4

Some writers have ridiculed that kind of outlook. The great French writer Voltaire made fun of optimism in *Candide*. "Optimism," he said, "is a mania for maintaining that all is well when things are going badly." A later writer, James Branch Cabell, did a turn on one of Voltaire's phrases when he quipped:

"The optimist proclaims that we live in the best of all possible worlds; the pessimist fears this is true."/5

A lot of college professors, too, can't resist the urge to jab a little at optimists. But I, for one, refuse to take them seriously. I like the remark made by literary critic and journalist Keith Preston: "There's as much bunk among the busters as among the boosters."/6

Some may like the cynicism of Voltaire or *Doonesbury* cartoonist Gary Trudeau. But optimism is the philosophy I like to hear preached. There was a grandmother who complained about the weather. "But, Melissa," said her friend, "awful weather is better than no weather at all." So quit complaining. Change the bad things in the world that you can, to be sure, but then work within the rest. And stop expecting the worst. Be the optimist who cleans his glasses *before* he eats his grapefruit!/7

When you're tempted to grumble about your rotten future, remember the doughnut. And, as Elbert Hubbard advised:

As you travel through life, brother,

Whatever be your goal,

Keep you eye upon the doughnut

And not upon the hole.

CHAPTER SUMMARY

1. Speeches on special occasions are usually grounded in ceremonies or rituals for defining and reinforcing a community's fundamental beliefs and values. We define ourselves by and live up to standards of behavior established by groups and institutions; thus, special-occasion speeches define and reinforce a community in important ways.

2. Typical speeches on special occasions include (a) speeches of introduction, (b) speeches of courtesy (welcomes, responses, acceptances, and toasts), and (c) speeches to entertain.

3. In speeches of introduction and courtesy, we see efforts to recognize and work within a group's standards for conduct.

4. In speeches to entertain, we see attempts to deflect a group's reservations, to create group cohesiveness, and even to critique and reform a group's practices.

KEY TERMS

community (p. 282)   speeches of courtesy (p. 286)
ritual (p. 284)   speeches of introduction (p. 284)
social construction (p. 283)   speeches to entertain (p. 290)

SKILLBUILDING ACTIVITIES

1. Your instructor will give you a list of special-occasion, impromptu speech topics, such as:

   a. Student X is a visitor from a neighboring school; introduce him or her to the class.

   b. You are Student X; respond to this introduction.

   c. Present your speech-critique forms to the state historical records office.

   d. You have just been named Outstanding Classroom Speaker for this term; accept the award.

   e. You are a representative of a speechwriters-for-hire firm; sell your services to other members of the class.

   f. You'll have between five and ten minutes in which to prepare and then present a speech on the topic assigned or drawn from the list. Be ready to discuss the techniques you used in putting the speech together.

2. Using the four-step procedure outlined on page 292, prepare and present to your classroom audience a simple speech to entertain based on one of the following topics or a similar one:

   a. You can't take it with you.

   b. The portion of campus I would not show to a visitor.

   c. What this country really needs is . . .

   d. My most idiosyncratic professor.

   e. The role of television in my life.

3. During the next round of classroom speeches, you'll be asked to introduce one of your classmates. Follow the suggestions in this chapter and, after learning the speaker's topic, plan an introduction that emphasizes its importance.

REFERENCES

1. David I. Kertzer, *Ritual, Politics, and Power* (New Haven, Conn.: Yale Univ. Press, 1988), 9.

2. Henry W. Grady, "The New South," *American Public Addresses: 1740–1952,* edited by A. Craig Baird (New York: McGraw-Hill, 1956), 181–185.

3. Based on part on material taken from *Friendly Speeches* (Cleveland: National Reference Library, n.d.) and on material developed for earlier editions of this book.

. . . . .

Public Group Communication

*W*hen Amy's public speaking instructor emphasized how much time people normally spend working in groups, Amy was skeptical. Then, Amy's
instructor asked everyone to jot down what they'd done during the previous
week. Amy's week began on Monday morning when her residence hall group
met to plan a Friday night party; later her biology class broke down into lab
groups; then she met with several of her sorority sisters after class to discuss
plans for homecoming. During the rest of the week, Amy participated in a
chapter of the campus Young Republicans, delivered a group report on an
advertising campaign in her marketing class, worked as a volunteer leader
with her troop of Girl Scouts, and gathered with some friends to study for a
Spanish examination. On Sunday, she attended a comparative-religions
study group and choir practice. As she thought about it, Amy began to realize how often she worked with groups of people.

As Amy discovered, there are many public speaking situations in which you'll be
participating in a different role—as part of a group rather than as a single speaker
addressing an audience. As a team member, you may present proposals to your
employer; you may join a group filing a grievance against a city council; or you
may be asked to justify your actions as part of an executive committee.

As a member of a group, you will participate in the discussion of ideas; you
may also address an audience as a representative of the group. In either case, your
role as a speaker will be changed by your relationship to others in your group.
You will need to understand the functions of public group communication. In
order to help you in this role, we will examine the responsibilities of participants
in group discussions, provide guidelines for developing a discussion plan, and
suggest ways to respond to audiences' questions and objections.

GROUP DISCUSSIONS

Business people and professionals depend heavily on oral communication for their success. Businesses and professional organizations rely on committees, task forces, and more informal groups to formulate ideas, evaluate courses of action, and put proposals into effect. These exchanges are generally termed **group discussions.** A group discussion is a communication transaction in which a small group of people exchanges and evaluates ideas and information in order to solve a problem. Usually group discussions involve four to six people. As many as 12 people can join the discussion, but as the number of participants increases, the efficiency of the group normally declines.

There can be many different goals for small groups—amateurs gather to discuss art, literature, or coin collecting, for example. Book clubs, genealogical societies, and religious instruction classes function to educate their members. While these are important goals, this chapter will focus on decision-making discussions.

In **decision-making discussions,** participants seek agreement on what the group should believe or do. These groups may also discuss ways of implementing their decisions. In discussions of this kind, participants examine conflicting facts and values, evaluate differences of opinion, and explore proposed courses of action for their practicality. The goal is to arrive at a consensus. A neighborhood homeowners' association may gather to evaluate a local sewer improvement

• Groups engage in discussion for many reasons. What kinds of group discussions have you engaged in recently?

project. A city council might plan for rezoning to control future growth. A sub-committee of an insurance association might search for ways to target the under-insured consumer. Once decisions are made, these groups may explore ways to implement their plans.

Responsibilities of Participants

When you participate in group communication, the most important requirement is that you be knowledgeable about the subject at hand. If you know what you're talking about, you're better prepared to contribute to the group process. For example, before you attend a discussion on locating a minimum-security prison in your neighborhood, you need to research the issue. You should find out how other neighborhoods have been affected by minimum-security prisons. You should investigate what measures will be taken to ensure the safety of neighborhood residents. You also will need to know what economic, environmental, and social impacts such a facility will have in your neighborhood. This information will help you contribute to the discussion.

It's equally important for you to practice good listening behavior as the discussion progresses. Unless you listen to what's going on, you'll forget what's already been said or lose track of the direction in which the group is moving. As a result, you may make redundant or irrelevant comments, require the restatement of points already settled, or misunderstand the positions taken by other participants. In any case, you won't be adding to the progress of the discussion. If you've seen a recent TV talk show, you've probably seen exactly how frustrated and angry people can become when they are ignored or misunderstood. Many times this frustration can be prevented if everyone listens carefully to the discussion.

You also should be aware of the dynamics of the group and its members. To the extent that you can acquaint yourself with group members' values and interests, you'll be able to judge more accurately the importance of their remarks. You'll also be able to determine the role you must play in order to make the group discussion profitable. If group members want to chat about the party last weekend instead of tackling the task at hand, you can remind them of the group's purpose; or if the atmosphere becomes tense or members show antagonism, you can relieve the strain by reminding everyone that the whole group will benefit from consensus or by redirecting the discussion until tempers have cooled.

The key to successful group communication experiences is *interdependency*. Even though discussions are sometimes competitive or hostile, they are ultimately a cooperative activity. You share with others; they share with you. Your ideas are deflected, reshaped, or accepted by others. In the end, they belong to everybody in the group. All group members leave parts of themselves in the final outcome. You are changed, even if just a little, by having worked as part of a team. When group members promote a sense of interdependency, the result is positive and productive.

Responsibilities of Leaders

Effective group leadership requires at least three basic talents. First, the leader of the group must keep the discussion moving. To do this, a leader should call attention to basic issues, remind members of what's on the floor, note common elements in diverse points of view, and strip controversial matters of their unnecessary complexity. It is important for a discussion leader periodically to summarize the results of the discussion. When the group has reached consensus, the leader might say, "Before we move on, let me summarize what I think we've decided." Such restatements will ensure that group members are in agreement and will reinforce the group decision for everyone.

Second, a discussion leader must be impartial. The leader needs to ensure that unpopular viewpoints are allowed expression. The leader must make sure that participants phrase questions and comments in neutral terms. Through the example of the leader, a spirit of cooperation and conciliation will be promoted among participants who may disagree. The leader may ask for opinions from individuals who have not yet contributed to the discussion or may remind the group that there are several different interpretations of an idea.

Third and finally, a discussion leader should encourage active participation. At the beginning of a discussion, the leader may be required to present background information to frame the issues. If individuals are hesitant to state their opinions, the leader may stimulate them to participate by asking questions such as, "Mary, do you agree with John's position?" or "John, will you give us reasons to consider your viewpoint?" A leader whose manner conveys confidence in participants may encourage group members who have ideas to contribute.

DEVELOPING A DISCUSSION PLAN

A carefully developed discussion plan will prevent wasted time and effort. Ideally, the entire group will cooperate in determining the discussion plan, but sometimes a leader must take the responsibility for formulating it. The plan can be used in most situations or modified to meet special needs.

Decision-making discussions characteristically raise claims of policy (see page 262). "What voice should students have in decision making in our college?" "How can our company meet competition from foreign imports?" "What should be done to control the escalating violence among American teenagers?" Answering such questions of policy requires answering secondary questions of fact and value.

The five steps in the following plan for decision-making discussions are adapted from John Dewey's analysis of reflective thinking.[1] This plan is one of several possible ways of deciding on a course of action and is intended to be suggestive rather than prescriptive. Any plan that's developed, however, probably should follow a problem-solution order.

Step 1: Defining the Problem

After the leader makes introductory remarks stating the general purpose of the discussion and its importance, the group should consider the following questions:

1. How can the problem for discussion be phrased as a question?
2. What terms or concepts should be defined?

If the question has not been phrased before the discussion begins, group members should start by developing it. The question should be specific yet allow for a variety of approaches. For example, it's better to phrase your discussion question, "What should be done to control the escalating violence among American teenagers?" than to phrase it, "Should we control violence among teenagers?" Clearly, you are encouraging many viewpoints when you ask, "What should be done?" Phrasing the question to require a *yes* or *no* answer limits the discussion.

To make the discussion flow smoothly, you will need to define the key terms in the discussion question. If your group is considering violence among teenagers, you will probably need to define *violence.* Will you consider vandalism as well as murder to be violence? Are you discussing both misdemeanors and felonies? Should you narrow your discussion to focus on assault with deadly weapons? Another term that probably requires definition is *teenager.* Will you use the legal definition, or will you expand your discussion to include 19-year-olds? As you define your terms, you may discover that the discussion question becomes clearer or even changes. It is easier to conduct a discussion if every group member understands what is meant by each of the key terms in the discussion question.

Step 2: Analyzing the Problem

This step involves evaluating the problem's scope and importance, discovering its causes, and setting up the basic requirements of an effective solution. The following questions are suggested for this step:

1. What evidence is there that a problem exists?
2. What are the causes of the problem?
3. What do we want a solution to accomplish?

First, your group must look closely at the problem to determine if it is real. Many factors could account for what seems to be an escalation of violent crime among teenagers. More careful record keeping, an expanded definition of *violent crime,* or the existence of more teenagers could all account for a bulge in the statistics.

If your group determines that a problem does exist, then you must identify its causes. Through research and discussion, you might decide that social and economic factors contribute to the problem. The increasing instability of the family, greater access to dangerous weapons, financially strapped schools, and greater poverty among the young may all be identified as causes of the problem.

At this point in the discussion, it is obvious that teenage violence has many roots. Your group will want to narrow the discussion by limiting the scope of the solution. It isn't feasible to control all of the factors contributing to the problem with one solution. You should decide *how much* of the problem to solve. For example, you may want to consider only solutions involving the school system, such as confiscation of handguns or stress on teaching moral principles. You might set up budget limitations or focus on one aspect of the problem, such as control of neighborhood gangs. Whatever your group decides, it should develop parameters for evaluating the solution.

Step 3: Suggesting Solutions

In Step 3, group members suggest a wide range of possible solutions and ask the following questions:

1. What are the various ways in which the problem could be solved?
2. What is the exact nature of each proposed solution? That is, what cost, actions, or changes does it entail?

At this stage, it is helpful to list all solutions, preferably on a chalkboard. Group members should volunteer ideas, withholding criticism or judgment until after all the possibilities have been listed. Some suggestions may trigger alternatives or other creative proposals. Other suggestions may come from policies or plans proposed by politicians, civic leaders, or friends.

After the proposed solutions have been listed, the group considers each in turn. Members expand the solution idea, alter it, or investigate its ramifications. For example, bullet rationing may be suggested as a solution to teenage violence involving handguns. When this solution is further investigated, group members would ask for development of the plan. How will bullets be rationed? How many bullets are now in circulation? How long will it take before bullet rationing makes handguns useless? Will the federal government control all bullet manufacturing? Can people manufacture their own bullets? Will some groups have unrestricted access to bullets? Will this create a black market in bullets? How will the armed services be treated? As you can see, there are a lot of questions to be answered about bullet rationing. The group proceeds through all the proposed solutions in this manner, asking questions and seeking full understanding of what each proposal entails.

Step 4: Evaluating the Proposed Solutions

After your group has fully developed each solution, compare solutions and try to agree on a mutually satisfactory plan. Your group may consider the following questions:

1. What are the similarities and differences among the proposed solutions?
2. How well do the various solutions meet the criteria set up by the group?
3. Which solutions should be eliminated and which ones retained for further consideration?
4. Which solution or combination of solutions finally should be approved?

A group begins selecting its solution by finding the common elements among all of the suggested solutions. For example, your group may discover that each solution focuses on controlling violence through limiting access to handguns. In addition, you may realize that many of the solutions involve creating zones of safety for teenagers, such as schools or recreation centers. Finally, your group has called for stiffer penalties than teenagers currently receive for serious crimes such as murder.

Since cost is an important criterion for adopting a solution, your group can eliminate some solutions immediately. Training a national police force for patrolling schools is costly. As a result, your group will cross this idea off its list of realistic solutions. On the other hand, establishing a uniform code for sentencing teenagers is less expensive. It also meets your group's endorsement of stiffer penalties for teenage crime.

The group may choose its final solution from among the ones proposed by group members, or it may compromise by combining several ideas to form a desirable answer to teenage crime. For example, your group may decide to prohibit teenagers from possessing handguns, to install metal detectors in all high-crime areas frequented by teenagers, and to enforce stiffer penalties for crimes teenagers commit with handguns. This solution meets your group's criteria, and it uses the best features of several proposed solutions.

As soon as your group reaches an agreement, the leader sums up the principal features of the accepted plan. If your group has no authority to act, this statement normally concludes the discussion.

Step 5: Deciding How to Put the Approved Solution into Operation

When a group has the power to put its solution into operation, the following additional questions are pertinent:

1. What is necessary to put the plan into effect? Does it require an official law, an appropriation of money, the formation of a committee, or other action?
2. When and where should the solution go into effect?

In this step, your group will discuss the procedures for implementing its solution. Sometimes your group will meet with other groups to iron out the details of the plan. For example, if you plan to place metal detectors in schools, you will need to estimate costs. You may require contractors to submit bids for the project. You must also arrange to start training school personnel to operate the equipment. When these matters have been decided, your group has finished its task.

PRESENTATIONS IN TEAMS: PANELS AND SYMPOSIA

When a group is too large for an effective discussion or when its members are not well informed on the topic, a **panel** of individuals may be selected to discuss the topic for the benefit of others, who then become an audience. Members of a panel may be particularly well informed on the subject or may represent divergent views. For example, your group may be interested in UFOs (unidentified flying objects) and hold a discussion for your classmates. Or your group might tackle the problems of tenants and landlords. Whatever your topic, the audience should learn the basic issues from your discussion.

Another type of audience-oriented discussion is the **symposium.** In a symposium format, usually three to five speakers present short speeches on different facets of a subject or offer different solutions to a problem. This format is especially valuable when recognized experts are the speakers. The symposium is commonly used at large-scale conferences and conventions. For example, if you attend a conference on education, you might learn from symposium speakers about careers for the next century or new technologies for teaching.

Various modifications of the panel and symposium formats are possible. Sometimes the two may be successfully combined. Frequently, the speeches of the symposium are followed by an informal exchange among the speakers. Then the meeting might be opened up for audience questions, comments, and reactions. The essential characteristic of both the panel and symposium is that a few people discuss a subject or problem for the benefit of a large audience.

Preparing for Panels and Symposia

As part of a panel or symposium team, it's important that you take others into account as you plan your remarks. The team approach involves several constraints that you don't face in other speaking situations. First, you have to fit your comments into a general theme. Suppose the theme of your panel is "Improving Health Care on Campus." This topic places on you certain substantial and stylistic limits. You'll be expected to talk about the current state of health care, requirements for good health care, personal responsibilities for improved health, and high-risk health practices.

Second, remember that you may be responsible for covering only a portion of a topic or theme. In most panels and symposia, speakers divide the topic into parts to avoid duplication. This also provides your audience with a variety of viewpoints. You might divide the responsibilities of a five-member panel as follows:

Speaker 1: The current status of health care on campus.

Speaker 2: Standards for effective health care.

Speaker 3: Changes needed in our campus health care system.

Speaker 4: Changing high-risk health behaviors among students.

Speaker 5: Paying for a campus health care system.

Third, the more you know about the subject under discussion, the better. You should be ready to discuss many facets of the topic in addition to the part of the discussion for which you are responsible. For each aspect of the subject or implication of the problem you think may be discussed, make the following analysis:

1. *Review the facts you already know.* Go over the information you've acquired through previous reading or personal experience and organize it in your mind. Prepare as if you were going to present a speech on every phase of the topic. You'll then be better qualified to discuss any part of it.

2. *Bring your knowledge up to date.* Find out if recent changes have affected the situation. Fit the newly acquired information into what you already know.

3. *Determine a tentative point of view on each of the important issues.* Decide what your attitude will be. Is health care on campus currently adequate? What changes are necessary? How will changes affect most students? What responsibilities can students take for their own health? Stake out a tentative position on each issue that is likely to come before the group. Have the facts and reasons that support your view clearly in mind. Be ready to contribute to the group whenever it's most appropriate.

4. *Anticipate the effect of your ideas or proposals on the other members of the group or the organization.* Will your proposal require people to change

Ethical Moments

Protected and Unprotected Speech

It is my legal judgment . . . that the testimony of Professor Hill in the morning was flat-out perjury. [Senator Arlen Specter]

If you . . . appear to have a closed mind, doesn't it raise issues of judicial temperament? [Senator Howell Heflin]

Did you ever have a discussion of pornographic films with Professor Hill? [Senator Patrick Leahy]

I felt I had to tell the truth. I could not keep silent. [Professor Anita Hill]

Law professor Anita Hill was grilled by members of the Senate Judiciary Committee in October 1991 after she alleged that Supreme Court nominee Clarence Thomas had sexually harassed her—with words. Not only was he alleged to have sought dates with her while he was her employer, but she said he talked trash—the language of "sexual overtures."

While the American doctrine of freedom of speech allows you to call people names, express your opinions, and declare your politics, it also limits your ability to threaten others with physical, economic, or even psychological harm. The courts have decided that personally aggressive speech, especially in situations of uneven power, is unprotected by the First Amendment's free-speech clause.

Clarence Thomas was recommended by the Senate Judiciary Committee to the United States Supreme Court. Yet, that fall, Anita Hill's testimony before millions of television viewers brought the issues of sexual harassment and harassing speech to public attention. In the long run, she achieved more than she probably could have imagined possible.

Material drawn from *Time* (21 Oct. 1991): 36–40.

their personal habits? What are the economic repercussions of changes in the health care system? Some forethought may enable you to adjust to possible opposition. The more thoroughly you relate your facts to the subject and to listeners, the more effective your contributions to the discussion will be.

Participating in Panels and Symposia

Present your point of view clearly and succinctly. Participation in a panel or symposium should always be guided by one underlying aim: to help group members think objectively and creatively so that they can analyze the subject or solve the problem at hand. To this end, present and organize your contributions in a way that will best stimulate people to think for themselves.

Your delivery will, of course, vary with the nature and purpose of the discussion and the degree of formality being observed. In general, however, speak in a direct, friendly, conversational style. As the discussion proceeds, differences of opinion may arise, tensions may increase, and some conflict may surface. You should be sensitive to the evolution of the discussion and make adjustments in the way you voice your ideas and reactions. You might calm participants by using humor or by suggesting a compromise on a difficult issue, for example.

Clearly organized ideas are easiest to understand and should stimulate group members to think for themselves. Inquiry order or elimination order work well. Begin by stating the nature of the problem as you see it; next, outline the various hypotheses or solutions that occurred to you; then, tell why you rejected certain solutions; and finally, state your own opinion and explain the reasons for it. In this way, you give other group members a chance to examine your thinking and to add other ideas. At the same time, you'll be making your contribution in the most objective and rational manner possible.

Remain sincere, open-minded, and objective. Above all, remember that a serious discussion is not a stage for prima donnas or an arena for settling personal problems. When you have something to say, say it modestly and sincerely. Always maintain an open, objective attitude. Accept criticism with dignity and treat disagreement with an open mind. Your primary purpose is not to get your own view accepted but to work out the best group decision. The best result is a team effort.

• Some audience members may ask for elaboration or explanation. What are the best ways to respond?

RESPONDING TO QUESTIONS AND OBJECTIONS

Direct feedback from listeners is often a part of public group communication. In meetings, listeners are usually given a chance to ask questions. Panelists frequently direct questions to each other; professors ask students to clarify points made in classroom reports; club treasurers are often asked to justify particular expenditures; and spokespersons usually field questions about statements they've made.

Sometimes, questions require only a short response—a bit of factual material, a *yes* or *no*, or a reference to an authoritative source. But at other times, questions from listeners require more fully developed responses. For example, some questions call for elaboration and explanation. After an oral report, you might be asked to elaborate on some statistical information you've presented. Other questions call for justification and defense. Politicians often must defend positions they've taken. In open hearings, school boards seeking to cut expenditures must justify their selection of school buildings to be closed. University officials might be asked to defend specific academic programs. In these special situations, a brief speech is called for in response to questions and objections.

Techniques for Responding to Questions

Responses to questions that call for elaboration and explanation are, in many ways, equivalent to informative speeches. Think about your responses as short informative speeches in which you offer listeners ideas and information in response to their needs and interests. Consider the following points on how to turn your responses into effective informative speeches:

1. *Give a whole speech.* Your responses should include an introduction, a body, and a conclusion. Even though a response is an impromptu speech, you're still expected to structure ideas and to present information clearly. An elaborated remark might take the following form:

   a. Introduction: A rephrasing of the question to clarify it for the other audience members; an indication of why the question is a good one; a forecast of the steps you will take in answering it.

   b. Body: First point—often a brief historical review; second point—the information or explanation requested.

   c. Conclusion: A very brief summary (unless the answer was extraordinarily long); a direct reference to the questioner to see if further elaboration or explanation is required.

2. *Directly address the question as it has been asked.* Nothing is more frustrating to a questioner than an answer that misses the point or drifts from the query. Suppose that, after you have advocated a pass-fail grading system for all colleges, you are asked how graduate schools can evaluate potential candidates for advanced degrees. The questioner is calling for information and an explanation. If your response is a tirade against the inequities of letter grades or the cowardice of professors who refuse to give failing grades, you probably won't satisfy the questioner. A better response would include all of the factors—letters of recommendation, standardized tests, number of ad-

Preparing for a Question-Answer Session

How can you best prepare for a question-answer session following a public presentation? Perhaps altering your perspective and thinking like a listener may help you to determine what your listeners will ask you. For a few minutes, pretend that you're a member of your audience. Answer these questions:

1. What would I ask if I were hearing about this topic for the first time?
2. What isn't covered in this speech that I want to know?
3. What could confuse me about this topic?
4. What is the most compelling argument developed on this topic?
5. If I disagreed with the subject development, where would I focus my disagreement?
6. What could I say to refute the position taken on the subject?

Once you've thought like a listener, you can begin to develop answers to the questions listeners are likely to ask you.

vanced courses taken, and so on—that graduate schools can use to evaluate candidates. If you're unsure what the point of the question is, ask before you attempt an answer.

3. *Be succinct.* While you certainly don't want to give a terse *yes* or *no* in response to a question calling for detail, neither should you talk for eight minutes when two minutes will suffice. If you really think that a long, complex answer is needed, you can say, "To understand why we should institute a summer orientation program at this school, you should know more about recruitment, student fears, problems with placement testing, and so on. I can go into these topics if you'd like; but for now, in response to the particular question I was asked, I'd say that. . . ." In this way, you're able to offer a short answer, leaving other listeners an opportunity to ask additional questions.

4. *Be courteous.* During question periods, you may be amazed to hear a person ask a question that you answered during your talk. Or another person may ask for information so basic that you realize your whole presentation was probably too complex. In these situations, it's easy to become flip or overly patronizing. Avoid those temptations: don't embarrass a questioner by pointing out that you've already answered the question; don't insult your listeners. If you really think it would be a waste of the audience's time for you to review fundamental details, simply say that you're willing to answer questions after the meeting.

Techniques for Responding to Objections

A full response to an objection has two parts: (a) it answers the objection (**rebuttal**) and (b) it rebuilds the original ideas (**reestablishment**). Suppose that at an office meeting you propose that your division institute a management-by-objectives system of employee evaluation. With this approach, the supervisor and employee together plan goals for a specified period of time. You contend that the approach tends to increase productivity, make employees feel they are taking part in determining their own futures, and make company expectations more concrete. During a question period, someone objects, saying that the approach means more busywork, that supervisors aren't really interested in involving employees in work decisions, and that job frustration rather than job satisfaction is the more likely result.

Your rebuttal rests on effective arguments (see Chapter 14). You can cite the results of studies at other companies similar to your own (reasoning from parallel case). You say that those studies conclude that paperwork doesn't increase, that supervisors like having concrete commitments from employees on paper, and that employee satisfaction probably increases because job turnover rates usually go down (reasoning from sign). Following your rebuttal, you reestablish your original arguments by reporting on the results of interviews with selected employees in your own company. They think the system would be a good one.

Successful respondents tend to adhere to the following communicative techniques:

1. *Be constructive as well as destructive when responding to objections.* Don't simply tear down the other person's counterarguments; constructively bolster your original statements as well. Reestablishment rationally shores up your position and, consequently, increases your credibility.

2. *Answer objections in an orderly fashion.* If several objections are raised by a single questioner, answer them one at a time. (You may need to jot down the objections as they are stated.) This approach lets you respond to each objection and helps listeners sort out the issues raised.

3. *Attack each objection in a systematic fashion.* Refutation usually proceeds in a series of four steps:

   a. State the claim that you seek to rebut: "Joe has said that a management-by-objectives system won't work because supervisors don't want input from their subordinates."

   b. State your objection to it: "I don't agree with Joe because I know of three studies done at businesses much like ours, and these studies support my position."

   c. Offer evidence for your rebuttal: "The first study that reinforces my point was done at the XYZ Insurance Company in 1991. This study was duplicated by subsequent studies at several other companies in 1993 and 1994."

   d. Indicate the significance of your rebuttal: "If our company is similar to the three I've mentioned—and I think it is—then I believe our supervisors will likewise appreciate specific commitments from their subordinates, quarter by quarter. I think we will have to agree that my position is most feasible."

4. *Keep the exchange on an intellectual level.* Counterarguments and rebuttals can degenerate into name-calling exchanges. Little is settled in verbal battles. Effective decision making is more likely to occur when the calm voice of reason dominates than when group members squabble.

Answering questions and responding to objections are vital parts of the group communication process because they allow us to interact directly with others. We are made accountable for what we say by questioners and counterarguers. Through verbal exchanges we can begin to weed out flaws in logic, insufficient evidence, prejudices, and unfeasible plans of action. By testing our ideas in the give-and-take of the public forum, we ultimately contribute to the group process.

CHAPTER SUMMARY

1. Decision-making discussions are communication transactions in which a small number of people exchange and evaluate ideas and information in order to solve a problem.

2. To be a successful participant in a discussion, you must know the subject, pay close attention to the progress of the discussion, and promote a sense of interdependency.

3. To be a successful discussion leader, you need to keep the discussion moving, to remain impartial, and to encourage full participation by group members.

4. A plan for a decision-making discussion requires five steps: (a) defining the problem, (b) analyzing the problem, (c) suggesting solutions, (d) evaluating the proposed solutions, and (e) deciding how to put the approved solution into operation.

5. When speaking as a member of a panel or symposium, fit your comments to the general theme, cover your portion of the theme, and develop a broad base of knowledge so that you can work well within the group.

6. When speaking on a panel or at a symposium, present your viewpoint clearly, succinctly, and fairly and maintain an attitude of sincerity, open-mindedness, and objectivity.

7. When responding to questions, give a brief but complete speech and answer the questions as they are asked.

8. When responding to objections, be both constructive and destructive, answer them in an orderly manner, attack each objection in a systematic fashion, and keep the exchange on an impersonal level.

KEY TERMS

decision-making discussions (p. 297) rebuttal (p. 307)
group discussions (p. 297) reestablishment (p. 307)
panel (p. 302) symposium (p. 302)

SKILLBUILDING ACTIVITIES

1. Join four or five of your classmates and select a topic for a decision-making discussion. Prepare a panel forum to present to your class. Decide how you will encourage audience involvement or critiques. Here are possible topics:

   a. How effective is our freshman orientation program?

   b. How well are American cities maintaining their infrastructures?

   c. What features make a speech great?

   d. What are the ethical implications of organ transplants?

   e. How can we reconcile the demands for both a healthy environment and more energy production in this country?

   f. What can be done about the cycle of welfare dependency?

   g. How can this speaking course be improved?

   h. What legal controls should be placed over pornography?

   i. What has the United Nations accomplished?

2. Conduct press conferences. Speakers will select or be given a description of a particular press conference situation. They will prepare an opening statement, and the rest of the class will serve as members of the press, asking clarifying or probing questions. The speaker might pretend to be the president disagreeing with legislation Congress has passed, an athlete explaining a controversial action, a governor asking for a property tax hike, or a board chairperson justifying a trade agreement with China.

3. As a class, choose a recent controversy in the news. Then divide the class into groups—pro and con. Begin with a spokesperson from one group who will give an impromptu argument on the topic. Alternate to a spokesperson from the other side who will refute the preceding argument and offer another. Continue alternating from one group to the other until everyone has practiced rebuttal and reestablishment of arguments.

REFERENCES

1. See John Dewey, "Analysis of Reflective Thinking," *How We Think* (Boston: D.C. Health, 1933), chap. 7. See also pages 244, 246–247 of this textbook, where these steps are discussed in connection with the motivated sequence.

Sample Speech Materials for Study and Analysis

Vice President Al Gore became the Clinton administration's expert on the so-called "information superhighway" as soon as the team moved into office. Even when fighting through many economic and social issues in Congress, the administration wanted the public to understand that new issues had to be faced as the country looked toward the twenty-first century. The linking together of computer-driven sound, pictures, and data-processing to form a powerful electronic network was a vision the administration wanted to communicate to the public. The vice president began the campaign to do just that late in 1993. The speech had to provide enough information so that the uninitiated could understand the foundational concepts underlying the information superhighway and yet enough in the way of direction to channel the efforts of the experts constructively. Explanations, illustrations, and analogies dominate the vice president's strategy as he seeks to instruct and inspire his audience. The following speech was the result.

A Speech to Inform

Remarks on the Information Superhighway
Albert Gore, Jr.

Thank you. It's a great pleasure to be here. I still have jet lag, though—nature's way of making you look like your passport photo./1

I'm happy to be home. And I'm particularly happy to be talking about telecommunications to people whose lives will be shaped by the changes ahead of us./2

I'm pleased to announce today that at the beginning of the year, President Clinton will present to Congress a package of legislative and administrative proposals on telecommunications. Today, I want to talk about the future we envision./3

But I'd like to start by talking about an incident from the past./4

There is a lot of romance surrounding the sinking of the Titanic 91 years ago. But when you strip the romance away, a tragic story emerges that tells us a lot about human beings—and telecommunications./5

Why did the ship that couldn't be sunk steam full speed into an ice field? For in the last few hours before the Titanic collided, other ships were sending messages like this one from the Mesaba: "Lat42N to 41.25 Long 49W to Long

50.30W. Saw much heavy pack ice and great number large icebergs also field ice."/6

And why, when the Titanic operators sent distress signal after distress signal did so few ships respond?/7

The answer is that—as the investigations proved—the wireless business then was just that, a business. Operators had no obligation to remain on duty. They were to do what was profitable. When the day's work was done—often the lucrative transmissions from wealthy passengers—operators shut off their sets and went to sleep. In fact, when the last ice warnings were sent, the Titanic operators were too involved sending those private messages from wealthy passengers to take them. And when they sent the distess signals, operators on the other ships were in bed./8

Distress signals couldn't be heard, in other words, because the airwaves were chaos—willy-nilly transmissions without regulation./9

The Titanic wound up two miles under the surface of the North Atlantic in part because people hadn't realized that radio was not just a curiosity but a way to save lives./10

Ironically, that tragedy resulted in the first efforts to regulate the airwaves./11

Why did government get involved? Because there are certain public needs that outweigh private interests./12

Today, as divers explore the hulk of the Titanic, we face a similar problem. A new world awaits us. It is one that can not only save lives but utterly change and enrich them. And we need to rethink the role of government once more./13

How do we balance private needs and public interests?/14

It's important in discussing the information age that we discuss not merely technology, but communications. Because from communications comes community. Not long ago, when travel was very difficult, communities were small and communication was personal and direct. It was between families, neighbors, business partners./15

Then the means of travel improved, moving us all away from each other, and making communication more difficult./16

Until recently, if an immigrant came to the United States, whether from Russia, or China, or England, it meant saying goodbye to one's parents and never having a conversation with them again./17

It is important in focusing on what's ahead in communications, to zero in not on the technology, but what we use technology for./18

No one says "Let's use the telephone." They say, "Let's call Grandma."/19

We haven't always kept that in mind./20

When the telephone was invented, stockbrokers in London said "Who needs so many telephones, we have messenger boys."/21

It didn't take long to see that there were some things messenger boys couldn't do—transmit both ends of a conversation, for example. We figured out new uses each time the telephone changed, from big wooden boxes on the wall, to desk phones, to ones with long cords . . . to the car phones and cellular phones that allow us to talk while we drive or walk./22

We will do this again with the changes in store over the next decade—one of the biggest changes the human species has ever faced./23

Most people today are primarily receivers of information. We watch TV. We listen to radio./24

In this decade we will transmit more and more as well./25

We'll send and receive, not just on the telephone but across the full range of the new technologies. We'll turn from consumers into providers./26

In a way, this change represents a kind of empowerment. The quality revolution in the factory treats each individual as a source of added value. The communications revolution recognizes each individual as a source of information that adds value to our community and to our economy./27

After all, interactive TV doesn't just mean yelling at the television when the referee makes a bad call. It means holding a business meeting without leaving your living room./28

It means that people at home can use their televisions not just as entertainment but as a tool./29

These changes have neither come overnight nor out of the blue. Rather, they are the outgrowth of a steady series of changes encompassing much of our history./30

It used to be that nations were more or less successful in their competition with other nations depending upon the kind of transportation infrastructure they had. Nations with deep water ports did better than nations unable to exploit the technology of ocean transportation. After World War II, when tens of millions of American families bought automobiles, we found our network of two-lane highways completely inadequate. We built a network of interstate highways. And that contributed enormously to our economic dominance around the world./31

Today, commerce rolls not just on asphalt highways but along information highways. And tens of millions of American families and business now use computers and find that the two-lane information pathways built for telephone service are no longer adequate./32

It is not that we have a shortage of information. Indeed, we often find now that we have a lot more than we know what to do with./33

John Stuart Mill, who lived through much of the 19th century was said to be the last man who knew everything. Since his time, no matter what your field, you have to resign yourself to the fact that a great deal will take place completely outside your awareness./34

Take the Landsat example. We're trying to understand the global environment, and the Landsat satellite is capable of taking a complete photograph of the entire Earth's surface every two weeks. It's been doing that for almost 20 years./35

Despite the great need for that information, 95% of those images have never fired a single neuron in a single human brain. Instead, they are stored in electronic silos of data./36

We used to have an agricultural policy where we stored grain in Midwestern silos and let it rot while millions of people starved to death. We now have an insatiable hunger for knowledge. And the data sits rotting away—sometimes literally rotting by remaining unused./37

Why?/38

Part of the problem has to do with the way information is configured and presented. Someone once said that if we tried to describe the human brain in computer terms, it looks as if we have a low bit rate but very high resolution. For example, the telephone company decided a few years ago that seven numbers were the most that we could remember. That's a low bit rate. Then they added three./39

On the other hand, we can absorb billions of bits of information instantly if they are arrayed in a recognizable pattern within which each is related to all the others—a human face or a galaxy of stars./40

In order to communicate richly detailed images that allow us to comprehend large volumes of data, we need to combine two technologies. Computers have an ever-growing ability to transform data into recognizable images. And we are making greater use of them every year./41

But to communicate these images among ourselves, we need networks capable of carrying those images to every house and business. We know how to do that technologically, but we have to unscramble the legal, regulatory and financial problems that have thus far threatened our ability to complete such a network./42

In the few places where this capacity now exists, we are already using them to communicate in ways that enrich and even save our lives./43

We use it with Matthew Meredith, a six-year-old boy who recently underwent a bone marrow transplant. His doctors recommended that he shouldn't begin his classes at Randolph Elementary School in Topeka. So the school and local telephone company teamed up to bring first grade to him through two-way video services and television camera./44

Matthew was able to take part in class. He used a fax to hand in class assignments. And the kids in his class got a glimpse of videoconferencing technology that will be common in a few years./45

In West Virginia, doctors are using the Mountaineer Doctor Television Project to link to specialists at West Virginia University. A while back, for example, two-month-old Zachary Buchanan had an irregular heartbeat. Using the network, his family doctor sent an image of his heart to a pediatric cardiologist 100 miles away. His diagnosis: the condition wasn't serious—and he didn't have to travel halfway across the state for treatment./46

All of these applications enhance the quality of life. Because they do, they will spur economic growth./47

After all, even the quickest glance at the telecommunications sector of the economy shows what it means for jobs. Over half of the U.S. workforce is now in information-based jobs. The telecommunications and information sector of the U.S. economy accounts for more than 12% of the GDP. And it's growing faster than any other sector of our economy./48

What about dollars?/49

Last year total sector revenues exceeded $700 billion. And we exported over $48 billion of telecommunications equipment alone./50

When AT&T sold the first cellular phone, they said there would be 900,000 of them by the year 2000./51

Well. We have 13 million now. And it's still 1993. The predictions for mobile telephone users for the year 2000 now total 60 million./52

This kind of growth will create thousands of jobs in the communications industry. But the biggest impact may be in other industrial sectors where those technologies will help American companies compete better and smarter in the global economy./53

Today, more than ever, businesses run on information. A fast, flexible information network is as essential to manufacturing as steel and plastic./54

Virtually every business and consumer in America will benefit dramatically from the telecommunications revolution. I see even Santa Claus is now on the Internet with his own E-Mail./55

If we do not move decisively to ensure that America has the information infrastructure we need, every business and consumer in America will suffer./56

What obstacles lie ahead in this rush to the future?/57

Systems of regulation that made sense when telephones were one thing and cable another may just limit competition in a world in which all information can flow interchangeably over the same conduits. To understand what new systems we must create, though, we must first understand how the information marketplace of the future will operate./58

One helpful way is to think of the National Information Infrastructure as a network of highways—much like the Interstates begun in the 50s./59

These are highways carrying information rather than people or goods. And I'm not talking about just one eight-lane turnpike. I mean a collection of Interstates and feeder roads made up of different materials in the same way that roads can be concrete or macadam—or gravel./60

Some highways will be made up of fiber optics. Others will be built out of coaxial or wireless./61

But—a key point—they must be and will be two-way roads./62

These highways will be wider than today's technology permits. This is important because a television program contains more information than a telephone conversation: and because new uses of video and voice and computers will consist of even more information moving at even faster speeds. These are the computer equivalent of wide loads. They need wide roads. And these roads must go in both directions./63

The new information marketplace based on these highways include four major components:

- First, owners of the highways—because unlike the interstates, the information highways will be built, paid for and funded by the private sector;
- Second, makers of information appliances, like televisions, telephones and computers, and new products of the future that will combine the features of all three;

- Third, information providers—local broadcasters, digital libraries, information service providers, and millions of individuals who will have information they want to share or sell;. . . and most important,

- Fourth, information customers, justly demanding privacy, affordability, and choice./64

At some time in the next decades we'll think about the information marketplace in terms of these four components. We won't talk about cable or telephones or cellular or wireless because there will be free and open competition between everyone who provides and delivers information./65

This administration intends to create an environment that stimulates a private system of free-flowing information conduits./66

It will involve a variety of affordable and innovative appliances and products giving individuals and public institutions the best possible opportunity to be both information customers and providers./67

Anyone who wants to form a business to deliver information will have the means of reaching customers. And any person who wants information will be able to choose among competing information providers, at reasonable prices./68

That's what the future will look like—say, in ten or fifteen years. But how do we get from here to there?/69

This is the key question for government./70

It is during the transition period that the most complexity exists and that government involvement is the most important./71

It's a "phase change"—like moving from ice to water. Ice is simple and water is simple, but in the middle of the change it's mush—part monopoly, part franchise, part open competition. We want to manage that transition./72

And so I am announcing today that the administration will support removal, over time, under appropriate conditions, of judicial and legislative restrictions on all types of telecommunications companies: cable, telephone, utilities, television, and satellite./73

We will do this through both legislative and administrative proposals, prepared after extensive consultation with Congress, industry, public interest and consumer groups, and state and local governments./74

Our goal is not to design the market of the future. It is to provide the principles that shape that market. And it is to provide the rules governing this difficult transition to an open market for information./75

We are committed in that transition to protecting the availability, affordability, and diversity of information and information technology, as market forces replace regulations and judicial models that are no longer appropriate./76

On January 11, in Los Angeles, I will outline in more detail the main components of the legislative package we will present./77

Today, though, I want to set forth the principles upon which it will be based./78

First, encourage private investment./79

The example of Samuel Morse is relevant here./80

Basically, Morse's telegraph was a federal demonstration project. Congress funded the first telegraph link between Washington and Baltimore./81

Afterwards, though—after the first amazing transmission—most nations treated the telegraph and eventually telephone service as a government enterprise./82

That's actually what Morse wanted, too. He suggested that Congress build a national system. Congress said no. They argued that he should find private investors. This Morse and other companies did. And in the view of most historians, that was a source of competitive advantage for the United States./83

We are steering a course between a kind of computer-age Scylla and Charybdis—between the shoals of suffocating regulation on one side and the rocks of unfettered monopolies on the other. Both stifle competition and innovation./84

The Clinton administration believes, though, that as with the telegraph, our role is to encourage the building of the national information infrastructure by the private sector as rapidly as possible./85

Second, promote and protect competition./86

I've talked about highways. All roads once led to Rome. But how many lead to each home? One, or two, or more? Whatever the answer, the same principle should apply: we should prevent unfair cross-subsidies and act to avoid information bottlenecks that would limit consumer choice, or limit the ability of new information providers to reach their customers./87

We can see aspects of this question in the debate over the powers of the Regional Bell Operating Companies; in the passage last year of the Cable Act of 1992; in the proposal to "open up" the local telephone loop./88

Third, provide open access to the network./89

Let's say someone has an information service to provide over the network. They should be able to do it just by paying a fair and equitable price to the network service provider./90

Suppose I want to set up a service that provides 24 hours a day of David Letterman reruns./91

I don't own my own network, so I need to buy access to someone else's. I should be able to do so by paying the same rates as my neighbor, who wants to broadcast kick-boxing matches./92

Without provisions for open access, the companies that own the networks could use their control of the networks to ensure that their customers only have access to their programming. We have already seen cases where cable company owners have used their monopoly control of their networks to exclude programming that competes with their own. Our legislation will contain strong safeguards against such behavior./93

Mitch Kapor, the founder of Lotus and head of the Electronic Frontier Foundation, has spoken about the need for the national information infrastructure to be an "open platform." The IBM PC is an "open platform" that any software programmer can use. They can develop software to run on the PC and if they developed a "killer application"—like Mitch did with Lotus 1-2-3—they could make millions of dollars./94

In the 1980s, thousands of programmers developed thousands of different programs, which have increased the productivity of our businesses, helped our children learn, and helped us balance our checkbooks./95

We need to ensure the NII, just like the PC, is open and accessible to everyone with a good idea who has a product they want to sell./96

This is essential if we are to have many information sources on it./97

Fourth, we want to avoid creating a society of information "haves" and "have nots."/98

You know, the original expression "haves and have nots" comes from Cervantes./99

But we're not tilting at windmills here./100

This is the outgrowth of an old American tradition./101

Broadcasts, telephones, and public education were all designed to diminish the gap between haves and have nots./102

In the past, universal service meant that local phone companies were required to provide a minimum level of plain old telephone service for a minimal price. State and federal regulations provided for subsidies to customers in poor and rural areas./103

The most important step we can take to ensure universal service is to adopt policies that result in lower prices for everyone. The lower the price the less need for subsidies. We believe the pro-competitive policies we will propose will result in lower prices and better service to more Americans./104

But we'll still need a regulatory safety net to make sure almost everyone can benefit./105

In the past it was relatively simple to fund universal service. The local phone companies were regulated monopolies that could be required to provide lifeline services. As more companies enter the market—as many of the regulations are removed—we have to find new ways of doing the same thing./106

Just last week, the National Telecommunications and Information Administration of the Department of Commerce held a hearing in New Mexico to examine just that question. Our bill will incorporate the findings from the hearing and others. It will reaffirm this administration's desire to see that all Americans benefit from the National Information Infrastructure./107

As we think about the future of universal service, we as a society ought to think about what kind of service, and on what group of people we must concentrate./108

Schools—and our children—are paramount./109

The new head of the FCC, Reed Hundt, recently said, "There are thousands of buildings in this country with millions of people in them who have no telephones, no cable television and no reasonable prospect of broadband services. They're called schools."/110

When it comes to ensuring universal service, our schools are the most impoverished institution in society./111

Only 14% of our public schools used educational networks in even one classroom last year. Only 22% possess even one modem./112

Video-on-demand will be a great thing. It will be a far greater thing to demand that our efforts give every child access to the educational riches we have in such abundance./113

The recent article in the *Washington Post* on the proposed video communication network in the D.C. area is a wake-up call to all of us concerned about "electronic redlining." If we allow the information superhighway to bypass the less fortuante sectors of our society—even for an interim period—we will find that the information rich will get richer while the information poor get poorer with no guarantee that everyone will be on the network at some future date./114

We cannot relax restrictions from legislation and judicial decisions without strong commitments and safeguards that there will be a "public right of way" on the information highway. We must protect the interests of the public sector./115

That's essential in building the information highway. That's essential in providing affordable services for public education, public health and government./116

The less fortunate sectors of the population must have access to a minimum level of information services through subsidies or other forms of a public interest tithe./117

Fifth and finally: we want to encourage flexibility./118

After all, flexibility and adaptability are essential if we are to develop policies that will stand the test of time. Technology is advancing so rapidly, the structure of the industry is changing so quickly, that we must have policies broad enough to accommodate change./119

Even though the Communications Act of 1934 could not anticipate many of the technological changes of the last 60 years, it was flexible enough to allow the FCC, state regulators, and the successive administrations to deal with those changes without rewriting the act every few years./120

As the administration develops its legislation we are trying hard to follow the example set by the authors of the 1934 act. We are trying hard to enunciate key principles of policy, identify which government agencies will implement that policy, and then leave many of the details to them./121

I don't want to sound like I've thought all these ideas up. The fact is, in Congress, several important pieces of legislation have already been introduced./122

I've already mentioned the Brooks-Dingell bill in the House. It and the Markey-Fields bill represent major steps forward, not to mention more than a year of hard work by other Congressmen including Congressman Boucher and Congressman Oxley./123

In the Senate, Senators Danforth and Inouye have introduced a major piece of legislation. Senator Hollings is working on another./124

Between now and the beginning of the next session, we'll be continuing our dialogue with Congress, industry, and public interest groups to formulate our proposal for legislative and administrative action that will clear the way for the communications marketplace of the future. And part of that effort will be to continue to publicly enunciate what we want and how we will achieve it./125

With high-level Congressional support, a growing consensus in industry, and leadership from the president, we have a unique opportunity. We can eliminate many of the regulatory barriers on the information highway—and perform the most major surgery on the Communications Act since it was enacted in 1934./126

We will do it by avoiding both extremes: regulation for regulation's sake, and the blind adherence to the dead hand of free market economics. We will do it with the principle that has guided so much of the administration's efforts over the last year: the urgent need to create flexible, responsive government./127

It's fitting that this address is being delivered here at the National Press Club. Almost every form of communication is present here, in this room. I'm talking to you orally. Some of you are taking notes—others are typing on laptops. Some of you will publish your observations through the use of printing presses, others through television or radio reports. People tuned into C-Span are watching on television. Still others are listening over a prototype of the NII—the Internet./128

All of these forms of communication bring us together—they allow us to participate in a virtually instantaneous dialogue. They will allow us to debate, and then to build a consensus, on the nature of the information infrastructure, on the details of legislation, on the nature of regulation./129

But even more, as I said at the outset, these methods of communication allow us to build a society that is healthier, more prosperous, and better educated. They will allow us to strengthen the bonds of community and to build new "information communities."/130

The challenge is not, in the end, the new technology. It is holding true to our basic principles. Whether our tools were the quill pens that wrote and then signed the Declaration of Independence or the laptop computers being used to write the constitutions of newly-freed countries . . . better communication has almost always led to greater freedom and greater economic growth./131

That is our challenge. That is what this administration—and the nation—will achieve./132

There's a story about Michael Faraday, the inventor of the electric generator. Once he was showing Benjamin Disraeli through his lab, taking great pleasure in demonstrating the effects he could produce. And at the end of the tour, Disraeli said, "Well, what good are all these things?"/133

Faraday answered, "What good is a baby?"/134

If we take the narrow view, it looks like telecommunications is well out of its infancy. But if we cast our eyes ahead a few decades—or centuries—we see that it's barely out of diapers. We need to look ahead, to protect it when it need protecting, but not get in the way when it needs to walk alone./135

Like those wireless operators should have done in the North Atlantic, we should be alert to where the collisions could be. And we shouldn't hesitate to chart a new course./136

If we do that, then much more than the telecommunications industry will grow strong. This country and much of the human race will, as well./137

In 1992 the five-hundredth anniversary of Columbus's "discovery" of the Americas generated a good deal of talk about relationships between the indigenous Indian populations that greeted the Columbian voyagers and the explorers and settlers who followed the Nina, the Pinta, and the Santa Maria. Those relationships are complicated by a history of exploitation, misunderstanding, and distrust. The anniversary celebrations in 1992 fostered informative exchanges. David Archambault, president of the American Indian College Fund, used those celebrations to present information to non-Indian audiences. In the following speech, he's sensitive to the need to answer the questions non-Indians would "most *like* to ask," to deal in a forthright fashion with the effect of the Columbian visits on Native Americans, and to project a positive future for Native Americans once relationships between them and Eurocentric citizens are improved. Note particularly how he uses information to provide the grounds for new beliefs and attitudes about Indian needs.

A Speech to Inform

• • • •
Columbus Plus 500 Years
Whither the American Indian?
David Archambault

Thank you and good afternoon. Hau Kola. That is how we Lakota say "Greeting, Friends." I am happy to be here today to represent Native American people. I am a Ikoeya Wicaska—an ordinary man. We think of an ordinary man as not superior to anyone else or for that matter to anything else. We—all people and all things—are related to each other./1

We begin our spiritual ceremonies with the phrase "Oni takuya Oyasi," which means all my relations. We believe that all people are ultimately part of one nation—the nation of mankind, but that this nation is only one of many nations that inhabit the Mother Earth. To us all living things are nations—the deer, the horses, things that crawl, things that fly, things that grow in and on the ground. All of these nations were created by the same Power, and none is superior to another. All are necessary for life. We are expected to live and work in harmony./2

In my travels I have learned that many Americans in mainstream society are uninformed or ill-informed about American Indians./3

So let me begin by responding to questions people most often ask about us—or questions people might most *like* to ask./4

No, we don't consider that Columbus discovered America. Estimates of the number of people who lived in the so-called New World at the time Columbus arrived run from 40 to 100 million or more. Hey, we knew we were here. It was Columbus who was lost. Maybe that poem ought to say,

> *"When Columbus sailed the ocean blue, it was he—not America—who got discovered in 14-hundred, ninety-two."*/5

Yes, American Indians are American citizens. After World War I, a nation grateful for the contributions of Indians to the war effort made all American Indians full citizens./6

No, we are not "prisoners" on the reservations. We can leave any time. Many have. But the rest of us don't want to. We don't want to be assimilated into the dominant culture. We want to preserve our own culture and traditions. I'll tell you later how we hope to do that./7

Yes, we have a unique status in the United States. We are both citizens and sovereign people. That comes from our history as nations—or tribes—defeated by Europeans, who, after giving up on trying to Christianize and civilize us, recognized our right to self-determination. I'll come back to this, too./8

No, not all Indians are alike. There is diversity among *tribal* nations just as there is among *European* nations. American Indians in 500 or so tribes speak more than 200 languages and dialects./9

Yes, many American Indians have an especially tough time of it today with alcohol and other health problems, with poverty and inadequate education- and job-opportunities, and with just trying to figure out their own identity. Only we Indians can provide the leadership needed to solve these problems./10

Finally, no, we don't care—at least most of us don't—whether you call us "Indians," "Native Americans," "Indigenous People," or "Amerinds." An Indian comedian tells it this way:

"I know why white people call us Indians," he says. "When Columbus got here, he thought he had arrived in the Indies, so naturally he called the inhabitants 'Indians.' I'm just thankful he didn't think he had arrived in Turkey."/11

Today I want to share with you some of our history and culture and our hopes for the future. It is important to American Indians—and I think to you as well—that *all* Americans know more about the first people to come to this land, about where we are and what we are doing and where we are headed. If we are to respect our differences and value what we have in common, we must begin with understanding./12

During this quincentenary of Columbus's voyage, attention is once again focused on what the white man brought to this land and on Columbus himself. This man who made such a remarkable journey has become the stuff of legend as well as history. He is admired and detested, exalted and condemned. Columbus Day will surely never be a favorite holiday among Indians, but we should consider Columbus for what he was—not for what we may wish he had been./13

Columbus was a skilled and courageous mariner who led his ships across unchartered waters. He found land and people unknown to Europeans. He discovered a sea route between Europe and America. Never mind that Norse explorers and perhaps others had made the trip earlier. It was Columbus who recorded ways for others to make it across the waters—and back again./14

Columbus came here, however, not to trade, but to conquer; he came to enrich himself and enslave his captives. His mission, in the words of his royal charter, was to "discover and acquire" all new lands as well as "pearls, precious stones, gold, silver," and other valuables. He would write back to Spain,

"From here, in the name of the Blessed Trinity, we can send all the slaves that can be sold."/15

Columbus was a man of his time. He felt inspired by his God, empowered by his monarch, and reassured by the rightness of his cause. He was sailing, as the saying had it, for "God, glory, and gold." If he had objected to enslaving others and taking their lands, someone else may have gotten that royal charter. To me, Columbus is neither hero nor villain, but rather a symbol of a world forevermore transformed. His culture and mine have never fully made peace./16

Tens of millions of native people would die during and after the years of Columbus's four voyages to our shores—die of gunfire from soldiers who wanted their lands and precious metals; die of maltreatment while forced to work as slaves; die of white man's diseases, such as smallpox and typhoid, for which they had no immunity./17

These native people had been hunters and fishermen and gatherers and farmers and weavers and traders. They had created stable, even advanced, societies. They had highly developed agricultural and trading systems. If was they who had grown the first potatoes and the first corn and the first tomatoes. They understood mathematics and architecture and calendar systems. They were rich in art and culture as well as in gold and silver. The Incas, the Mayans, the Aztecs, and many others—civilizations all destroyed, their people subjugated./18

In North America, too, Indians lost their lands, their economy, and their freedom to Europeans. At times, the new settlers were not quite sure what to do about these native people. The Indians had welcomed them, fed them, traded with them. They were people who respected their environment. They had developed intricate political and social systems. The Iroquois, for example, had the world's only true democracy—a Supreme Chief, a legislative council, and a judicial branch as well as universal suffrage and direct representation. It was a system the Founding Fathers of the new nation would study and learn from./19

But the Indians were in the way—in the way of new settlements and new riches. So for a long time, the objective was to get rid of the Indian. "The only good Indian is a dead Indian," the saying went. Whites even slaughtered the buffalo so the Indian could not hunt. The Indians fought back—often ferociously. But they lacked the manpower and the arms to resist./20

Sometimes they pleaded. In a remarkable speech in 1879, Chief Joseph of the Nez Perces addressed his conquerors with these words:

"All men were made by the same Great Spirit Chief," he said. *"They are all brothers and all should have equal rights. . . . Let me be a free man, free to talk and think and act for myself—and I will obey all of your laws."*/21

Often they made treaties: 800 of them, in fact—nearly half of which were ratified by the U.S. Senate in full accord with the federal Constitution. Each of these treaties—every one—was violated by a nation that prides itself on keeping its word./22

The Indians could not resist, but they could not be exterminated either. And so the government moved them to reservations—a movement with a long and sordid history. One of the most notorious chapters in that history was recorded in the 1830s when tens of thousands of Cherokees, Choctaws, and Creeks were forcibly moved from the Southeastern United States to what is now the state of Oklahoma. The Cherokees called it the "trail of tears." Along the way, nearly one-quarter of them died of starvation and disease./23

The reservations were run by those who believed the way to "civilize" us was to take away our language and culture and religion. Our children were called savages and taken from us. They were put in boarding schools where they were educated—dare we say "brainwashed?"—with the white man's ways. Their teachers vowed to "kill the Indian and save the child." The idea was that if the white man couldn't get rid of the Indian, perhaps he could at least get rid of the Indian's culture./24

Not until the 1930s was an effort made to give Indians limited sovereignty, allowing them to carry on their traditions and pass along their culture to their children./25

But by the 1950s, the new watchword was assimilation. Break up the tribes, move Indians into mainstream society. In other words, make them "real Americans." Once again, the emphasis was on destroying Indian culture./26

Only during the past several decades has there been a growing realization that we American Indians must determine our own destiny. We must be free to cherish our traditions and our culture, but also learn to live and work with the society around us. We must learn to walk in both worlds./27

Can we do it? Yes, we can. It will require education for economic development and self-sufficiency. It demands that we create opportunity and hope for future generations./28

This idea is not original with me. It was taught to us by a great leader of the Lakota people—my people—the great Chief Sitting Bull. He taught us that Indian children could succeed in modern society and yet retain the values of their culture, values such as respect for the earth, for wildlife, for rivers and streams, for plants and trees; and values such as caring for each other and for family and community./29

He taught us that we must leave behind more hope than we found.

"Let us put our minds together," he said, "and see what life we can make for the children."/30

That is why there is an American Indian College Fund. It is to carry out the dream of Sitting Bull: to bring together the best minds in the Indian and non-Indian world to build a better future for our children. Our mission is twofold: to raise badly needed funds, of course, but also to help the general public understand the heritage of American Indians./31

There are 26 colleges located on or near reservations in the United States. They were created by and for Indians. Three are four-year colleges; the others, two-year schools. Most are fully accredited and the rest are earning accreditation./32

In the schools, our children are prepared for both worlds. The schools maintain a rigorous academic discipline while preserving Indian heritage and culture. Our students study math and science and business management, as well as American Indian philosophy, traditions, and language. They learn what it means to be Indian—and gain greater understanding of the world around them./33

And it's working. Young American Indians who attend our colleges go on to further education and employment. They become productive, active citizens with confidence and pride in their tribal heritage. Many return to the reservation to work. Above all, they learn to value learning and to value the wisdom of those who came before us./34

The colleges do something more. They serve their communities. They offer job training and day care, health clinics and counseling services, public-affairs and literacy programs. They provide leadership and support for economic development of the reservations. In short, they are committed to service and renewal./35

Not long ago researchers from the Carnegie Foundation for the Advancement of Teaching spent two years studying our colleges. The schools, the Foundation concluded,

"are crucial to the future of Native Americans and to the future of our nation."

The Foundation called accomplishments of the schools "enormously impressive" and said they

"give hope to students and new life to their communities."/36

But the report also pointed to the need for expanded science labs and libraries and other facilities and urged the federal government to keep promises it has made. Congress had authorized payment of nearly six-thousand dollars for each full-time equivalent student at tribal colleges. But the amount actually appropriated is only about half that./37

I feel a special commitment to the work of these colleges—not only because I temporarily head the effort to raise private funds and public awareness for them but, more important, because of what they mean to my life and the lives of my people./38

More than 100 years ago, our great chief Sitting Bull was murdered. His people—frightened that they too would be killed—set out on foot across South Dakota along with Chief Big Foot. Carrying their children, they fled across the frozen prairie through the bitter subzero cold 200 miles to seek refuge on the Pine Ridge reservation in southwestern South Dakota./39

On December 29, 1890, near a creek now known to all the world as Wounded Knee, Chief Big Foot and his followers were massacred. No one knows who fired first, but when the shooting was over, nearly 300 Indians—men, women, and children—lay dead and dying across the valley. Their bodies were dumped into a mass grave. The survivors were unable to hold a burial ceremony, a ceremony we call the wiping away of tears. It meant the living could never be free./40

On the 100th anniversary of the massacre at Wounded Knee, several hundred of us on horseback retraced the journey of Big Foot and his band during those final days. We arrived at dawn at the site of the mass grave at Wounded Knee and completed the wiping of tears ceremony. The Si Tanka Wokiksuye, the Chief [Big] Foot Memorial Ride, was a mourning ritual that released the spirits of our ancestors and closed a tragic chapter in our history./41

We have the opportunity now to help rebuild our nation. And I do not mean just the Indian nations. On this 500th anniversary of Columbus's voyages, we together can build a better America, a nation enriched by the diversity of its people and strengthened by the values that bring us together as a community./42

Let us make this anniversary a time of healing and a time of renewal, a time to wipe away the tears. Let us—both Indian and non-Indian—put our minds together and see what life we can make for our children. Let us leave behind more hope than we found. I think Sitting Bull would be proud of us all. Thank you. Tosha Akin Wanchin./43

Architect Myron Goldman's speech, "We Shape Our Buildings, and Thereafter They Shape Us," is an excellent example of a speech to orient an audience about to be exposed to a variety of speakers. It opened a symposium on the revised architectural master plan for the city of Columbus, Indiana. He designed it to orient the audience to the value of the dual architectural concerns for utility and aesthetic appeal. Notice how he uses his introduction to stress the importance of his subject and to forecast the development of his speech, carefully divides the body of his speech into "utilitarian" and "aesthetic" considerations, and presents a short conclusion (because the other presenters presumably will develop more particular conclusions). The resulting speech is short, clear, and effective.

Presentation to a Symposium

• • • •
We Shape Our Buildings, and Thereafter They Shape Us
Myron Goldsmith

The theme of our symposium is "We Shape Our Buildings, and Thereafter They Shape Us." I would like to explore the truth of that statement in terms of architectural merit and the architecture of your community./1

Scholars all over the world study the impact of environment on human behavior. It is a new and burgeoning field of research activity for anthropologists, sociologists, psychologists, and communication specialists. For these scholars, it is a fresh areas of inquiry that is enjoying a surge of attention and scrutiny. It is widely covered and discussed in journal literature, in publications, and in symposiums such as the one we enjoy today./2

But the impact of environment on human behavior is *not* a new idea to architects: It's something we've known for hundreds of years. I will address its significance in reference to the two broad aspects or dimensions of architecture—the utilitarian and the aesthetic—and I will explain why I think great architecture combines both of these./3

First, the utilitarian. In the field of domestic architecture, we know that some houses are easier and more pleasant to live in than others and promote positive interaction among family members. The large kitchen of our past and its legacy in the post-World-War II family room encourage family interaction. On the other hand, a too-formal and forbidding room can discourage use. A similar effect occurs in a neighborhood. Arrangement of houses in a common cul-de-sac promotes interaction among families and children in the cul-de-sac. Or, dwellings can be set back—behind fences, through gates. Such devices provide greater privacy and security; they convey messages that say: Stay Out./4

In places of work, we know that a pleasant, well-organized factory or office fosters better efficiency, happier employees, and less absenteeism. The layout of a building can promote or restrict accessibility to people. In some banks, for example, the president is in the open, accessible to any person who wants to discuss something. The opposite can also be true, where top executives are on the upper floor of a building, reached only through a battery of receptionists and secretaries, or even in a separate building with separate dining and parking facilities. This too affects interaction, the style of management, and the priorities of the corporation./5

I know of a conglomerate that was nearly ruined because all the top managers of the constituent companies were moved to a single, isolated building on the theory that the interaction of the top management was the most important priority. For them, horizontal communication at the upper echelons was more important than vertical communication. And meanwhile, no one was minding the company store./6

In other words, we have learned and are learning by trial and error about architectural spaces—public and private, accessible and formal. We understand more about what makes a building function well and efficiently./7

What about the aesthetic? In the best architecture, the utilitarian is combined with the aesthetic. And when that occurs, architecture represents more than the sum of its parts. While it is easy to define and evaluate the functional aspect, it is much more difficult to define and evaluate the aesthetic aspect. To do this, we must be able to recognize and make informed judgments about aesthetics and decide how much we are willing to invest in it. The return may be many times the investment in the improved quality of life./8

How does the aesthetic aspect serve us and our community? Does it only give people pleasure? Or does it meet other basic human needs as well? The most dramatic example of this concept is the church or cathedral. How can one explain Chartres Cathedral, built 700 years ago in a town the size of Columbus, Indiana? What prompted the prodigious effort in engineering and craftsmanship, in art and architecture? What made those people build a nave over

120 feet high, the height of a 12-story building, and towers almost 300 feet high? If the utilitarian dimension was the sole criterion, they could have built a nave 15 to 20 feet high. But there were other things at stake in the 13th century—the glory of God and civic pride, to name but two. The worship of God was heightened and exalted by the beauty of man's unparalleled artistic achievement. And the pride of the community was enhanced by the size, the proportions, and the majesty of the cathedral—bigger and more beautiful than its counterpart in Paris, only 40 miles away./9

But we need not go to thirteenth century France to see a proper example of the combination of the utilitarian and the aesthetic in historic architecture. Your own county courthouse, built in 1874, is a good example. Not to put it in the same class as Chartres, but it is a fine building. It provides centralized, efficient working space for the county functions, but it also aesthetically represents a good example of late nineteenth century civic architecture. Buildings constitute a large part of the tangible reality we experience. Size and scale are not necessarily the measure of their significance./10

Your own town is a notable example of the impact of a distinguished architectural environment on the quality of community life: where informed clients and distinguished architects have confronted with honesty and solved with integrity the problems of space and use, where the functional and aesthetic aspects of architecture have forged a standard of excellence that any community in the world might envy. Through a combination of clear vision, good fortune, and unusual circumstances, you have provided for your citizens the finest our profession has to offer in churches, schools, and buildings—public, commercial, and industrial. You have given your young people something beautiful to grow up with, and you have given your own population something beautiful to live with./11

So, then, what value do we place on the environment where we live and work and learn? How important is it that the community as well as the leadership—clients, architects, teachers, and business people—are knowledgeable about architecture and have some aesthetic judgments? It is of immense value and in Columbus you are better informed about architecture than any city I know of. Columbus is the proper training ground for the architects and clients of the future. You shape your buildings, and thereafter they shape you./12

Associate Professor of Art Harold Haydon offered the following remarks at the unveiling of *Nuclear Energy,* a bronze sculpture created by Henry Moore and placed on the campus of the University of Chicago to commemorate the achievement of Enrico Fermi and his associates in releasing the first self-sustaining nuclear chain reaction at Stagg Field on 2 December 1942. The unveiling took place during the twenty-fifth anniversary of that event. Notice in particular how he verbally controls the way the audience is to see—to understand, interpret, and evaluate—*Nuclear Energy.* The first three paragraphs examine the historical foundations and present-day functions of commemorative sculpture. He next reviews the spiritual side of scientific discovery, the controversy surrounding nuclear energy, and then the importance of artistic recognition of creativity no matter what its field. Haydon thus brings together the heroic aspects of science and art, controlling his listeners vision of both.

A Dedicatory Speech

• • • •   ## The Testimony of Sculpture
Harold Haydon

Since very ancient times men have set up a marker, or designated some stone or tree, to hold the memory of a deed or happening far longer than any man's lifetime. Some of these memorial objects have lived longer than man's collective memory, so that we now ponder the meaning of a monument, or wonder whether some great stone is a record of human action, or whether instead it is only a natural object./1

There is something that makes us want a solid presence, a substantial form, to be the tangible touchstone of the mind, designed and made to endure as witness or record, as if we mistrusted that seemingly frail yet amazingly tough skein of words and symbols that serves memory and which, despite being mere ink blots and punch-holes, nonetheless succeeds in preserving the long human tradition, firmer than any stone, tougher than any metal./2

We still choose stone or metal to be our tangible reminders, and for these solid, enduring forms we turn to the men who are carvers of stone and moulders of metal, for it is they who have given lasting form to our myths through the centuries./3

One of these men is here today, a great one, and he has given his skill and the sure touch of his mind and eye to create for this nation, this city, and this university a marker that may stand here for centuries, even for a millennium, as a mute yet eloquent testament to a turning point in time when man took charge of a new material world hitherto beyond his capability./4

As this bronze monument remembers an event and commemorates an achievement, it has something unique to say about the spiritual meaning of the achievement, for it is the special power of art to convey feeling and stir profound emotion, to touch us in ways that are beyond the reach of reason./5

Nuclear energy, for which the sculpture is named, is a magnet for conflicting emotions, some of which inevitably will attach to the bronze form; it will harbor or repel emotion according to the states of mind of those who view the sculpture. In its brooding presence some will feel the joy and sorrow of recollection, some may dread the uncertain future, and yet others will thrill to the thought of magnificent achievements that lie ahead. The test of the sculpture's greatness as a human document, the test of any work of art, will be its capacity to evoke a response and the quality of that response./6

One thing most certain is that this sculpture by Henry Moore is not an inert object. It is a live thing, and somewhat strange like every excellent beauty, to be known to us only in time and never completely. Its whole meaning can be known only to the ever-receding future, as each succeeding generation reinterprets according to its own vision and experience./7

By being here in a public place the sculpture *Nuclear Energy* becomes a part of Chicago, and the sculptor an honored citizen, known not just to artists and collectors of art, but to everyone who pauses here in the presence of the monument, because the artist is inextricably part of what he has created, immortal through his art./8

With this happy conjunction today of art and science, of great artist and great occasion, we may hope to reach across the generations, across the centuries, speaking through enduring sculpture of our time, our hopes, and fears, perhaps more eloquently than we know. Some works of art have meaning for all mankind and so defy time, persisting through all hazards; the monument to the atomic age should be one of these./9

Kim Patterson of Miami University in Ohio wanted to talk about something she saw as a cruel hoax—fertility clinics that promised much more than they could deliver to couples wanting children. She opens with an emotional illustration, develops her central idea and a forecast for the rest of the speech in paragraph 3, devotes six paragraphs to developing the problem, sets out institutional solutions in paragraphs 10 to 12, and talks to her immediate audience about its personal activities in two paragraphs. She then is ready to conclude by returning to her opening illustration. The motivational appeals are clear, as is the state of mind she expects the audience to be in by the end.

A Speech to Persuade

• • • •

Fraudulent Fertility Clinics
Kim Patterson

Debbie and Steven Gregory can't have a baby but want one desperately, which is why they trusted the doctor who treated Debbie with large doses of fertility hormones. Three times, Dr. Cecil Jacobson told Debbie she was pregnant; he even showed her ultrasound pictures of her baby to be. And yet, each time, Debbie was told she had miscarried. During her third supposed pregnancy, Debbie decided to see another doctor. He told her the truth—Debbie had never been pregnant./1

Debbie and Steven Gregory are just one of a growing number of infertile couples who are being exploited by the doctors and fertility clinics which are supposed to be helping them. But instead of bringing home a little bundle of joy, most couples leave these clinics childless and heartbroken. In fact, the March 13, 1989 issue of *Time* reports that fertility clinics have become a "prescription for disaster."/2

In order to better understand the extent of fertility fraud, let's first examine the three problems plaguing infertility treatment: the falsified information, the medical hazards, and the astronomical costs of this new reproductive technology. After looking at the problems, we can then discuss some solutions to prevent infertile couples from becoming the victims of these so-called infertility specialists. Perhaps then we will understand that the cost of fighting infertility is a often a price too high to pay./3

Most of us probably want to have children at some point in our lives, and we just assume that we'll be able to have a baby when we decide the time is right. But that may not necessarily be true, because infertility is on the rise in the U.S. The December 4, 1989, *Wall Street Journal* reports that infertility has tripled among 20-to-24-year-olds primarily because of the rise in sexually transmitted diseases. The March 1989 issue of *Changing Times* magazine reports that one out of every six couples is infertile. If this doesn't directly affect you, just think of any six couples you know, chances are that one of them has had or will have problems with fertility. We need to be aware of the problems of fertility treatment in order to protect ourselves and our loved ones from such deception. The first of these problems is falsified information./4

Most clinics have become experts at either lying about or disguising their success rates, especially where the procedure of in-vitro fertilization is concerned. IVF is a process in which the egg is removed from the woman, fertilized with the man's sperm in a petri dish, and then placed back into the woman. But ask any clinic its success rates with IVF and you may get figures calculated almost any way. For example, many clinics like to brag about their pregnancy rates. But what they don't tell you is that 20–35% of all IVF pregnancies result in miscarriages, as reported in the January 22, 1988, issue of the *Journal of the American Medical Association.* Or they may give you figures for pregnancies which aren't really pregnancies. Take the case of Debbie Gregory. She was given a fertility hormone which caused her to mimic the symptoms of pregnancy, including weight gain and testing positive for pregnancy. Remember those ultrasound pictures Dr. Jacobson showed Debbie? Well, when another fertility specialist saw those pictures, he said they looked more like weather reports than a fetus./5

Very few clinics will give out their actual take-home-baby rates. This may be because there aren't any babies to tell you about. The March 13, 1989, issue of *Time* reports that over half of the nation's 200 IVF clinics have never even produced a baby. And yet, women entering many of these clinics are led to believe that they will soon become pregnant. You see, clinics are literally allowed to give this misleading information because they're not regulated. The October 28, 1989, issue of *The Lancet* reports that IVF clinics don't have to be certified and doctors don't even have to follow any professional guidelines./6

Even more outrageous than these falsified success rates are the health hazards posed by fertility hormones. Clomid is a widely used fertility drug which has been taken by millions of women over the past 20 years. But a recent study by Gerald Cunha at the University of California in San Francisco shows that Clomid may cause malformations in the reproductive organs of a female fetus, thus leading to future fertility problems. However, Cunha believes that Clomid won't cause birth defects as long as it's not given during pregnancy./7

However, many doctors continue to prescribe Clomid long after conception takes place. Kathy from Bridgeport, Connecticut, was treated with Clomid but was never tested for pregnancy. Then one day, Kathy was taken to the emergency room, delirious with pain. She had miscarried a 6-to-8-week-old fetus. Kathy says, "They give out Clomid's like M&Ms. I keep thinking I might have had a baby by now. I can't help but be angry about that."/8

This, coupled with the emotional stress of not having a child, is further exaggerated by the third problem of fertility clinics—the astronomical costs of these often fraudulent procedures. The Office of Technology Assessment reports that the nation's 2.4 million infertile couples spend over $1 billion a year on treatment. And yet, after all the money sacrificed, only 5% of them will bring home a baby. You see, each IVF procedure costs over $5 thousand, and many women undergo five or six attempts before either becoming pregnant or giving up hope. Clearly, the infertility industry is a booming billion-dollar business, where doctors have all the money to gain and patients have everything to lose./9

With such widespread fraud on the levels of false information, health hazards, and financial costs, it would seem to be difficult to prevent clinics from taking advantage of the childless. But there are measures which can be taken in three areas to prevent infertile couples from being exploited when they're most vulnerable. The first step lies with the government. The December 3, 1989, issue of *The New York Times* reported that a congressional committee has recognized the fertility fraud problem. However, proper action remains to be taken. They must go beyond mere acknowledgement and legislate solutions that will regulate this industry. But we can't wait while thousands of couples fall prey to unethical practices./10

So we must focus our attention on solutions which will produce results in the near future and turn to the medical community. The American Medical Association must demand that clinics adhere to professional guidelines. For instance, they must require all clinics to undergo professional auditing. (These results can then be published in a directory, so the public would know a clinic's IVF attempts, the number of pregnancies achieved, and the actual number of births.) This will ensure that statistics given to potential clients are indeed fact and not fiction./11

Secondly, they must investigate any fraud. For over seven years, several doctors knew about Jacobson's false pregnancies, and yet absolutely nothing was done until some of his patients decided to sue./12

But solutions on these levels are never enough. In order to ensure that we or our loved ones don't become yet more victims of fraud, we need to take an active role in combatting this problem. First and foremost, if you plan on having children any time in the future, be aware that 20% of all infertility is caused by sexually transmitted diseases, as reported in the May 21, 1988, issue of *Science News*. Taking the proper precautions now may help to eliminate heartbreak in the future./13

Next, if you know any couples who are currently seeking the help of a fertility specialist, warn them of the fraud which surrounds this field. Encourage them not to be embarrassed to ask questions about the clinic's practices. By knowing the right questions to ask about pregnancy success rates and by understanding the risks involved, you can help them make more educated choices about one of the most important decisions of their lives. Until steps such as these are taken, clinics will continue to go unregulated and couples will continue to go home childless./14

Perhaps one of life's greatest gifts is the birth of a child. It's painful enough when couples can't conceive a child naturally, but when they are given unrealistic hopes by falsified statistics and misleading doctors, that pain can turn into a living nightmare. By examining the problem of fraudulent fertility clinics and by adopting solutions, perhaps cases like Debbie and Steven Gregory's will become obsolete. And instead, fertility patients will get a happy return on their emotional and financial investments./15

While you've probably heard people talk about the need to support the arts, supporting the artistic development of the disabled is an unusual topic for most listeners. Erik Anderson of Grand View College in Iowa wanted to make sure his listeners had the background they needed to act on his recommendations. Notice his use of poetry and lists of specific instances, in particular, as ways of making the problem concrete and yet elevating our sense of its importance. His visualization of the problem and possible solutions is very well developed, although his call to action probably could have had more punch. The speech, nonetheless, is fascinating and quite different from the usual Interstate Oratorical Association student contest speech.

A Speech to Actuate

· · · ·

A Plea for the Arts
Erik Anderson

Let's say that you have a dream. That dream is to be a professional performing or visual artist. Perhaps you want to be a singer or a dancer, or maybe you might want to be a painter or a sculptor. Some people would tell you that this is an unrealistic dream and that you should concern yourself with more important things. Now, let's also say, for the sake of argument, that you have a physical or mental disability. Should that dream be any less realistic or any less attainable? It certainly would not be any less important to you./1

I would like to look at the issue of arts for the disabled. I would like to show you that the arts are vitally important to special populations, and that the disabled are capable of a wide range of creative expression. More that just the "arts and crafts" that are sometimes associated with them. Finally, I would like to show you not only how to be involved with arts for special populations, but also why you should./2

There's something locked up deep inside.
Won't you help me find the key
That opens doorways where I hide,
And treasurechests of me./3

Artistic expression is important for everyone. It provides us with a way to feed our need for self-improvement and self-esteem, and sometimes even peer approval. For the disabled, however, it can be even more important because other avenues of expression are sometimes limited./4

Artistic creativity and disability have long been tied together. After all we have all heard that you must, as the cliché says, "suffer for your art." Dr. Phillip Sandblom, in his book *Creativity and Disease,* maintains that "because disease (in this case, disability) limits other activity, it figures heavily into artistic creativity." For the disabled, the arts provide a vital means of expression and achievement. Sandblom also suggests that persons with disabilities have a great need to excel. Often this is to compensate for things they feel that they lack. Lord Byron, who had a club foot, put it this way: "Deformity is daring. It is its essence to o'ertake mankind by heart and soul and make itself equal—aye, the superior to the rest. There is a spur in its halt movements to become all that the others cannot, in such things as still are free to both." I can attest to this myself. You cannot know what it means to me to be able to stand here today and compete on an absolutely equal footing./5

Because the arts are such an accessible means for the disabled to build their self-esteem, they are often used as a tool in therapy. Availability of arts experiences for special populations is vital./6

Homer's *Iliad* and *Odyssey,* Da Vinci's *Mona Lisa,* the famous *Fifth Symphony* by Beethoven,—what do these great works have in common? Handel's *Messiah,* Milton's *Paradise Lost,*—certainly they are all classics. Each one of them is a masterwork, a testament to its creator's timeless artistic skills. But what else do they have in common? The *Telltale Heart* by Edgar Allen Poe, *Tartuffe* by Moliere, *Robinson Crusoe* by Robert Louis Stevenson, even Stevie Wonder singing *Ebony and Ivory*—what do they have in common? These are the works of disabled artists./7

As with any group, disabled artists display a wide range of creative capabilities. Our culture has benefited greatly from the works of these disabled artists, and we are proud to list them among our number. But these are only a few. The number of disabled artists is staggering./8

Whistler	Monet	Renoir
Chopin	Vivaldi	Paganini
Byron	Mattisse	Van Gogh

Schumann	Sir Walter Scott	Emily Dickinson
D. H. Lawrence	Chekov	Mozart
Sarah Bernhardt	Toulouse-Lautrec	Helen Keller
Lionel Barrymore	Ronnie Milsap	Ray Charles
Stevie Wonder	Jose Feliciano	Billy Barty/9
Itzhak Perelman		

And these are still only a few! Disabled artists are capable of truly great things. Availability of arts experiences for special populations is vital./10

With paint and crayons I will draw
A world of beauty, strength and awe.
With costumes, makeup, words to say,
I'll be an actor in a play.
With just one lesson, just one chance,
I'll twirl and swirl in wondrous dance.
With instruments and with my voice,
I'll make the music of my choice.
With just a little of your time,
I'll be a silent, perfect mime.
The arts will let the whole world see,
Beyond the "dis" is "ability!"/11

Fortunately, there are things that we can do to ensure that the arts continue to be available to special populations. There are a number of organizations whose purpose is to provide services for the disabled. Monies for these organizations are always less than what is needed. And if you cannot make a financial contribution to help provide arts opportunities to the handicapped or if you wish to help further, they always need volunteers. It isn't difficult to become involved. All you have to do is ask, "How can I help?" I have been involved for the past ten years with an organization called Very Special Arts. It is an international organization that exists specifically to provide arts experiences to the handicapped./12

Another thing that we can do is support legislation designed to provide equal opportunities for the disabled. This may not have a direct effect on arts opportunities, but it will affect our society's perception of special populations over time. As our society comes to see the disabled, not as people who lack ability, but people, who like everyone else, are simply doing the best they can with what they have; then art will, as it often does, imitate life./13

The question then becomes "Why should I become involved if I don't have a disability?" Maybe you will become involved because you know someone with a disability whose quality of life could be improved through exposure to the arts. Maybe you will become involved because it will nurture your own sense of achievement and self-esteem. Or maybe you will become involved because you, or someone you know, may become disabled, and you will realize then what an important role the arts play for the disabled. Whatever the reason, become involved. Availability of arts experiences for special populations is vital./14

I cannot hear, I cannot talk, I cannot even see.
I cannot run, I cannot walk, but look inside of me!
For through I think uniquely, and I travel in a chair,
My journey's filled with passion and with bold artistic flair.

I long to leap, unfettered, on flights of fancy free,
To mold the lifeless clay to visions only I can see.
To paint with strokes of wisdom, to pen the purest page,
To play the ageless actor on the timeless human stage.

To sing and play and juggle!
To dance and shout and mime!
To share my spirit's struggle
In my very special rhyme!

I am the Child Disabled, I am your brother-son:
I am your sister-daughter, the world's forgotten one.
So bring the arts unto me! The barriers destroy!
The handicap of yesterday is Tomorrow's Child of Joy.

So, upon examination of the issue, there is no argument that the arts are vitally important to special populations. And certainly our culture has benefited a great deal from the contributions of disabled artists. Their work establishes beyond question that the disabled are capable of great things. And considering how important it is to support arts for the disabled, I urge you to <u>BE</u> involved.

In closing, I would like to again quote Father Gander whose poetry I have been using as illustration. He said, "Perhaps, armed with the knowledge that our culture has benefited immeasurably from these special people, we will nurture the opportunities of their artistic heirs of tomorrow . . . perhaps we will be their patrons . . . their audiences . . . their advocates . . . their fellow artists . . . their friends."

TEXT—Vice President Albert Gore, Jr., "Remarks on the Information Superhighway," 21 Dec. 1993, delivered to the National Press Club, Washington, D.C. Available on the National Information Infra-structure, through American Communicating Electronically (ACE), on the Internet.; David Archam-bault, "Columbus Plus 500 Years," *Vital Speeches of the Day,* 58 (1 June 1992), 491–493.; Myron Goldsmith, "We Shape Our Buildings and Thereafter They Shape Us." Reprinted by permission of Myron Goldsmith.; Harold Haydon, "The Testimony of Sculpture," © 1968, *The University of Chicago Magazine.* Reprinted by permission from *The University of Chicago Magazine.*; Kim Patter-son, "Fraudulent Fertility Clinics," speech prepared for speech contests, Miami University, Oxford, Ohio, 1993. Reprinted by permission of Kim Patterson.; Erik Anderson, "A Plea for the Arts," *Winning Orations 1992.* Reprinted by permission of Larry Schnoor, Executive Secretary, Interstate Ora-torical Association, Concordia College, Moorhead, Minn.

PHOTOS—1: David Young-Wolff/Photo Edit; 7: Michael Newman/Photo Edit; 10: Dion Ogust/The Image Works; 14: Richard Hutchings/Photo Edit; 24: Robert Brenner/Photo Edit; 28: Bob Daemm-rich/The Image Works; 34: Robert Brenner/Photo Edit; 35: Paul Conklin/Photo Edit; 36: Bob Daemmrich/Stock Boston; 50: Mark Richards/Photo Edit; 58: Wampler/Sygma; 65: Bob Daemm-rich/The Image Works; 72: Michael Newman/Photo Edit; 75: David Young-Wolff/Photo Edit; 91: Lonnie Duka/Tony Stone Images; 95: D. Ogust/The Image Works; 102: Elizabeth Crews/Stock Boston; 107: John Curtis/The Stock Market; 111: Bob Daemmrich/The Image Works; 127: Charles Feil/Stock Boston; 131: Sohm/The Stock Market; 136: Eastcott/The Image Works; 142: Larry Down-ing/Sygma; 152: Michael Newman/Photo Edit; 156: Starr/Stock Boston; 159: Bob Daemmrich/The Image Works; 164: Eastcott/The Image Works; 174: Mark Richards/Photo Edit; 176: David Young-Wolff/Photo Edit; 178: B. Mahoney/The Image Works; 183: Rhoda Sidney/Stock Boston; 194: Jose Paelez/The Stock Market; 198: Courtesy of Pearson Yachts, Portsmouth, R.I.; 208: Matthew Borkoski/Stock Boston; 212: Michael Newman/Photo Edit; 214: Jeff Greenberg/Photo Edit; 224: Jim Pickerell/The Image Works; 235: Bob Daemmrich/The Image Works; 236: R.Maiman/Sygma; 243(all): Courtesy, Foote, Cone & Belding; 259: Bob Daemmrich/The Image Works; 260: P.F. Gero/Sygma; 264: Mark Reinstein/The Image Works; 281: David Young-Wolff/Photo Edit; 282: Phil McCarten/Photo Edit; 288: Bob Daemmrich/The Image Works; 296: Jon Riley/Tony Stone Images; 297: J. McNally/Sygma; 305: Don & Pat Valenti/Tony Stone Images.

INDEX

• • • •